Ireland in
Prehistory

Figure 1 Map of the counties and provinces of Ireland.

Ireland in Prehistory

Michael Herity and George Eogan

Routledge & Kegan Paul
London, Henley and Boston

First published in 1977
by Routledge & Kegan Paul Ltd
39 Store Street,
London WC1E 7DD,
Broadway House,
Newtown Road,
Henley-on-Thames,
Oxon RG9 1EN and
9 Park Street,
Boston, Mass. 02108, USA
Set in 11 on 12½pt Photon Baskerville
and printed in Great Britain by
The Camelot Press Ltd, Southampton

ISBN 0 7100 8413 7

Contents

Illustrations

Figures

Preface

Though the last forty years have seen a great acceleration in archaeological discovery in Ireland, no work of synthesis covering the whole prehistoric period in the island has appeared since the publication of Raftery's *Prehistoric Ireland* in 1951. Irish archaeologists have been very active in this period however; a growing body of professional workers – there are now forty-five – have been accumulating a formidable body of primary evidence from both field and museum studies. Chance discovery and planned excavation have both contributed their share of information. The present work was conceived from the realization that a general prehistory was needed to order the large body of fact and to provide new orientations. Though this book is designed primarily to serve the large numbers of young people who are now studying archaeology in our universities, it is hoped that the general reader also will find the story of prehistoric Ireland told in its pages of interest.

The writers both specialize in the prehistoric period: Herity's work is related mainly to the Neolithic, and he has written chapters 1–4 and 11; Eogan's work centres upon the later Bronze Age, and he has written chapters 5–10. The material presented in a book of this kind is inevitably only a selection, and both writers are well aware that alternative selections of material and other interpretations can be put forward, particularly in the areas in which they are not specialists. It is hoped, however, that the present compilation will at least have indicated Ireland's wealth of prehistoric material and raised new questions about pre-Christian Ireland.

The writers are indebted to their colleagues in the Department of Archaeology at University College, Dublin, for their willingness to discuss numerous points during the writing of the book. The bibliography is an eloquent tribute to the work of individual prehistorians in Ireland.

Acknowledgments

We are grateful to the Director (Dr A. T. Lucas) and the Keeper of Irish Antiquities (Dr Joseph Raftery) for providing facilities to study prehistoric material in the National Museum of Ireland; we also wish to thank them for providing photographs (Plates 12a and b, 13a and b, 14b).

For facilities to examine material in their care we wish to thank the authorities of the following Museums: The Ulster Museum, Belfast (Mr Laurence Flanagan), The County Museum, Armagh (Mr Roger Weatherup), The British Museum, London (Dr Ian Longworth), The Ashmolean Museum, Oxford (Mr Humphrey Case), The University Museum of Archaeology and Ethnology, Cambridge (Miss Mary Cra'ster).

For permission to reproduce copyright photographs of Irish monuments and landscapes we are grateful to the Commissioners of Public Works in Ireland (Plates 5b, 6b, 7b, 10b, 15b, 16), Dr J. K. St Joseph (University of Cambridge Aerial Photography Collection, Plates 1a, 5a, 6a, 10a, 11a and b), Mr Seán Ó Nualláin (Plate 4), Mr A. E. P. Collins (Northern Ireland Archaeological Survey, Plate 8b) and Dr Daphne Pochin-Mould (Plates 9a and b). We should also like to thank the following individuals and institutions for permission to reproduce portraits, Miss Saive Coffey (Plate 3c), Mrs Mary Cooper (Plate 2c), Royal College of Physicians in Ireland (Plate 3b), Royal Dublin Society (Plate 2d) and Royal Society of Antiquaries of Ireland (Plates 3a and 3d).

Many of the drawings which illustrate this volume are based on material published in the following journals – *Acta Archaeologia Austriaca, Archaeologia Cambrensis, Archaeological Journal, Journal Cork Historical and Archaeological Society, Journal Kildare Archaeological Society, Journal Royal Society of Antiquaries of Ireland, Palaeohistoria, Proceedings of the Royal Irish Academy, Sibrium* and *Ulster Journal of Archaeology*.

For permission to reproduce copyright drawings we wish to thank Professor M. J. O'Kelly and *Journal of the Cork Historical and Archaeological Society*, and Dr Joseph Raftery and Batsford Ltd.

All the other drawings are the work of Fionnuala Williams, Ursula Mattenberger, Alacoque O'Connell and Kevin O'Brien.

For typing the manuscript we are most grateful to Miss Margaret O'Brien.

CHAPTER ONE

The Background, Geographical and Historical

Ireland is an island in the Atlantic. She lies immediately to the west of Britain. Her sea-indented west coast is continuous with that of Atlantic Europe and with the west of Scotland and Norway, this whole long seaboard united from Cadiz to Bergen by the Atlantic Ocean. The eastern half of the country has been left far richer by Nature than the west, and it looks across a less hazardous sea towards Britain, and beyond to the Low Countries and Jutland and the mouths of the rivers Rhine and Elbe.

Two hundred and fifty million years ago, when the Silurian and Devonian epochs had passed, the mass on which Ireland's foundations lie had been roughly sculpted. Her mineral wealth had already been created: the copper deposits of Avoca in Wicklow's Caledonian foldings, the gold which presumably lies at the margin of the Leinster granite close by and, in the Armorican foldings of the south, the Silvermines deposits of Tipperary and the copper of west Cork and Kerry (Fig. 2b).

A relatively short hundred million years ago, the chalk of Antrim and Derry with its layers of flint nodules had been formed at the bottom of a Cretaceous sea (Plate 1a). Later, the ice came. An ice sheet, 300 m thick, ground and smoothed the mountains, leaving a broad central plain, opening to the sea on the east but otherwise surrounded by a ring of mountains. Most of the country was covered over with a generous depth of rich glacial mud and clay (Fig. 2a; Plate 1b).

Only in winter, and then only occasionally, does Ireland today feel the intense cold of the North European Plain; even then, her western seaboard tends to remain under the influence of the mild and moist south-westerlies that blow in over the warm Gulf Stream. These winds and ocean currents have brought to Ireland a dramatic link with the flora of Spain and Portugal and even of America, for several Lusitanian and American plants exceptional in these latitudes are found in the south-west and west of Ireland (Fig. 2c). Nature has thus been generous with Ireland, endowing her with gifts of minerals, land and climate; she is 'rich in pastures and meadows, honey and milk'

1

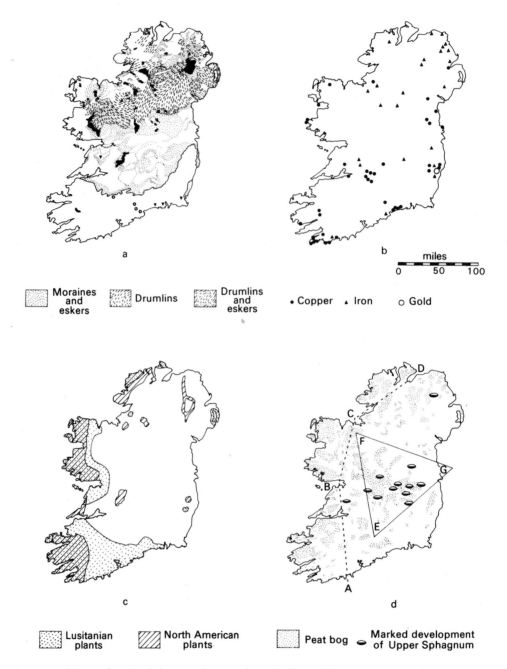

Figure 2 Maps of Ireland showing (a) extent and effects of the most recent glaciation (after Charlesworth); (b) Ireland's mineral resources; (c) the extent of plants of Lusitanian and North American origin (after Charlesworth); (d) Irish peat deposits.

as Gerald the Welshman described her in 1185, having within her shores the best cattle-land in Europe.

Climate History

The science of pollen analysis has enabled workers in Ireland to chronicle the history of climatic change from the end of the Ice Age onwards in a series of successive eras, called zones. Raised bog deposits which began to form in the hollows of the central plain as soon as they were free of ice have grown steadily from then on to the present day, trapping and preserving on each new surface the pollens of trees and other plants which grew to windward (Fig. 2d). The analysis of these pollens under the microscope enables us to reconstruct the varying representation of significant plants as time went on and broadly to deduce a history of vegetation and climate. The detailed examination of layers of mud formed at the end of the Ice Age in Scandinavia (Varves) and the new technique of radiocarbon dating allow us to locate each pollen-zone precisely in time (Clark 1960, 143–9, 156–9; Jessen 1949; Mitchell 1951).

The story thus documented opens after the retreat of the ice-sheet with an open tundra vegetation, including dwarf willow (*salix herbacea*), covering Ireland. A new warmer zone began at 10,000 B.C. and lasted to 8800 B.C.; grasses and herbs appeared and birch and juniper were common. A third stage, ending at 8300 B.C., showed a regression to the earlier, open tundra vegetation, suggesting the return of a very cold climate for a brief period at the very end of the last Ice Age. Some oceanic influences can be discerned at this stage. It marks the end of the Palaeolithic or Old Stone Age in these latitudes.

With the beginning of neothermal times, in Zone IV, birch re-appeared and aspen and heather grew for the first time. This Pre-Boreal phase (8300–7500 B.C.) was still significantly colder than modern times. An expansion of hazel indicates a climatic improvement at the beginning of the Boreal phase, named from *Boreas*, the north wind of the Greeks (7500–6900 B.C.). In this zone, birch began to decline and oak and elm reached Ireland and grew in small numbers. By this stage, the climate was as warm as it is today. The climatic improvement continued in the next phase, still Boreal (Zone VI: 6900–5200 B.C.). Summer temperatures then reached a point at which they were higher than today, and the wind system tended towards the oceanic, favouring the growth of holly and ivy. The first signs of man are claimed for this phase, which belongs to the Mesolithic or Middle Stone Age.

An Atlantic phase, Zone VIIa (5200–3000 B.C.), in which alder flourished, brought a climax in the warm oceanic climate. In this phase the sea rose to a maximum post-glacial inundation of the coasts of the north-east of Ireland, leaving behind on its retreat the Larnian raised beaches. Periwinkle (*litorina littorea*), a lover of warm waters, was now as common on these shores as it was in the contemporary Litorina raised beach of the Baltic.

Whereas in the period that has gone before, Nature has determined the changes in

3

vegetation, it is probably the influence of man in initiating forest clearance that gives rise to the next or Sub-Boreal phase (Zone VIIb). The arrival of the farmers of the Neolithic or New Stone Age period may have thus caused the elm decline sometimes taken as the distinguishing mark between Zone VIIb and the preceding VIIa. This phase (3000–1000 B.C.) was drier and warmer, as much as 2.5° C. better than today, with less oceanic wind-cycles. Oak was very common, and birch and pine grew 1000 ft above their present limits on the mountain sides. A return to the wetter, temperate climate of today came with the Sub-Atlantic, about 1000 B.C. (Zones VIII–X). It was about this time, or a little before, that the blanket bogs of the higher mountains and of the west of Ireland started to grow, enveloping the tombs and farmsteads of the first farmers and their successors and thus preserving them. The population by now had grown to proportions big enough to have an even more significant influence on the vegetation through tree clearance and the growing of crops.

It was against this backdrop of changing climate and plant life that ancient man in Ireland acted out his story, looking to the land, the riches within it, and the plants, crops and animals feeding off it, for his material necessities. We turn now to another story, the history of how our present knowledge of the ancient drama has developed over the last centuries.

The story of antiquarian thought can help us to appreciate the kind of questions asked in modern archaeology. It can also indicate sources in which useful information about the context of older finds may be obtained, and give us significant insights into the cultural history of Ireland. Although things ancient were much prized in the Celtic tradition, a study of modern Irish antiquarianism can conveniently begin about the year 1600.

History of Irish Archaeology

The English antiquarian tradition, newly begun by William Camden and the Elizabethans, was taken up in Dublin at the beginning of the seventeenth century by Ussher and Ware. Both these men made contact with the scholars of the native Irish tradition who could interpret for them the old Irish chronicles and the mythical Celtic history of Ireland's origins. The native tradition was dying with the break-up of Irish society after the Flight of the Earls in 1607, and the Franciscans, like Colgan on the continent and the Four Masters at home, whose *Annals* were compiled at Bundrowes in Donegal between 1632 and 1636, were doing what they could to commit authoritative versions of it to paper before it was lost forever. Sir James Ware (Plate 2a), whose *Antiquities* was first published in 1654 and in a revised version in 1658, employed as his interpreter An Dubhaltach Mac Fir Bisigh, one of the Mac Fir Bisigh family of Lacken, near Ballina in Co. Mayo, the hereditary learned family of the O'Dowdas (Herity 1970a), one of whose forbears, Giolla Íosa Mór, had written the *Great Book of Lecan* in 1418.

When the Dublin Philosophical Society was founded by William Molyneux and Sir

4

William Petty in 1683, this collaboration between the new and the native antiquarian traditions was continued: Thady Rody of Fenagh in Co. Leitrim was asked to write descriptions of his native county and of Longford, and Roderick O'Flaherty, who was at that time finishing his *Ogygia* (1685), wrote a description of Iar-Connacht. Though the new spirit recognized the value of legendary history, this attitude did not bring any significant results in Ireland until the coming of Edward Lhuyd in 1699. Lhuyd, who was Keeper of the Ashmolean Museum at Oxford, and who had conceived a plan of investigating the language, customs, antiquities and flora of Wales, Scotland and Ireland, was to spend almost a year in Scotland and Ireland. In August of that year, Lhuyd arrived in Dublin with three young helpers, David Parry, Robert Wynne and William Jones. There they split forces: Jones and Wynne were sent west and south with specific instructions to reconnoitre and record the geology, botany, history, antiquities and folklore of the country, while Lhuyd himself and Parry went northwards to Antrim and into Scotland to return to the north and west of Ireland in January of 1700 (Campbell 1960). Though Lhuyd's original notebooks have almost entirely perished, several letters of his are extant as well as copies of the drawings made by the party, which were rescued by John Anstis immediately after Lhuyd's death in 1709 (British Museum MSS. Stowe 1023, 1024). Among the antiquarian drawings and descriptions are several of New Grange, of the High Crosses at Monasterboice, of the monuments around Cong in Co. Mayo, of megalithic tombs around Donegal Bay, and of the monastic remains at Clonmacnois on the Shannon. Lhuyd's observations were perceptive and rational (Herity 1974, 1–2). In all, about sixty monuments are drawn in the Anstis notebooks, a cross-section of Ireland's monuments not equalled until the Ordnance Survey began its work in the late 1820s. Volume 1 of the *Archaeologia Britannica*, embodying some fruits of his linguistic researches, was published in 1707, and he died in 1709. Had Lhuyd lived to complete Volume 2 of this work, an incisive analysis of the monuments, their folklore and their legendary history would have been produced. As it was, this was not to be done until O'Donovan and Petrie began their work with the Ordnance Survey well over a century later.

The eighteenth century began with the issuing of a number of editions of Ware's *Antiquities* translated into English. Sir Thomas Molyneux, a medical doctor, who became the state physician in Ireland, and brother of William Molyneux, also republished Gerard Boate's geographical work, the *Natural History of Ireland*, published originally in 1653 for the benefit of Cromwellian planters; with this he included several articles written under the aegis of the Dublin Philosophical Society and published in the *Philosophical Transactions* of the Royal Society, as well as his own essay asserting the Danish origin of the Round Towers and of New Grange, the *Discourse concerning the Danish Mounts, Forts and Towers in Ireland* (1726).

Walter Harris, who brought out the most extensive and useful edition of Ware's *Antiquities* (1764), was one of the members of another Dublin group, the Physico-Historical Society, a society consisting mainly of noblemen, who met for the first time in the Lords' Committee Room of the Parliament House in Dublin in April 1744. Its members described themselves as 'a voluntary society for promoting an enquiry into the Ancient and Present State of the several Countys of Ireland'. Harris, a Dublin lawyer, and Charles Smith, an apothecary from Dungarvan in Co. Waterford, published a description of Co. Down in 1744. Smith went on to publish descriptions of Cos Waterford (1746), Cork (1750), and Kerry (1756), and to assemble the materials for a description of the rest of Munster. James Simon's *Coins* was also published under its aegis (1749) but, had he not communicated them to the Society of Antiquaries at London, drawings and descriptions of several Irish prehistoric antiquities found about that time would have been lost. Several valuable accounts written by Dr Pococke, Bishop of Ossory, would also have been lost had they not been communicated to the same Society (Pococke 1773; Herity 1969).

About 1770, the new romantic spirit brought a surge of interest in the past. In that year, Major (later General) Charles Vallancey began the publication of his *Collectanea de Rebus Hibernicis* of which six volumes in all were to appear by 1804 (Plate 2b). The first publication was Sir Henry Piers's *Chorographical Description of the County of West Meath* written for the Molyneuxs in 1682. The title page of volume 1 describes Vallancey as *Soc. Antiq. Hib. Soc.*, but apart from other equally oblique references, little is known of this Hibernian Antiquarian Society. The original purpose of the *Collectanea* (1770–1804) was to publish the writings of earlier workers like Ware, Camden and Lhuyd, but soon the only contributions were those of Vallancey himself, 'inspired omniscient antiquary', whose quotations in Arabic, which he had learnt during a sojourn in Gibraltar before coming to Ireland, were to exhaust the stocks of Arabic type in all the Dublin printing presses:

> THE Author, desirous of printing the Arabic words in their proper characters, prevailed on the printer to borrow all the Arabic Types, this city afforded; after all endeavours to compleat the alphabet, but one *Kaf*, and no final *Nun*, could be found, and several deficiencies in the points appeared. We were therefore under the necessity of writing most of the Arabic words in Roman letters, adopting the sound in the best manner we could.
>
> (*Collectanea*, vol. 5, iv)

In May 1772, the Royal Dublin Society, which had been established in 1731 for the improvement of farming and industry, founded a Committee of Antiquities. Joint secretary with Vallancey was Edward Ledwich, Dean of Aghaboe and author of the *Antiquities of Ireland* (1790). Not to be outdone by Vallancey, he deciphered writing 'in Bebeloth characters' on the face of one of the High Crosses at Castledermot. As the Molyneuxs and the Physico-Historical Society had earlier done, this committee sent out a questionnaire seeking antiquarian information; its most important act, however, was to advertise in the continental gazettes seeking manuscripts which would have been taken abroad by Irish noblemen, soldiers and clerical students after the Williamite Wars and during the Penal times.

6

Some of the most valuable work done in this period was done under the influence or patronage of William Burton Conyngham of Slane in Co. Meath, who was a Lord of the Treasury at Dublin Castle and who, after coming into his inheritance in 1779, devoted much of his private money to antiquarian research (Plate 2c). He engaged two artists, Gabriel Beranger (Plate 2b) and Angelo Bigari, a scene-painter at the Smock Alley Theatre, and sent them on two tours, one to Sligo and the west, the other to Wexford, to plan and describe antiquities (Wilde 1870). Bigari's drawings were afterwards published in full by Grose (1791), but not Beranger's, though a number of his were used by Vallancey and, afterwards, by Petrie. This group of 'Castle' antiquaries included Austin Cooper, who was a clerk in the Treasury at Dublin Castle and who also acted as a landlord's agent. A number of his published drawings indicate the interests of a typical antiquary of this school and period: old castles, churches and towers, earthworks like Norman mottes and ring-forts and megalithic tombs (Price 1942). Because of the difficulties of travelling, many of the drawings in his collection are copies from those of other artists and antiquaries; several of Cooper's, for instance, are the work of Vallancey, Lord Carlow, Jonathan Fisher and of Cooper's cousins Turner and Walker.

The Royal Irish Academy, founded in 1782, had a good deal in common with the contemporary movements. The scholars connected with it were mainly from Trinity College and they included Antiquities with Polite Literature in the scope of their inquiries; their *Transactions*, the first volume of which commenced in 1785, contained an account of a Bronze Age Urn from Kilranelagh in Co. Wicklow. Other objects donated as a result of the investigations of Vallancey and Conyngham were placed in the Trinity College Museum for safe-keeping. A scholar who was sought after by all the different bodies of Dublin antiquaries was Charles O'Conor of Belanagare in Co. Roscommon, an Irishman trained in the native learning, the equivalent in the eighteenth century of Mac Fir Bisigh, Rody and O'Flaherty in the seventeenth, whom the Dublin antiquaries of that day had also sought out.

The Ordnance Survey

With the passing of the Act of Union in 1800, the Ascendancy *dilettanti* left Dublin for London and antiquarian work went into decline for want of private patrons. When the Ordnance Survey was set up in 1823, it was now the turn of the State to provide the patronage. Travel was becoming easier in this century, with the building of roads and canals and, later, railways. Printing technology was improving and wider markets for printed works were being created with the growth of popular education: the Irish National Schools system was set up in 1829.

The Irish Ordnance Survey was founded to provide a set of detailed and authoritative maps on which a new valuation of land could be based. The trigonometrical survey was begun in 1824 under the direction of Colonel Thomas Colby, who commanded the Survey Corps, a branch of the army with headquarters at

Mountjoy House in the Phoenix Park in Dublin. In 1828, Lieutenant Thomas Larcom was appointed to assist Colby in the work of surveying and engraving the large-scale maps, the work for which was at that time being begun in the north of the country. Notes were to be taken by the surveyors of the natural resources, population, economic potential and the historical and archaeological monuments of each parish as they surveyed it. Because of the importance attached by Larcom to the marking of the names on the maps, he undertook the study of the Irish language in 1828. The teacher he chose was John O'Donovan (1807–61).

O'Donovan was born in Attateemore in Co. Kilkenny and received a good education in Irish and in the Classics. In 1830 he joined the Survey in the Placenames and Antiquities section: his job was to follow the surveyors into the field, to determine the pronunciation and derivation of the names collected by them and noted in a Namebook for each of the 2400 Civil Parishes in the country, and to suggest a suitable English rendering of each name for the maps.

The basic map of the Survey was engraved at a scale of six inches to the mile (1 : 10,560). On it was marked every field and farmhouse in the country and all antiquities and other features noted by the surveyors. Even today, this is the best basic survey of field antiquities in Ireland. O'Donovan's vast experience of the country is attested by the great number of letters written by him from the field to Larcom at Mountjoy House: so extensive was his knowledge of Irish monuments that he was able to suggest authoritative identifications for most of the hundreds of sites mentioned in the pages of the *Annals of the Four Masters*, which he edited in 1849. In 1851 he became Professor of Celtic at the new Queen's College in Belfast.

The Ordnance Survey thus brought an ordered and sustained effort to bear on the study of field antiquities on a countrywide scale. The Heads of Inquiry issued as guidelines to the officers listed the principal requirements as drawings and descriptions and a note of local traditions in respect of 'Ecclesiastical Buildings', 'Military Buildings', 'Remains of Pagan, or unknown origin' and 'Miscellaneous'; while the Survey personnel were enjoined, 'a good drawing is more valuable than an inscription and well preserved tradition than doubtful history.'

George Petrie (1789–1866), who had begun life as an artist and had been drawn into the study of antiquities in the 1820s, became head of the Placenames and Antiquities section of the Survey in 1835 (Plate 3a). His clear-minded approach and his respect for Baconian logic helped to bring Irish antiquarianism from the extremes of the romantic phase into harmony with the more logical and scientific spirit of nineteenth-century science. Both his great published works benefited from the collaboration of O'Donovan and the exact mensuration of the surveyors. His *History and Antiquities of Tara Hill*, published by the Royal Irish Academy in 1837, is a detailed description of the monuments remaining on the hill and an identification of these with a *Dindseanchas* description written by an antiquary of the old Celtic tradition about the year 1000.

Petrie's *Essay on the Round Towers* was first written for a competition of the Academy in 1832: the prize was a gold medal and £100. In the published version he argued three major conclusions based on the siting of the towers in ancient monasteries, on the fact that many bore Christian ornament and on the nature of their architectural construction. His conclusions were as follows:

I That the Towers are of Christian and ecclesiastical origin and were erected at various periods between the fifth and thirteenth centuries.

II That they were designed to answer, at least, a two fold use, namely, to serve as belfries, and as keeps, or places of strength, in which the sacred utensils, books, relics, and other valuables were deposited, and into which the ecclesiastics, to whom they belonged, could retire for security in cases of sudden attack.

III That they were probably also used, when occasion required, as beacons, and as watch-towers.

(1845, 2)

Petrie supported his arguments with several passages from ancient historical sources and noted that his conclusions were supported 'by the uniform and concurrent tradition of the country'. The essay, published in 1845, brought order and logic to a subject that had long excited antiquarian attention. By the time of its publication, the large-scale maps of the Survey had been engraved for all thirty-two counties and many of the personnel disbanded.

Eugene O'Curry (1794–1862) joined the Survey late, in 1837. A scholar in the native tradition, he had learnt Irish from his father at his home at Doonaha in the south-west of Co. Clare. After leaving the Survey he was employed with O'Donovan editing Irish texts at Trinity College, and in 1854 he became Professor of Irish History and Archaeology at Cardinal Newman's Catholic University in Dublin. Two series of his lectures were afterwards published: *Lectures on the Manuscript Materials of Ancient Irish History* (1861) and *On the Manners and Customs of the Ancient Irish* (1873).

With the publication of the Ordnance Survey maps, a basic document was available from which the study of field antiquities could be begun. John Windele of Cork was using the Ordnance Survey maps of Kerry as early as 1848 and, later in the century, Wood-Martin, Westropp and Borlase were to make extensive use of these valuable maps.

The coming together of Petrie and Larcom with O'Donovan and O'Curry reflects the meeting of the more scientific antiquarian spirit with the native tradition begun more than two hundred years before. In the Ordnance Survey, the sustained and disciplined efforts of these men extending over a period of at least ten years' full-time work brought Irish antiquarianism on to a new plane. Yet, their very success with Tara and the Round Towers had within it a weakness that was to retard progress later on.

Ancient Objects, Collectors and Museums

Chance finds of ancient objects were recorded long before the establishment of our

9

first museum: a sword found at Eamhain Macha in 1111, a gold horse-bit presented by Strafford to Charles I, gold objects, including a Tara-type torque from Ballymorris in Co. Laois, the subject of a Treasure Trove inquisition in 1673, a Late Bronze Age horn found in a cairn near Carrickfergus and drawn and described by Lhuyd in 1699. Before Lhuyd's visit, a Food Vessel found in a Passage Grave at Waringstown in Co. Down had been presented to the Dublin Philosophical Society and was housed in the Library of Trinity College with a small collection of other antiquities.

With the acceleration of land clearance and agriculture in the eighteenth century, the finding of objects also increased and the few records we have of the finding of gold objects are probably only the tip of the iceberg. Several are recorded in the Minutes of the Society of Antiquaries at London (Herity 1969), and many of those in the collection of the Royal Dublin Society, founded in 1731 for the improvement of agriculture, may have come from there as it was the only scientific Society with which the finders had any contact. There are many accounts, however, of objects that came into private collections and have since disappeared, and many others of objects which came into the hands of jewellers and were melted down into bullion. Such was the fate of a massive treasure of Viking armlets of gold, found on an island on the Shannon in 1803 and weighing 160 oz (5 kg), which was melted down by Delandre, a Dublin jeweller, because he could not find a collector to pay a small premium on the bullion value, say £700 in all (Vallancey, *Collectanea*, vol. VI, 255–65). Happily, objects like the Clones gold fibula, which weighs 15 oz, came into the possession of the Hibernian Antiquarian Society and were preserved in Trinity College and the Royal Irish Academy at the end of the previous century, before the Union.

In the 1830s, interest in the Academy's collections was revived and a new policy of acquisition was begun. In 1837, a collection of antiquities was bought from Underwood, a Dublin jeweller, and two years later the Cross of Cong was acquired from the representatives of Fr Prendergast, the last abbot of Cong, who had died some years earlier. In the same year, two gold torques found at Tara were bought for £150 from West, the Dublin jeweller: these had been found in 1810 and had been more or less continuously in West's possession since then. In 1842, the Academy raised over £1000 by subscription for the purchase of an extremely valuable collection, that of Dean Dawson of St Patrick's Cathedral in Dublin.

Victorian drainage works on the Bann and the Shannon brought up quantities of objects which had been lost at prehistoric crossing-places: these, too, were added to the Academy's museum, so that when William Wilde (Plate 3b) was commissioned to edit the catalogue of the Academy's collections in March 1857, in preparation for the visit of the British Association, the collections had grown to something approaching those of Copenhagen, the foremost prehistoric museum in Europe. Wilde chose to order the objects by simple categories; stone, earthen, vegetable and animal materials; copper, bronze, silver and gold (1857, 1861, 1862), despite the fact that Thomsen's Three Age system was gaining acceptance all over Europe and had been promulgated at the Academy itself in 1847 by Worsaae (Daniel 1964, 47; Wilkins

1961). His choice of this arrangement may have been dictated by the necessity for speed: the resolution to spend £250 'in the arrangement and cataloguing of the Museum' was taken on 16 March 1857, and the first section of the *Catalogue*, amounting to 250 pages, was ready for printing by August, at the end of which month the British Association met in Dublin.

The thirty years ending in 1860 had brought Irish antiquarianism onto a new plane of development largely through the efforts of the Ordnance Survey and the Royal Irish Academy: Wakeman's assessment was that it had been shown 'that Ireland contains an unbroken series of monuments, many of them historical, which lead us back, step by step, to a period long before the conversion of her people to Christianity', that museums had been formed and that annals and manuscripts relating to her history and antiquities had been translated (1848, viii). New antiquarian societies had been founded. In Belfast, the Natural History and Philosophical Society was founded in 1821; by 1831, its members were ambitious and energetic enough to collect £10,000 to build a public museum, and between 1853 and 1862 a first series of the *Ulster Journal of Archaeology* was published under the editorship of Robert MacAdam. In Cork, the Cuvierian Society had encouraged antiquarian work from 1836 on, and in Kilkenny a local antiquarian society, founded in 1849, began the publication of its own journal, which now continues as the *Journal of the Royal Society of Antiquaries of Ireland*. Excavations with a more or less scientific purpose began to be made: at Lagore, under Petrie and Wilde in 1839, at Dowth, by Frith for the Academy's Committee of Antiquities in 1847, and at Ballynahatty in 1852 under MacAdam and Getty. Public interest was certainly enlightened, as Thomas Davis's essays in the *Nation* newspaper (1842–5) testify. The very success of Petrie's essays of 1837 and 1845 may have done much to foster an insular climate of opinion in which it was easy silently to reject Thomsen's Three Age system. The archaeological arguments in the Round Towers essay were strongly supported by a wealth of quotations from historical sources, as well they might be, for the towers probably began to be built about A.D. 900, by which time the Irish annals were well established. In the Tara essay, Petrie had an illusory success. Following on Petrie's success, O'Curry ascribed Bronze Age weapons to the Celts in his *Manners and Customs* and accepted the mythical chronology of prehistoric Ireland devised by the pseudo-historians as having historical validity. He was followed by Eugene Conwell, the schools inspector who described the Loughcrew Passage Graves in Co. Meath, who identified Cairn T, the focal tomb on Carnbane East, as the tomb of the mythical Celtic figure, Ollamh Fodhla (1873).

Petrie, O'Donovan and O'Curry, who had dominated for three decades, all died in the 1860s and Irish archaeology lost impetus after their deaths. They were followed by a generation of field-workers, Conwell, James Fergusson, a Scottish architect (1872), W. G. Wood-Martin, a Sligo landlord, who in his *Rude Stone Monuments* (1888) followed a lead given by Fergusson, and fell in with the European vogue for lake-dwelling archaeology in his *Lake-Dwellings of Ireland* (1886). Westropp's work in the field, which began before 1890 and continued well into the twentieth century, is typical also of the period. The finest of all of these field syntheses was written by a Cornishman, William Borlase, whose compilation, *The Dolmens of Ireland*, is a most thorough corpus of 898 Irish megalithic tombs (1897).

Fieldwork, George Coffey and R. A. S. Macalister

The search for the earliest man in Ireland was largely conducted in the implementiferous raised beach gravel of Antrim and Down from about 1870 onwards. Collectors in that area, follo ving the work of de Perthes, de Mortillet, and Lartet and Christy, searched for flint tools of primitive aspect in the hope that these might parallel those of the French cave and drift deposits which had been recognized as of great antiquity only about 1859 (Daniel 1964, 45). William Knowles, a landlord's agent from Ballymena, was a central figure in these investigations and also in a series of parallel examinations of the sandhills deposits of the same area, conducted by a Committee of the Royal Irish Academy and modelled on the contemporary Kitchen-midden Commissions of Denmark. As had earlier happened at Meilgaard, the first of these kitchen-middens to be scientifically investigated in Denmark, and in the Swiss lake-dwellings investigations which began in 1854, archaeologists and natural scientists worked in collaboration, and the theoretical basis of Irish archaeology may have benefited from this contact with the more developed natural scientific disciplines.

By 1895, archaeological knowledge had advanced to the stage where it was possible for W. G. Wood-Martin to publish his *Pagan Ireland*, the first extensive work of synthesis on Irish prehistoric archaeology. The great antiquity of man was recognized, and the study of his remains was allied to the study of modern so-called primitive peoples, while the uncritical acceptance of Celtic myth was castigated. The story was not yet conceived in sequence, however; his chapters were mainly descriptive, treating of the different categories of monuments and museum objects.

In 1897, George Coffey (1857–1916) was appointed Curator of the Royal Irish Academy's collections, which by then were housed in a new Museum of Science and Art set up by the government. Coffey, the first professional archaeologist since O'Curry, had studied engineering at Trinity College, Dublin, and had been called to the Irish Bar in 1883 (Plate 3c). He was a member of the circle of literary men and artists who fostered the Celtic Revival in Dublin and he frequently exhibited at the Royal Hibernian Academy. He devoted himself to continuing the cataloguing of the collections begun by Wilde, and in 1909 he brought out his *Guide to the Celtic Antiquities of the Early Christian Period*. His description of New Grange and other Irish Passage Graves, *New Grange and other Incised Tumuli in Ireland*, sub-titled 'The Influence of Crete and the Aegean in the Extreme West of Europe in Early Times' (1912a), probably shows the influence of the notion *ex oriente lux* of Oscar Montelius, the dominant figure of northern prehistory, with whom he corresponded. In *The Bronze Age in*

Ireland (1913), he adopted Montelius's five-period division of the Bronze Age in Britain and Ireland.

Coffey conceived his three books as complementing one another in delineating the history of ancient art in Ireland and in relating Irish remains with those of the European continent and the Mediterranean (1913, vi); now, in the age of Montelius and of the French synthesist Joseph Déchelette (1861–1914), the prehistory and proto-history of Ireland could be conceived in sequence.

Coffey's assistant from 1907, who became Keeper on his retirement in 1914, was E. C. R. Armstrong (1879–1923). He studied archaeology in Germany, and is probably best known for his *Catalogue of the Gold Ornaments in the Collection of the Royal Irish Academy* (1920). In 1922, he resigned the post to become Blue Mantle Pursuivant of Arms at the Heralds' College in London, and he died shortly afterwards.

A great stimulus was given to archaeological work in Ireland with the appointment of R. A. S. Macalister (1870–1950) to the chair of Celtic Archaeology (interpreted in the older sense of prehistoric archaeology) at University College, Dublin, in 1909 (Plate 3d). For the previous nine years he had worked in Palestine as Director of the Palestine Exploration Fund and he was to teach at University College until 1943. His *Ireland in Pre-Celtic Times* (1921a) is an interesting combination of the historical and anthropological approaches, with chapters on the 'Stone and Bronze Ages', 'Ornament and Symbolism', 'Social Organisation', 'Pottery', 'Dwellings and Fortifications', and 'Religion and the Disposal of the Dead', an arrangement foreshadowed in Wood-Martin's *Pagan Ireland*. In the same year, he published the first volume of a projected but unfinished *Textbook of European Archaeology* (1921b), an excellent summary of the Palaeolithic and Mesolithic. The notion of an archaeological culture so familiar today had not been realized in 1921, and Macalister referred only to *societies* and *states*. Besides continuing his Near Eastern work, he kept up a constant flow of articles in the fields of Celtic Studies and archaeology (Brennan 1973). His *Archaeology of Ireland* (1928) and *Ancient Ireland* (1935) continued the synthesis of prehistory and early history begun in his earliest lectures, which were published in instalments in the *Irish Monthly* in the years before 1920. Archaeology was established as a degree subject in all of the colleges of the new National University with the founding of Chairs at the Cork and Galway colleges (Clark 1939, 193–4).

The Period 1930 to the Present

It was in 1932 that fieldwork on the sustained scale that is normal in modern times began, for in that year two young members of the staff of Queen's University, Belfast, Estyn Evans of Geography and Oliver Davies of Classics, collaborated in the excavation of a Neolithic Court Cairn at Goward in Co. Down. In the following decade, they conducted several excavations, mainly in tombs, and provided much of the driving force behind the survey of monuments begun under the auspices of the Belfast Naturalists' Field Club. Of this a first instalment was published by Evans and

13

Gaffikin (1935) and an enlarged version in the *Preliminary Survey* (Chart 1940). To all these workers goes the credit for reviving the *Ulster Journal of Archaeology* in a third series which began in 1938, and the creation of a lectureship in archaeology at Queen's University, Belfast, in 1948.

In 1927, a Committee of Inquiry which included Professor Nils Lithberg of Stockholm among its members was set up by the Minister for Education to inquire into and report on the main purposes that should be served by the National Museum in Dublin, and the needs of the Museum in the light of these purposes. Several recommendations were made by the end of the year: a Board of Governors should be appointed, public lectures should be given and the staff of the Antiquities Division should consist of a Keeper and six Assistants. In that year also, Dr Walter Bremer had been appointed to the Museum, but he died soon afterwards and was succeeded by Dr Adolf Mahr, who increased dramatically the numbers of acquisitions to the Museum, initiated the Album of Christian Art (1932; 1941) and also made an outstanding contribution in his review *Prehistory in Ireland* which was published by the newly formed Prehistoric Society in London during his presidency of that body (1937).

An enlightened National Monuments Act in February 1930 defined a national monument as a monument or its remains 'the preservation of which is a matter of national importance by reason of the historical, architectural, traditional, artistic or archaeological interest attaching thereto.' The Act also provided for the guardianship, preservation and acquisition of national monuments, restricted the export of archaeological objects and provided for the licensing of excavations.

In 1932, the Harvard Archaeological Expedition began work in Ireland. This was part of a broader campaign that also included surveys in physical and cultural anthropology. Several excavations were conducted by Hencken of megalithic tombs, Bronze Age cairns and crannógs (lake-dwellings), and by Movius on Larnian shoreline sites and in the Bann Valley.

A further impetus was given to archaeological excavation by the provision in 1934 of government funds for excavation in areas where there was unemployment. The first excavation under the scheme was that of Leask and Price at the Labbacallee wedge-shaped tomb in Cork (1936). Expenditure under this head has grown from about £500 in 1934 to about £50,000 in recent years.

Since 1945, the pattern of large-scale excavations has increased dramatically, field surveys have been begun by the Megalithic Survey under the auspices of the Ordnance Survey at Dublin – three volumes have been published – and county surveys have been under way since 1950, from Belfast where the volume on Co. Down has been published (1966) and from Dublin where several counties have been surveyed under the Office of Public Works. The publication of these surveys and of corpus studies of museum objects will bring prehistoric studies in Ireland on to a new plane and facilitate and broaden the scope of future syntheses of our prehistory.

The reconstruction outlined in the following pages begins, after a short prologue dealing with the hunter-fishers of the coasts of Antrim and Down, with the arrival of the first farmers before 3000 B.C. Apart from the fact that their tools were of stone, their way of life differed little from that of many small farmers in Ireland up to the beginning of this century. Before the end of that Neolithic era, at 2000 B.C., the potential of the land of Ireland for farming had twice been realized by colonists from Atlantic Europe, and the exploitation of the metal resources of Leinster and of the lands bordering the Irish Sea had been begun. The prospectors who found the Irish El Dorado came, not from Atlantic Europe, but along the Elbe and across the North Sea and Scotland from Central Europe. The story of the metal ages which follow is in large measure a story of Ireland's relations with these two major areas of prehistoric Europe, now looking south to Iberia, now east to Bohemia and beyond, as far even as Transylvania and the east Mediterranean. Ireland's relations with Britain oscillate after a similar pattern, looking now south to the richer lands of Wessex and now to a northern province. The mythical colonizations of Ireland invented by the pseudo-historians of the Christian period bring colonists from both Iberia and Scythia: perhaps at the root of these inventions there are folk memories from thousands of years earlier in the prehistoric period?

Stone Age Beginnings: Hunter-Fishers and First Farmers

During the last Ice Age, which ended gradually in Britain and Ireland over the period between 12,000 and 8000 B.C., only the part of Ireland south of a line from Wexford to Tralee had been free of ice. Here, the reindeer, the brown bear, the mammoth, the lemming, and the Arctic fox lived in a rich tundra vegetation, using the many caves of the area as places for shelter. As the ice receded northwards, the giant Irish deer (*cervus giganteus*) flourished in the open, unforested terrain of the country, but was occasionally trapped and suffocated in the raised peat-bogs which began to form in the hollows as the ice continued to recede.

With the coming of a warmer climate, a new fauna found it possible to immigrate into Ireland, probably across a short-lived land-bridge between north Antrim and Kintyre. One result of the early separation of Ireland and Britain is that Ireland has today a much narrower range of plants and animals than has Britain. The most notable absence is that of wild ox, which has never been found in Ireland despite many thorough examinations of the fauna of late-glacial and post-glacial times found in caves (Movius 1942, 74, 91; Herity 1970b, 29–30). A special Lusitanian fauna, derived from the Atlantic coast as far south as Portugal and flourishing along the western seaboard, derives from Ireland's position on the Atlantic façade of Europe (Fig. 2c).

Only the faintest record of the presence of Ice Age man can be detected. Recently, a waste flint flake struck in Clactonian style was picked up on the surface of glacial gravel deposited as early as 200,000 B.C. near Drogheda in Co. Louth (Mitchell and Sieveking 1972). The flake shows faint signs of rolling, and was probably transported with the gravels in which it was found from somewhere to the east of the find-spot. It documents the existence of man in middle Palaeolithic times close to the basin of the Irish Sea. Claims for an inter-glacial immigration by Mousterian Man into Ireland about 40,000 B.C., made on the basis of limestone flakes found near the shore in the Sligo area, have been disposed of by Charlesworth and Macalister (1929).

Tratman's excavations at Kilgreany Cave in Co. Waterford recovered a skeleton, Kilgreany B, which was claimed by him to be Palaeolithic because of its association with late-glacial animals, now extinct. No Palaeolithic implements were found (1928). Movius's excavation at the same site in 1934 showed that the skeleton was probably associated with a hearth which yielded oak, ash and hazel charcoal typical of warmer post-glacial climates, and that bones of domesticated ox were found nearby (Movius 1935a; 1942). This new evidence would suggest that the skeleton belonged to the Neolithic period, which began about 3000 B.C. Though a Palaeolithic date, before 8000 B.C., has again been recently claimed for the skeleton on the basis of a flourine test (Raftery 1963, 103), it seems reasonable, because of the uncertain nature of that method, not to alter Movius's view.

Larnian and Mesolithic

In the old shoreline on the coasts of Antrim and Down opposite Scotland, where the shortest of the sea-crossings to Britain can be made, the implements of a flint industry have been discovered. These deposits are found as far south as Dublin and as far north-west as Donegal. The industry they represent has been labelled 'Larnian' from the extensive deposits found at Curran Point which is situated in the modern harbour of Larne, sheltered by the Island Magee peninsula. The greatest part of this material is found in the storm beach deposits of the old shoreline, and is consequently much battered, making it difficult to distinguish between artifacts and waste material. This north-eastern area is also the area of easiest availability of fresh flint in Ireland (Fig. 3).

The raised beach in which the Larnian material is found was formed after the end of the last Ice Age. When the ice-cap retreated, its meltwater was added to the seas and oceans, raising their level and drowning great areas of low-lying coastal land. With the release of the ice-cap's pressure, the earth's crust re-asserted itself, raising parts of the landmass out of these newly deep seas. Raised beaches and old shorelines are the tangible results of this series of oscillations, and their history is particularly well recorded in Scandinavia, where they culminated in four minor transgressions of the warm Litorina sea towards the year 2000 B.C. In Ireland the Larnian raised beach was first inundated and later, over centuries, raised up to 9 m at its highest above the present level of the sea in Antrim. From the association of Neolithic material of the first farmers with the storm beach which marks the maximum point of this inundation at Sutton, north of Dublin, it can be dated about 3000 B.C.

The Larnian material consists of the battered remnants of both flint artifacts and waste material which had been lying on the shore before it was rolled into the storm beach. Sites like Sutton, Rough Island in Co. Down, and Glenarm and Island Magee in Co. Antrim, have remains of this kind. Extensive mounds of seashells, presumably the refuse of communal eating, are associated with the Sutton and Rough Island sites. Related sites on the nearby coasts of Scotland are those of Campbelltown in Kintyre

17

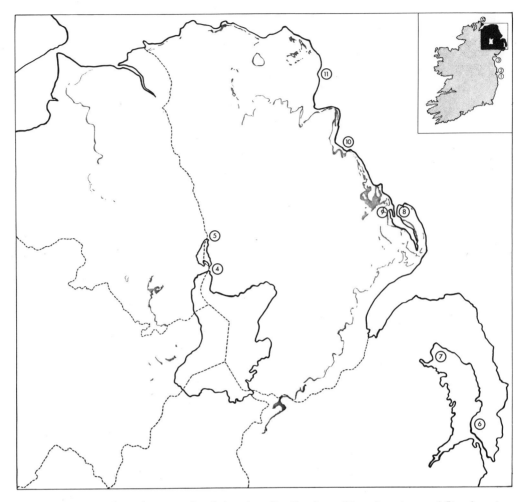

Figure 3 Map of north-east Ireland showing distribution of Larnian sites and flint-bearing chalk deposits. Inset shows Larnian sites outside the north-east: 1 Dalkey Island; 2 Sutton; 3 Rockmarshall; 4 Toome Bay; 5 Newferry; 6 Ringneill Quay; 7 Rough Island; 8 Island Magee; 9 Curran Point, Larne; 10 Glenarm; 11 Cushendun; 12 Culdaff.

and the shellmounds of the west coast near Oban (Lacaille 1954). A much deeper stratigraphy is provided by the more sheltered site of Larne, and by Cushendun where the strata were built up in lagoons and at the estuary of the Dun river.

At Cushendun, a site with a series of deposits piled up in the estuary by sea and river action at the time of the transgression was investigated by Movius (Fig. 4a). His Horizons 1–3 are the relevant layers and these total 7·96 m in depth (1942, 126–9). The lowest layer, Lower Lagoon Silt, formed during a climate milder than today's,

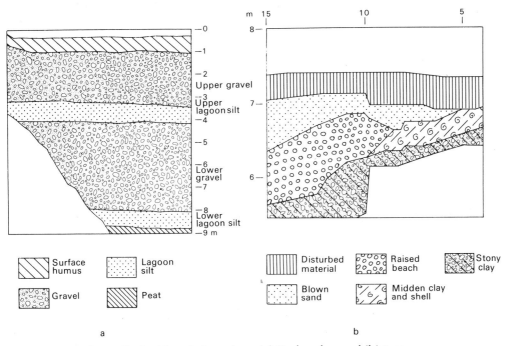

Figure 4 Sections of raised beach deposits at (a) Cushendun and (b) Sutton.

was assigned to the end of the Boreal period (pollen Zone VI) by Jessen, about 5200 B.C. (1949, 135–9). Movius found here three unrolled implements: an unworked leaf-shaped flake, a second leaf-shaped implement with slight secondary working on the edges, and a parallel-sided blade. Horizon 2, a very prolific stratum of Lower Gravel, 3·58 m thick, overlay this; it yielded several well-struck blade implements of light 'Early Larnian' type, and three microliths (Fig. 5, 12–14).

A lagoon was then formed, 0·77 m deep, then quickly silted up, to be overlain by Upper Gravel thrown up as a storm beach; in this, Horizon 3, were found the crude, much-rolled flakes which Movius assigned to his 'Late Larnian'. During the formation of these layers the sea encroached to a height of about 4 m.

At the site on the Sutton isthmus north of Dublin between Howth and the mainland, Mitchell excavated a number of raised beach deposits and an associated shell midden (1956; 1972). This shellmound was accumulating before the maximum of the sea's transgression, as it was cut into by the sea and overlain by a storm beach (Fig. 4b). Parallel-sided blades and leaf-shaped points were found in both the midden and the raised beach, with an obliquely truncated blade, a transverse arrowhead and a number of plunging flakes. There were also in the midden two polished stone axeheads of dark green quartz-chlorite schist and a number of bolster-shaped 'limpet-hammers'. The arrowhead and polished stone axeheads clearly place the site

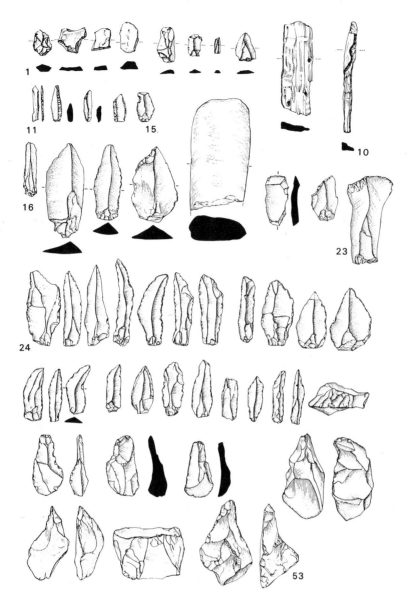

Figure 5 Irish Early Stone Age material: 1–10 objects of flint and wood from Toome Bay, Co. Antrim; 16–23 polished stone axehead, *petit tranchet* arrowhead, obliquely truncated flake and flints of Larnian type from Sutton, Co. Dublin (after Mitchell); 11–15, 24–53 flints of Movius's Early Larnian type from Cushendun, Rough Island and Island Magee (after Movius). ($\frac{1}{3}$)

in the Neolithic, and a recent radiocarbon determination accords with this, indicating a date of 3000 ± 100 B.C. for the midden.

Movius's study divides the material into Early Larnian, light and relatively unrolled, and Late Larnian, heavier and showing much greater signs of battering in the beach gravels during the storms immediately before the maximum (1942, 148). It can be claimed, however, that this division is a product of sorting by sea action rather than by human activity. Certainly the general categories of the flint material ascribed to both the Early and the Late Larnian are broadly comparable (Figs 5, 6) and both are therefore combined in the description which follows.

By far the most numerous category is composed of primary parallel-sided or leaf-shaped flint blades, flakes, and points. This accounts for 95 per cent of Movius's Early Larnian and a similarly large proportion of his Late Larnian. A series of larger and heavier flakes, a number of them cello-shaped and many with the cortex of the parent flint nodule adhering to them, form a large part of the remainder; these are variously called plunging flakes, rostrates, and Larne and Cushendun picks (Fig. 6). Core scrapers and axeheads of *core tranchet* type are the implements made from flint cores. The typical flake implements are perforators, notched scrapers, and side- and end-scrapers. Easily the most diagnostic implements in the whole of the series published by Movius are four microliths with one edge blunted for hafting found at Cushendun and Rough Island (Fig. 5, 11–14). The industry, then, is characterized by a very large quantity of both primary flakes and trimming material. The few conventional implements, amounting to very much less than 5 per cent of all the material, provide little opportunity for comparison with other approximately contemporary implement assemblages in north-west Europe. The few *core tranchet* axeheads and the microliths with blunted backs (*dos rabattu*) may indicate some connection with the Mesolithic tradition of the north European plain, the Maglemosean, which is found at sites like Star Carr in Yorkshire (Clark 1936; 1954).

A central question is whether we should reconstruct the Larnian merely as an industry or as a full culture. It seems better to regard the Larnian material as the products of a flint industry based at those places at which fresh flint nodules are plentiful, where they fall naturally from the chalk cliffs. The large quantity of what would conventionally be regarded as waste products might lead us further to regard the relics of this Larnian industry as consisting mainly of *debitage*, the central objects having been exported; it might well then be that axe-production or the trimming of cores for export was the main goal of this industry. The almost complete absence of organic material from these sites makes it difficult to derive conclusions about either economy or date. There are, however, a small number of ox-bones, probably food remains, which may be particularly diagnostic from the cultural point of view.

Movius's dating was arrived at on the basis of pollen analysis, a correlation being made between the composition of the small samples of pollen recovered from the beach deposits and the sequence in a master diagram largely derived from raised bog deposits in the central plain (Jessen 1949). The small size of the samples would itself

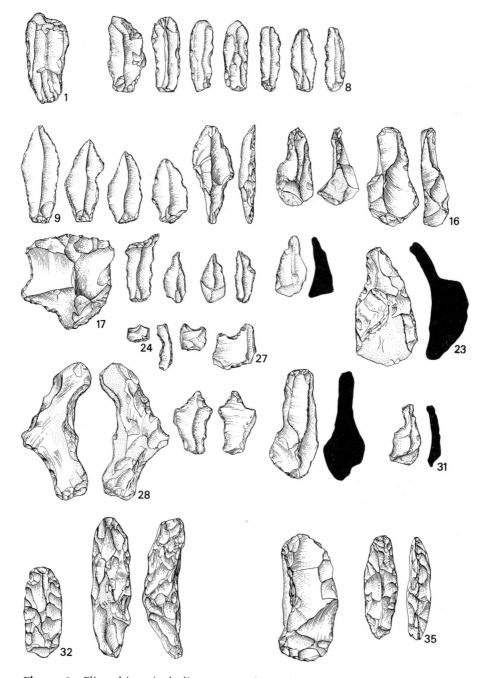

Figure 6 Flint objects including *core tranchet* axeheads of Movius's Late Larnian type from Cushendun, Larne, Glenarm, Island Magee (after Movius). ($\frac{2}{5}$)

make them unreliable for dating purposes. Differences between shore and inland pollen spectra would also arise through the very different environment of the coastal areas (Morrison 1959), and because of the fact that some pollens, like pine, float in water and may therefore be deposited in a very uneven fashion. The new radiocarbon process had not been devised when this dating was done; determinations more recently made by this method for Dalkey Island and for Sutton near Dublin indicate dates of 3340 ± 170 B.C. and 3000 ± 100 B.C., respectively. Neolithic axeheads and arrowheads and remains of domesticated ox (*bos taurus*) found with the Larnian material at Sutton and Dalkey and at the site of Ringneill Quay in Co. Down (Stephens and Collins 1960) confirm their Neolithic status. Ox-bones from the Larnian sites at Rough Island and Glenarm are probably also of domestic rather than wild ox, as the latter are not found among the post-glacial animals in Irish caves. However, the great depth at which Larnian artifacts occur at both Curran Point and Cushendun indicates that material was deposited at these sites for a very long time before the sea's maximum transgression; the very depth of this stratigraphy might still evidence a Mesolithic date for these sites.

In 1951 Mitchell carried out an investigation on an ancient sandy spit off the shore at the inland site of Toome Bay north of Lough Neagh, near to which Whelan had earlier found a number of flint artifacts (1955). At one site he found a group of large stones, possibly a hearth, beside which was a large piece of charcoal; this was dated by the radiocarbon method to 5725 ± 110 B.C. In a second cutting a steeply backed nosed scraper with narrow flutings was found on basal sand below mud with a pollen assemblage apparently of Zone VIb date. A third cutting yielded material associated with pollen of Zone VIc type: three parallel-sided blades, a burnt and broken leaf-shaped point, a bifacially flaked 'scraper' and a quartz hammer-stone with some worked wood. There was a flat, rectangular hazel tablet pierced with three holes, and a pine rod which may have been grooved to take microliths and pierced to take the thong of a harpoon (Fig. 5, 1–10). These finds may indicate the presence of a group of hunter-fishers on the shores of Lough Neagh in Mesolithic times, soon after 6000 B.C. The parallel-sided blades and leaf-shaped point may also link this site with the Larnian of the coast, and the earliest levels at Cushendun might then be correlated with this inland Mesolithic site of Toome.

A detailed study of the archaeological remains and of the pollens found at a site near Newferry on the east bank of the river Bann above Lough Beg has been published recently by Smith and Collins (1971). In a series of ash and charcoal layers formed in the diatomite during seasonal flooding, a number of flint artifacts were found, mostly leaf-shaped points of Larnian or Bann type. The upper layers contained Neolithic polished stone axeheads and a plano-convex knife. The published radiocarbon determination indicates a date of 3330 ± 170 B.C. for this layer. A single parallel-sided flake probably belongs to the end of the Boreal period (Zone VIc) and eight other flakes may belong to the earliest part of the Atlantic period (Zone VIIa); this, then, is another inland Mesolithic site yielding leaf-shaped points related to those of the Larnian tradition a little distance north of Mitchell's Toome Bay site.

Whereas the Larnian material discussed above is assigned to the Mesolithic period on the basis of pollen analyses and some radiocarbon determinations, the material itself being almost entirely *sui generis*, the flint assemblage found at the newly discovered site of Mount Sandel, Co. Derry, at the mouth of the river Bann, can be compared with the material of the well documented Mesolithic of the north European plain, the Maglemosean (Clark 1936; 1975). Here, microliths and *tranchet* axeheads have been discovered in excavations by Collins and by Woodman, the first time an extensive assemblage of the kind has been investigated in modern excavations in Ireland. A number of round huts, each about 6 m across, with central hearths, were found by Woodman (1974). These contained the bones of fish and birds, while the bones of mammals were relatively rare, suggesting that their occupants subsisted on a harvest of the sea. Several hundred microliths, some flint axeheads and a bone point were also found. A second site nearby, the stratigraphy of which is still doubtful, may have had, associated with the characteristic microliths, pottery of the first farmers, whose culture and impact on the landscape are now described.

The First Farmers and the Neolithic

In the centuries before 3000 B.C., the arts of farming and a new technology in pottery and stone arrived simultaneously in the northern part of Ireland. They were brought by mixed farmers, whose equipment, labelled Neolithic A by Childe (1931) and Piggott (1931), embraced shouldered and flat-based pottery, polished stone axeheads, flint knives and scrapers and kite-shaped projectile-heads. This assemblage is clearly related to those of the British Primary Neolithic and of Childe's West European Zone, while also projecting an insular Irish image. Though the tomb-builders of this province exhibited certain regional morphological preferences in Ireland, the Isle of Man and south-west Scotland, their burial mode, communal burial by a mixture of cremation and inhumation in megalithic tombs covered by trapezoidal long cairns facing east, is also standard in the Western Neolithic Zone. The relatively indestructible nature of these long cairn graves has made them, with the centres of the stone industry and their products, the most readily discoverable relics of this culture, settlements and houses being poorly documented. A realization of this imbalance between habitational and burial evidence has led to a recent orientation of research towards the discovery of settlement evidence. This research has included the use of pollen analysis and radiocarbon dating towards the delineation of the earliest farming culture in Ireland.

Land-Clearance and Cereal-Growing

Since 1941, when Iversen pointed out that the phenomena of the clearance of forest with the resultant increased growth of scrub, grasses and cereals, as documented by fluctuations in the pollen record of trees and grasses, could be interpreted as the making of clearance-patches by farmers, attention has been directed towards the recognition of this land-clearance or *landnam* phenomenon. In 1951, Mitchell noted that the pollens associated with agriculture appeared a short time after the beginning of Sub-Boreal (Zone VIIb) vegetation at Treanscrabbagh, below the Carrowkeel Passage Graves in Sligo and at Ravensdale Park in Louth (1951, 199), and later showed that the sciences of pollen analysis and radiocarbon dating could be combined to provide a hypothetical time-scale within which the earliest occurrences of farm clearance could be correlated (1958).

The investigations of Smith and Willis at Fallahogy, west of the Bann and three miles south of Kilrea in Derry, detailed, from the pollens in the raised bog peat, the impact of early agriculturalists on the area (Fig. 7): a stage of clearance had been followed by a stage of agriculture attested by abundant pollen of ribwort plantain, a weed indicating cultivation; then in the third stage the forest encroached on the abandoned clearance (1962). The clearance stage began with a decline of elm and a related rise in the pollens of grasses. The date of the transition between this stage and the next was determined roughly as between 3350 and 3200 B.C. Elm was the tree selected for clearance, the stands of oak and alder being left to grow throughout this phase. As soon as the clearings were made, digging of the soil brought on the rapid growth of plantain, while nettle and sorrel also appeared. About 2900 B.C., the forest began to encroach again, bringing about the disappearance of the plantain and sorrel and eventually of the grasses and nettles. Hazel quickly grew to a maximum, the elm re-asserting itself more slowly in the clearings, till a balance resembling that of the forest before clearance came about. The date of the second clearance in the area was determined at about 2500 B.C. Though no cereal pollens were recovered at Fallahogy, the pollen diagram documents the classic *landnam* or land-clearance of Iversen (1941; 1949).

More widespread application of the technique has led to the recognition of the same phenomenon at Newferry, also in the Bann Valley, where cereal pollen has been found (Smith and Collins 1971) and on a site close by ApSimon's Neolithic house at Ballynagilly in Tyrone. Comparably early bog sites at Beaghmore in Tyrone and Ballyscullion in Antrim have also been recently investigated, and at these sites and at Ballynagilly the palaeo-botanists have found evidence suggesting that a phase of cultivation and of mainly arable farming may have preceded a phase of pastoral farming lasting as much as 400 years (Pilcher et al. 1971). Other radiocarbon estimates indicate elm clearance near Redbog in Co. Louth at 3210 B.C., near Lomcloon in Offaly at 3200 B.C., and near Treanscrabbagh in Sligo at 3010 B.C. (McAulay and Watts 1961). These sites are relatively widely dispersed in the area north of the central plain and provide evidence for the widespread immigration of groups of farmers. Though the 'dates' arrived at by radiocarbon determinations need not be regarded as absolutely equivalent to calendar dates, it is evident from the present trend of the

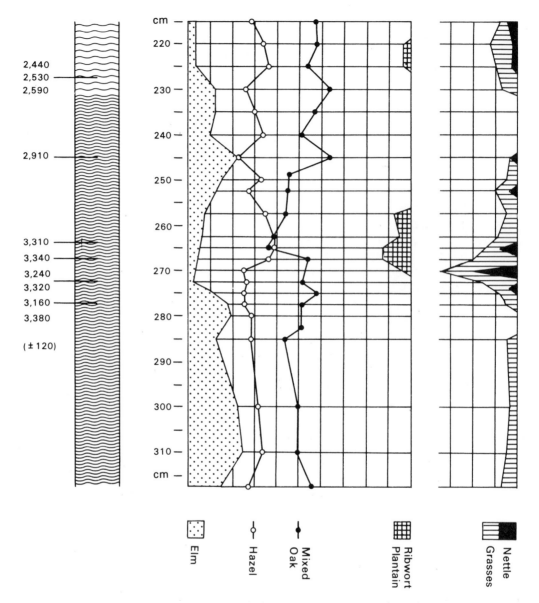

Figure 7 Pollen diagram documenting *landnam* or land-clearance phenomena, Fallahogy, Co. Derry (after Smith and Willis).

determinations that this immigration probably took place in the centuries before 3000 B.C.

Material Culture

Because the evidence brought forward by these natural scientists is derived largely from bog deposits, there arises the difficulty of correlating the phenomena they chronicle with the farming events which took place some distance to windward on arable ground. When the remains of these farmsteads are recovered, preservation of pollen is much poorer in the tilled soils than it is in the bogs nearby and the task of producing a fuller combined record from both sources is thus a difficult one. At present, a correlation is achieved by the somewhat arbitrary method of regarding those sites which have produced comparable radiocarbon determinations as being contemporaneous. Cereal grains have been found on Irish Neolithic habitations, but only infrequently; indeed more extensive evidence of the use of cereals has been found in the form of impressions made casually in the walls of pottery vessels (Jessen and Helbaek 1944). The bones of domesticated animals are rather more frequently preserved.

The search for diagnostic evidence leads us now to examine the more durable remains: a range of monuments and objects made possible by the religious ideals and efficiency of these first farmers and containing the Primary Neolithic assemblage of plain pottery, polished stone axeheads and leaf arrowheads. This assemblage, defined as primary by Childe in 1931, is also dated by radiocarbon to the centuries before 3000 B.C. at the earliest, at several sites in Britain and Ireland. As they afford the clearest evidence of the distribution of the Neolithic A in Ireland and contain many everyday artifacts, the long burial-cairns are the first Neolithic monuments to be described.

Long Burial-Cairns in the North: the Court Cairns

The primary group of long burial-cairns in Ireland consists of Court Cairns. Three hundred and ten are known in the area north of a line from Westport to Dundalk, no more than six lying south of this area (Fig. 17). The cairn has a long trapezoid or double trapezoid shape with a formal outer edge contained by orthostats (standing slabs of stone) or dry-walling. The long axis lies east–west and there is a general emphasis on the eastern end (de Valera 1960; de Valera and Ó Nualláin 1960, 1964, 1972) (Fig. 8).

Within this trapezoid cairn were built one or two courts of roughly oval outline or shaped like a segment of this oval cut on a chord parallel to the short axis. The main burial-chambers opening off this on the long axis were arranged in one or two galleries normally made up of two or four chambers. The burial-gallery, 2 m to 3·5 m wide, was entered between well-matched portals roofed with a flat lintel and often

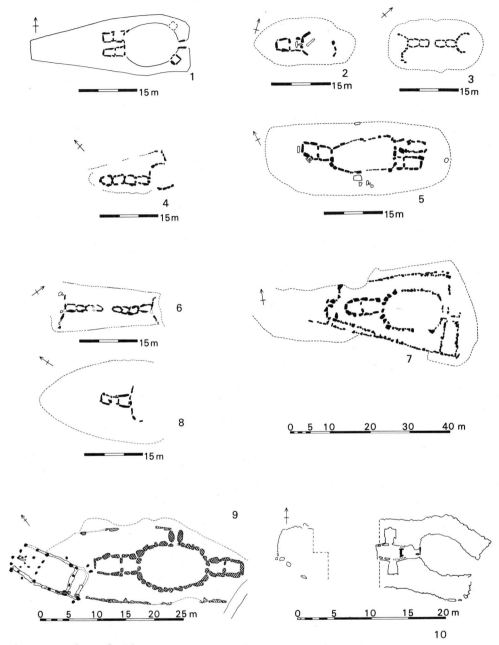

Figure 8 Plans of Irish Court Cairns: 1 Malin More, Co. Donegal; 2 Arnasbrack, Co. Sligo; 3 Ballywholan, Co. Tyrone; 4 Browndod, Co. Antrim; 5 Deerpark, Co. Sligo; 6 Audleystown, Co. Down; 7 Creevykeel, Co. Sligo; 8 Ballyalton, Co. Down (after de Valera); 9 Ballyglass, Co. Mayo (after Ó Nualláin); 10 Behy, Co. Mayo (after de Valera and Ó Nualláin).

flanked on either side by matched stones which reached as high as the top of the lintel to form an impressive entrance façade. This façade was designed to contain the cairn where it rose to its highest point to cover the roof of the gallery. The gallery chambers were normally divided one from another by a low sill between two upright jambs and they were roofed with large corbels set in a number of courses. This corbelling is at its most magnificent where split glacial boulders were used. The segmenting jambs and the endstone were frequently gabled to accommodate the corbelling.

A small proportion of galleries in Mayo and Sligo are transepted or cruciform in ground plan. Both façade and gallery show best the confidence of the earliest megalith-builders in Ireland in handling apparently awkward stones. Variant single burial chambers are occasionally placed with an entry opening from the court or, more commonly, from the outer edge of the cairn behind the main gallery.

Creevykeel, situated 30 m (100 ft) above the sea overlooking the natural harbour at Mullaghmore in Sligo, had a trapezoidal cairn 55 m long (Fig. 8, 7). It was excavated by Hencken of the Harvard Expedition in 1936 and 1937 (1939). A short passage through the broader east end gave on to an oval court, its orthostats rising to a massive flat façade at the west end. The entry to the two-chambered gallery, 10 m long and 3 m wide, and segmented roughly halfway along its length by gabled jambs and sill, was under a massive lintel running 1·50 m back over two low jambs 1·50 m high. Large ice-boulders split in two were used to roof the chambers, the rounded surfaces resting on both the cairn and the low orthostats which formed the chamber sides, and then reaching inwards over the gabled backstone. Three subsidiary chambers, two on the north side and one on the south, were inserted in the tail of the cairn to the west of these main chambers. The evidence of burial was five small pockets of cremated bone in the main chambers; the great quantities of pottery in the north-eastern subsidiary chamber may have been deposited with inhumed burials which have now disappeared.

Clearly the open court was designed to accommodate the mourners at a funeral – it would hold about fifty people comfortably; indeed, this court was paved near the entrance to the burial-gallery. Its sacred character is emphasized by a polished diorite axehead buried at the entrance.

A smaller and simpler variant of Creevykeel lies under a peat cover at a height of 120 m to 150 m (400 ft to 500 ft) above the Moy estuary at Carrowleagh on the slopes of the Ox Mountains. The tomb is buried in blanket peat and enclosed within a short trapezoid cairn only 25 m long. The court, ill-defined under its cover of peat, is only 7 m on the longer, east–west, axis, and gives on to two chambers in line measuring 8 m from front to back. The front chamber has lost its roofstones; the corbels, however, are still in position and the commodious rear chamber, today used as a shelter by turf-workers, is still completely roofed. Three courses of split granite boulders with smaller stones between form corbels over which are set two massive flat roofing-slabs spanning well over the 2 m width of the chamber.

The economy in cairn-building of Carrowleagh is repeated at Behy, 150 m (500 ft) up on the side of Maumakeogh and to the west of the concentration of about thirty tombs in the Killala focus. This tomb was also built on the old glacial deposits and was covered long after its abandonment as a tomb in an envelope of blanket peat. Here the coffin-shaped double-trapezoid cairn was 28 m long, its dry-walled revetment enclosing both an oval court, 7·50 m by 5 m, and a transepted gallery, rising to its highest (2 m) and widest (11 m) at the transepts (Fig. 8, 10). The flattened façade of the dry-walled court at the entrance to the gallery had a peculiar bottle-shape, and its long axis diverged from that of the chambers by about fifteen degrees, two features which are repeated in many other Court Cairns. The segmentation between the two chambers was effected by the jamb and sill arrangement, but in this tomb the jambs were set parallel to the line of the side-walls rather than at right angles to them. Behind the segmentation in the gallery the well-constructed side-chambers, built of quarried gritstone slabs, like the rest of the megalithic construction, opened north and south.

Tombs with this transeptal arrangement – a feature much more familiar in Irish Passage Graves and among the Cotswold–Severn tombs of southern Britain – are known at eight sites, seven in Mayo and one in Sligo (de Valera 1965). All are concentrated close to the great Killala focus, which probably included some of the earliest Irish Court Cairns.

The grand style of the Court Cairn architects, a centre-court variant with a different arrangement of court and chambers, is found in the area of the tombs' most dense distribution along the shores of Donegal Bay. In this type, two-chambered galleries are set east and west on either side of a massive court entered from one side. This arrangement is found in the excavated tomb of Ballyglass II in Mayo (Ó Nualláin 1972) (Fig. 8, 9; Plate 4a), Ballymunterhiggin south of Ballyshannon in Donegal, and Farranmacbride in the south-west corner of Donegal, where a symmetrical arrangement of four unusual single-chambered subsidiaries also opens off the court. The famous Deerpark tomb, sited in a limestone area of great natural beauty overlooking Lough Gill in Sligo, has twin, parallel, two-chambered galleries on the east side of its court opposed to the single western gallery. Here the court is entered from the south side (Fig. 8, 5).

The siting and general magnificence of the architectural conception and construction of these centre-court tombs suggests that they belong to a mature phase, well after that of the pioneers, when the builders' economy had been secured. At the same time, the freedom to experiment which their builders enjoyed in placing the various elements of the tomb suggests that they were built early in the tradition, too early for rigid academicism to have set in. Their siting in the centres of greatest population in the west reinforces this notion.

At a time when this freedom was still in the air, a version with a court at either end and galleries placed back to back, the dual Court Cairn – the inverse of the centre-court version – grew up in Mayo, and was disseminated inland along the drumlin and lakeland area between Lough Allen in Leitrim and the inlet of Carlingford on the east coast; examples are found at Carbad More near Killala, Glenmakeerin in Antrim and King Orry's Grave on the Isle of Man. In the confusion resulting from the fact that this tomb-type faced both to the east and to the west, it was perhaps inevitable that a loss of the rule of eastern orientation standard in the west of the country should occur. Its construction probably influenced that of multiple-chambered galleries like those of Aghanaglack in Fermanagh, Cohaw in Cavan and Audleystown in Down, and of the much reduced courts in the east.

This preference for more than two chambers in line is expressed most clearly at the east end of the group diffused across mid-Ulster to Antrim, where tombs like Browndod and Ballymarlagh have four chambers; further on, East Bennan on the island of Arran in Scotland and Cashtal yn Ard on Man each has five chambers.

From the very density of distribution in Mayo, Sligo and Donegal, from the presence there of the greatest numbers of finely built tombs, from the strongest adherence in that area to the rule of eastern orientation, to the building of full rather than open courts and to the two-chambered burial element as standard, de Valera has argued the primacy of the western tradition of that region (1960, 45). An additional determinant of early typological date are the transeptal sites like Behy found in the primary area. From this area two clear lines of eastward diffusion showing progressive loss of primary traits can be established: a dual-court line just north of the Central Plain and a line north of this across Fermanagh, Tyrone and Derry to Antrim. The building of subsidiary chambers remained a feature of this more northerly group.

In early studies of the north-eastern tombs Evans noted their siting 'on the fringes of the uplands' at elevations varying between 400 ft and 800 ft, 'in the light stony soils intermediate between the out-cropping rocks of the hills and the deep glacial drifts of the lowlands' (Evans and Jope 1952, 79). De Valera noted a similar pattern towards the west (1960, 40). In their discussion of the Mayo pattern, he and Ó Nualláin described the preference for siting on 'long esker ridges which would have provided better-drained soils than otherwise available on the wide water-logged moorlands' and the avoidance of the drumlin area in the triangle between Killala, Crossmolina and Ballina (1964, 115).

Occasionally, commanding situations were chosen, like those of Deerpark in Sligo and Tullyskeherny in Leitrim, 225 m (750 ft) up. The tombs are seldom grouped even in pairs; Browndod Hill in Antrim, with three tombs, being the exception that proves the rule. The distribution pattern is very much in keeping with the picture of small communities of peasant farmers. This pattern is also clear in the finds from the tombs and in the other features of the culture of the tomb-builders.

Burial Ritual and Finds

The earliest excavations of Court Cairns were confined to the chambers. Bell recorded such investigations early in the nineteenth century at Ballymacdermot and Annaghcloghmullin in Armagh and Ballybriest in Derry, all of which appeared to be

31

confined to the galleries. Later in the century, work at Moyaver and Dunteige (Cairnasegart) in Antrim was similarly confined. It was only after 1930, with the renewed work begun by Evans and Davies and the Belfast Naturalists' Field Club, that investigations of both the courts and the surrounding cairns were begun, giving an opportunity of discovering more than merely the burials.

It might be thought strange that the burials noted in the Court Cairns so far excavated do not normally number more than three, with the exception of Creevykeel (5), Ballyalton (6/8), Ballymacaldrack (5/6) and Audleystown (30/33). It was observed in many excavations, however, that there had been a good deal of later disturbance in Neolithic and Bronze Age times, as well as in more recent illicit digging. The inundation of many tombs by acid peat and destruction by wild animals would also be inimical to the preservation of inhumed burials. It is hardly surprising, therefore, that burial by inhumation is attested at only five sites, and that no burial evidence at all was found at Kilnagarns Lower, Ballywholan and Browndod.

In six tombs, a protective paving appears to have been laid over the original burials in the manner of the stones covering the much larger deposits in Passage Graves. Several tombs give evidence of continuance of burial in the original rite to a level well above the first deposits, indicating a long use of the tomb. The typological diversity of pottery styles found in many tombs also implies a very long use for them. Collins, however, was inclined to the view that the unusually large number of burials, both cremated and inhumed, at Audleystown were buried in a single act of deposition (1954).

Intermingled with the burials, and presumably deposited as the personal equipment of the dead in the main chambers and also in the subsidiary chambers, are found quantities of pottery, stone and flint artifacts (Figs 9, 10) as well as a few ornaments and some food offerings. Scattered finds of the same assemblage are found in levels of the courts and both in and under the cairns of these tombs.

The handful of personal ornaments found (Fig. 10, 13–20) contrasts with the many items of practical everyday equipment also found with the burials, and also with the large numbers of beads and pendants from the Passage Graves described in chapter 3. Their fewness may indicate a peasant conservatism, if not indeed puritanism.

It has been suggested that the broken condition of much of the pottery found in these tombs argues deposition in terms of a rite in which the pottery was smashed at the burial ceremony. Though this suggestion is not excluded, it may be that a number of vessels were deposited whole. The single open shouldered bowl found at Cohaw, for instance, with its suspension-holes under the rim, may have been used as a hanging bowl and may even have been left as such in the tomb, to break on the ground when the suspension string rotted.

Though both round- and flat-based pottery vessels are found in a variety of forms and in plain and decorated styles, by far the most common pottery type found in these tombs is the undecorated shouldered bowl; this is found in all tombs which yield significant quantities of pottery (Fig. 9). Bowls open at the mouth are commonest,

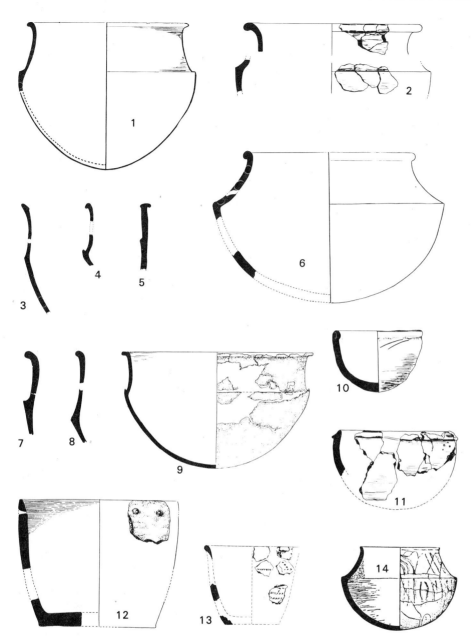

Figure 9 Court Cairn pottery finds: 1 Browndod, Co. Antrim; 2 Creevykeel, Co. Sligo; 3 Tamnyrankin, Co. Derry; 4, 9 Ballyalton, Co. Down; 5 Ballymacaldrack, Co. Antrim; 6, 13 Ballybriest, Co. Derry; 7, 8 Ballymarlagh, Co. Antrim; 10 Clady Haliday, Co. Tyrone; 11 Ballymacdermot, Co. Armagh; 12 Legland, Co. Tyrone; 14 Beacharra, Mull of Kintyre, Scotland. ($\frac{1}{3}$)

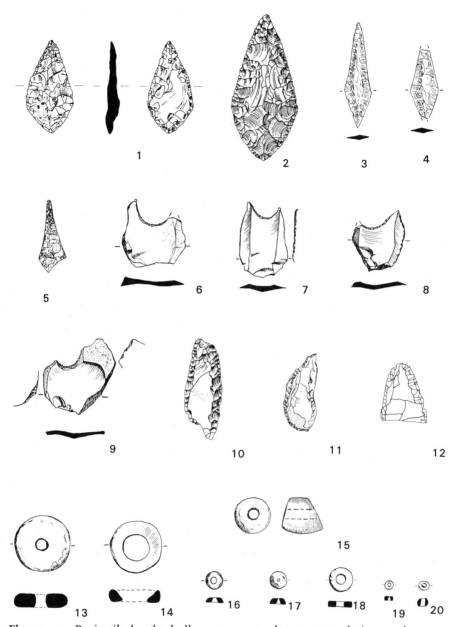

Figure 10 Projectile-heads, hollow scrapers, plano-convex knives and ornaments from Irish Court Cairns: 1 Kilnagarns Lower, Co. Leitrim; 2, 10 Audleystown, Co. Down; 3, 4, 6–9 Cairnasegart, Dunteige, Co. Antrim; 5 Clontygora Large, Co. Armagh; 11 Legland, Co. Tyrone; 12, 13 Ballyalton, Co. Down; 14 Clady Haliday, Co. Tyrone; 15,16 Ballymacaldrack, Co. Antrim; 17 Aghanaglack, Co. Fermanagh; 18 Creevykeel, Co. Sligo; 19 Ballymarlagh, Co. Antrim; 20 Mourne Park, Co. Down. $(\frac{2}{5})$

only four plain vessels of Piggott's Form J, in which the mouth is smaller than the neck, being found at Creevykeel, Ballyreagh, Ballybriest and 'Larne'. The rims tend to be simple. The exaggerated shoulder noted by Davies and Evans (1934), Clark (1937) and Hencken (1939) as characteristic of Irish Neolithic pottery is as marked in Court Cairn finds as it is elsewhere, but not in the western tombs. This form is also found in the Isle of Man, and may indicate a regional development characteristic of the lands around the northern part of the Irish Sea. It probably resulted from making the neck and the body of the pot separately and from interaction with the closed bowls of Piggott's Form J style.

Fifteen other tombs have yielded plain unshouldered bowls. The rims of these are usually pointed and slightly inturned, the walls thicker than normal. They appear to have been used as mugs or soup-bowls, in contrast to the shouldered vessels, which may have been used for cooking. One of the Ballymacdermot vessels has an unusual ledge rim, and two bowls found at Audleystown are exceptional in having lugs like Scottish vessels found in similar tombs at Clachaig, Torlin and Sliddery. The ornamented variants of the simple bowls are normally decorated in channelled or corded technique and, with few exceptions, can be assigned to the Late Neolithic on the basis of the cord technique and of the motifs and their arrangement.

The shouldered decorated pottery, styled Beacharra ware by Childe from the prolific eponymous Scottish site on the Mull of Kintyre (1940, 53), is most elegant and commonest in its narrow-mouthed Form J variant (Fig. 9, 14). Few complete Irish examples are decorated in the 'purer' channelled technique but examples are known from 'Larne', Ballyutoag, Ballymacaldrack, Clontygora Large, Barnes Lower and Audleystown. Fingertip fluting on three vessels at Audleystown may be a variant of channelling and brings these vessels into the same range as similar vessels found at the Lyles Hill settlement in Antrim, at Nether Largie and Easterton of Roseisle in the east of Scotland and in the Mull Hill Circle on the Isle of Man. Many of these, however, show some development in rim or shoulder form, implying a typological development from the ideal simple ancestral form found at Beacharra itself (Scott 1964, 151).

Thick-walled vessels with flat bases have been found at seven sites in Down, Armagh, Derry and Fermanagh, in most of these cases associated with other Neolithic vessels or in the earliest levels distinguishable in the tombs (Fig. 9, 12). Several other Irish Neolithic sites have also yielded this pottery, which appears to have been a coarser kitchen storage ware. Similar flat-based ware occurs at a few Neolithic sites in Scotland. It appears that the ware is characteristic of an Irish-Scottish province, being absent from the otherwise closely comparable Neolithic of southern Britain. A few vessels of this class found in Fermanagh, Derry and Antrim are decorated. A pair of elegant decorated flat-based vessels from the Creevykeel Court Cairn are *sui generis* in the Irish Neolithic.

The range of flint implements found is almost identical with that of everyday habitation sites: the assemblages from Kilnagarns Lower, Dunteige (Cairnasegart)

35

and Audleystown exhibit the range well (Fig. 10). Kite-shaped projectile-heads are found with hollow scrapers, plano-convex knives and axeheads of flint and stone. Six sites have yielded javelin-heads, projectile-heads more than 5 cm long. The classic kite-shaped javelin-head with polished faces, so characteristic of the north-east of Ireland, was found at Kilnagarns Lower and Clady Haliday. Unpolished examples of similar shape were found at Creevykeel, Kilnagarns, Aghanaglack and Audleystown. Unusually large ovoid examples came from the west at Creevykeel and Behy, one Behy example being heavily burnt.

As with the javelin-heads, the smaller arrowheads (less than 5 cm long) tend to be kite-shaped, and only three true leaf-shaped arrowheads are known in the Court Cairn range, from Kilnagarns and Ballybriest. The two barbed-and-tanged arrowheads found at Aghanaglack in apparently early stratigraphical association must, like the rest of their class, belong to the Early Bronze Age.

The characteristic Irish hollow scraper, found at twenty-one Court Cairns, is more numerous than projectile-heads and as widespread. Nine sites produced end-scrapers of classic horseshoe form. Fourteen plano-convex knives, many with unreduced longitudinal flake-scars, indicate complete conformity with the non-burial monuments of the local Primary Neolithic. One found at Legland in Co. Down was heavily burnt.

Only two flint axeheads, found with a hoard of flint artifacts and flakes at Ballyalton, are known; all others are of stone. The Tievebulliagh factory in Antrim was the source of two found at Ballymarlagh, otherwise diorite and epidiorite from unidentified sources was used for axeheads found at Creevykeel and Ballymacaldrack. A faceted shape was preferred at Creevykeel, Behy and Ballymacaldrack, where a roughout was also found. A single adzehead of epidiorite came from Clontygora Large. At both Dunloy and Creevykeel the axehead assumed the role of magical guardian of the tomb.

The faunal evidence from Court Cairns gives a much fuller record than is available from the habitations described below, despite the fact that ritual preferences for particular animals might have reduced the range deposited with burials, animal bones, probably the remains of funeral feasts, being found at eight sites, Clontygora Large, Ballymarlagh, Audleystown, Ballyalton, Goward, Mourne Park, Aghanaglack and Deerpark. All eight, except Clontygora and Deerpark, yielded evidence of ox-bones, presumably domesticated, while bones of sheep or goat were identified at Clontygora Large, Audleystown and possibly also at Deerpark; these are presumably also the remains of domesticated animals. Bones of pig and dog or wolf from both Audleystown and Ballyalton may indicate the hunting of wild animals, as do the deer-bones from Aghanaglack. Bird-bones were identified at Audleystown. If this sample is representative of the meat-eating habits of the tomb-builders, hunting maintained a high priority side by side with the rearing of domesticated cattle and sheep or goats.

Industries: the Exploitation of Stone and Flint

A central item in the tool assemblage of the first Irish farmers was the axehead of polished stone, one of the prime indicators of Childe's Western zone (1931). From the sites of Tievebulliagh and Brockley in the north-east, rough bars of igneous rock were traded to be polished as need arose by buyers in bulk, or to be retailed by our first itinerant traders. This pattern is similar to that established in Britain, where evidence of a similar trade from factory sites has been found, and in Brittany, where workers at Rennes have recently established the existence of such a factory at Séledin near Bénodet (Le Roux 1971).

At the site of Tievebulliagh, 1000 ft up on the side of a mountain overlooking Cushendall in north-east Antrim, the potential of outcrops of porcellanite was realized in providing numerous axeheads. This site, discovered by Knowles at the beginning of this century, has a thick deposit of *debitage*, flakes and half-finished bars discarded in the roughing-out process. At Brockley on Rathlin, E. E. Evans has discovered another factory site where porcellanite petrologically indistinguishable from that of Tievebulliagh was exploited (Knowles 1906; Jope 1952).

Here the stages in the production of an axehead before polishing can be deduced from partly finished examples: after roughing out a massive keeled block of stone, the keel was reduced by transverse flaking which became progressively shallower as the plano-convex roughout shape was approached (Fig. 11).

Most of the products of Tievebulliagh and Brockley are found in Co. Antrim and the neighbouring east Derry area immediately west of the river Bann. Examples of porcellanite axeheads have been found well outside that area of primary dispersal at Beltany in Donegal and Carrickbanagher in Sligo to the west, at Coomnacloughy in Cork, Lough Gur in Limerick and Killamoat in Wicklow to the south, and in Britain as far south-east as Kent. At least a dozen have been recognized in the area of south-west Scotland which the Court Cairn builders colonized (Scott 1969a) (Fig. 12).

No polished axeheads have so far been found at the factory sites themselves. Hoards of polished axeheads, some of them partly finished, found at places like Portglenone and Newferry, where a hoard of six axeheads had been left close to a polishing stone hollowed out of sandstone like a saddle-quern, may indicate that trimming and polishing was done on the habitations themselves, though it might also be interpreted as evidence of a rudimentary retail trade. A chipping and polishing site found under a cover of later blanket peat at Loughaveema in Antrim might well have been the station of a packman. Dramatic evidence of the transport of polished axeheads has come to light recently at Aghintemple near Ardagh in Co. Longford, where a circular or oval basket, woven of alder rods and bound probably with rushes, was found about 4 m deep in a bog. Inside the bag was a small polished limestone axehead of D-shaped cross-section (Raftery 1970a). Could this be the last axehead in the stock-in-trade of an itinerant trader?

The deposits dredged up in Victorian drainage operations at prehistoric river-

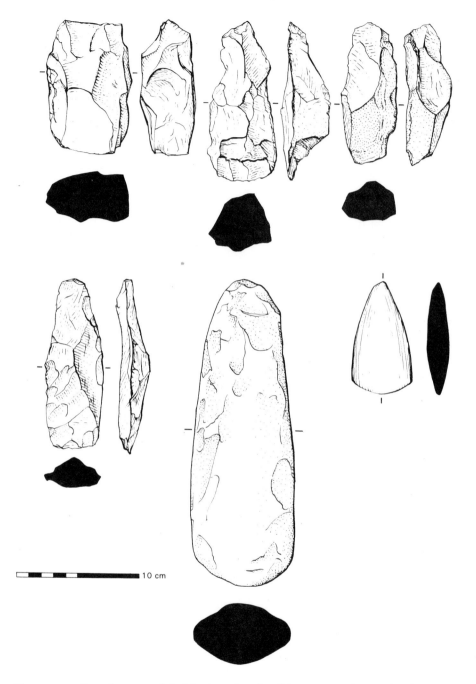

Figure 11   Roughouts and finished axeheads of igneous rock, north of Ireland, showing stages of axe manufacture (after Jope).

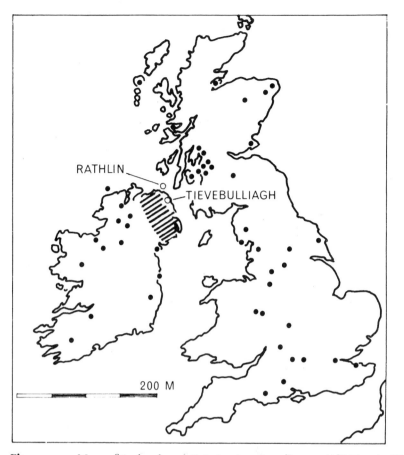

Figure 12 Map of Ireland and Britain showing dispersal of Tievebulliagh axeheads (after Rynne). Area of densest distribution in the north-east of Ireland hatched.

crossings on the Bann and the Shannon at Toome, Portglenone and Keelogue, for instance, have included rich assemblages of polished stone axeheads. The richness of these deposits is to be expected on the Bann river, but the many axeheads found in the Shannon are perhaps unexpected evidence of a much-used ford on the esker system between Dublin and Connacht and indicate a demand for axeheads presumably in Connacht which was filled from an easterly source (Griffith 1844) (Fig. 17).

The insular industry seems to have satisfied the needs of the Irish communities, as there is little evidence for the importation of axeheads from the prolific British factories, not even from nearby Graig Lwyd in north Wales nor from Cumberland; Jope noted the existence of only four British axeheads in his survey (1952, 48). However, some community of tradition between the Cumbrian area and the north-east of Ireland is indicated by the similar flat-sided shape of some products of both areas.

39

Many Irish axeheads are made from materials other than porcellanite. Jope mentions the use of clay-slate and mudstone, of green stone from a source near Creeslough in Donegal, of an epidiorite presumably glacial in origin, and of the pink Mourne granite of Co. Down (1952). Rynne has identified the use of dolerite from Donard in Wicklow and Jackson has noted numbers of axeheads made from the porphyry of Lambay Island off the north Dublin coast (Lucas 1968, 94), and from a green stone in Limerick (Raftery 1969, 94). To judge from the number of axeheads of stone other than porcellanite, it is likely that further Irish factory sites have yet to be discovered; Jope has hinted at the presence of one near Clogh, Co. Antrim.

The normal method of hafting is indicated by complete examples from Maguire's Bridge, Co. Fermanagh and Ehenside Tarn in Cumberland, and a broken alder handle recently found at Edercloon in a Co. Longford bog (Raftery 1967, 2) (Fig. 13). These hafts are curved upwards, away from the plane of the blade, at the end farthest from the handle in the manner of stylized representations of axes on a number of Breton Passage Graves like Mané Kerioned and La Table des Marchands (Péquart *et al.* 1927, Pls 37, 43). The majority of Irish axeheads were made to fit into hafts of this kind though Jope noted just a few examples which appear to have been sleeved (1952, 41). Normally the axeheads range between 7·5 cm and 17·5 cm long, though exceptional ones reach 30 cm in length. Such massive axeheads have been found at Armoy and Danesfort in Co. Antrim and with a Passage Grave pottery vessel at a hearth under a bog at Lislea in Monaghan. Besides the flat-sided form already noted, Irish axeheads tend towards a D-shaped cross-section which is claimed as being the best for tree-felling. In modern experiments these apparently crude axeheads have been shown to be surprisingly effective for forest clearance: in a Danish experiment three men cleared over 500 square metres of silver-birch forest in four hours, one Neolithic axehead felling more than 100 trees without breaking.

The durable rock of Tievebulliagh was not used exclusively for the making of axeheads: adzeheads and chisels of this stone have also been found. While the adzeheads are clearly designed for specialized woodworking, the chisels may have been used, with some axeheads, for digging the soil in preparation for the sowing of crops.

Though these axes are typical of Primary Neolithic sites, they continued in use into the Early Bronze Age, as associations of polished stone axeheads with some Food Vessels, as at Trillick, Co. Tyrone, indicate. If proof were needed that axes were in everyday use, their occurrence on the settlements of Goodland and Lyles Hill in Antrim, Ballynagard and Ushet on Rathlin, and at Lough Gur and Island MacHugh should be convincing. They have also been found in contexts presumably implying habitation at Newferry and Loughanisland on the Bann and with Neolithic A pottery at Tyrone House in the south suburbs of Belfast. Though their deposition at the Court Cairns of Creevykeel, Ballymacaldrack, Ballymarlagh and Tamnyrankin may be ascribed to everyday use or even to habitation, the placing of axeheads in the entrance to the court of Creevykeel and the gallery entrance at Ballymacaldrack may indicate a

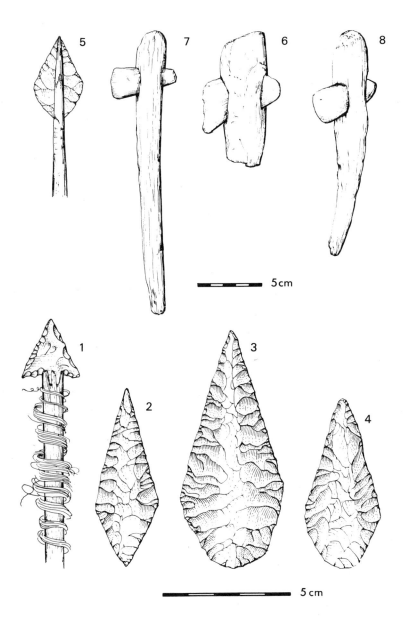

Figure 13 Neolithic hafted arrowheads and axeheads: 1 Ballykillen Bog, Co. Offaly (after Wilde); 2–4 Craigs Bog, Teeshan Bog and near Glarryford, Co. Antrim (after Knowles); 5 Fyvie, Aberdeenshire (after Anderson); 6 Edercloon, Co. Longford; 7 Maguire's Bridge, Co. Fermanagh (after Raftery); 8 Co. Monaghan (after du Noyer). (The arrowhead in the top row has the same scale as those in the bottom row.)

magical use akin to that carried into recent times: a Tievebulliagh specimen from Killamoat in Wicklow had been placed under the doorstone of an old farmhouse (Rynne 1964b).

Side by side with these igneous rock industries, the flint sources of the same north-eastern area were exploited. They provided the material for an assemblage of axeheads and smaller flint tools in the pattern established in Britain and western Europe and including leaf-shaped arrowheads and end-scrapers with the classic insular flint tool, the hollow scraper, and another insular form, the plano-convex knife. Outside the Antrim area, the poorer flint from the glacial drift was used in conjunction with black chert from the plentiful limestone deposits and, exceptionally, quartzite was brought into play to satisfy the demands of the large farming population. Fresh flint was also traded from Antrim into these areas for the making of larger objects like the fine kite-shaped javelin-heads with polished faces.

A narrow band of chalk limestone extending under the edge of the basalt deposit in Antrim, east Derry and north Down (Fig. 3) is the only source of fresh flint which was exploited in Ireland in ancient times; great numbers of flint implements are thus found in the area where porcellanite axeheads are commonest. The need for sinking mine-shafts from which galleries to exploit the stratified flint deposits would have been thrown did not arise in Ireland as was necessary at sites like Grimes Graves in England: coastal exposures on the chalk cliffs of Antrim apparently did away with this need. Near the largest of all these exposures of chalk now partly buried under blanket peat between Knockdhu and Ballygalley Head, four miles north of Larne on the Antrim coast, the Court Cairn of Cairnasegart at Dunteige yielded an austere Neolithic A assemblage in excavations by Lord Antrim and Dr Holden in January 1870 (Herity, Evans and Megaw 1968). The raw material may have come from a system of open-cast flint mines on nearby Ballygalley Head from which Collins has reported Neolithic A pottery (1958). Other large deposits under Crockanore, inland from Murlough Bay, along Church Bay on Rathlin, and above Whitepark Bay may have also invited prospectors. The inhabitants of Lyles Hill may have drawn their flint from deposits under the modern village of Templepatrick, while those of the nearby Squires Hill may have looked for their flint to the narrow band of chalk running along the face of Ligoniel by Cave Hill to Carnmoney Hill on the higher ground to the north-west of modern Belfast.

Though many projectile-heads have been found in bogs, little evidence of arrowshafts has been recovered. The tanged arrowhead, presumably of Early Bronze Age date, found beside a trackway in Ballykillen Bog near Edenderry in Offaly, and now in the Cambridge University Museum, had a briarwood shaft tied with gut (Wilde 1857, 254). Knowles noted an ashwood shaft about 75 cm long and a hollow-based arrowhead of similar date found at a depth of about 2 m at Kanestown Bog in Antrim. He described the shaft as split at the top, the arrow cemented into the split and the shaft bound with animal sinew for a distance of about 10 cm from the head in order to prevent it splitting (1909).

A similar method of hafting was used on the kite-shaped arrowhead of yellow flint found at Blackhillock, Fyvie, in Aberdeenshire, in 1875 (Anderson 1876, 508–13). This was found between 2·4 m and 3 m deep in the bog; the shaft was cleft at the end and ran along to the point of the arrowhead on both faces to form a sort of strengthening midrib. Three Neolithic arrowheads in Knowles's collection had 'shadows', presumably the stain of the cement used in this method of hafting; in each case the 'shadow' ran to the tip of the arrowhead and indicated a similar method of hafting. These were found at Craigs Bog, at Teeshan Bog near Ballymena, and in a bog near Glarryford, all in Co. Antrim, and ranged between 6 cm and 8 cm in length (Knowles 1909). Knowles also noted similar staining on a javelin-head 7·5 cm long at Curncarney near Kells in Antrim. No bow of this early date has been found in Ireland, but presumably the form of the Irish bows was similar to the Neolithic examples described by Clark from Ashcott and Meare in Somerset (1963).

Polished javelin-heads of distinctively insular form, so large that they must have been made from fresh nodules of flint, are common in the Bann and Braid valleys in Antrim and generally in the north-east. Occurrences outside that area can be taken to indicate the dispersal of fresh flint or of finished artifacts from the north-east in the manner of the Grand Pressigny trade from its source in the Loire valley in France. The Derry, Tyrone, Down, Cavan and Sligo examples noted by Evans and Jope (1952), with those noted from Court Cairns above, thus indicate a trade in flint parallel to that in stone. The trade-routes did not end with the provinces of Ulster or north Connacht, however, as examples from the south are known from counties Cork, Wicklow, Meath, Galway and Roscommon.

A Late Neolithic hoard consisting of thirteen hollow scrapers, seven end-scrapers, one *petit tranchet* derivative arrowhead and three flakes with secondary working found at the Three Towns, near the head of the valley of the Braid river in central Antrim (Fig. 14), is interpreted by Flanagan as a personal hoard rather than as indicating trade because of the lustre showing wear on the cutting edge of one of the hollow scrapers (1966b). It would be surprising, however, in view of the widespread dispersal of stone and flint, if fresh flint was not similarly diffused, probably in the form of near-finished or finished objects. One example of this is the 'Killybeg' hoard, probably from mid-Antrim, which consisted of six finished end-scrapers, a polished stone axehead of mudstone and a dozen blanks for hollow scrapers which appear to have been found in a wooden box (Woodman 1967). What itinerant crafts-man/retailer lost this and where was he bound?

It is clear that many of the Larnian deposits along the north-east coast from Dublin to Donegal belong to this Neolithic period rather than to the earlier Mesolithic; they are then part of the industrial superstructure of this farming society.

The range of Neolithic A flint implements is the same as that found in the Court Cairns: plano-convex penknives, some of which show evidence of hafting, together with the hollow scrapers, projectile-heads and axeheads described above. It may be that a search for implements designed specifically for agricultural use will result in the

43

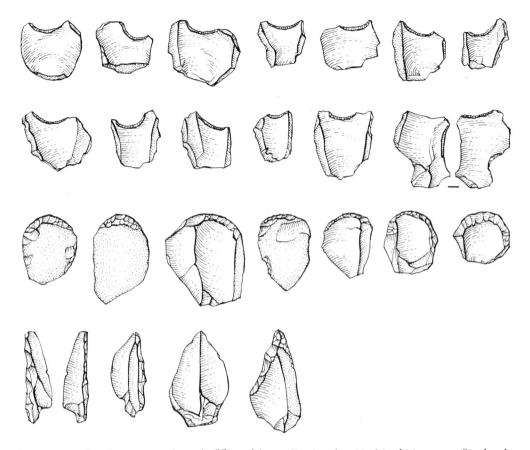

Figure 14 The Three Towns hoard of flint objects, Co. Antrim, National Museum of Ireland (after Flanagan). ($\frac{3}{4}$)

recognition of our first Neolithic sickles; these may well have been composite if we are to judge from the small size of most of the objects in our flint assemblage.

Habitations, Houses and Farmsteads

Though the burials and industrial sites of the first Neolithic people were undoubtedly matched in antiquity by habitations and farmsteads outnumbering these at least tenfold, evidence of houses is hard to come by in Ireland as elsewhere in western and northern Europe. The imbalance can be readily understood: the wooden houses of the Neolithic were neither built as durably as the stone burial structures nor had they the same easily recognizable features. If it is stated that in the otherwise well documented Primary Neolithic of lowland Britain not a single house structure is

44

known, it can be seen how fortunate Ireland is in having even four sites at which Neolithic houses are recognized.

Habitational evidence ranges from the well preserved and well documented sites recovered in modern excavations like Lough Gur to stray finds of Neolithic pottery or flint implements like those discovered in the excavation of Early Iron Age hill-forts or of ring-forts, and to well preserved material found under burial-mounds and cairns. There are also many old finds, the sites of which might yet yield a rich reward in modern excavations.

Because of the unchanging nature of the material found on these sites it is difficult to assign them to specific stages in the Primary Neolithic tradition, which may have lasted as long as a millennium in Ireland. Regional specializations can hardly be assigned an absolute date, neither can typological developments, and the major problem is to isolate the complete assemblage of the original farmers; so far, the main interpretations hold that this should have a 'pure' aspect (Childe 1931; Piggott 1931; de Valera 1960, 1961; Case 1961, 1969). But it seems certain that too much emphasis has been placed on assigning all 'pure' forms to the earliest period; such forms are found in undoubtedly late contexts in association with materials and monuments of clearly Late Neolithic date (chapter 4). For this reason it seems best to assign sites to the Primary Neolithic *tradition*, rather than to Primary Neolithic *phase*.

The general distribution of pottery, stone and flint finds indicating Neolithic A habitation in Ireland, including the stray finds of these artifacts, is concentrated almost exclusively north-east of a line from Westport in Mayo to Waterford. It thus coincides with the distribution of burials of the long cairn tradition in the northern part of Ireland and in the Irish Sea Zone. In the absence of other forms of early Neolithic burial, there seems little doubt that the long cairns are as much a part of a homogeneous Neolithic A culture in Ireland as are the stone and flint industries.

Several habitations were recorded imperfectly by antiquarians who, in the fashion of their time, concentrated on the lithic technology and recorded little else. Towards the end of the last century, Gray recorded the finding of several polished stone axeheads on the ridge of glacial sand along which the Malone Road runs south of the Lagan in Belfast. 'Several Urns' were found at Pleasure House Hill on this road and, nearby, in the space of eight square feet, ten polished stone axeheads, all beautifully finished, the longest 32 cm and weighing 4 kg (8 lb), the shortest 24 cm. Gray noted that each stood 'on its end in the sand with its edge turned upwards' and that there was nothing near to indicate a burial nor was there any waste from which the working of the axeheads might be deduced. Though no hearth was reported, the site is probably a habitation (1872).

A brief account by Andrews and Davies described a Neolithic A assemblage with hearths in the grounds of Tyrone House in the same area (1940). Beside a hearth 3 m in diameter and 1 m below the present surface were a hammer-stone, some mullers, a basalt slab with lozenge and triangular scorings, and several fragments of Neolithic A

45

pottery; a large rimsherd with characteristic simple rim, burnished surface and pointed shoulder was published with drawings of a kite-shaped arrowhead of white flint and the broken end of a plano-convex flint knife. There was also a rough axehead of fine-grained stone. An earlier find at the site reported by Evans was a finely made honey-coloured kite arrowhead only 3 mm thick and with an expert S-twist along the long axis.

The Dunmurry site, 15 m above the Glen river, a tributary running from the hills near Black Mountain south into the Lagan, is only two miles west of these Malone Road sites. This prolific hearth-site, investigated in the late 1920s by Whelan, was 2 m in diameter and 15 cm thick in the centre, and yielded both pottery and flint artifacts, but no bone or other refuse. The pottery is well made, and in some cases has marked quartz gritting in the fabric. The rims are pointed or rolled over and the vessels have the characteristic pointed shoulder of the north-east of Ireland. There are two or more Form J vessels in the assemblage. An end-scraper and a broken javelin-head of grey flint were associated with these. The excavator mentions 'certain $3\frac{1}{2}$ in blades, found with sides serrated and worn back by use as knives'; it may be that these were parts of composite sickles (Whelan 1928).

Several other Neolithic A sites, though discovered recently, were so poorly preserved as to give a mere record of finds. Finds of Neolithic pottery and leaf arrowheads have been made in the excavation of Navan Fort, while similar finds have been uncovered at Castle Skreen in Down (Dickinson and Waterman 1960), Dún Ailinne in Kildare (Wailes 1970), and at Dressogagh Rath in Co. Down where, under the old turf-line, Collins found sherds of Neolithic A type and a Tievebulliagh axehead (1966). At Langford Lodge, on the east shore of Lough Neagh, Waterman discovered a series of Neolithic pits and part of a ditch of the same date (1963). Associated with these were several sherds of plain Neolithic pottery having rolled rims and pointed shoulders. The small flint assemblage included a plano-convex knife and porcellanite flakes indicated a connection with the stone axe trade. A similar Neolithic A layer yielding characteristic pottery with pointed rims, two plano-convex flint knives and some end-scrapers was found under the Early Bronze Age burial monument of Dún Ruadh in Tyrone (Davies 1936).

Extensive evidence of Neolithic A habitation has been recovered at two open hilltop sites at which no evidence for houses has come to light. Neolithic A pottery has been found at several places in the eighteen-acre enclosure on the flat hilltop of Lyles Hill a few miles north-west of Belfast overlooking the village of Templepatrick (Evans 1953). In the excavation of the hearth-site D3, Evans discovered 600 sherds of the burnished pottery characteristic of the site. Sherds of Neolithic A ware and of coarse ware were also found in a number of cuttings across the north-west face of the low embankment which surrounded the site. The circular burial-cairn at the highest point of the hilltop, 225 m (750 ft) up, appears to have been built in the Late Neolithic period.

A similar concentration of Neolithic material was recovered on top of Feltrim Hill,

45 m (150 ft) high, under an Early Christian habitation-layer. Several pottery vessels of the Primary family with pointed and rolled rims and the usual stepped shoulders were found with three rimsherds of coarse ware, eighteen axeheads and a large collection of implements made of drift flint: leaf- and kite-shaped arrowheads, plano-convex knives and thumb-scrapers. The thirty arrowheads discovered is an unusually high number for a habitation. The extensive use of local Lambay or Portrane porphyry for the making of axeheads, fourteen of which were made of this material together with the use of local flint, shows a great self-sufficiency on the part of these Dublin farmers (Hartnett and Eogan 1964).

Habitation layers revealed in the excavation of Court Cairns at Ballybriest, Ballymarlagh and Ballymacaldrack probably belong to the builders of these tombs, the material from habitation and tomb being culturally similar in all three cases. Under the partly destroyed east court of the Ballybriest tomb lay a circular layer of charcoal 13 m in diameter in which there were a number of stone-lined hearths. Lumps of potters' clay and several Neolithic A sherds were found. A cooking-pit 45 cm in diameter at the mouth, 50 cm deep, and stone-lined, yielded hazel charcoal and carbonized hazel-nuts as well as burnt flints and sherds of Neolithic A pottery.

Under Ballymarlagh was a good deal of oak and hazel charcoal with a number of burnt and unburnt flint flakes and sherds of seven shouldered Neolithic A vessels. A few remains of pottery were found in and under the Dunloy (Ballymacaldrack) cairn including the rolled rim J and an unpolished stone axehead. The destroyed site at Edenville, Ballygraffan, Co. Down, had a similar black layer with burnt flints and 'Western' pottery (Collins 1957a).

The number of finds at these sites is no more than would be expected in a short period of habitation necessary to prepare for the raising of the tomb and resembles the short-period habitations similarly preserved under the Passage Graves of Townleyhall in Louth and Bryn Yr Hen Bobl in Anglesey (chapter 3). It is clear that the plain grave-assemblages of the Court Cairns are matched by an equally spartan assemblage in the habitations.

The rectangular house, 13 m by 6 m, with its entrance in the narrow north-facing side, which was discovered in Ó Nualláin's excavations under Ballyglass Court Cairn in Mayo, in 1970, was supported on a framework of wooden posts set upright in postholes up to 70 cm deep (Fig. 15; Plate 4b). Wall-trenches between the posts probably held a timber wall, though no trace of this was found. The house yielded Primary Neolithic pottery with pointed rims, and a flint assemblage similar to that in the centre Court Cairn above (1972). Though a relatively long span of habitation, say even a century, is implied in the permanence of such a well built house, there is no need to regard it as other than the house of a family of Neolithic A farmers, the most extensive evidence for which so far is the thirty Court Cairns in the area.

The Ballynagilly habitation, sited above 180 m (600 ft) up on a low glacial hillock with a strong spring of clear water near Cookstown in Tyrone, gave evidence in ApSimon's excavations (1969a) and in the associated palaeo-botanical investigations

47

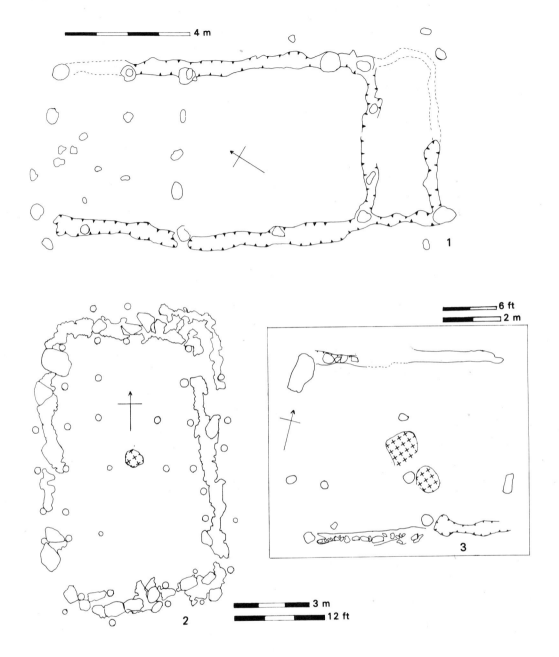

Figure 15 Plans of rectangular Neolithic houses, Ireland: 1 Ballyglass, Co. Mayo (after Ó Nualláin); 2 Lough Gur, Site A, Co. Limerick (after ÓRíordáin); 3 Ballynagilly, Co. Tyrone (after ApSimon).

in the nearby bogs of two phases of early Neolithic settlement. Two widely separated pits and a hearth with plain Neolithic pottery all gave radiocarbon estimations of an unexpectedly early date between 3700 B.C. and 3800 B.C. for the beginnings of farming activity on the site.

Whatever the controversy which will surely attend such unusually early determinations, the date of the house estimated at 3300/3200 B.C. by the same radiocarbon method seems reasonable. The house was rectangular, 6·5 m by 6 m (Fig. 15). Its long sides were supported by corner posts standing at the ends of two parallel wall-trenches 3 cm deep which held oak timbers dated 3215 ± 50 B.C. Two post-holes in the centre of the house probably supported the roof-tree of a Neolithic A roof. There were two hearths and pits which yielded Neolithic A pottery with heavy, insular rims, a flint industry of narrow flakes and blades and six 'leaf' arrowheads. In the nearby bog, a phase of forest clearance by burning, dated by radiocarbon to this period (3195 ± 70 B.C.), probably represents a *landnam* (Pilcher *et al.* 1971). An unusual correlation of habitational and palynological evidence is thus established. A later phase on the habitation site with Sandhills pottery was dated 2930 ± 110 B.C., though this pottery would elsewhere be dated circa 2200/2000 B.C. (chapter 4).

Slieve Breagh in Co. Meath, excavated between 1959 and 1961, yielded evidence of several cooking-pits and of two circular post-built houses 5 m in diameter, on the south-facing slope about 210 m (700 ft) above sea-level. The range of artifacts comprised Neolithic A pottery, a good deal of coarse flat-borromed ware and a large number of end-scrapers of flint with kite-shaped arrowheads and peculiar tanged dart-heads of flint and chert (Lucas 1960). There were also a few polished stone axeheads.

Though the famous sites at Knockadoon beside Lough Gur in Co. Limerick have been regarded as part of the Neolithic A culture in Ireland, the occurrence in many of them of Late Neolithic heavy-rimmed Class Ia pottery and of other Neolithic material in association with sherds of Early Bronze Age Beaker and Food Vessel indicates that they fall late in the Neolithic (Ó Ríordáin 1954; Herity 1970c). Only one notable site, Site A, can be regarded as of the Primary Neolithic family because of the 'pure' nature of the material associated with it.

The rectangular house at Site A had a framework of posts set to an average of 25 cm deep in the ground and about 17 cm in diameter. The house was 14 m by 4·5 m in extent, measured on the outside of the low wall-footings built around the wall-posts. Inside, four parallel rows of posts ran north–south along the long axis to support the A-roof (Fig. 15). The house was entered through a door in the south-west corner and had a central hearth. Neolithic A pottery (the local Class I) was found with some coarse (Class II) sherds, plano-convex knives, end-scrapers, a broken kite-shaped arrowhead of flint, a broken greenstone axehead and a slate spear-head. About 1000 fragments of ox-bones and two fragments of the teeth of a young horse were also found.

Lough Gur is an isolated site in an extremely rich area far removed from the northern region of Primary Neolithic colonization in Ireland. The Neolithic land-clearance recorded by Mitchell at Littleton Bog, near Thurles (1965), may document farming by Lough Gur farmers; alternatively it may record the activities of people of Passage Grave tradition or of the Late Neolithic, who colonized that area in greater strength.

A new possibility of extending our knowledge of prehistoric habitations has been opened up by a survey of ancient field-systems in the west of Ireland. In the knowledge that many Neolithic Court Cairns had been built on what were once good soils on hillslopes, later to be invaded by sub-Atlantic blanket peat, and that some field-walls could be traced under this blanket of peat, a systematic survey of these walls was initiated by the writer and Mr Séamas Caulfield (Herity 1971). The result has been the recognition of walls and enclosures on the old land-surface under peat at over thirty sites. Fuller excavations of the sites of Behy/Glenulra and Glenree have delineated the nature and extent of two farmsteads; land-use studies are continuing side by side with a search for the habitations which must lie close by. At the Mayo site of Glenree, a mile south of the Carrowleagh tomb described above, a large acreage of ridge-and-furrow cultivation extending over at least three fields of a farmstead was arranged on the south-facing slope of a low knoll.

Though it is difficult to assign the building and use of these fields specifically to the earliest farmers, it is hoped that further investigations will lead to the finding of farmhouses, the technology of whose builders can be linked with the earliest Neolithic. The occurrence of many of the systems in areas also thickly peopled by Court Cairn builders indicates that this hope may well be realized.

Relations with South-West Scotland

A Neolithic technology closely related to that of the Irish phenomena described above, and found in the Clyde region of south-west Scotland, is placed by a few radiocarbon estimates roughly parallel to the Irish complex, roughly between 3200 B.C. and 2000 B.C. Though attention there has concentrated on tombs and pottery, the assemblage of stone implements deserves some study, as Scotland appears to have provided a big market for Irish flint, having little or none herself, as well as for Irish and Cumbrian stone axeheads.

Irish porcellanite axeheads were disseminated into this area, nineteen occurrences being noted (Ritchie 1968, 123–6; Scott 1969b, 228), the diffusion continuing further into Aberdeenshire in east Scotland. Three black basaltic axeheads, probably from the Clough factory mentioned by Jope (1952, 37), and a flint adzehead, presumably of Antrim flint, were found on the Mull of Kintyre, fifteen miles across the channel from north Antrim. Of the six arrowheads in Kintyre described by Scott (1969b, 242), four are clearly made in the distinctively Irish kite shape, one from Kilblaan Farm being polished on one face in typical Irish fashion. The arrowhead from the Sliddery tomb is similarly kite-shaped as are three of the four found in the Giant's Graves tomb in

Arran (Fig. 16). Scottish craftsmen, however, appear to have preferred the plano-convex flint knife to hollow scrapers, nine of these being known in the area, eight in the tombs of Giant's Graves, Torlin and Tormore on the island of Arran and one in Kintyre. However, several stray finds of crude hollow scrapers have been made in Scotland; a total of about thirty was counted by the writer in the National Museum in Edinburgh.

The differences between Irish and Scottish tombs have been stressed more than the similarities. The movement from Antrim, Derry and Down to Scotland indicated by these tombs seems justified on the distributional evidence (Fig. 17), though there are slight dissimilarities in the method of segmentation of one chamber from another in Scottish galleries, the Scottish builders using imbrication, a kind of telescoping of the walls of each segment into the next; Achnagoul II in mid-Argyll has the Irish style of jamb and sill, however (Scott 1969a, 216). There is also a general similarity in the plain pottery found in the tombs in both areas, lugged 'Beacharra A' bowls being found in Ireland at Audleystown and Ballymacdermot, and in Scotland at Clachaig, Torlin and Sliddery (Bryce 1902). Fluted shouldered pottery is found at Cairnholy and Monamore, though stratigraphically late in both, while sherds of a plain shouldered bowl and a coarse ware sherd have come from the Cragabus tomb on Islay. The decorated pottery in both areas is quite similar.

A strong community of tradition between north-east Ireland and Scotland can thus be argued. The Isle of Man, where pointed-shouldered pottery, hollow scrapers and Bann flakes of Irish style are commonly found, and where two Court Cairns of Irish-Scottish style have been excavated, falls clearly into this Irish/Scottish region. When the features of the Neolithic A of this region are contrasted with those of the other major regional group of the earliest farmers in these islands, that of southern Britain, the unity of the Irish/Scottish province is even more closely underlined.

Measured against the total range of activities for a modern so-called primitive community, our picture of the culture of this earliest province is a well-rounded one. The economy was based on mixed farming. The stands of elm in the forests were cleared for grazing and agricultural plots by at least 310 communities of small farmers, comfortably off, who established themselves on the light upland soils of the north in the manner characteristic of the Western Neolithic communities of Europe, reaping and grinding their cereals with composite sickles and with saddle querns, and keeping cattle and sheep. Their technology was a well developed one, providing a wide range of flint and stone tools and using with confidence even cherts and quartzites when the flint ran out. Pottery utensils were also made with obvious pride in craftsmanship, and excellent bog preservation gives us glimpses of craftsmen of a high order making at least basketry bags. The higher building skills were utilized more in the building of tombs than of houses. A primitive trading network was set up for the dissemination of stone and flint within the province and outside it.

From the size of the houses they built, that at Ballyglass being 13 m by 6 m with two

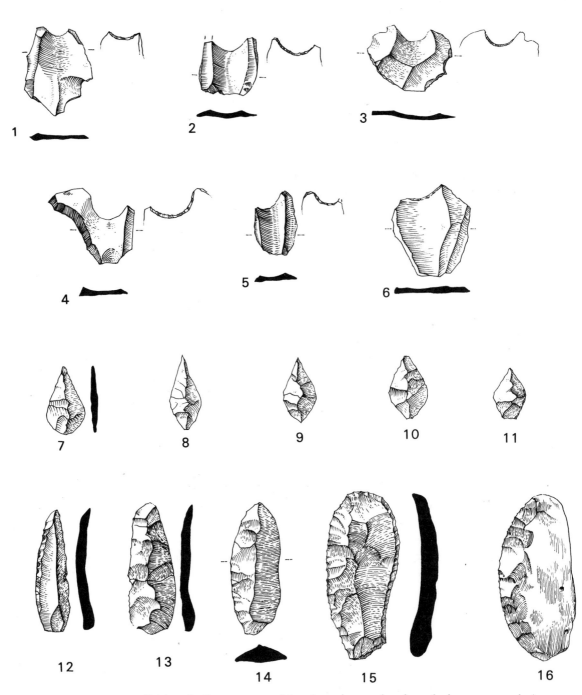

Figure 16 Neolithic A hollow scrapers, kite-shaped arrowheads and plano-convex knives from tombs and habitations, Scotland and Isle of Man: 1 Luce Bay; 7, 16 Sliddery; 8–11 Giant's Graves; 12, 13 Tormore; 15 Torlin; 2, 3 Ronaldsway; 4 Cashtal yn Ard; 5, 14 Mull Hill; 6 Cronk y Chule. ($\frac{1}{2}$)

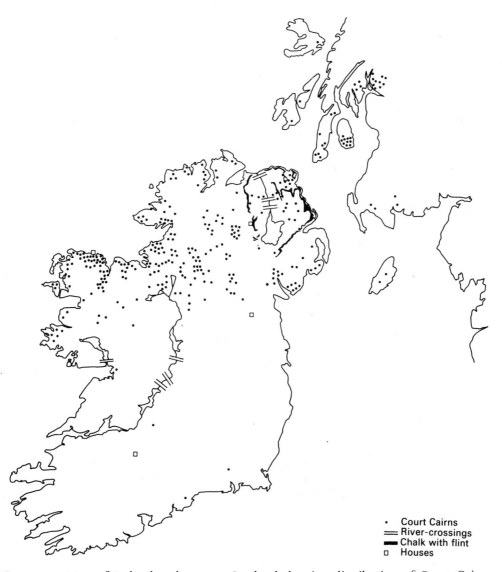

Figure 17 Map of Ireland and western Scotland showing distribution of Court Cairns, Neolithic habitations, chalk outcrops and river-crossings.

- • Court Cairns
- = River-crossings
- ▬ Chalk with flint
- □ Houses

rooms, that at Site A, Lough Gur, being a one-roomed structure just a little larger, we can hardly picture any more than a single natural family living in them, these small families uniting in community effort into efficient *meitheals* or work-gangs under a chief or elder for the more skilled and demanding job of tomb-building. It is very likely that a specialized priest/architect class existed. The size of such a community was

53

probably organized around the labour of fifty to 100 able-bodied men; in any generation there might be no more than 600 such, indicating a total population of about 3000 or, at most, 5000 at any one time.

A strong belief in the after-life and in the magical powers of the sun were the mainsprings for the erection of their tombs, in which architectural imagination and a feeling for natural scenic beauty is clearly evidenced. So far as we can know, the art of the two court-stones in the Cloghanmore tomb in Donegal is unique, and personal ornaments are rarely found. Solid craftsmanship in wood, pottery and stone was respected; nothing for the living was ostentatious. This was a solid, hard-working peasantry respecting sober, if not puritan, values.

Contrast with the First Peasants of Southern Britain

Though a generalized comparison can be drawn between the Irish-Scottish province and its analogue in lowland Britain, the differences are sufficient to distinguish the two cultures as cousinly streams in the general West European Neolithic defined by Childe. Clear parallel streams are implied in the common use of east-orientated trapezoid burial cairns or mounds with transeptal burial-galleries and, frequently, subsidiary chambers in both areas. These burial-mounds are found with chambers both of stone and wood in Britain (Daniel 1950, Fig. 33). In the scattered distribution of these burials near light upland soils, in the general 'Western' appearance of the pottery, in the organization of a common method of production and distribution of polished stone axeheads and in the general kite or leaf shape of the projectile-heads used for hunting, both communities reveal their common ancestry (Piggott 1954, chapters 5 and 6).

The distinguishing differences between the two provincial groups is evident in the presence of a marked court-feature in the tombs of the Irish-Scottish province, in the Irish preference for cremation as against English inhumation, and in the distinctive rim and shoulder development of Irish pottery. Angular kite-shaped arrowheads, sometimes polished, contrast with the leaf profiles of English types, and other differences in tool-assemblages are epitomized in the absence of a recognizable analogue for the Irish hollow scraper in England. Meanwhile, British causewayed camps, large hilltop enclosures, find no recognized alternative in Ireland. Environmental differences may in part have influenced the differing development of the two streams: the Irish lance-head may have been developed for the hunting of the large numbers of wild animals in Ireland, while the development of chalk long barrows with wooden chambers in southern Britain was presumably influenced by local geology. The isolation of the two traditions one from another is sufficient to account for other cultural differences. Theoretically, both traditions should be most closely comparable at their respective points of entry. A significant indicator of this community in tomb-building traditions, the presence of transeptal chambers in the presumably primary areas of both, has been discussed by de Valera (1965).

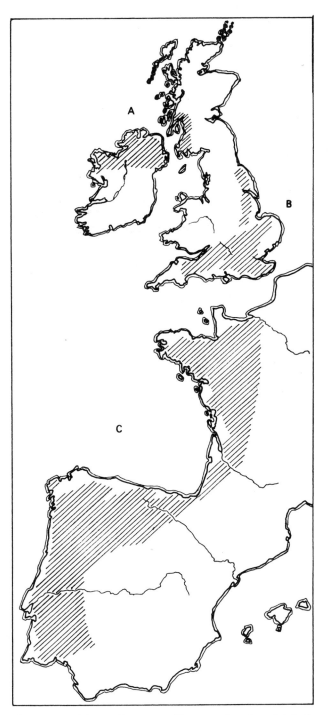

Figure 18 Map of western Europe showing Irish-Scottish province (A), south English province (B) and West European Zone (C).

Origin in the Western Neolithic Zone

In almost every one of its features the culture of the Irish Primary Neolithic peasants can be compared with Childe's Western Zone (1931). Their pottery is Western: the 'leathery' appearance noted by Childe is commonly produced in Ireland by burnishing. Their preference is for the upland territories. In their industries, a version of the leaf arrowhead is the normal projectile type, while axes of pointed oval section are produced; and now a continental factory has been discovered in Brittany (Le Roux 1971). Burials are made communally in long cairns, many of the features of which can be derived from north-west France (de Valera 1960, 1965). Only in the absence of fortified camps, transverse arrowheads and sleeved axeheads in its primary phase does Ireland fail to conform to the model set up by Childe. The evidence of pottery, long burial cairns and the manufacture of axeheads relates Ireland to an Atlantic dispersal-point somewhere in the north-west of France (Fig. 18) though, as in 1931, the popularity of transverse arrowheads and the fewness of leaf arrowheads in that area makes it difficult to pinpoint the ancestral area exactly or with complete confidence.

CHAPTER THREE

The Boyne Culture:
Passage Grave Builders in
Ireland and Britain

About 2500 B.C., the Passage Grave builders arrived in the Irish Sea from Brittany, and built their first tombs on the Menai Straits between Anglesey and the mainland of Wales and on the opposite shore of the Irish Sea in Ireland. Unlike the builders of other megalithic tombs, these people grouped their graves in cemeteries, their first insular Irish one clustered tightly around imposing central tombs set in commanding positions in the valley of the Boyne river. Here, in this first eastern cemetery, they secured a powerful economy and constructed massive tumuli which, in the elegance of their structural and artistic features, reveal their builders' sophistication and the richness and maturity of the culture they established in Ireland.

As their culture became more firmly rooted in the country, vigorous moves inland brought groups of these Boyne people first to the Loughcrew cemetery, then to Carrowkeel, and finally to the Atlantic coast at Knocknarea above Sligo. In these cemeteries the distinctive Boyne features of nuclear cemetery and mountain-top siting are realized in conjunction with pronounced insular traits: a peculiar art idiom, a preference for cruciform tombs and a sophisticated series of grave-goods.

This unique assemblage of material is found within the Passage Graves with the cremated remains of the dead: heavily decorated pottery called Carrowkeel Ware, personal ornaments, curious stone and chalk balls. Noteworthy is the complete exclusion of all other stone implements, weapons and tools from the sacred ambience of the burial-place. By some fortunate finds we are enabled to link tombs and habitations, and although none has yet been discovered it seems clear that we should expect eventually to find townships. However, there is evidence that their industrial dynamism led these Passage Grave builders to take over the flint deposits of counties Antrim, Derry and Down in the north-east.

Their mural art, a series of symbols combined in complex designs including some abstracted human figures is, at its best, effectively and even dramatically placed within the tombs and reveals their Atlantic ancestry. The assemblage of tomb plans, art motifs and ornaments further indicates the ties which these Irish Sea tombs and their builders have with those on the Gulf of Morbihan in the south of Brittany (Powell 1938b; Childe 1940; Daniel 1941; de Valera 1965; Herity 1974).

The Passage Grave people built many of their tombs in the orthodox megalithic style, rectangular or round burial chambers approached by long passages and covered with round mounds. In Anglesey and on the east coast of Ireland as far north as Antrim they observed Breton norms, siting their tombs on promontories overlooking sheltered water, setting their chambers asymmetrically to the passages, and edging their tumuli with drystone walls. Ystum Cegid Isaf in Caernarvon, Bryn Celli Ddu in Anglesey, Knocklea on the Dublin coast and Carnanmore on an Antrim promontory are all orthodox, simple Atlantic Passage Graves. They also introduced transeptal forms like the tomb of Barclodiad y Gawres above Trecastle Bay in Anglesey, the art on which is executed in a style resembling that of the simple tomb of Le Petit Mont which stands high on the promontory of Arzon at the mouth of the Gulf of Morbihan in south Brittany (Powell and Daniel 1956; Lynch 1967). Similar ornamentation is found on the angled and transeptal Passage Grave of Seefin, 600 m (2000 ft) up on the mountains south of Dublin, in the simple, lopsided Dowth South tomb in the Boyne Valley, and in the exceptional, unroofed, pear-shaped chamber with side-recesses of Fourknocks, also in Co. Meath. This combination of ornamentation, tomb-plan, drywalled kerb and siting in the Breton style found in Anglesey and eastern Ireland may well reflect, with the simple Broadstones tomb near Paignton in Devon (Radford 1958), the initial stage of the Atlantic Passage Grave builders' move into the Irish Sea and Ireland.

The Boyne Valley and the Insular Spread

The first phase of insular tomb building is embodied in the three massive tumuli at the Bend of the Boyne near Slane in Co. Meath. Set prominently on three knolls about a mile apart, these tombs each cover an area approaching an acre and a half, 6500 square metres. Here, a new kind of insular cemetery came into being with the clustering of smaller tombs around each of the three larger ones: in the generations after the initial settlement, for example, about seventeen smaller satellite tombs were built close against the kerb of the massive Knowth tumulus. Throughout the spread of the Passage Graves, cemeteries of this kind became standard in Ireland (Coffey 1912a; Ó Ríordáin and Daniel 1964; C. O'Kelly 1967; Herity 1974).

The New Grange tumulus, a pear-shaped heap mainly of water-rolled pebbles, has a diameter of roughly 80 m and was built to a height of about 15 m (Plate 5a). The edge of the mound is revetted by a kerb of oblong boulders, averaging 3 m by 1 m. Most of these bear designs; three, the entrance stone and numbers 52 and 67, are exceptionally well ornamented. The monumental tumulus, which required the labours of at least several hundred workers to pile up its 200,000 tons, contains at least three times the material of Gavrinis and Le Petit Mont, the largest tumuli of this class in Brittany. The ornamented kerb encircling it displays the standard art motifs of the Irish *ateliers* in the open air, but the display is overshadowed by the tumulus above. The tomb underneath has a passage 19 m long entering a cruciform chamber 6·50 m wide and 6 m high (Plate 5b). An angular, hexagonal vault roofs the chamber, springing from the endstone of the smaller left-hand recess and the lintel of the larger right-hand one. It is built of corbelled blocks each weighing up to a ton and bedded on large pebbles which have been crushed by the weight of the roof and the tumulus above. This vault, an insular translation of the Atlantic drywalled beehive (*tholos*) roof of L'Ile Longue in Brittany and Romeral in Spain, integrates the central chamber and the three side-recesses into a single unit.

The ornamentation of this chamber is not of the same exceptional standard as its imaginative architecture, its skilled building, and the artistry of its entrance stone, its clearest feature being the embellishment of the horizontals of lintels and corbels above eye level. An accomplished triple spiral is hidden away inside the end-recess and the lightly incised designs – including an abstracted human face – on the roofstone of the right recess would have been more striking if placed in an architecturally more prominent position.

That this chamber was a burial-place is clear from fragments of cremated human bone found in the recesses in recent excavations. With them were a few ornaments which had been heat-cracked on the funeral-pyre. In each of the three recesses are stone basins – there are two, one on top of the other, in the right-hand recess, laboriously hollowed out from large granite boulders, which are best explained as the repositories in which each new cremation was placed during the burial ceremony.

The creative energies of an artistic genius in the New Grange community were reserved for the ring of kerbstones which girdled the tumulus at its completion. His masterpiece was the entrance stone, set on a slight incurve of the kerb against the backdrop of the doorway, the fanlight above, and the receding walls of the façade. Five spirals, a group of three and group of two, with a vertical groove separating them, form the central motifs of a design which is completed with lozenges and with nested arcs undulating to the edge of the stone and then dispersing. The spiral motif is also engraved on Stone K52 at the north-west side of the tumulus. The division into two parts which is a marked feature of the entrance stone is executed with even more formality here. To one side of the central groove a net-pattern of lozenges is grouped below a pair of opposed spirals. On the right of the groove a series of three shields filled with rows of cupmarks nests within an arrangement of grouped arcs. The shields and grouped arcs are both Breton in character, their arrangement and the lozenge and spiral of the other half of the stone insular. Kerbstone K67, nearby, has a shallower design, an insular face made by combining an S-shaped pair of spirals with a pair of lozenges. To one side of this is a net-pattern of lozenge and triangle. Both these kerbstones have the appearance of being experiments through which the confident artistry of the entrance stone was developed.

At New Grange, then, an adventurous and imaginative architect, adapting a Breton

59

plan, designed and built a transeptal tomb into which he incorporated an Irish version of the Atlantic beehive roof, constructed of rough ice-boulders rather than neat building stones, and an approach passage the equal in length of any yet built in Atlantic Europe. He aligned this passage to face the rising of the midwinter sun, and later had to incorporate the fanlight over the doorway to compensate for the slope on which the tomb was built in order to allow the rising sun to play on the centre of the chamber floor on midwinter's day. The religious fervour of the people of the Boyne moved them to crown this tomb with a massive tumulus more imposing than any yet erected in Europe. The artist of New Grange came too late on the scene to influence in any significant way the ornamentation of chamber and passage. He did, however, evolve a new, insular idiom in which the spiral became a dominant motif, and he realized his potential in the conception and execution of the entrance stone, a marvellous primitive abstract. The circular peristalith of thirty-five pillars set standing free 10 m to 15 m outside the edge of the tumulus was a later addition built by the Beaker people of the Early Bronze Age.

At Knowth the Breton traditions of building and placing of ornamented stones within the tomb were more closely adhered to. The plan of Knowth West is that of a Breton *allée coudée* like Les Pierres Plates and Luffang, but 34 m long and with the bend of its passage much less marked. Its bottle-shaped chamber and heavy slab roof are also Breton, as is the idea of placing the ornamental stelae in dramatic positions deep in the recesses of the tomb (Eogan 1967b). A design of boxed rectangles on the entrance stone is repeated on the sill and backstone of the chamber.

At the eastern side of the mound another incurve in the kerb signals the entrance of Knowth East, a cruciform tomb measuring 40 m from entrance to endstone. In plan, scale and roofing it resembles New Grange; the right-hand recess here also is larger than that on the left. From endstone to endstone of the side-recesses the width is 8 m and the heptagonal corbelled roof rises to almost the same height. In the right-hand recess is a high stone basin, far finer than any yet found in Ireland, the sides and hollow of which are carved with a homogeneous design of broad bands.

This broad band style and the related false relief style are typical of the work of the Knowth artist. A greater number of the kerbstones than at New Grange are expertly carved here. And in the ornamentation of this kerb it is as if the mistakes of New Grange had been recognized; the Knowth kerbstones have a boldness and simplicity designed to be appreciated from a distance and forming a zone of ornamentation which would not be dwarfed by the mass of the layered tumulus above. The false relief *marmite* of the left-hand chamber stone of Knowth West is typically Breton, the analogue of similar designs at Mané Rutual near Locmariaquer and at Gavrinis on the Gulf of Morbihan.

Around this tumulus, which is even larger than New Grange, are seventeen smaller tombs, grouped close against the larger, parent tomb. Four of these satellites were built to a cruciform plan; all the others have the simple plan of Knowth West (Eogan 1967b, 1974a).

The Dowth tumulus, 84 m in diameter and the largest of the three, stands on a third knoll at the east end of the cemetery. Like Knowth, it covers two Passage Graves, here set side by side in the west side of the tumulus facing New Grange. The smaller South tomb has a short passage leading into a circular chamber 5 m across, which was built with a corbelled roof. At the south side of this chamber is a single side-recess giving the lopsided plan typical of Brittany. On three orthostats opposite the entrance of the main chamber, bold poster designs of lozenge, chevron and spiral lightly ornament the surface of the stones.

The larger North tomb has a passage only 14 m long, segmented with high sillstones, leading into a cruciform chamber 6·50 m across. The lofty vault roof of New Grange and Knowth East was not attempted here; instead, an unambitious corbelled roof reaches a bare 3 m from the floor. But in laying out this cruciform chamber the builder of Dowth North innovated an Irish norm (to be followed later at Loughcrew, Carrowkeel and Carrowmore) of setting four tall pillars on a lozenge plan to outline the walls of the central chamber, leaving four gaps between for passage and recesses. The ornamentation of this North chamber, though poorly executed, is found on three of these four pillars and shows some sense, though a poor one, of an ideal of enhancing the impact of the architecture. A curious L-shaped extension to the south is an idiosyncratic feature of Dowth. Only one kerbstone is in any way accomplished; this is the one at the east side of the tumulus which has five delicate rayed circles on its smoothed surface.

Two satellite tombs are found on this east side of Dowth, one of them, Coffey's Site J, having a complex comparted plan.

The founders of the Loughcrew dynasty appear to have taken much of their inspiration from Dowth, for the comparted plan and the rayed circles are prominent features of architecture and art at this north Meath site (Fig. 19). The builders of Loughcrew pushed forty miles inland and chose the three highest hilltops in Co. Meath on which to site their first focal tombs. Around these the cemetery grew in later generations, many more than thirty tombs being eventually built there (Plate 6a; Fig. 20, 8, 9, 10) (Conwell 1873; Frazer 1893; Rotherham 1895; Coffey 1897, 1912a).

The Loughcrew community began with the central summit, Carnbane East, 275 m (904 ft) above sea-level. There they built a neat cruciform tomb, Cairn T, 10 m long, and much like Dowth North in its proportions and in the high sillstones of its passage. This they covered with a cairn 35 m in diameter. Like New Grange, this tomb faced slightly south of east and, like Dowth North, the chamber was planned around four central orthostats, each side-recess being built of three upright slabs and corbelled independently of the main chamber, the roof of the central chamber a neat heptagon beehive poised on the lintels over the opes of passage and recesses. The proportions are very much those of Dowth North, overall width being 5 m and height 3·05 m, but the building is much more accomplished.

In this tomb glacial boulders of sandstone were selected to bear the ornamentation.

Figure 19 Map of Passage Graves of the Boyne tradition in Ireland and Britain. Symbols with circles denote cemeteries.

Central motifs are the rayed circle, flower-patterns, curvilinear designs and shields, while multiple arcs grouped in the style of Gavrinis and L'Ile Longue in the Gulf of Morbihan are also common. The discrete idiom of Loughcrew is probably best

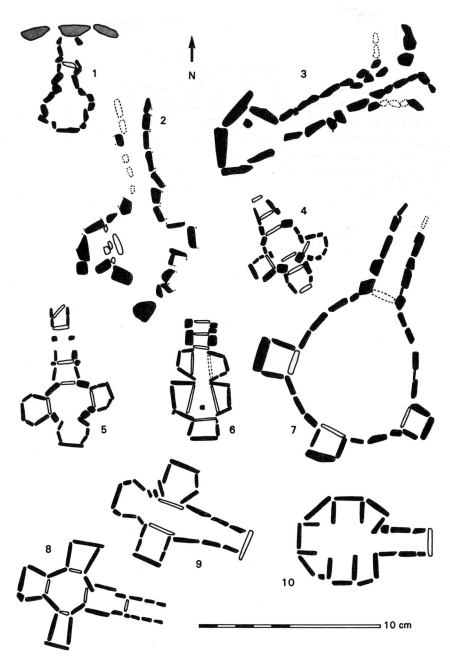

Figure 20   Plans of Passage Graves in Ireland and Anglesey: 1 Baltinglass; 2 Barclodiad y Gawres; 3 Bryn Celli Ddu; 4, 5, 6 Carrowkeel; 7 Fourknocks I; 8, 9, 10 Loughcrew.

expressed on the backstone of the end-recess, where a pattern of chevrons, rayed circles and grouped arcs is arranged around pairs of flowers-in-circles and shields on a pre-smoothed surface. The primary purpose of the artist, the depiction of these standard designs within the burial area, is realized, but he has failed to achieve the coherence that his ancestors in the Boyne Valley had so evidently mastered. This tomb was kerbed with a number of oblong ice-boulders, many of them split in half to reduce their mass and to give a flat surface more suitable for tomb-building.

Around this tomb were grouped six smaller ones, in all of which rounded ice-boulders, either whole or split in half, were utilized. As in Cairn T, it was the more suitable sandstones which were chosen for ornamentation. Cairn U, only 13 m in diameter, sited north of Cairn T with its passage facing in the same easterly direction, is the most noteworthy of these. Its plan has two pairs of transepts in a tomb 9 m long. By the time this tomb was built, the school of art founded at Cairn T had grown to a new mastery of abstract expression and understood the canons of scale and positioning. The masterpiece of Cairn U is an owlish face/figure of grouped arcs, a distortion in which the arcs of Gavrinis are combined with the outlines of the menacing female depicted on an orthostat of the angled tomb of Luffang in Brittany, now in the Carnac Museum.

In the last century, there were over twenty tumuli on the next highest summit of Patrickstown, 265 m (885 ft) high, of which the remains of only four can now be traced. Cairn Y, on the summit, was 31 m in diameter. Thirty-five metres to the west are the remains of three others, X, Xa and Xb. Cairn X, which faced west, was 12 m across and still has at its centre a sandstone boulder, the last remains of the chamber, on the flat, inner face of which was placed an elaborate rayed circle, one of the finest single designs in the whole repertoire of Irish Passage Grave art.

The largest concentration of tombs still preserved is on the summit of Carnbane West, 252 m (842 ft) high. Here are two foci, one arranged around the massive Cairn D, 55 m in diameter, now largely destroyed. The other focus, a little to the east, has Cairn L at its centre. Cairn L, set on the rocky east edge of the summit, is built in the comparted plan of Site J at Dowth and covered with a tumulus 40 m in diameter. In this focus also, the central and earliest tomb, Cairn L, was ornamented by an artist whose style was as yet unformed; here again, it was the later tombs like Cairn I that witnessed the maturer phase of the school's style. The comparted plan is favoured also in Cairns I and J, where the rayed sun and flower motifs are displayed prominently on the narrow edges of the slabs which separate each recess from the next.

In choosing the highest hilltops in Meath for the focal tombs of their cemetery, these Loughcrew builders set a new fashion which took insular Passage Graves on to the highest summits in the parts of the country they colonized. This insular exaggeration also led to the growth of a new kind of extended cemetery, with the earliest tombs on the summits and those of later generations on the slopes around them.

Their next move brought the Passage Grave builders to Keshcorran and Carrowkeel on the summits of the limestone Bricklieve Mountains overlooking Lough Arrow in Sligo (Fig. 20, 4, 5, 6). Here, the focal tomb, Keshcorran, is 362 m (1188 ft) up. On lower summits, and set on the north-facing promontories of a high limestone plateau, are the Carrowkeel tombs, while on the drumlins below are Seelewey, Sheerevagh and Ardloy. Beside these is the massive Heapstown Cairn, 60 m in diameter and the largest tumulus outside the Boyne Valley, but very atypically sited in the lowlands at the head of Lough Arrow. It may be a Bronze Age cairn covering single, cisted burials.

Cruciform tombs are again commonest in this cemetery, which was investigated in 1911 by Macalister, Armstrong and Praeger (1912). The finest is Cairn F, with a limestone covering-cairn 26 m in diameter. This was a double-transepted tomb roofed with a corbelled vault almost as fine as those of the Boyne. A pillarstone which stood upright in the chamber opposite the end recess carried on a tradition found earlier at Bryn Celli Ddu in Anglesey and at New Grange.

On the next promontory to the east are the classic cruciform tombs, Cairns G and K. Cairn K is the larger, 21·50 m in diameter, with a chamber laid out in the Dowth manner around four tall orthostats. The three recesses are pentagonal, the chamber being 5 m wide and the roof rising to a height of 3·60 m. Cairn H in this focus repeats the Breton *allée coudée* plan of Knowth West (Fig. 24, 7). If Cairn H brings Carrowkeel close to the earliest stages of the Irish Passage Grave tradition, the atypical Cairn E may represent a link with an even earlier tomb-tradition, that of the Neolithic A. This is a cruciform Passage Grave which yielded the conventional Irish Passage Grave find-assemblage but was atypically set in the north end of a long parallel-sided cairn. Perhaps the long cairn represents cultural mixture, possibly intermarriage with the earlier Court Cairn builders, perhaps even a link with de Valera's group of western transeptal Court Cairns (1965; chapter 2 above).

The largest of the Irish cemeteries was that begun with the building of the great Maeve's Cairn on the summit of Knocknarea, 328 m (1078 ft) above Sligo town (Wood-Martin 1888, 108–15). Here and on the glaciated plain of Carrowmore below almost 100 tombs were built, many of them extremely simple 'dolmen' forms constructed with the large rounded granite boulders of the area (Plate 6b). There are six tombs on the summit of Knocknarea: Maeve's Cairn in the centre is 55 m across, while Tomb 7 of Wood-Martin's account is a cruciform tomb of limestone slabs in a cairn 32 m in diameter (Piggott and Powell 1947).

The Carrowmore tombs below are laid out around Listoghil, Petrie's No. 51, a simple pentagonal tomb built of quarried slabs under a cairn 45 m across, kerbed also with slabs (Wood-Martin 1888, 71–4). Around this are the eighty 'dolmens', simple denuded tombs expertly built with the awkward split granite boulders, most of them having no formal passage, but with a single capstone covering the chamber, and rounded boulders forming a massive kerb. No. 7 is 13 m across, with a pentagonal chamber of narrow pillar-like boulders standing 1·30 m tall, with their flat surfaces facing inwards. The half of a large granite ice-boulder forms the roof and a single stone south of the entrance to the chamber and outside it indicates a token passage. Despite the difficulties presented by the use of this awkward boulder building material, the building of two cruciform tombs, Nos 27 and 63, was carried through to completion. In Tomb 27 the Dowth lozenge layout of four central pillars was repeated and a cairn 18 m across, kerbed with thirty massive boulders up to 1·80 m in height, was thrown up over it.

Cloverhill, standing alone, 500 m east of Tomb 27, has three decorated orthostats in its simple bottle-shaped chamber, one with two ornamented faces at the right of the entrance, and two facing each other in the chamber itself. The designs, though unusual, are carved on sandy boulders with the sense of scale and positioning that is so much a feature of Irish Passage Grave art (Coffey 1912a, 109–11). The remains of a cairn still exist around the chamber.

The traditions of the Boyne were also borne to the hills south of Dublin, where the tombs of Fairy Castle, Seehan, Seefin, and Seefingan were built to accord with insular canons on summits close to the 610 m (2000 ft) contour. The double-transept tomb of Seefin was 12·5 m long in a cairn twice that diameter and had two angular figures like those of Barclodiad y Gawres in Anglesey set opposite one another in the passage (Macalister 1932, 1937; Rynne 1963a). Further south, an extended Wicklow cemetery, including Lackan, Church Mountain and Tournant, set on commanding heights, ran as far south as Baltinglass Hill (Fig. 20, 4) (Walshe 1941). Here was a complex cairn in which a cruciform tomb was in turn supplanted by one of double-transept plan and then an elegant version of Mané Rutual in Brittany. Its simple ornamentation and its stone basins link this tomb with the earliest Irish Passage Grave traditions. Beyond Baltinglass the Passage Grave builders pushed south into Kilkenny and Tipperary and west as far as Temple Hill in Limerick where they placed their tumulus on a summit 786 m (2579 ft) high.

Though the greatest concentration of Irish Passage Graves is to be found in the four great cemeteries between the Boyne and Sligo, very many are to be found, grouped in smaller cemeteries, in north Louth and in Ulster. At least a quarter of the total number were built in this area. On the hilltops of the Louth–Armagh border, builders from the Boyne erected ornamented tombs on the summits of Killin Hill, Vicar's Cairn and Aughnagurgan, with others at Clermont mountain, Carnvaddy and Slieve Gullion. Three basins in the Boyne tradition were carved for this cruciform tomb at Gullion. Once assigned to the simple *tholos* class, this tomb has proved in a recent investigation to have a cruciform plan, with a fine roof about 4 m high (Collins and Wilson 1963).

A group of tombs in south Down includes Millin Bay and Ballynoe (Collins and Waterman 1955), and Slieve Donard, at 852 m (2796 ft) the highest in Ireland. In north Down they built a group at Ballynahatty, outside Belfast, one of which was later encircled in Beaker times by the Giant's Ring. The simpler plans were more popular in the north-east, 'dolmens' not unlike those of Carrowmore at Sligo crowning the chalk summits of Antrim and Derry and controlling much of the flint wealth of Stone Age Ireland. The concentration of tombs in this area may represent as much a takeover of lands already colonized by the Neolithic A farmers as of the precious flint deposits of the area.

North-east Antrim may well have been colonized direct from Anglesey; the promontory tomb of Carnanmore (Evans 1945), with its simple rectangular chamber, has the plan of Bryn Celli Ddu and is ornamented, while its promontory siting is that of Bryn Yr Hen Bobl above the Menai Straits, of Le Petit Mont on the Morbihan coast, and of Le Rocher at the junction of the Auray and Bono rivers in the Morbihan.

Beyond Gullion and the Armagh group lies a remarkable south Tyrone group, sited around the focal Knockmany tomb, which has several ornamented orthostats (Coffey 1912a, 98–105). It includes the simple bottle-shaped Sess Kilgreen, on the twin backstones of which are the female figure of Cairn U, Loughcrew, placed side by side with the angular icon of Barclodiad, Seefin, Fourknocks and Dowth South. Beyond are the cruciform tombs at the ends of the Passage Grave spread, at Belmore in Fermanagh, at Finner on the Donegal coast, and at Kilmonaster in north Donegal (Ó Nualláin 1968a).

Burial Rite and Finds

The Passage Grave builders burnt their dead before burial and placed large numbers of cremated remains in the side and end-recesses of their cruciform tombs, filling up the space behind the sillstone at the end of the passage in the simpler tombs. The stone basins which are found in the Boyne Valley and within the semi-circle between Slieve Gullion, Loughcrew and Baltinglass appear to have played a part in the rituals surrounding the actual deposition of the burnt remains of the dead (Plate 7b). Well preserved deposits recovered in the excavations at Carrowkeel, Fourknocks and Tara give us an impression of the numbers of people buried: the small tomb at the Mound of the Hostages, Tara, may have housed as many as 200 burials.

The personal ornaments of the dead were burnt with them on the funeral pyre and then buried with their cremated remains. These ornaments consisted of antler hair pins and necklaces made up of beads and pendants frequently made of semi-precious stones and carved in a variety of finished shapes imitating larger tools (Fig. 21). Many of the eighty known pendants were made in the shape of pestle-hammers, others appear to represent the waisted shape of a miner's maul, but a great many are of simpler shapes. Three recovered from Cairn G in Carrowkeel by Macalister are imitations of the Breton *hache à bouton* or knobbed axe.

Those miniatures which reproduce metalworkers' tools paradoxically indicate an interest in the country's metal resources by a group of people whom we regard as formally belonging to the Stone Age. This paradox is heightened by the fact that the pestle pendants are found even in the earliest tombs of the tradition in the Boyne Valley, which appear to date to about 2500 B.C. (O'Kelly 1973).

67

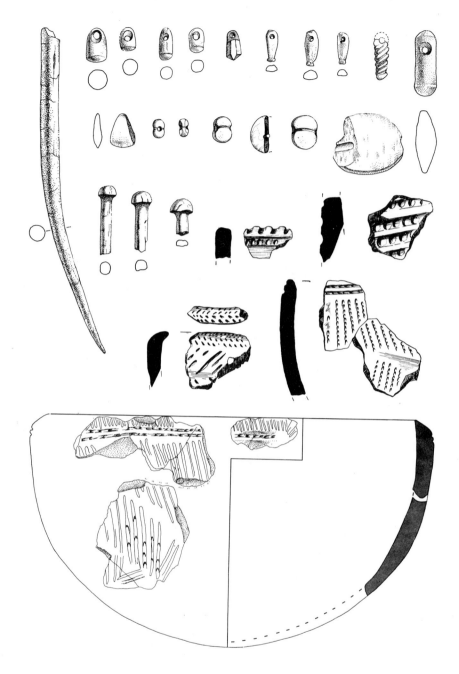

Figure 21 Passage Grave finds: pendants, antler pins and Carrowkeel Ware, Loughcrew, Carrowkeel, Fenagh Beg and Carrowmore. ($\frac{2}{3}$)

The antler pins are normally mushroom-headed, about 15 cm long and peg-like in shape (Fig. 21). These, too, have invariably been burnt, so they were apparently personal ornaments, possibly for the hair. The standard mushroom shape of the head may be a phallic representation; one example from Fourknocks I in Meath has a series of chevron incisions not unlike the grooving on the stone phallus found recently at Knowth. An extremely large example, 50 cm long, was found at Carrowmore by Wood-Martin.

Stone and chalk balls also showing signs of burning are found with the burial deposits. They are often no more than 2 cm in diameter and frequently made of chalk presumably imported from the Antrim/Derry deposits. A few examples are paired; perhaps these should be related to the antler pins and also interpreted as having a phallic significance?

Hemispherical bowls of thick friable ware ornamented all over the outer surface – the only pottery vessels associated with Passage Grave burials – are the typical vessels of the Passage Grave people (Fig. 21). The ware is called Carrowkeel Ware after the Sligo cemetery, and the normal bowl is open with a bevelled rim between 10 cm and 25 cm in diameter. Ornament on these vessels is executed in a stab-and-drag technique, and the motifs, chevrons and loops, are simpler versions of those on the tomb walls. Common are one or two horizontal rows of stab-and-drag under the rim. The vessels are sometimes gritted with crushed seashells. Sherds of this ware are frequently found in the burial deposits, indicating that they were used to bear individual burials to the tomb, or possibly as the containers for offerings of food or drink to accompany the dead. The ware occurs with at least twelve Passage Grave burials and is found as far south as Baltinglass in Wicklow, as far west as Carrowmore, and as far north as Rathlin Island in Antrim; it is also found with habitation deposits at several sites in Ireland, and at Bryn Yr Hen Bobl in Anglesey.

In contrast with other countries, no flint or stone tools or weapons are found with Passage Grave burials in Ireland. This can be best interpreted as a record of fastidiousness involving the ritual exclusion of these mundane objects, the assemblage being very much in keeping with the supreme sophistication of Passage Grave ornament and the general magnificence of the tombs. If the record of the activities of the Passage Grave builders were confined to the restricted material in these burial deposits, the reconstruction of their everyday life would be made difficult; we are fortunate, therefore, in having discovered material from a few habitation deposits located mainly under the tombs themselves.

Habitations, Industries and Contacts with the First Farmers

On the analogy of Los Millares near Almeria in Spain and the Camp de Lizo overlooking the Crach river in Brittany, one would expect the Irish Passage Grave builders to have lived in agglomerated settlements, while the size of the Boyne tumuli would suggest that their builders lived in townships. No such township or settlement can as yet be identified with certainty in Ireland, though it seems likely that the forty-seven circular enclosures on the limestone promontory of Mullaghfarna below Cairn O of the Carrowkeel cemetery in Sligo was one. These circles range between 6 m and 13 m in diameter and many of them are now covered in blanket peat. Unfortunately, those with no peat covering appear to be quite denuded and give little promise that finds would be recovered in an excavation (Macalister *et al.* 1912, 331–2).

It might be inferred from the siting of these tombs on hilltops that their builders were ranging farther into the lowlands than did the earlier Neolithic A farmers. The territory dominated by three of the major cemeteries, Loughcrew, Carrowkeel and Knocknarea, is a heavily-glaciated lowland one, suggesting that the Passage Grave builders commanded a farming technology suitable for exploiting its wealth. Finds under bogs at Bracklin in Westmeath and Lislea in Monaghan offer some confirmation of this view; both are located in the lowlands at some distance from the nearest Passage Grave cemetery. The Lislea find was made in the 1860s; at a hearth 6 m under a bog near Clones in Co. Monaghan were a Carrowkeel Ware bowl with panelled ornament, a second pottery vessel and two fine polished axeheads of green stone: the remains of a camp-site of a small group of Passage Grave folk (Coffey 1904) (Fig. 22).

The other important Passage Grave settlements were found under four tombs, Baltinglass Hill, Fourknocks II, Townleyhall II and Bryn Yr Hen Bobl (Walshe 1941; Hartnett 1971; Eogan 1963; Hemp 1935). Though the Baltinglass Hill tomb is sited 383 m (1258 ft) up on an exposed summit, two large fireplaces, indicating a fairly lengthy stay by its builders on the summit before the tomb was erected, were found under its cairn. The objects associated with these were a polished stone axehead, a flint javelin-head and several flint scrapers. A wooden container in which wheat had been brought to the hilltop had also been abandoned in this temporary settlement before the building of the tomb.

In the covering-mound of the Fourknocks II monument, Carrowkeel Ware of a rather rougher variety than that normally found with the burials was discovered in contexts suggesting that it may have been domestic refuse (Fig. 22). There were also a polished stone axehead and a number of end-scrapers and hollow scrapers of flint.

Under the ruined simple Passage Grave of Townleyhall II, Eogan discovered the most extensive remains of a Passage Grave settlement yet recovered in Ireland. This site is on the north edge of the Boyne Valley looking southwards to Dowth, only a mile away. The habitation material covered an oval area 16 m by 11 m and was up to 15 cm thick. In all there were nine hearths, two of them cobbled, suggesting that the settlement had some permanency. But, though 142 stake-holes were found, no reasonable hut-pattern could be reconstructed, and it must be concluded that the settlement was no more than a temporary encampment to plan for the erection of the tomb which was to cover it over and preserve it, and later lead to its discovery. Among the very many flint artifacts found were forty-six hollow scrapers and three *petit tranchet* arrowheads (Fig. 22, 9, 10). Sherds of at least twenty-four pottery vessels were

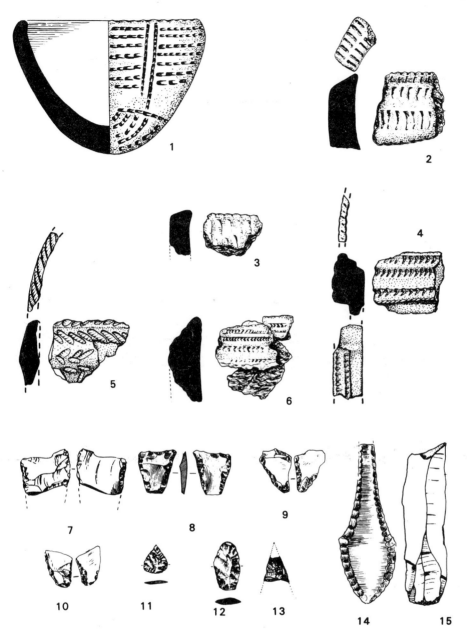

Figure 22 Material from Passage Grave habitations, Ireland and Anglesey: 1 Lislea, Co. Monaghan; 2, 3, 6 Fourknocks II, Co. Meath; 4, 5, 8, 11, 12 Bryn Yr Hen Bobl, Anglesey; 7 Millin Bay, Co. Down; 9, 10 Townleyhall II, Co. Louth; 13, 15 Druid Stone, Co. Antrim; 14 Carrowmore, Co. Sligo. ($\frac{3}{4}$)

recovered, ten of which were of Carrowkeel Ware, some resembling the vessel from Donegore in Antrim, while the remainder consisted of a few Neolithic A sherds and several Late Neolithic vessels of the Sandhills variety described in the next chapter. Wheat grains were also found at this site.

Under the 'terrace' of Bryn Yr Hen Bobl, an unusual long mound built at the same time as the Passage Grave and its tumulus, a similar habitation was discovered. There were extensive remains of occupation and fires, an ox-bone and several seashells. The artifacts were mainly arrowheads of both the leaf and *petit tranchet* varieties, with four well made polished stone axeheads of the local Graig Lwyd rock. The Carrowkeel Ware from the site is closely comparable with that found at Loughcrew Cairn R2 and Fourknocks II (Fig. 22, 4, 5, 8, 11, 12); a few sherds of Neolithic A ware of the local variety imply some contact with indigenous Primary Neolithic tradition.

The indications of mixture with the Neolithic A indigenes found at Bryn Yr Hen Bobl, Townleyhall II and Fourknocks II are found also under smaller satellite tumuli at New Grange and Knowth. The insular form of the pottery, the kite arrowheads and the hollow scrapers at these sites suggests that the indigenous Primary Neolithic culture had developed a clearly insular aspect before the arrival of the Passage Grave builders and the meeting of the two peoples. Seventy Passage Graves were constructed in the north-east of Ireland, an area already extensively colonized by the Neolithic A folk; a takeover by these later arrivals of an area already pioneered in the earlier phases of the Neolithic may be suggested by this evidence. The most attractive riches of the area may have been its flint, found in chalk deposits in counties Antrim and Derry and in the north of Co. Down (Figs 3, 20). Thirty-three of the thirty-six tombs in this area are sited on or overlooking the chalk deposits; the remaining three are spread in a line running west across the Bann at Movanagher. Could this be the beginnings of a traders' route westwards which brought the fresh flint from which the polished javelin-head of Listoghil, the principal tomb of the Carrowmore cemetery, was made? It may be that the hints of industrial potency in the polished stone axeheads of Lislea and Bryn Yr Hen Bobl are even more dramatically illustrated in the distribution of Passage Graves in the industrial north-east. An excavated tomb in north Antrim, the Druid Stone at Ballintoy, yielded only Neolithic A material from a small habitation deposit underneath (Mogey 1941); the hollow scraper from the Clegnagh 'dolmen' has the same Primary Neolithic affinities (Chart 1940, 4, 5). A mixed assemblage containing Neolithic A and Carrowkeel wares was found by Whelan in the Ballynagard settlement on Rathlin Island (1934a).

The scanty evidence available from Passage Grave habitations shows that cereals were grown to provide part of the food supply: evidence of wheat was found at Baltinglass Hill, at New Grange and possibly at Townleyhall II. At Treanscrabbagh, near Carrowkeel, there are signs of early clearance in the bogs; these probably indicate that the builders of that cemetery also grew cereals (Mitchell 1951, 199). The bones of oxen were found at nine sites, Dowth, Fourknocks I, Loughcrew R2 and D, Carrowkeel, Carrowmore 19 and 27, Bryn Celli Ddu and Bryn Yr Hen Bobl. These must have been domesticated as were the sheep or goats whose remains were found at six sites, and the pig found at ten sites. Hunting on a large scale is also attested by the finding of the meatbones of several wild animals, including those of bear at Carrowkeel. The larger animals were hunted with javelin-heads like those found at Baltinglass and Listoghil in Carrowmore (Fig. 22, 14), the smaller with the native leaf arrowhead of the Neolithic A tradition and a new kind of arrowhead introduced from Brittany, the *petit tranchet*. Several hafted implements with polished midribs, mainly knives, in the tool assemblage of these people were presumably used to skin and butcher animals; examples were found at Loughcrew and Carrowmore.

An unexpected addition to the diet of the inland Passage Grave people was shellfish, attested by quantities of seashells found with the funeral deposits at Loughcrew and Belmore Mountain and by the fact that seashells were used as gritting in the pottery of the Carrowkeel cemetery. Seashells were also recovered from the Anglesey tombs and Carrowmore. At Knocklea on the north coast of Dublin, Newenham recorded a great quantity of seashells under the cairn of the simple grave which he examined at that site. Harvesting of shellfish must have been a normal part of life for Irish Passage Grave builders; in this activity they stand clearly apart from other Irish tomb-builders. If the shellmound at Sutton, in which Mitchell found a *petit tranchet* Passage Grave arrowhead, is typical, then it may be that some coastal shellmounds can be attributed to them.

Art and Ornamentation

Passage Graves are unique among Irish tombs in their ornamentation. Art is found in profusion on the tomb walls, on sills and lintels and on the kerbstones surrounding the tombs, spirals, grouped arcs, serpentiform lines, chevrons, lozenges and triangles being the main elements used to build up the motifs and figures of this school. In its best achievements the designs cover the whole surface of orthostats and kerbstones with abstract patterns, as on the entrance stone to New Grange. A number of the designs have the appearance of stylized representations of the human face and form (Fig. 23).

Artist and architect worked in harmony on these tombs, the architect reserving for the display of the artist's work those spaces where its impact would be most striking, the artist carving his designs to a scale dictated by the size and proportions of the tomb. In the Barclodiad y Gawres tomb in Anglesey, three anthropomorphic stelae were positioned at the junction of passage and chamber to strike the eye of the viewer looking back towards the entrance. Stone 22 has two double serpents running vertically towards the base of the stone on either side of a pair of double lozenges. Above is a horizontal chevron continuing on to the narrow sides of the stone in the manner of the double serpent on the right. The whole stele resembles a stylized human torso and the similarity is heightened by the lightly incised spiral on the right above the chevron. Stone 6 of the same tomb places emphasis on a face of paired

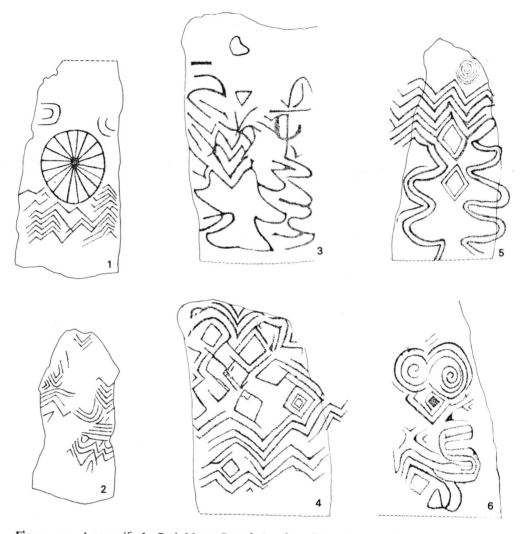

Figure 23 Art motifs, Le Petit Mont, Dowth South and Barclodiad y Gawres.

spirals and a lozenge above a contorted torso. As Lynch has pointed out, these stones are clearly related in design to those of Le Petit Mont on the Arzon peninsula at the mouth of the Gulf of Morbihan in Brittany. Stone 5 of Dowth South, one of a group of three placed opposite the entrance to this large circular chamber which is 5 m in diameter, is intelligible as a more discrete version of the same figure (Lynch 1967). A pair of stelae placed opposite one another in the passage of Seefin are simple designs of grouped lozenges giving the same impression, though poorly positioned for viewing in the narrow passage (Rynne 1963a).

The Fourknocks I tomb was built spaciously, with a diameter of about 6 m, probably to provide the artist with a unique gallery for the exhibition of his work. Inside this chamber, on the left of the entrance, a comical face and the suggestion of a torso are engraved on a simple stele. But there are no more figures of this kind, only the striking ornamentation on the lintel stones of the centre and right-hand recesses, comprising rectilinear compositions of lozenge and chevron. In the depiction of abstract rectilinear designs in a narrow horizontal frame, the artist developed his finest production – the primitive abstract of simple chevrons designed as a lintel for the inner end of the passage. Here at Fourknocks a more striking artistic effect was achieved by choosing stones with a smooth sandy texture and grey colour for ornamentation and contrasting them with the rougher texture of the split limestone glacial boulders which line the chamber walls.

Knowth West exhibits a close harmony between art and architecture in an extremely long tomb 34 m from entrance stone to endstone, the first Irish version of a Breton *allée coudée*. A bold design of nested rectangles is repeated three times, on the entrance stone, on the sillstone of the chamber and on the backstone. The most striking pictures are displayed in the deepest recesses of the tomb; a *marmite* set in relief in the centre of the innermost left-hand stone of the chamber, and a wraith-like human figure on the right towards the inner end of the tomb. As in Brittany, the finest art is reserved for the area beyond the angle in the passage, where its impact on the votaries would be greatest.

The desire to embellish the grand monuments of the Boyne Valley led the Passage Grave artists of this area to devise a new display-place, the kerb of boulders which encircled the tumulus. Some hesitation on the part of the artists in developing this new feature can be deduced from the stones of the New Grange kerb, while those of Knowth show a greater confidence in displaying bold motifs on the kerbstones (Plate 7a). The finest achievement of New Grange, and also possibly the latest, is the entrance stone.

Though the magical motifs of the Passage Grave repertoire are found in the main centres of primary dispersal, the best traditions of the Boyne reach only to the Loughcrew cemetery and the south Tyrone tombs. The insular stone basins of the burial ritual follow the same limited distribution. At Loughcrew the range of motifs, like the tomb-plans, is very much that of Dowth. On the western summit the rayed circles of Dowth are displayed in a charming manner on the narrow edges of the uprights within the chamber; on the eastern summit they are combined with tiny shields into the designs of Cairns T and U. One of the uprights of Cairn U bears a design of grouped arcs, a combination of designs from Gavrinis and Luffang in the Morbihan, in a form resembling a steatopygous female. And in the simple chamber of Sess Kilgreen, fifty miles to the north, a voluptuous female like that of Cairn U is engraved large on a granite boulder with, beside her, the angular male figure of Barclodiad, Dowth and Seefin.

An analysis of the Irish art reveals a small corpus of curvilinear and rectilinear elements. Circles, sometimes with cupmarks, sometimes rayed, and also arcs, sometimes rayed, are most frequently displayed in groups. Lozenges and triangles are the main elements of the rectilinear group. The corpus is completed with spirals, a very common motif in Ireland, and with chevrons and serpentiform lines. The individual elements and the simpler motifs of the repertoire are so frequently depicted on their own that it can be assumed that they once had a meaning, and it is reasonable to regard them as magical symbols whose message has been lost. The same message was projected by the ornamental designs on some personal ornaments and on the pottery. It is only at the centres where the best art is found that effective and harmonious combinations of these symbols are engraved, and the highest artistic achievements of the school are those described above.

The insular character of the school is probably most clearly epitomized in the depiction of spirals. Only four of these were engraved on the walls of Gavrinis in Brittany, but in Ireland this became a central motif. In Ireland, the spiral replaces the paired oculi of Iberia in representations of the human face, the Irish artist preferring to combine spirals and lozenges in a new, insular face design as on Stone K67 of the New Grange kerb.

The Irish tombs are so well preserved that much of the art can be seen today in its original freshness, enabling us to study the techniques used. Incised lines were used to mark the patterns which were then picked out with a point of flint or quartz. At New Grange a number of the grooves thus picked out were smoothed with sand and water. In the most accomplished schools false relief is found: the picking away of the area surrounding a design which then stands in relief. The converse of this, area picking, was also practised. Pick-dressing to remove the glacial patina from the whole surface of ornamented stones is a technique found on the important kerbstones of New Grange as well as on the passage orthostats there (Shee 1973).

Some of the simpler of the curvilinear elements of this mural art can be compared with the limited range of symbols depicted in rock art mainly in the south-west of the country. This art is found on exposed surfaces of the living rock at about 100 sites and appears to be related to the similar rock art of Galicia in the north of Spain. In so far as the simpler elements in the two schools overlap, a relationship, possibly cultural, can be claimed, and Shee and O'Kelly have demonstrated the similarity of a more complex rayed circle motif with cupmarks, common in Irish and Galician rock art, with a single motif in Loughcrew Cairn T (1971). It would appear, however, that the case for more than the merest cultural overlap has yet to be demonstrated.

Origins

Tombs of the Passage Grave family are found in three concentrations on the continent of Europe: in Iberia, Brittany and Scandinavia (Fig. 25). In general, the graves are grouped fairly close together in cemeteries which presumably represent large agglomerations of people. In all three areas they are found relatively close to the sea. In contrast with other megalithic people, their builders show a high regard for the adornment of the person and for ornamentation of the walls or furniture of the tomb. Paired *oculi*, staring eyes around which the outlines of stylized human faces can be discerned, are at the centre of the commonest set of ornamental motifs in which the human face or figure is depicted. In Iberia and Scandinavia, at the ends of the distribution, these depictions are found on mobiliary art; in Brittany and Ireland they are found on the tomb walls. In both Brittany and Ireland the same canons of harmonizing art and architecture and of portraying the human face or figure are central. Display is important in the best tombs of both areas: at Les Pierres Plates it is the chamber stones which are ornamented, and at La Table des Marchands the most accomplished stone in its tomb is the massive ogival backstone (Péquart *et al.* 1927).

The small number of *allées coudées* between Locmariaquer and Auray embody this feeling for dramatic positioning of the art most clearly, their stelae being normally placed in the darkened area beyond the angle close to the chamber (Fig. 24). This group may have been built to an angled plan in order to provide the maximum length of passage in the minimum tumulus; unlike other tombs, their end-chambers are very close to the edge of the circular tumulus covering them. It is noteworthy that when the type is transmitted to the Boyne Valley in Ireland, the tumulus is no longer minimal: at Knowth West an *allée coudée* only slightly angled and 34 m long was placed back to back with a similarly impressive cruciform tomb in a tumulus 80 m across. The unique accomplishments of the artist of Gavrinis on an island in the Gulf of Morbihan had a great influence on the school of ornamentation which grew up in the Boyne Valley milieu. This is perhaps most clearly seen in the peculiar interpretation of the human torso through the use of grouped arcs, and in the spiral unique to Gavrinis which becomes the favourite Irish motif.

The tombs of the Irish province can be classed in two groups: those with simple, rectangular or round chambers (some tombs of this class have only a minimal passage) and those with a number of recesses off the main chamber, the cruciform shape being classic. The Breton tombs can also be subdivided in this way, but in that area the simple tomb is commonest (Fig. 24), whereas in Ireland the comparted tomb dominates. It seems as if this change in preference for comparted rather than simple plans took place with the initial insular adaptations in the Boyne Valley, when the spiral motif proliferated and the close-knit Irish cemetery developed. The find assemblage shows a similar pattern. The Irish personal ornaments are developed from the necklaces of Brittany, but are then highly regionalized, and the *petit tranchet* arrowhead is presumably also introduced from that region.

The dynamism of this Boyne Valley tradition, manifest in tomb art and architecture, is best exemplified in the massive tumuli built there. If each of the three central tumuli is built of up to 200,000 tons of material, a large, semi-urban population must have lived within easy reach of these sites. If no more than a generation is allowed for their piling-up, a work force of several hundred must be

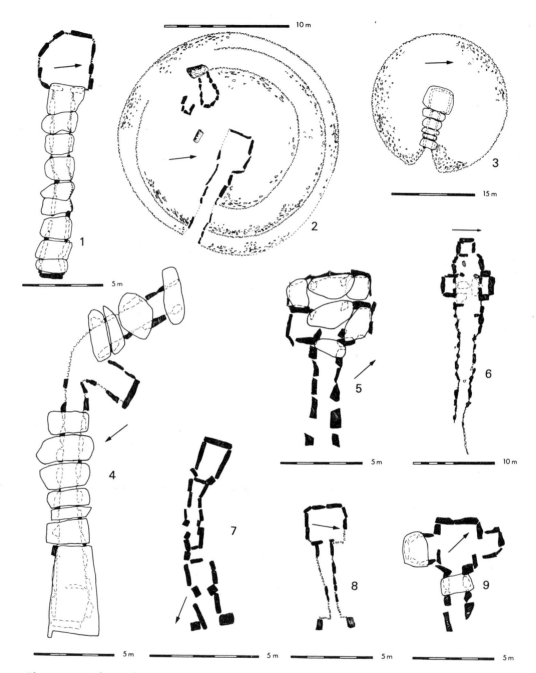

Figure 24 Plans of Breton Passage Graves: 1 L'Ile Longue; 2 Le Noterio; 3 Kercado; 4 Les Pierres Plates; 5 Mané Gros; 8 Le Petit Mont; 9 Locqueltas, with 7 Cairn H, Carrowkeel and 6 La Hougue Bie, Jersey.

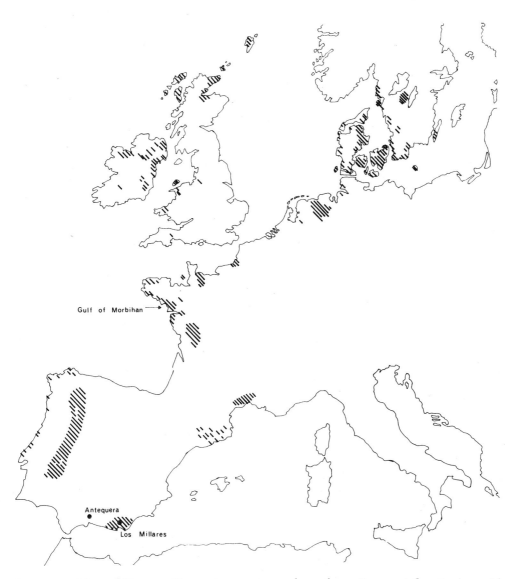

Figure 25 Map of Passage Graves in western and northern Europe (after Kaelas, with additions for Ireland and Britain).

envisaged for each of the tumuli. It seems unlikely that the Neolithic A people, who were already established in the country, could alone have so readily re-organized their society into a labour pool of this size and order. Though they undoubtedly contributed to it, did not new professionalism and dedication come from a large force of Passage Grave people of Breton ancestry?

CHAPTER FOUR

Late Neolithic: Single Burials, New Technology and First Central European Contacts

A new stage, the Late Neolithic, is discernible in the centuries immediately before 2000 B.C. It is marked by the appearance of a new set of flint tools and a variety of novel pottery forms and decorative devices, some of which, like the predominant cord ornament, can be traced to the Baltic lands. At this time, two new burial modes became fashionable: the inhumation of single males, accompanied by elaborate hanging vessels and new personal ornaments, in small stone chambers (cists) under round tumuli, and a single-chambered megalithic tomb, the Portal Dolmen, which was roofed with a massive capstone and set, like the Court Cairns of the Neolithic A tradition, at the east end of a long cairn. The bearers of both these burial modes exploited fresh territories, travelling south along the axis of the Irish Sea, the Portal Dolmens being found in Leinster, Waterford and Cork as well as in Anglesey, Merioneth, Pembroke, Cornwall and Dorset, and the Single Burials being found chiefly in Leinster, particularly in the area west of the Wicklow Mountains. River-valleys and glacial sands and gravels were the chosen environment of the builders of both Portal Dolmens and Single Burial mounds in Leinster.

An apparently new bias towards coastal living can be deduced from the large numbers of habitations among the coastal sandhills along the North Channel and Irish Sea coasts as far south as Dublin; these also yield a new pottery and flint assemblage. Meanwhile, the traditions established by the first farmers a millennium before were not immediately displaced: land-clearance in the old mode continued, the traditional insular Neolithic A assemblage of shouldered pottery, hollow scraper and kite-shaped arrowhead was still in use, and burials were still being made in the Court Cairns of this earliest farming tradition. Some Passage Graves, like those at Tara and Townleyhall II, were also being built at this time.

New Burial Traditions

Single Burials

Several typical Single Burials under round tumuli have been found, many of them during the course of gravel-digging, since the first discovery of this rite at Drimnagh, in the southern suburbs of Dublin, in 1938 (Kilbride-Jones 1939). The Drimnagh mound was sited on a low esker, 61 m (200 ft) above sea level and the highest point in the area. A stone grave in the shape of an irregular triangle had its walls made of limestone slabs, doubled at some places; these leant inwards, their upper edges were levelled, and the grave was then roofed with two large limestone slabs (Fig. 26, 2). In this cist was found the skeleton of a well developed man between thirty and forty years old, 1·65 m (5 ft 5 in) in height, and having a skull tending towards a round shape. Osteomyelitis of the vertebrae of his thoracic region probably indicated that the man was used to hard manual labour and the lifting of heavy objects. The heels of the skeleton had been doubled up behind the thighs and an elaborate hanging bowl had been placed near the feet.

Around this primary cist a small oval cairn had been built, 4·2 m on its longest axis; above this a mound 22 m in diameter and 3 m high, built entirely of sods, had been raised, in which long timbers mainly of alder had been laid radially, wigwam fashion. A few bones of pig and sheep and some sherds of Neolithic A pottery were incorporated into this sod mound.

A secondary burial, cremated and accompanied by a Bronze Age Vase Food Vessel, had been inserted in a shallow grave on the south-east side of the mound. Later, a secondary mantling mound of gravel taken from a surrounding ditch dug to an average depth of 1·2 m had been built over the primary one to a height of 4·4 m; this averaged 30·8 m in diameter. This secondary mantling seems to have been built to cover the cremated burial of an adult male deposited in a Bronze Age Collared Urn which had been placed on the apex of the primary sod mound beneath. Two inhumed burials were later inserted just east of its centre.

The hanging pottery vessel which was found with the primary burial in the cist is an elaborate necked vessel with four lugs beneath the shoulder and four suspension-holes in the neck close to the shoulder, one to each lug (Fig. 27, 1). The slightly raised collar is ornamented with three rows of oblique stabbing interrupted by plain areas. Beyond this on the neck, radial grooves, alternating with free spaces, continue the design to the shoulder. The lugs, decorated above and below with oblique slashings, dictate the ornamentation of the bowl, a quadripartite design borne by four ribs from lugs to base. The base is a slightly flattened lozenge bounded by ribs, the space inside being filled with radial channelling on the main ribs and a swastika pattern of short stabs. The part of the bowl between base and shoulder has a circumferential ladder pattern on two quadrants, a similar design bisected by a radial ladder pattern on a third and a plainer design of circumferential grooves on the fourth.

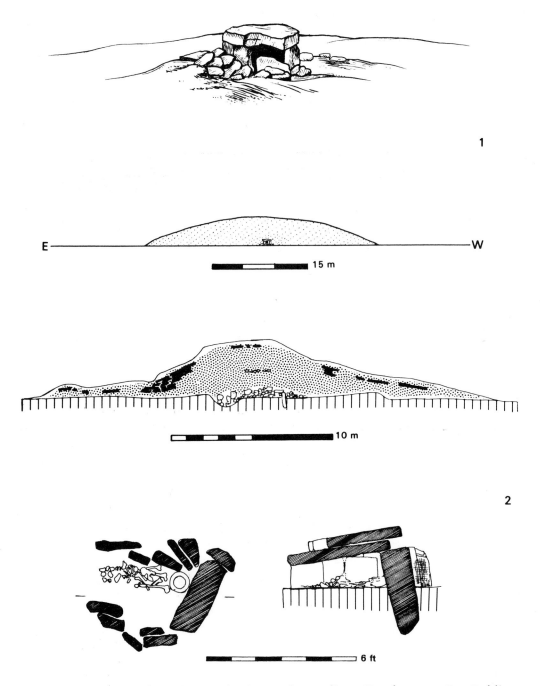

Figure 26 Sections of Single Burial, cists and tumuli: 1 Knockmaree, Co. Dublin; 2 Drimnagh (after Kilbride-Jones).

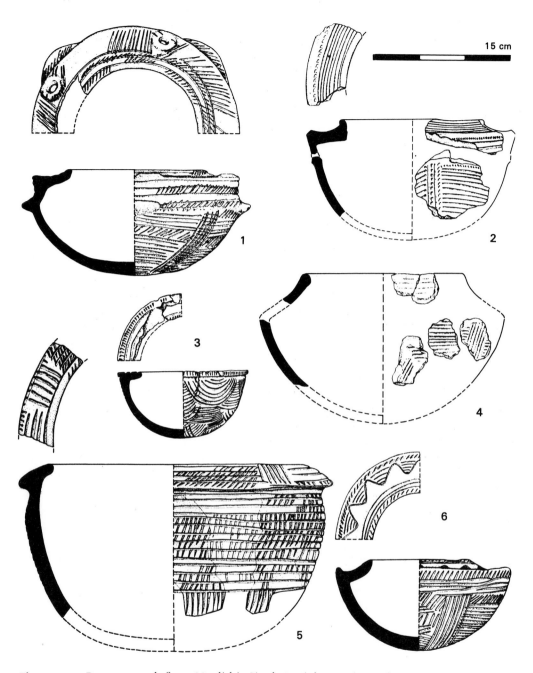

Figure 27 Pottery vessels from Neolithic Single Burials: 1 Drimnagh, Co. Dublin; 2 Kiltale, Co. Meath; 3 Baunoge, Co. Carlow; 4 Norrismount, Co. Wexford; 5 Linkardstown, Co. Carlow; 6 Ballintruer, Co. Wicklow.

83

Many of the distinctive features of the Drimnagh burial are repeated in a group of five similar burials discovered in the province of Leinster, all of them south of Dublin. These are Linkardstown, Co. Carlow, discovered in 1944 (Raftery 1944a), Norrismount, Co. Wexford, which came to light in 1949 (Lucas 1950), and Ballintruer in Wicklow, Jerpoint in Kilkenny and Baunoge in Carlow, all excavated since 1971 (J. Raftery 1973; Ryan 1973; B. Raftery 1974). Cremated and inhumed burials have been found with related pottery at Rath, Co. Wicklow, and Kiltale, Co. Meath (Prendergast 1959; Hartnett 1951), and pottery vessels found in later Celtic sites on the hilltops of Rathgall and Dún Ailinne south of Dublin may originally have belonged with Single Burials of this kind.

All six burials had the typical central cist with inclined slab walls, frequently doubled, containing the flexed skeletons of adults. All had the large covering tumulus with typical layering of compacted turves and radial and arc-shaped settings of stones, ranging between 20 m and 35 m in diameter. The burials were of men in the prime of life, between their twenties and their fifties.

The pottery found was also distinctive, most vessels being elegant hanging-bowls, decorated regularly all over the outer surface, with a marked shoulder from which the neck projects horizontally inwards. The ornament is frequently arranged in a tripartite or quadripartite system, especially on neck and base (Fig. 27). Only the Linkardstown vessel, which has a flat T-rim with channelled ornament and channelling arranged in a ladder-pattern below the cavetto neck, and the two vessels found at Rath are somewhat different.

A pair of burials found at Knockmaree in the Phoenix Park at Dublin in 1838 seem also to belong to this group (Fig. 26, 1). Under a round tumulus 33·5 m in diameter and over 4 m high, sited on a gravel ridge above the river Liffey and only about two miles from the Drimnagh burials, was a cist 1·8 m by 1 m, roofed with a flat slab 2 m by 1 m. A drawing made at the time, now in the Royal Irish Academy (MS. Antiq. Portfolio I) shows at least two courses of subsidiary slabs laid at an angle against the walls of the cist in the manner of Drimnagh and Jerpoint and surrounded by the remains of the earthen mound. In this central cist were two male skeletons, their heads to the north; both were probably contracted to fit in a cist only 1·8 m long. Both wore necklaces of *Nerita* shells, one of 195, the other of 274 shells. There were also a barbell bone fibula 6·7 cm long (Fig. 40, 8) and a plano-convex knife of flint. With these were the tops of the femora of another human skeleton and an animal bone, possibly of a dog. Elsewhere in this mound, and presumably secondary to the two central inhumation burials, were four stone cists in which were 'sepulchral vases, containing ashes and burned bones'; three of these were Bronze Age Food Vessels and are now in the National Museum (Wilde 1857, 180–3, 191–2).

This new rite breaks with the tradition of multiple burial in a megalithic tomb which was standard in the earlier part of the Neolithic tradition in Ireland, and the small finds, a lignite toggle from Baunoge and barbell bone fibulae from Knockmaree and Jerpoint, are new kinds of ornament in Ireland. The rite looks forward to a new

Single Burial mode which is to become the standard method of burial in the Bronze Age and with which the secondary Food Vessel and Urn burials inserted into the mounds of Drimnagh and Knockmaree are continuous (Herity 1970c).

Portal Dolmens

The standard megalithic burial tradition of this Late Neolithic period in Ireland is represented by the Portal Dolmen, a single-chambered tomb in which the finest achievements of megalithic building anywhere are economically matched. A stout pair of pillarstones were set as jambs on either side of a doorstone slab and flanked by the orthostats of a reduced semi-circular court; this formed the impressive façade of a magnificent building which was lintelled by the uptilted heavier end of the capstone covering the chamber behind (Fig. 29). In its classic form, this chamber was formed of two slabs set longitudinally and resting against the outer sides of the upright portal-stones and either edge of a gabled backstone. Slab corbels carried the side-walling to the level of the capstone, and the grave was sealed and enclosed with a long cairn resembling that of a Court Cairn. This is the tomb which, denuded, excited most of the imagination of the antiquaries of the Romantic Period of the late eighteenth century, who idealized in their drawings its rugged grace, the dynamism of its economic style and the charm of its classic lowland siting.

The sureness with which the capstone is poised on backstone and portals in such tombs as Legananny, Co. Down, Proleek, Co. Louth, Glendruid, Co. Dublin, Pentre Ifan in Pembrokeshire, and Trethevy Quoit in Cornwall, and the very weight of the capstones themselves – weights of up to 40 tons are common enough and the most massive, at Brownshill in Carlow, weighs over 100 tons – has understandably given rise to speculation about the means whereby they were so dramatically poised. Though the raising of the capstone could have been achieved by lifting it vertically on a rising bed which was then removed after the stone had been securely propped over the site of the proposed chamber, it is more likely that the capstone was normally levered into position on rollers over an inclined plane which was probably provided by the base of the half-finished covering cairn piled up at the back of the chamber.

In Ireland, concentrations of Portal Dolmens are recorded in the Malinmore region of south-west Donegal, in the Carlingford area, in the Dublin region, on the Leinster granites of west Wicklow and Carlow along the rivers Barrow and Nore, and in the Tramore region of Waterford. De Valera and Ó Nualláin estimate that there are 151 in Ireland, and have pointed out that the distribution is strong in the Court Cairn province north of the central plain, extending somewhat further south than the Court Cairns of the Primary Neolithic into Cavan and Longford (de Valera 1960, 69; de Valera and Ó Nualláin 1972, 166–7). Concentrations are known in Wales at the north end of Cardigan Bay and in Pembrokeshire, and also in Cornwall (Lynch 1969, 146, Herity 1970b, 32). In all there are probably 200 of these tombs in Ireland and Britain (Fig. 28).

85

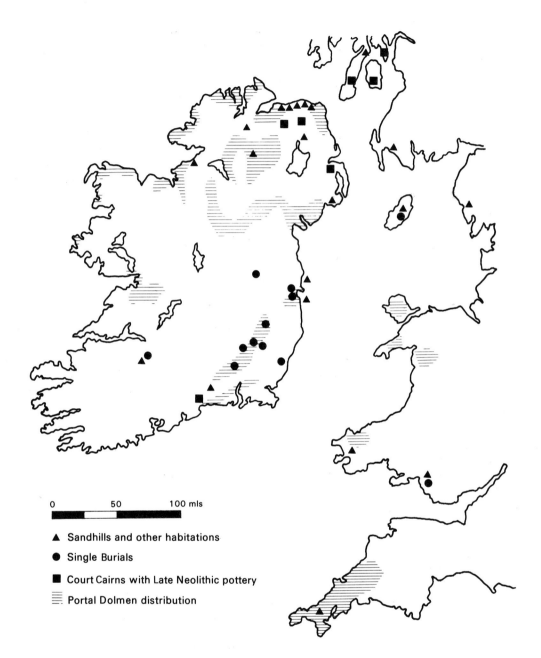

Figure 28 Map of Ireland and the Irish Sea in Late Neolithic times showing habitations, Single Burials, Court Cairns yielding Late Neolithic pottery and Portal Dolmen distribution.

86

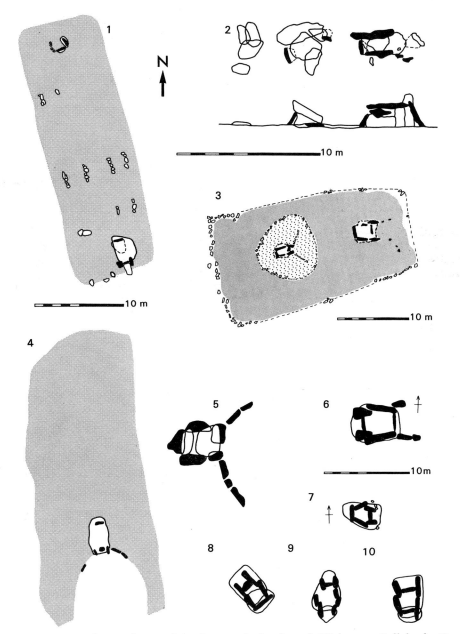

Figure 29 Plans of Portal Dolmens, Ireland and Wales: 1 Ballykeel, Co. Armagh; 2 Trefignath, Anglesey; 3 Dyffryn Ardudwy, Merioneth; 4 Pentre Ifan, Pembrokeshire; 5 Ticloy, Co. Antrim; 6 Brennanstown, Co. Dublin; 7 Gaulstown, Co. Waterford; 8 Knockeen, Co. Waterford; 9 Haroldstown, Co. Carlow; 10 Kilmogue, Co. Kilkenny (after Collins, Lynch, Powell, Grimes and Evans).

They are normally built in lowland situations, the classic siting being near a stream: Glendruid, one of a group of seven Portal Dolmens near Dublin, stands only a few paces from the edge of a stream in a small natural amphitheatre. The Drumanone tomb in Roscommon, excavated by Topp, is sited overlooking the Boyle river on the southern slopes of the Curlew Hills and close by Lough Gara, its lowland siting being reflected in the finds from the tomb, which include a pair of fish-spears, one of chert and one of flint (1962). The name of Tawnatruffaun in Co. Sligo, meaning literally 'the grassy mound by the stream', encapsulates this typical siting. Powell has noted the fact that many of these tombs were faced against the slope of a low rise as were Dyffryn, Tan y Muriau and Pentre Ifan in Wales, and Ballykeel, Drumanone and Bree Hill, Co. Wexford, in Ireland (1963).

The Ballykeel dolmen, excavated by Collins in 1963, was sited immediately west of Slieve Gullion on a level terrace with some granite outcropping on the 90 m (300 ft) contour and above a small stream. The rectangular cairn was 27·5 m by 9 m and was built of granite slabs and boulders to a plan which was laid out along four parallel lines of stones spread symmetrically on either side of a central axis (Fig. 29, 1; Plate 8b). Some habitation debris with Neolithic A and coarse pottery was scattered under this cairn. The portals of the main chamber at the south end of the cairn were well bedded in sockets dug 30 m into the till and filled with packing-stones. The three-quarter doorstone had fallen outwards and the backstone had collapsed into the chamber, allowing the capstone, 2·9 m long by 2·5 m broad, to slip back off the portals (Fig. 29, 1). Though no sidestones had survived, it was clear from the distribution of finds, including the beautiful decorated bowls described below, within the general area between the backstone and the portals that chamber walls had existed originally. Phosphate analysis of the soils from this area showed a large concentration compared with the average values from the pre-cairn turf-line, probably indicating that inhumed burials had been placed there. A small cist about 1·25 m square had been built at the north end of the cairn in which a few sherds of a Goodland bowl decorated with filled triangles, a small flint javelin-head and a discoidal bead had been deposited at a date close to that of the main chambers (Collins 1965a).

Pentre Ifan, situated near the Clydach, a tributary of the Nevern river, a few miles inland from Newport on the north coast of Pembrokeshire, had a chamber of imposing dimensions not unlike that of Legananny in Co. Down. This was situated at the south end of a long cairn, 39 m long by 19·50 m wide, and faced uphill. Its semi-circular façade was marked by two uprights on either side of the portals (Fig. 29, 4; Plate 8a). Shouldered Neolithic A pottery, a triangular flint arrowhead and a flint point were found in excavations by Grimes (1949).

Tawnatruffaun, sited west of the Ox Mountains in Sligo, has triangular portals set longitudinally to a relatively short and high chamber. The capstone, roughly sculpted to a vertical face at the front end, is gracefully tilted over the upright boulder backstone. Though a modern wall masks many of the features of this tomb, one of a small group in Sligo and Mayo, it is clear that it originally had a long cairn.

88

The most impressive of the Irish Portal Dolmens is capped with a massive granite boulder and stands at Brownshill, two miles east of Carlow town in Leinster and about four miles from the site of the Baunoge Single Burial. A standard pair of squat portals with a square doorstone between dictates the façade, which also has a low flanking stone at the south of the shallow east-facing court. It is doubtful if the rear end of the 100-ton granite capstone was ever raised off the ground. In the last century, a subsidiary chamber stood some distance behind the chamber; this, with the cairn, has long since disappeared (Borlase 1897, 438).

One of the most magnificent monuments of this class was the Malinmore long cairn, now standing denuded near the seaward end of and on the southern slope of the valley of that name at the south-west tip of Donegal (Ó Nualláin 1968b, 298). The western chamber had the characteristic tall twin portals supporting the higher end of a gigantic block of quartzite, the rear end of which rested on a second, lower capstone, flat and slab-like, placed over the matched sidestones and the backstone. Twin flanking-stones, slightly higher than the portals, stood one on either side of the entrance. The northern portal has now collapsed, bringing with it the forward capstone. A rather more ruined tomb of equal size, having the characteristic double capstone roofing, stands facing in the same direction as its twin, 90 m to the east. Around this eastern chamber are the remains of the cairn which probably originally enclosed these two monuments. Four smaller chambers, resembling the subsidiary tombs of Court Cairns, can still be seen between the two large endchambers.

On the west coast of Wales, at Dyffryn Ardudwy in Merioneth, two Portal Dolmens arranged tandem fashion like those at Malinmore have been excavated by Powell (1963, 1973; Lynch 1969, 133–6). They stand 13 m apart in a rectangular cairn 27 m long facing uphill and to the east (Fig. 29, 3). The monument is within sight of the sea. Powell's excavation showed that the west chamber had a wide V-shaped forecourt in which there was a pit containing fine Neolithic A pottery. A small oval cairn surrounded this first tomb. The larger eastern chamber, almost 2 m square, was built next, and then the enclosing rectangular cairn which was edged with small boulders.

A similar tandem arrangement can be seen in Tan y Muriau nearby, and the 'long graves' of Trefignath and Din Dryfol in Anglesey probably represent a local exaggeration of this style (Lynch 1969, 114). The Ballyrenan tomb in Tyrone has a similar arrangement (Davies 1941). The tandem arrangement, then, was used at a number of widely separated sites throughout the Portal Dolmen distribution. Such a clearly defined arrangement can hardly have had a mere *ad hoc* status; it seems more likely that this is a style developed by the Portal Dolmen builders and implemented on both sides of the Irish Sea. The succession of building, burial and enclosure implied for the earlier chambers in these tombs seems to be a new feature in the burial rites associated with the long cairns of these islands, possibly a version of the earlier tradition of incorporating laterals or subsidiary chambers in the long cairn.

These tombs' long cairns, their distribution in the Court Cairn area, their eastern orientation and their façades, which are reduced courts, all suggest a relationship with the earlier Court Cairns. The finds from both tomb classes accord broadly. The biggest difference between the two classes is in the form of the burial element: the Portal Dolmen has a single chamber with a massive capstone and emphatically portalled façade, whereas the Court Cairn has a multi-chambered gallery with an imposing façade. But even these Portal Dolmen chambers relate to the Court Cairns both in their ground plans, which are the same as those of the subsidiaries of many Court Cairns, and in their roofing, which includes the use of corbelling as a standard feature. We can thus argue the derivation of Portal Dolmens from Court Cairns, indicating the virtual identity in ground plan that exists between the subsidiary chambers of the Tullyskeherny Court Cairn in Leitrim and many Portal Dolmens, and the fact that many Portal Dolmens retain the ancestral link in an even stronger form by themselves having subsidiaries: Ticloy in Antrim, Ballywholan in Tyrone, Melkagh in Longford and Ballykeel in Armagh (Evans 1938a; de Valera 1960, 66; de Valera and Ó Nualláin 1972, 165).

The two-chambered examples at Brennanstown in Dublin, Sunnagh More in Leitrim, and Gwern Einion in Wales suggest that the Portal Dolmen builders may not always have regarded themselves as quite distinct from the Court Cairn folk, even if they did move away from the Court Cairn area in Ulster into an Irish Sea region. This impression is strengthened by the similarity between the later, east chamber of Dyffryn Ardudwy and the chamber of the Ballynamona Lower tomb, located in the area of the Tramore Portal Dolmen group in Waterford. This tomb, though formally a two-chambered Court Cairn, is exactly the same size as the larger Dyffryn chamber, less than 150 miles away by sea (Powell 1938a, 1963, 1973). The segmentation between the two chambers in the burial-gallery at Ballynamona is atypical of Court Cairns, however, being a single high septal rather than the usual jambs and sill. The pottery vessel found in this Ballynamona tomb belongs to a type characteristic of the Portal Dolmens, suggesting that the tomb was built at a time when Portal Dolmens were current and by people familiar with the constructional methods and pottery fashions of the Portal Dolmen builders.

The fashion for roofing the single chambers of some Portal Dolmens with two capstones, like Malinmore, Dundonald in Down, Kilmogue in Kilkenny and Knockeen in Waterford, relates these tombs to two-chambered Portal Dolmens, and with them suggests even more strongly a derivation from the multi-chambered Court Cairns. As at Malinmore, the two capstones are arranged in standard fashion, a smaller slab being placed over the rear end of the chamber, with the tail of the larger capstone resting on this and projecting over the portals (de Valera 1960, 66).

Because of the denuded state of many of these tombs and the vulnerability of the chamber deposits, which in the nature of things are not protected by the small debris of fallen roofing as they might be in other megalithic tombs, evidence of burial deposits in the chambers is often poorly preserved. Inhumed burials may have been more vulnerable to robbing and decay in this class of tomb than in others. Some unburnt human bones found at Ballywholan and the massive concentration of phosphates in the Ballykeel tomb may indicate that inhumation was practised as it was in the Court Cairns. Cremation was certainly common, being recorded in eight Irish sites (Herity 1964).

The Neolithic A and coarse pottery found at six Irish sites, together with kite-shaped javelin-heads, plano-convex knives and hollow scrapers from a number of others, suggests continuity with earlier insular traditions (Fig. 30). The very small number of beads from three sites implies the sober attitude to personal adornment that is characteristic of the Neolithic A farmers. Coarse ware with cord chevrons, hollow-based arrowheads and the elaborate corded vessels of necked shape found at Ticloy, Ballynahatten and Ballykeel, together with the massive corded rim of Sandhills pottery from Greengraves, all suggest a strong Late Neolithic admixture and a relationship with the new Single Burials. Bann flakes found at Ticloy, Aghnaskeagh and Drumanone imply a similarly late date; if they were fish-spears, they also accord with the lowland siting near water of many of these tombs. Carbonized wheat-grains found at Clonlum and a possible sickle-insert from Ballykeel suggest the continuance of the farming traditions established at the beginning of the Neolithic. On the other hand, hones found in the chambers at Dyffryn and Zennor Quoit imply continuity with the Bronze Age which follows.

It is in the use of the new decorated wares that the separateness of the Portal Dolmen people from the old Neolithic A tradition is most clearly seen. The massive Sandhills rim from Greengraves, Co. Down, ornamented with a hurdle pattern in cord technique is new, as is the specialized coarse ware with cord chevrons on the rim from Zennor and Kiltiernan. Most clearly Late Neolithic are the three exotic bowls from Collins's sensitive excavation of the front chamber at Ballykeel in Armagh (1965a), three of the finest prehistoric bowls ever recovered in Ireland (Fig. 31). All three had the same hard ware, steeply inturned neck, marked shoulder and a combination of channelled and corded ornament. Their closest affinities in Ireland lie with the shouldered Single Burial vessels from Leinster.

The first of these had close-set vertical incised channels converging on the base from two horizontal corded lines below the shoulder. Above the shoulder, there were nine lines of twisted cord encircling the neck and its beaded rim. Three semi-circular *oculi* made with applied strips of clay were set at equal intervals on the neck; these are clearly 'unintelligent local renderings of the marks seen on some face vases of the late Passage grave period in Denmark' (Collins 1965, 68). The sherds of this bowl and the next were concentrated towards the right of the chamber.

This next vessel had the same hard fabric, grey in colour. Below the neck there projected three flat lugs like those of the Drimnagh vessel (Fig. 27, 1) at equal distances around the bowl. On this bowl the channelled ornament was arranged hurdle-fashion in a pattern reminiscent of basketry. The ornament on the neck, set almost at right angles to the body, was arranged in a tripartite hurdle pattern of alternating circumferential and radial lines, the radial patterns being arranged opposite the lugs.

91

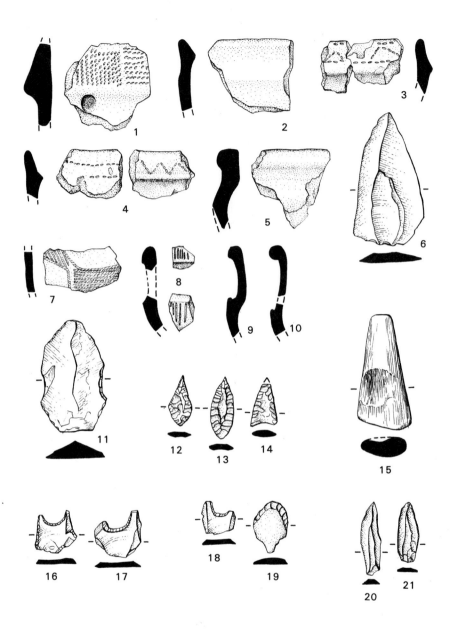

Figure 30 Pottery, flint and stone finds from Irish Portal Dolmens: 1 Greengraves, Co. Down; 2 Kilfeaghan, Co. Down; 3–5, 14, 16–19 Kiltiernan Domain, Co. Dublin; 6, 7, 13 Ticloy, Co. Antrim; 8–10, 12 Ballyrenan, Co. Tyrone; 11, 15 Drumanone, Co. Roscommon; 20, 21 Aghanaskeagh A, Co. Louth. ($\frac{1}{3}$)

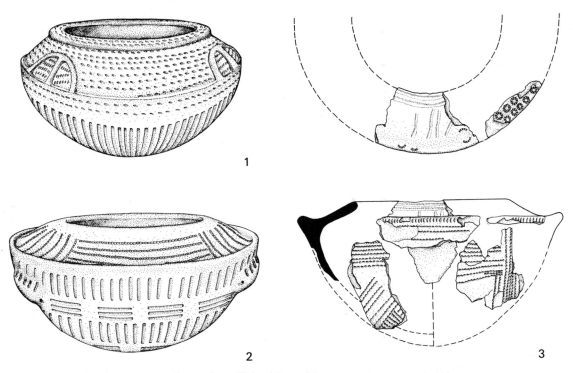

Figure 31   Cord-ornamented vessels, Ballykeel Portal Dolmen, Co. Armagh. ($\frac{1}{3}$)

The third vessel, found at the back of the chamber, had corded ornament on the bowl arranged in a rough basketry design, some of its radial lines being placed on slightly raised ribs. A single row of close-set vertical impressions ornamented the shoulder; the rim had a pattern of radial lines joined to a pair of circular grooves at the rim. In the hollow between neck and shoulder were two rows of stamped rosettes, made probably with the notched end of the shaft of a tubular bone. Sherds of a fourth ornamented bowl, a 'Goodland' bowl (Case 1961, 193–4) decorated with filled triangles of fine twisted cord arranged around the rim as on a vessel from Tamnyrankin Court Cairn (Herring 1941, Vessel I), were found in the northern subsidiary chamber.

Late Court Cairn Deposits

The three bowls found at Ballykeel are matched by others found in the Court Cairns of Annaghmare in Armagh and Clachaig on the island of Arran in Scotland (Fig. 32, 5, 6). A number of the fine vessels from a tomb near Larne are also comparable (Herity, Evans and Megaw 1968), while the Single Burial bowls from Kiltale, Baunoge, Ballintruer, Norrismount and Drimnagh can be classed with these on the basis of their shape and the regularity of their ornamentation. Vessel E, found in the front chamber of the Ballymacaldrack Court Cairn in central Antrim, resembles the

93

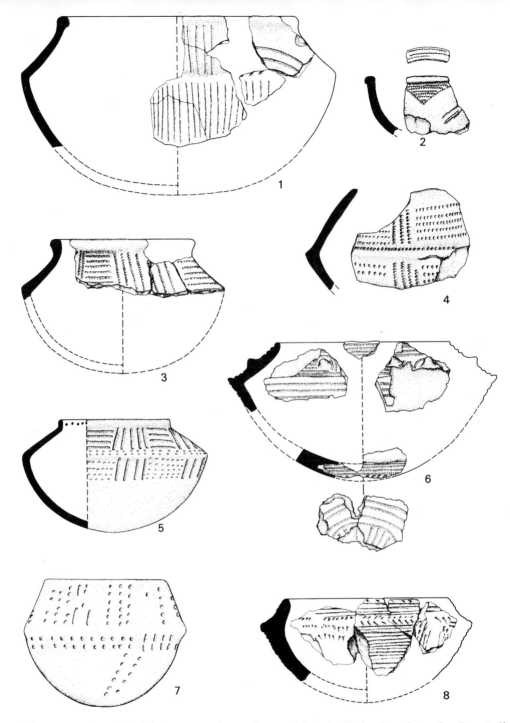

Figure 32 Late Neolithic pottery from Court Cairns in Ireland and Scotland: 1 Bally-macaldrack E, Co. Antrim; 2, 3, 4 'Larne', Co. Antrim; 5 Clachaig, Arran; 6 Annaghmare, Co. Armagh; 7 Bickers Houses, Argyll; 8 Ballynamona, Co. Waterford. ($\frac{1}{4}$)

94

Ballykeel decorated bowls very closely. Its neck is set at a more upright angle than those of the Ballykeel bowls, but it is ornamented in a pattern of alternating radial and curved lines in whipped cord technique; the bowl has regular incisions running radially (Fig. 32, 1).

With this Vessel E at Ballymacaldrack were four other vessels of rather a different tradition which is also found at the Ballyalton Court Cairn in east Down. Their unshouldered shape places them in a different class to the Ballykeel vessels, though the regularity of their corded ornament implies some community of tradition; these vessels are probably most interesting in that they can be clearly paralleled in Denmark. These four upright-walled vessels (A–D) were found high up in the front chamber of Doey's Cairn at Ballymacaldrack; it appears that they had been placed there at the same time (Evans 1938b, 64). Vessel A, the finest of the four, is made of reddish fine-gritted ware, and is a deep upright bowl (Fig. 33, 2). Oblique cord-impressions cover the thickened rim. On the body are several vertical lines of whipped cord; these are interrupted by two opposed panels of horizontal corded lines with pinched-up ribs on either side of them. The top of each rib splays into something resembling an eyebrow motif. Below the rim between each pair of ribs there are three suspension-holes.

A horizontal row of similar suspension-holes is placed below the pointed rim of Pot B, which is similar in shape to A, if somewhat shallower. The outer surface below the rim is scored with shallow, vertical lines, crossed near the base by two or three similar scorings encircling the base. Vessels C and D are plain but similar in shape.

Another cord-ornamented bowl was found in excavations by Davies and Evans above a paving in the front chamber of the Ballyalton Court Cairn near Downpatrick in Down (1934, 97). The primary levels of this tomb yielded the standard Neolithic A assemblage, pottery with pointed shoulder, a kite-shaped arrowhead, two plano-convex knives and hollow scrapers. The corded vessel is an upright, open bowl with a slight carination between neck and bowl and five lugs set vertically on the carination (Fig. 33, 1). The upper part of the vessel is ornamented with eleven horizontal rows of twisted cord resembling stab-and-drag decoration. Twin vertical channels in the same stab-and-drag technique run from the rim downwards on to each of the lugs.

The subsidiary chambers at the west end of the Tamnyrankin Court Cairn on the east Derry uplands yielded two pottery vessels (A and I) of particular interest in this connection. Vessel A resembles the Ballymacaldrack Vessel A: oblique lines of cord ornament the upper surface of the thickened rim; horizontal rows of cord form the basic ornamental scheme on the body, fringed near the unusual flat base with vertical channelling; there are two opposed sets of three perforations each enclosed within a panel of five vertical ridges; the pot is quadranted by pairs of vertical ribs with parallel rows of whipped cord (Herring 1941). The other vessel, Vessel I, is a bowl of Case's Goodland class (1961) with corded pendant triangles fringing the rim (cf. Fig. 32, 2). Gordon Childe commented on the pendant triangles and the form: 'extraordinarily

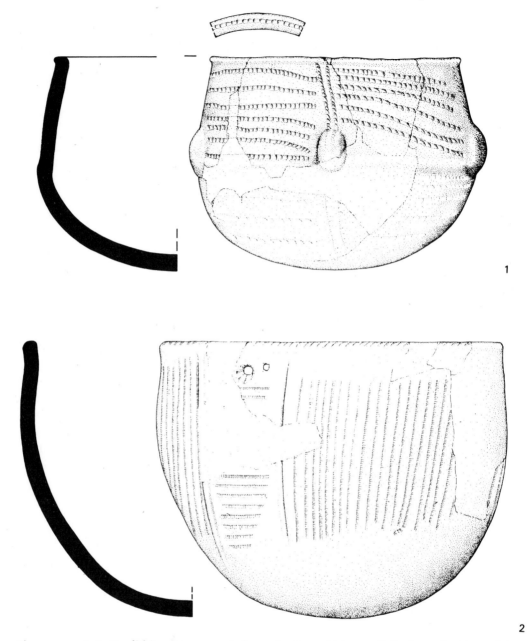

Figure 33   Late Neolithic pottery vessels from the Court Cairns at Ballyalton, Co. Down (1) and Ballymacaldrack (Dunloy), Co. Antrim (2). ($\frac{1}{2}$)

Central European or even Russian . . . to get anything so round-bottomed and neckless, you must go to Fatyanovo or the Pontic steppes' (Herring 1941, 46).

Habitations

The Sandhills

The well known habitation sites of the sand-dunes of the coast of north-eastern Ireland, which show up as black layers of organic refuse against the light-coloured sand, appear to come first into prominence in this Late Neolithic phase. Similar sites are found on the nearby Scottish and Manx coasts. The attractiveness of the decorated pottery and of the flint artifacts which they yield, the ease with which they can be excavated and their position close to modern seaside resorts have all combined to bring large quantities of the material to the hands of private collectors and to our museums. A Sandhills Committee of the Royal Irish Academy, composed of both archaeologists and natural scientists, produced four reports, the last of them in 1901 (Knowles 1889b, 1891, 1895, 1901), a year after the appearance of the report on the famous Danish excavations at the kitchen-midden of Ertebølle in north Jutland (Madsen et al. 1900). Two recent excavations by Collins at sites in the Dundrum Sandhills give the detailed information which serves to control that provided by the older collectors.

On the sandy spit of Murlough, 500 m south of the Portal Dolmen of Slidderyford in Co. Down, Collins excavated at six sites in the dunes within 200 m of the modern shore, where sherds of the distinctive heavy-rimmed pottery had previously been found (1952, 1959). A lower turf-line, in which several characteristic finds were made, had a number of roughly made furrows about 1·30 m apart in its surface, possibly indicating ancient agriculture. The remains of two post-built shelters, one U-shaped about 1·20 m across, the other a flimsy dwelling possibly as much as 2·50 m in size, were found. Someone had gathered a heap of beach-pebbles of flint close by one of them. These and other sites investigated yielded sherds of heavy-rimmed Sandhills pottery (Fig. 34, 7, 8), hollow scrapers, plano-convex knives, horseshoe scrapers and *petit tranchet* derivative arrowheads in typical Late Neolithic styles. A cist in which an adult female had been buried had an encircling ditch 5 m in diameter dug in the sand. A second cist contained the burial of a male adult.

A collection of pottery and stone objects from Lambay Island described by Macalister probably came from a similar Sandhills habitation (1929). The collection comprised several sherds of typical pottery with club rims carrying panelled ornament (Fig. 34, 4–6), seven polished stone axeheads of local porphyry, three massive and awkwardly made kite-shaped javelin-heads up to 14 cm long, several plano-convex knives and scrapers and a number of limestone rings of a type sometimes found with Early Bronze Age burials. Some finds from the nearby island site of Dalkey, at the south end of Dublin Bay, are of the same heavy pottery, and there

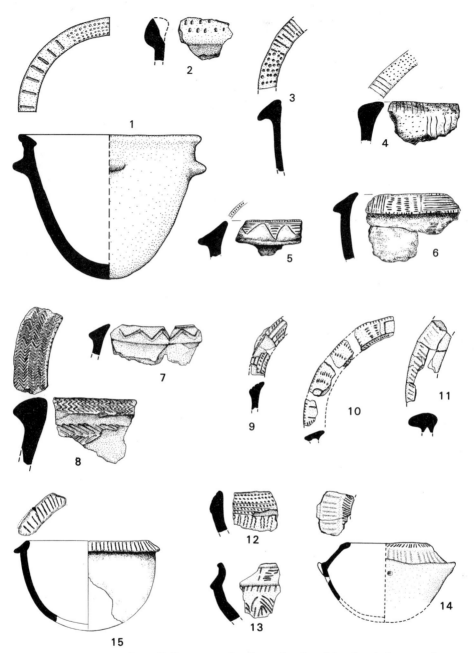

Figure 34   Pottery of Sandhills type, Ireland, England and Scotland: from settlements at 7, 8 Dundrum, 4–6 Lambay Island, 9–14 Dalkey Island, 2 Ehenside Tarn, 3 Rothesay; and from Court Cairns at 1 Beacharra, Mull of Kintyre, and 15 Ballyedmond, Co. Down $(\frac{1}{3})$

is even a plain vessel of Ballykeel type and a typical Neolithic A sherd with pointed rim (Liversage 1968) (Fig. 34, 14). Though twenty-three axeheads were found, there is not a single one of Tievebulliagh stone, nine being of shale or mudstone and fourteen of amphibolite or hornblende schist.

An important site in Antrim which yielded evidence of much more permanent habitation was investigated over a period of six days in 1897 by Plunkett, Haddon, Coffey, Knowles and Oldham (Knowles 1901, 333). Twenty circular hut-sites 6 m in diameter were mapped by the party at the centre of Whitepark Bay (Fig. 36). Fourteen of these were in a rough line parallel to the shore about 500 m long; six others stood behind. Nine other sites were found at the east end of the bay. Over 500 manufactured flint implements were collected, consisting of varieties of scrapers, arrowheads, knives, hollow scrapers and dressed flakes, with fragments of pottery, bones, teeth, and shells.

While shells of oyster, mussel, limpet, periwinkle and cockle have been found at several northern sites, indicating the exploitation of this obvious food-source, other material like the three saddle-querns found at Ballycastle and Whitepark Bay suggests strong contacts with an inland Neolithic (Knowles 1889b, 175; MacHenry 1888, 463). Bann flakes, *petit tranchet* derivatives and flake *tranchet* axeheads are frequently mentioned in the reports, with accounts of flint debris indicating the making of flint objects on the strand. A cylinder of birch-bark found at Ballintoy was probably used as a source of resin used for cementing arrowheads into their shafts (Knowles 1878, 205).

Typical heavy-rimmed Sandhills pottery of the kind found at Dundrum and other sites has also been recovered at the habitation of Townhead near Rothesay on the island of Bute in the Clyde estuary (Marshall 1930; Scott 1964, Fig. 11). Similar club-rimmed pottery has also been found at a number of sites not far from the shore in the Isle of Man, but associated with rectangular houses similar to those at Ballyglass, Ballynagilly and Lough Gur, Site A. The post-built rectangular house at Ronaldsway was located a short distance above the line of the raised beach and was 7·3 m long and 4 m broad, with a central hearth. The food remains included several ox-bones and bones of sheep and pig. Other artifacts included elongated kite-shaped flint arrowheads, hollow scrapers, polished flint knives and serrated flakes, possibly from composite sickles; the axeheads included several extremely small examples of flint with polished cutting edges, which were probably sleeved in the same manner as the stone axeheads of the Swiss lake-dwellings.

The Glencrutchery dwelling, built in the sand, also on Man, yielded a broken polished flint chisel and a broken hollow-based arrowhead of late date (Bruce *et al.* 1947). There are indications that the single cremation, contained in the characteristic club-rimmed pottery vessels deposited mouth upwards, is the normal burial rite of these people (Bersu 1947, 161–9). A cemetery of these burials at Ballateare yielded a bone barbell pin of the same kind as those found at Knockmaree and Jerpoint in Ireland.

It might be possible to include the inland site of Ehenside Tarn near St Bees in Cumberland with this group of north Irish Sea habitations, as one of the sherds found there during the last century can be reconstructed as the heavy club-rim of a Sandhills vessel with bird-bone ornament (Darbishire 1873) (Fig. 34, 2). Two inland lake sites in Derry and Tyrone, excavated by Davies, have yielded the same pottery, confirming the impression derived from the siting of Portal Dolmens that the people of this period preferred lowland sites near water. Halfway between Omagh and Strabane in Co. Tyrone, Davies excavated Island MacHugh, which was apparently artificially formed and measured about 60 m at its maximum dimension. Typical corded Sandhills pottery was found at an area of rough cobbling with some timber posts 5 cm to 7 cm in diameter. The flint industry comprised kite-shaped arrowheads, including the classic variety with polished faces, end-scrapers, plano-convex knives and at least 120 hollow scrapers, many of them serrated (Fig. 35, 39–42) (Davies 1950). A natural island of similar size in Lough Enagh, Co. Derry, yielded corded sherds, a few Bann flakes and twenty-three hollow scrapers (Davies 1941).

The typical pottery found at the Dundrum Sandhills and at Lambay Island and Dalkey Island near Dublin is hard, well baked and fairly thick; most frequently the profile is a deep bag shape with a heavy club or T-rim. Ornament is normally confined to the top of this rim and has in general the same characteristic panelled arrangement that is found on the Linkardstown T-rim. Chevrons and filled triangles sometimes ornament these rims and cord is a relatively common technique. Exotic variants are found at sites like Murlough in Co. Antrim and at the inland site of Island MacHugh in Co. Tyrone, where the T-rim is placed above a short cavetto neck and the native shoulder (Case 1961, Fig. 20).

The motifs found on these exaggerated rims, and the techniques in which they are executed, can be closely compared with those of the necked vessels found with Late Neolithic burials. Panelling is common, as on the largest of the Lambay sherds and one rim from Dalkey. The ornament is arranged in a chessboard pattern on another of the Lambay club-rims in a manner reminiscent of one of the sherds found in the Rothesay settlement on Bute, but perhaps even more closely resembling the necked vessel found in the tomb at Bickers Houses in Kintyre (Fig. 34, 4, 6; Fig. 32, 5, 7). A third Lambay sherd and others found at Dundrum (Fig. 34, 5, 7) have filled triangles with notches on the point of the rim, very closely comparable with the design on the neck of the Ballintruer Single Burial pot. Pots of this elegant necked Single Burial shape were found on the Dalkey Island habitation (Fig. 34, 14) and in the Dundrum Sandhills. The club-rims of these pots seem to be shortened versions of the necks of the burial vessels on the one hand, and thickened versions of the T-rims of Linkardstown and Lough Gur Class Ia on the other.

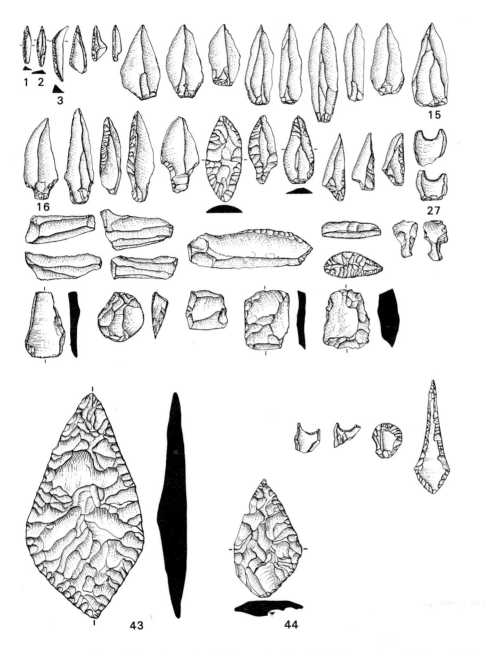

Figure 35 Flint objects from Sandhills and other habitation sites: Whitepark Bay, Co. Antrim; Grangemore, Portstewart, Castlerock, Co. Derry; Dundrum, Co. Down; Narin, Co. Donegal (after Knowles); Island McHugh, Co. Tyrone (after Davies); Lambay Island, Co. Dublin; Carn Brea, Cornwall. (All $\frac{2}{3}$ except nos 1, 2, 3, 43 and 44, $\frac{3}{7}$.)

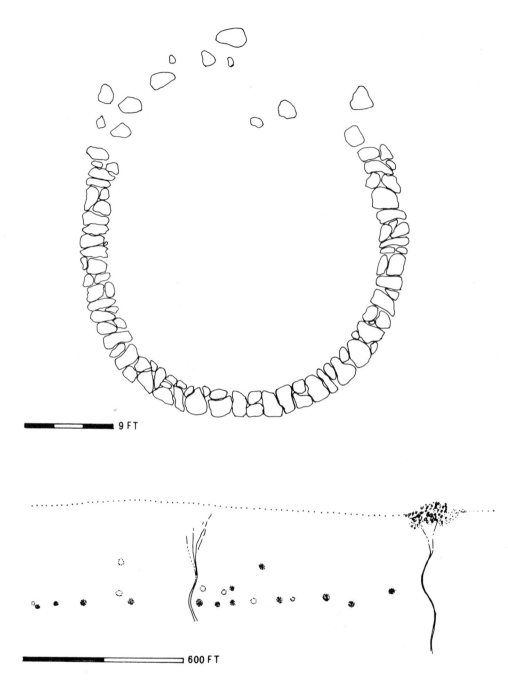

9 FT

600 FT

Figure 36   Sketch map showing position of hut sites above high-water mark at Whitepark Bay, Co. Antrim with plan of one site (after Knowles).

102

The Bann Fisheries

At several sites in the valley of the Lower Bann between Lough Neagh and Kilrea, a flint assemblage has come to light which is characterized by leaf-shaped Bann Points. These are primary flakes sometimes found with trimmed and reduced butts which may have been used to arm fish-spears (Fig. 35, 7–20). Associated with these are leaf and lozenge arrowheads and flake *tranchet* axeheads. The flint nodules from which these were made probably came from the nearby chalk deposits at Slieve Gallion in Co. Derry. Massive stone axeheads up to 43 cm long are also characteristic of this industry (Movius 1942, 239–52).

A site at Newferry on the Bann north of Lough Neagh, where the extensive diatomite deposits have long been known by collectors as a rich source of Bann Points, yielded a number of these points together with three polished stone axeheads of basalt in excavations by Movius in 1934. Nearby, associated with a hearth at the base of the diatomite, a stroke-ornamented, lugged bowl with a large rim related to the Sandhills style was found (1936). Hearths have been found in several different layers of these diatomite deposits which were presumably formed during the winter flooding, the hearths then indicating temporary summer stations of fisherfolk. The few flint flakes and points found by Smith and Collins in the lowest layers of a nearby site can be assigned to the Mesolithic period (1971). It may be that some Bann Flakes were used as knives for filleting fish which were then cured by smoking them over the hearths (Movius 1942, 250). The presence of Bann Points, flake *tranchet* axeheads and Sandhills type pottery suggests a connection with the Sandhills sites of the coast, and it is worth noting that the Bann Point has been found at several places in the Isle of Man (Clark 1935, 74–5). Movius has suggested that both the Bann and the Sandhills folk owe something to the earlier, coastal Larnian tradition (1942, 251, 254). The apparently early finds made by Smith and Collins at Newferry reinforce the suggestion that the Bann material has some roots in the Mesolithic and is linked with the Larnian of the coast. Some modification of the traditional view may be necessary in view of the proven Neolithic status of so many of the coastal Larnian sites. If, however, a Mesolithic content is recognized in the Sandhills and Bann assemblages, this complex fulfils the standard model of Secondary Neolithic in which it is supposed that indigenous Mesolithic traits are effectively mixed with those of the incoming Neolithic A people (Clark 1936, xvi). Certain traits, like the dependence on both lake and sea fishing evidenced in the siting of the habitations and the equipment found in them, may, however, be derived from the Neolithic of the Nordic area, where the flake *tranchet* axeheads, some of the pottery, the decorative techniques, and the burial rites of this Late Neolithic phase are current at the end of the third millennium (Piggott 1954, chapters 10 and 11).

Lough Gur

The extremely attractive light limestone soils in the neighbourhood of Lough Gur in Limerick brought Late Neolithic farmers to the promontory of Knockadoon which was probably inhabited already by Primary Neolithic farmers (Plate 9). On three sites on that promontory, B, C and D (Fig. 37), many thousands of artifacts with animal bones were found in the foundations of houses in a series of excavations by Seán Ó Ríordáin (1954); the occurrence on these sites of a distinctive heavy-rimmed Limerick style pottery (Class Ia), which in its exaggerated rim resembles the Linkardstown bowl, indicates that they flourished in the Late Neolithic (Fig. 38). Beaker and Food Vessel pottery of the Early Bronze Age seems to be associated with the Late Neolithic material at sites C and D. Single, flexed burials found in shallow graves at Sites C and D also connect them with the Leinster group of Single Burials (Ó Ríordáin 1954).

Site B, between Site A and the lakeshore, had a rectangular house about 6 m wide, its southern wall marked by a double row of postholes, its northern by a wall-trench. The 650 sherds found here were mostly of the local version of the shouldered Neolithic A style (Class I). With them were a number of the distinctive Class Ia shouldered vessels with a marked club- or T-shaped rim having radial or concentric stroke ornament sometimes resembling the ladder pattern of Linkardstown, sometimes the chevron of the Dundrum Sandhills. Normally these were about 2·50 cm across, but a pair of exceptional rims measured 7·50 cm. Parts of eleven polished stone axeheads, mostly of greenstone, a flint kite-shaped arrowhead, a chert plano-convex knife, and four flat stone beads were associated with the pottery. Ox-bones predominated among the food remains, with a few fragments of sheep or goat, pig and red deer, barnacle goose and mallard.

Site C was a little to the north-west of Site A and yielded a total of 15,000 sherds. Class II ware, a coarse bucket-shaped, flat-based kitchen ware like that found in the Court Cairns, far outnumbered the Class I and Ia pottery, 2000 sherds being found here in the 1949 season against the combined total of 1200 for the two shouldered classes. Two hundred and fifty sherds of Beaker and Food Vessel pottery were found in that season with ten Early Bronze Age hones and one barbed-and-tanged arrowhead. Three circular houses about 5 m in diameter with central hearths and post-built walls, set either in wall trenches or individual postholes, housed the inhabitants of this site. Leaf- and kite-shaped arrowheads were found and some apparently Neolithic green glass beads. The limestone soil had preserved many animal bones, 95 per cent of which were of ox, with 4 per cent pig and the rest sheep or goat.

At the north-western corner of the site the skeleton of a youth of fourteen years was found in a grave 1 m deep; the body lay on its left side facing north with its legs slightly flexed and drawn up against the chest. At its head was a Class Ia bowl 21 cm across the

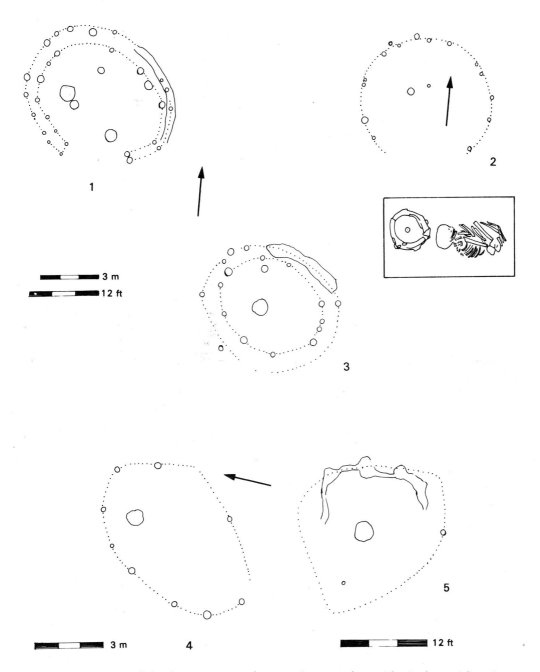

3 m
12 ft

3 m   4   12 ft

Figure 37   Late Neolithic houses at Lough Gur, Sites C and D, with Single Burial at Site C (after Ó Ríordáin).

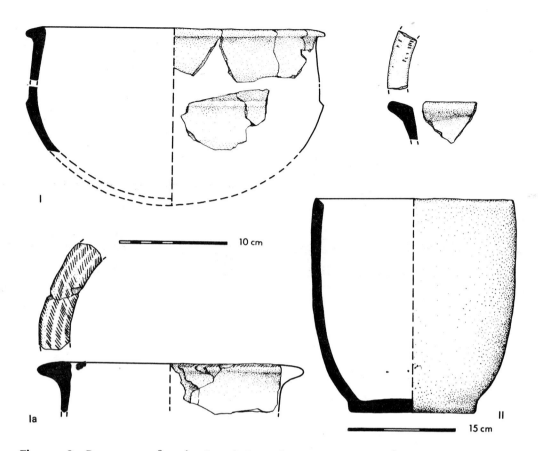

Figure 38 Pottery types found at Lough Gur, Classes I, Ia, II (after Ó Ríordáin).

rim, which was of T-form with a chevron ornament on top. The shoulder of the vessel was extremely pronounced and was quadranted by four equally spaced sets of three vertical ribs. The burial is clearly a single one, and related to those in Leinster.

Two Neolithic circular houses were again discovered on Site D, a little to the east of Site C. The first was a post-built oval 7·3 m by 6·1 m and the second D-shaped and about 5·5 m across. A third was probably built in the Late Bronze Age. Four thousand Neolithic sherds were found, indicating the same intensity of occupation as on Site C. Class II was much less common here; only a dozen typical Class Ia sherds were found and there was a good deal of Beaker. Two children had been buried beside the second house: the first, aged four to five, was accompanied by some sherds of Class I pottery; the second, between five and six years old, had no accompanying finds. Both skeletons were flexed.

The special environment of Knockadoon evidently supported a large population in Late Neolithic times. The Class I plain shouldered pottery and the Class II flat-based kitchen ware are related to the insular Neolithic A tradition of the north, as are the kite-shaped arrowheads, the plano-convex knives and the polished stone axeheads. The Limerick Class Ia style is a local development but, as Ó Ríordáin has pointed out, its exaggerated rims are probably influenced by the Linkardstown and Dundrum styles (1954, 454). The flexed single burial at Site C and its associated ribbed and quadranted bowl suggest that the burial rite appropriate to this phase at Lough Gur is the Leinster Single Burial rite. A Neolithic A bowl found with a polished stone axehead under a round earthen burial-mound at Rathjordan nearby may have been originally deposited with an inhumed burial (Ó Ríordáin 1947a). If this was so, the suggestion that the Single Burial rite was the customary one of the Late Neolithic dwellers at Lough Gur is strengthened.

Insular Adaptations, the Irish Sea and Origins

The new material found in these Late Neolithic contexts has a great diversity of form and decorative technique, a diversity which is one of the characteristic marks of the whole period. A number of pottery styles can be clearly distinguished, however, which may help us in delineating the genesis of the new forces which are clearly at work.

The first of the new forms is the necked bowl of Ballykeel type found also in the Leinster Single Burials at Martinstown, Drimnagh, Ballintruer, Baunoge, Norrismount and Jerpoint, and in Court Cairns at Annaghmare, 'Larne', and Ballynamona, as well as at Clachaig in Scotland. The Ballykeel and Single Burial vessels of this variety have a well marked collar and an elaborate shoulder. The Clachaig vessel, in particular, in its profile and in the regularity and disposition of its ornament, invites comparison with the angular vases of the Danish Passage Graves, like the hanging bowl from Skalkhøj Mose near Ringkøbing (Glob 1952, No. 174) (Fig. 39, 2).

The second variety, discovered exclusively among the latest deposits in Court Cairns, can also be related to Danish types. It is found in the front chamber of Ballyalton and Ballymacaldrack, and also at Tamnyrankin, Aghanaglack and Clontygora Large. Within this variety the Ballymacaldrack and Tamnyrankin bowls compare closely in the hurdled arrangement of their corded ornament and in the pairs of diametrically opposed suspension-holes below their rims as well as in the vertical ribbing on their outer surfaces. The Ballymacaldrack vessel can be compared with one of the Doune Food Vessels from Perthshire, but much more closely with the vessel from Mogenstrup Passage Grave near Randers in Denmark (Glob 1952, No. 152). The corded Ballyalton vessel has an upright profile with slight shoulder on which five solid lugs are set vertically, and it has a horizontal cord pattern on most of its surface which is broken by pairs of vertical cord lines at the lugs. A similar, quadranted vessel was found in a round burial mound at Faelledskovhuset near Jaegerspris. The Aghanaglack corded bowl compares closely with one found in a Jordgrav at Ettrup near Viborg (Glob 1952, No. 160) (Fig. 39, 5).

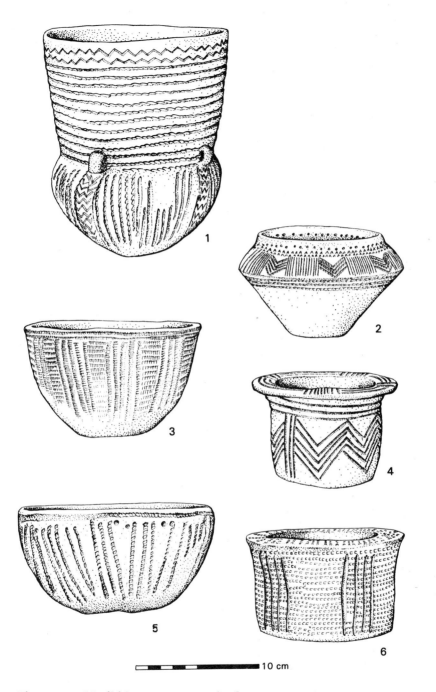

Figure 39 Neolithic pottery vessels from Denmark: 1 Harreby; 2 Skalkhøj Mose; 3 Mogenstrup; 4, 6 Hagebrogard; 5 Ettrup (after Glob).

The large vessel found with the Linkardstown Single Burial in Carlow represents a third class, its T-rim and cavetto neck comparing with those of similar, though somewhat smaller, Straight-walled Beakers in the Copenhagen Museum. The pattern on the rim, circumferential groovings slashed radially and quartering it, compares with that of a literally straight-walled vessel of this class found at the Hagebrogård Passage Grave in Jutland (Glob 1952, No. 470) (Fig. 39, 4, 6). Another vessel from this same Danish tomb has horizontal cord decoration interrupted by groups of four vertical grooves like the designs on the Ballymacaldrack and Tamnyrankin vessels (No. 472). The T-rimmed Class Ia vessels which are a component of a local Limerick style in the Lough Gur area appear to be related to the Linkardstown vessel; however, on these vessels the rim ornament is normally a chevron pattern like those on the Dundrum Sandhills bowls and they are shouldered in the Irish Neolithic A manner. Vertical ribbing which quadrants the Class Ia bowl found with the burial of a youth at Site C harks back to Ballymacaldrack and Tamnyrankin.

In contrast with the three styles described above, the club-rimmed Sandhills vessels are designed for kitchen use in a habitation context. They are normally ornamented on the rim only, while the body has a deeper and baggier profile than the funerary vessels described above. The character and disposition of their ornament relates them to the T-rimmed vessels of Linkardstown/Lough Gur type, but there are strong reminiscences of the necked vessels of Ballykeel style in the motifs which ornament some of them. The filled triangle ornament of one of the Lambay vessels is the same design as that found on vessels from Dundrum, Co. Down, and the Ronaldsway settlement in the Isle of Man. It is closely comparable with that on the neck of the Ballintruer Single Burial vessel from Co. Wicklow and on the little Tamnyrankin bowl, while the chessboard pattern on the rim and wall of another of the Lambay vessels can be compared with the very similar design on the neck and shoulder of a pipkin found in the Bickers Houses Court Cairn in Scotland. The deep Beacharra heavy-rimmed bowl from the Court Cairn of that name in Kintyre resembles these Irish Sea Sandhills vessels as do similar T-rimmed vessels from the habitation of Rothesay in Bute (Marshall 1930; Scott 1964).

In these four styles, particularly in the first three, which are more deliberately ornamented funerary bowls, two principal traits stand out, the regularity of their ornamentation and the fact that they were designed as hanging vessels. Function and ornamentation are combined in these two traits, for the arrangement of lugs, suspension-holes and rims frequently dictates the disposition of the ornamental panels. Even where lugs and perforations are absent, the same regularity is adhered to in the tripartite and quadripartite divisions of the ornament, as on the vessels from Tamnyrankin and Linkardstown. Basal ornamentation is also symmetrical, being combined with functional ribbing at Drimnagh.

Though a number of distinct new traits are clearly present in this Late Neolithic phase in Ireland, a characteristic feature at this time is the persistence of the island's Neolithic A traditions. *Landnam* or land-clearance in the style introduced by the people of the Neolithic A is documented towards the Late Neolithic at sites like Fallahogy (Smith and Willis 1962), and the pollen of ash trees appears in quantity (Smith 1970). Many of the new phenomena of the period are found in the north of the country in the area of greatest Primary Neolithic influence, and Neolithic A pottery and flint objects are found associated with the new material in Sandhills sites and in burials. This strong insular culture clearly absorbed the new rituals: Nordic hanging vessels were placed, presumably with burials, in the old Court Cairns, and the insular tomb form, the Portal Dolmen, embodied the assimilation of new ideas into the older framework. Some new cereals may have been introduced from Scandinavia also: impressions of Small Spelt wheat were detected by Jessen and Helbaek on pottery found in the Ballymacaldrack Court Cairn in Antrim, the first traces of this class outside Denmark (1944), while Emmer wheat was also noted at the same site (Evans 1946, 89). An impression of Naked Barley was observed on a pot found at the Whitepark Bay Sandhills site, and Island MacHugh yielded evidence of wheat (Davies 1950). An impression of Charlock was noted by Jessen and Helbaek on a vessel found in the Portstewart Sandhills.

The strong movement south into the Irish Sea evident in the distribution of Portal Dolmens and Single Burials underlines both the separateness of these from the older tradition and the momentum of the new influences; the single chamber, tall portals and heavy capstones of these tombs further evidence this momentum. In south Leinster, at the western edge of Wicklow and in Carlow and Kilkenny, Portal Dolmens and the new Single Burials are never sited far apart, implying that both groups together pioneered this new move south along the Irish Sea. The same necked pottery may well have been a characteristic funerary ware of both, implying a ritual ambivalence on the part of its makers.

This move down the Irish Sea creates a route never before exploited in Irish prehistory, extending along the north–south axis of this sea rather than from shore to opposite shore at its narrowest points. At the northern end of this route, Sandhills habitations from Dalkey and Lambay north as far as Rothesay appear to have housed the people of these new funerary traditions; at its southern end, the massive javelin-heads of Lambay are found also at the settlement of Carn Brea in Cornwall where they are associated with shouldered pottery familiar to these Irish Sea people. The hones found in the Portal Dolmens of Zennor in Cornwall and Dyffryn in Wales, if they do not indicate that the builders of these tombs were exploiting the tin of Cornwall and the copper of Waterford, Wicklow and Anglesey on the fringes of Mackinder's Inland Mediterranean, at least suggest the same continuity with the Early Bronze Age as the Leinster Single Burials betoken.

The siting of both habitations and burials on this 400-mile long axis is on the lower eskers and into the river valleys beside sea, rivers and lakes. At many of the habitation sites new flint types are found: massive javelin-heads, flake *tranchet* axeheads, tiny sleeved axeheads of the type found at Ronaldsway, arrowheads or knives of the *petit tranchet* derivative class (Fig. 35, 3–6, 24–26). The new pottery styles found with the burials, with their strong Nordic appearance, and the new rites of burial both have an exotic appearance; even the peculiar mixture of new Single Burial and old collective burial in megalithic tombs is itself alien.

The north of Jutland seems to be the proximate origin-place of a significant number of the new styles and rites: certain of the pottery styles, the flake *tranchet* axeheads, the mixture of burial rites, all are present there in the period immediately before 2000 B.C. Certain features of the new Irish Single Burial rite can be traced further afield to Bohemia and Saxo-Thuringia, where Corded Ware burials under round tumuli are laid out in the same flexed attitude, the heels drawn up behind the hams. Characteristic ornaments in the Central European Corded Ware complex are mother-of-pearl discs, apparently breast ornaments, having a pair of central thread-holes and a cruciform pattern, analogues of the Irish gold sundiscs of the Early, Bronze Age (Buchvaldek 1967, 55) (Fig. 40, 3). The Bognaesgaard clay disc found in Jutland has the same pattern (Fig. 40, 4): can it then be regarded as the representation of a new Central European motif in course of transmission towards the western world (Butler 1963, 171)? Barbell pins of bone are a characteristic ornament at Ronaldsway, Knockmaree, Jerpoint and at the site of Caherguillamore in Limerick (Hunt 1967). These too have their analogues in Bohemia, but in the single burials of the Unetician culture of later date than the Corded Ware burials (Fig. 40, 5–8). Single burial is the rite which is to become standard in the Bronze Age of Ireland in the years following 2000 B.C., after its adoption from the Beaker people, who themselves owe something to the Corded Ware complex of Bohemia for their beginnings. Can it be that what we are witnessing is the first interest of people from Central Europe in the lands along the Irish Sea (Fig. 41), pioneers and prospectors travelling up the Elbe into Jutland, venturing across the North Sea and Scotland, then turning confidently south for Wicklow and Cornwall? Does this mark the first tentative steps along what is to become a much-travelled trade route in the mature Bronze Age, the bow wave of a much larger Beaker incursion? Is it Wicklow gold and copper and Cornish tin which attracts these argonauts? But, then, no metal is documented in any of the Irish Sea burials or habitations; these remain ostensibly Late Neolithic.

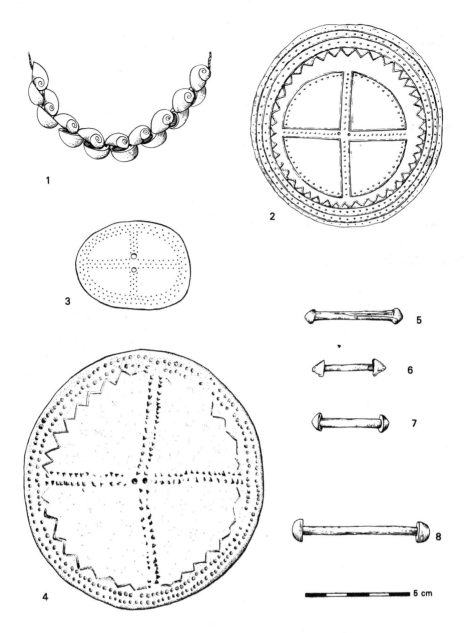

Figure 40   Irish gold sun-disc from Kilmuckridge, Co. Wexford (2), pottery disc from Bognaesgaard, Jutland (4), and mother-of-pearl ornament, Corded Ware Culture, Bohemia (3); shell necklace and bar bell pin, Knockmaree, Co. Dublin (after Wilde) (1, 8), and Aunjetitz sites, Bohemia (5, 6, 7) (after Moucha and Pleinerová).

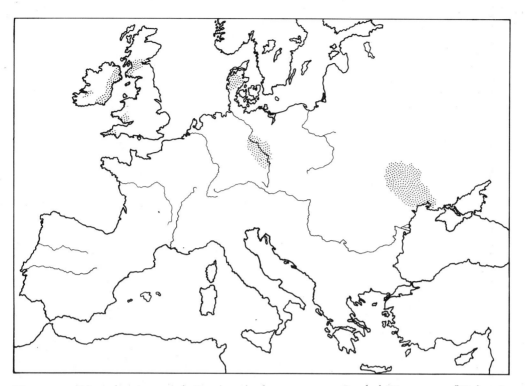

Figure 41 Map showing south Russian single-grave area, Corded Ware area of Bohemia and Saxo-Thuringia, single grave area of north Jutland and Late Neolithic area, Irish Sea.

CHAPTER FIVE

Beaker Peoples and the Beginnings of a New Society

Background

Knowledge of metallurgy is an important adjunct to any society and in Ireland it appears that the introduction of metal-working can be attributed to the arrival of new peoples and the establishment of new societies. Metallurgy is one of the facets of these new societies; single-grave burial (especially in the eastern part of the country) is another. As the origin of the single-grave burial rite ultimately goes back to that great complex of single-grave cultures of northern continental Europe it is the rise and regeneration of single-grave 'cultures' that is the theme of study for most of Ireland during most of the 'Bronze' Age. These single-grave societies, especially the more metallurgically advanced Food Vessel and Urn people, had an abundance of metal artifacts and large-scale metal production must have been taking place. As the Bronze Age proceeded industrialization increased. Towards the end the increase became more marked and the culmination was the revolution of the eighth–seventh centuries B.C.

The discovery of the nature and use of metals was 'one of the most important stages of man's mastery of natural resources' (Piggott 1965, 71). It made possible the production of artifacts *en masse* and, furthermore, a more serviceable type of artifact could be produced, such as a cutting tool with a sharper and harder edge. Man developed a fuller understanding of nature and its resources. People were no longer totally dependent on agriculture, as they had been during the Neolithic period, for the rise of metallurgy enabled communities who were occupying poor agricultural areas to become rich by the exploitation of mineral resources. The Near and Middle East was a key area for the emergence of metal-working and in that area but also in the Aegean copper-working was widely practised by the third millennium. A number of natural deposits of copper could have been available to Early Bronze Age metallurgists. Cyprus, Spain, the Alps and the Carpathians were rich in ores. Ireland also had large deposits of copper, notable areas being the Avoca region of Co. Wicklow and in the peninsulas of west Cork and the adjoining parts of Co. Kerry. But copper occurs at a number of other places in Ireland such as in Co. Waterford between Dungarvan and Tramore, the Silvermines region of Co. Tipperary, around Lough Corrib in counties Galway and Mayo, Loughshinny, Co. Dublin, the Beauparc–Brownstown area, Co. Meath and in Co. Tyrone (Clark 1952, 187–8 and references; Harbison 1966).

Jackson has recognized twenty-five ancient mines on the eastern side of Mount Gabriel, Co. Cork (Plate 10a). These have a narrow entrance, that of Mine No. 1 is 77 cm (2 ft 6 in) in width. From the entrance the floors of the mines slope downwards and the sides widen. Mine No. 1 is 9 m (29 ft) long and 1·54 m (5 ft) in maximum height above the rubble that covers the floor (Fig. 42). The ores include sulphides, chalcocite,

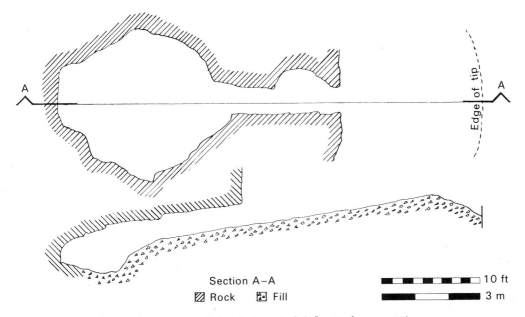

Section A–A

▨ Rock   ▨ Fill   ▬▭▬▭▬▭ 10 ft   ▬▬▬▬▬ 3 m

Figure 42   Copper mine, Mount Gabriel, Co. Cork (after Jackson 1968).

chalcopyrite, tetrahedrite. Fire was used to loosen the rock but as the mine got deeper stone mauls may have been utilized. This material was then taken outside the mine and broken up so as to extract the ores. For this purpose stone mauls, which were fashioned from beach pebbles, were used. The waste was thrown to one side and gradually small dumps of this material formed (Jackson 1968; Deady and Doran 1972; see also Coghlan and Case 1957). Casting could also have taken place close to the mines. At least in the manufacture of some objects that were used by people of the Eastern Province of the Early Bronze Age (p. 139) open stone moulds were used (cf.

115

Fig. 54). These moulds have been found in various places (Fig. 53, left), so there is the possibility that itinerant smiths were also in operation.

Copper on its own has disadvantages: for instance, it is soft so in order to produce more serviceable artifacts a quantity of tin was mixed with the copper and this produced bronze. Deposits of tin in Europe are scarce but tin is known from Bohemia, north-western Iberia, the Breton peninsula and Cornwall. The tin used in Ireland was probably imported from Cornwall (on Cornish tin trade see Hencken 1932, 158–88).

Gold was also readily available to Bronze Age craftsmen. Despite large-scale melting down of artifacts after discovery, especially in the last century, around 800 pieces survive. At present gold occurs, but in small quantities, in different parts of Ireland (Reeves 1971; Briggs, Brennan and Freeburn 1973). In relatively recent times gold was exploited commercially in Co. Wicklow. Prospecting during the century after 1775 in the gravels of the Aughatinavought, or Gold Mines, river and its tributaries between Croghan Kinshelagh and Wooden Bridge has yielded between 7400 and 9000 ounces troy of gold. These and other sources were probably exploited by Bronze Age man. Hartmann (1970), however, has claimed that analysis has shown that the composition of gold ornaments and Wicklow nuggets is different. He has put forward the view that the Bronze Age ornaments were made from gold other than Wicklow, very likely gold that was imported from the continent. But if large quantities of gold were being imported into Ireland it seems strange that craftsmen of contemporary industries in Britain did not also acquire gold. In Britain the vast majority of ornaments were made from bronze. It would then seem that Irish craftsmen had at home a natural supply of gold. As in modern times, it is likely that the gold used during the Bronze Age was acquired by sieving or 'panning' the gold-bearing river gravels. Alluvial gold is rarely found in nugget form. Usually it consists of small flakes or grains. When a sufficient amount was collected this was melted into an ingot and from that it could have been hammered or cast into the required shape.

The existence of about 2000 copper or bronze artifacts and around 100 gold objects is clear evidence that large-scale metal production took place during the early stages of the Bronze Age.

During the last centuries of the second millennium B.C. many significant changes took place in different parts of the world. In western Asia and Egypt the rich Early Bronze Age civilizations collapsed (Kenyon 1966). In northern Europe, from the North Sea to Russia, there was a complex of single-grave cultures – Globular Amphorae, Corded Ware and Battle Axe people. These people were mainly stone-using pastoralists but they had the occasional metal artifact. The burial rite was inhumation. The body was placed in a crouched position in a grave, together with goods such as a pottery vessel, a stone battle axe or a V-perforated button. Usually a mound was constructed over the grave (Childe 1957, 158–74; Piggott 1965, 84–91). Developments in the single-grave cultures, especially the Corded Ware culture, took place towards 2000 B.C. in north-western Europe and as Lanting, Mook and van der

Waals (1973) have demonstrated the ensuing culture is a Beaker culture (Harrison 1974, for the complexities of Beaker development).

Beaker cultures occur over large parts of Europe, from south Scandinavia to north Africa and from Ireland to Russia (Piggott 1963, Fig. 12). It was Beaker people that disseminated a single-grave culture to areas which had previously been outside its orbit. Beaker people have been described as nomadic traders and warriors but there is evidence to show that they were settled pastoralists. Their most characteristic feature is their pottery and, although a number of styles developed, there is a basic pan-European Beaker, the so-called Bell Beaker. In the main 'funerary' Beaker pottery is characterized by its thinness and fineness. The Bell Beaker has an ovoid body and this curved gently into an everted rim so that the profile is in the form of a continuous S-shaped curve. The surface is decorated. The patterns are simple and they are usually executed by imprinting a 'comb' to give a continuous hyphenated line, by impressing a cord in the soft clay before firing or by incising a line.

It appears that it was Beaker people who introduced the knowledge of metallurgy into Ireland but this was not a unitary event either in time or place. One group, possibly the earliest, arrived in the south-west directly from the continent. Another group (or groups) arrived in the east from Britain. This led to the emergence of two provinces (de Valera 1968, 80).

The Western Province

Burials and their Content

A type of megalithic tomb, termed a wedge-tomb, provides the chief evidence for a Western Province (de Valera and Ó Nualláin 1961, xiii; 1972, xiii, Fig. 86 for distribution). The burial chamber usually has an ante-chamber or portico at the entrance end. In a limited number of tombs there is a closed end-chamber at the rear. The division between the main chamber and the portico normally consists of a slab but in some tombs jambs occur. Usually the main chamber narrows and decreases in height from the portico inwards. The tomb is roofed by slabs which rest directly on the orthostats. Very often one or more wallings of orthostats, or internal revetment, is found a short distance out from the sides of the chamber. The covering cairn varies in shape, but a D-shaped or a short oval form are common. The straight front of the cairn faces westward and it has an orthostatic façade. Some cairns have a kerb. The tombs also vary in size. For instance, the tomb at Labbacallee is a large structure at least 13·75 m (45 ft) in length (Leask and Price 1936). But in the Burren area of Co. Clare, due to local geology, the chambers are small simple structures that consist of a slab on each side and at each end and roofed by a single slab (de Valera and Ó Nualláin 1961).

Between four and five hundred wedge-shaped tombs are known (cf. Fig. 43). The

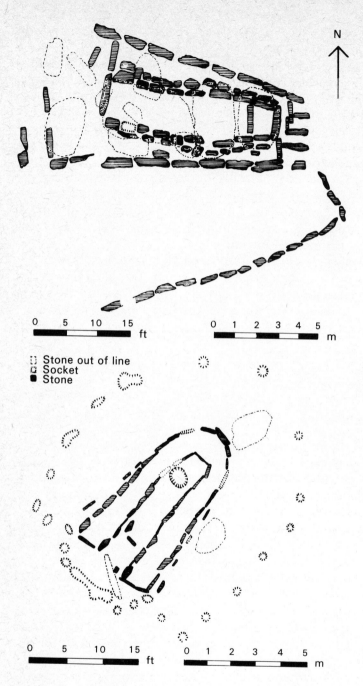

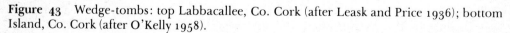

Figure 43 Wedge-tombs: top Labbacallee, Co. Cork (after Leask and Price 1936); bottom Island, Co. Cork (after O'Kelly 1958).

largest concentrations occur in west Cork, in east Clare and the adjoining parts of Tipperary, the Burren country of north-west Clare and in the Sligo/north-east Mayo region. By and large the wedge-graves occur singly. In Clare, however, groups of tombs occur but there is no cemetery complex. The siting of tombs varies but as de Valera and Ó Nualláin (1961, 107–11) have demonstrated the tombs mainly occur on high pasture lands, on sandstones or on limestones that had a thin covering of soil. Tombs are rarely found on rich, heavy lands such as the Golden Vale in Co. Tipperary. On the other hand the high mountain lands, such as parts of Kerry, were not settled, though the copper-rich area of west Cork and east Kerry was attractive for settlement.

The tombs were used for communal burial, and both inhumation and cremation were practised. At Moytirra, Co. Sligo (Madden 1969) the inhumed remains of four adults and one child occurred. Inhumation was also the rite at the Lough Gur 'wedge' (Ó Ríordáin and Ó h-Iceadha 1955) where at least twelve persons were interred. There was also one cremation burial in the tomb. Cremation was the burial rite at both sites at Loughash, Co. Derry (Davies 1939b; Davies and Mullin 1940) and probably at Ballyedmonduff, Co. Dublin (Ó Ríordáin and de Valera 1952).

A number of excavated sites have produced finds. These consist of pottery and flints. As de Valera and Ó Nualláin (1961, 113–15, with references) have pointed out, Beaker, both fine and coarse varieties, is the main type of pottery represented.

Amongst the finer Beaker wares Bell Beakers were the predominant type (de Paor 1961; Madden 1968). These have a smooth surface and the body is decorated. The ornament often occurs in bands with undecorated zones in between. The band consists of horizontal and diagonal lines, lozenges and criss-cross hatching (cf. Fig. 46, 1, 3, 5). The coarse ware consists of vessels with flat bases. The walls may be upright or splay outwards slightly. Decoration in the form of incised or grooved lines or finger-tip impressions sometimes occurs (Case 1961, 198–200, 206–8, Rockbarton and Kilhoyle pots).

Sherds of Food Vessel and Cinerary Urn document the use of these tombs later than Beaker times, while the few sherds of Neolithic pottery indicate some survival from the Late Stone Age. The flints include barbed-and-tanged arrowheads and thumb-scrapers.

Farming

The distribution of the wedge-tombs shows that the areas settled contained good pasture lands. It would appear that tillage was of secondary importance (de Valera and Ó Nualláin 1961, 111–12). Trees may have been cut down with flat thick-butted copper axeheads (Case 1966, 142–9, Type A; Coghlan and Case 1957, 102; Harbison 1969b, 10ff, Lough Ravel type; Britton in Allen, Britton and Coghlan 1970, 52–6; see Fig. 44, 4–5). Axes of this type have a wide distribution in Ireland and they are known from western and central Europe. The place of origin is probably western Asia (cf. Bar-

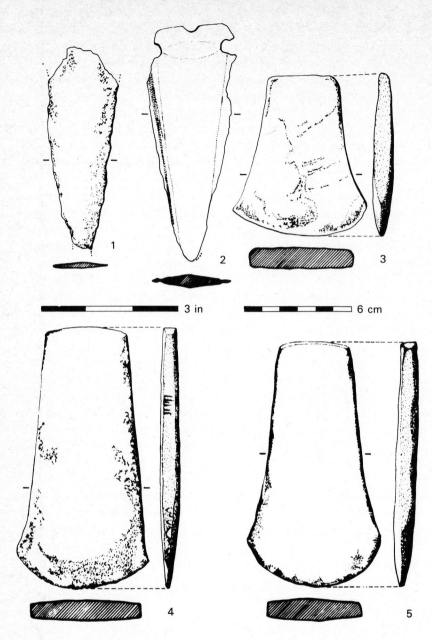

Figure 44 Hoard from Whitespots, Co. Down: 1 tanged knife-dagger; 2 riveted knife-dagger; 3 thick-butted axehead with concave sides, sub-type Ballybeg (N.M.I. P.1949: 1–3); 4–5 thick-butted axeheads of primary form (Lough Ravel Type) found together at Castletown Roche, Co. Cork (Ashmolean Museum 1885: 747–8).

Adon 1962, 218–26; Hestrim and Tadmor 1963, 265–88). Axes of this type are rare in Britain. This, and the fact that axes that more closely resemble the continental trapeze shape are more common in Munster (Case 1966, 149), suggests that the thick-butted axe was introduced into the south of Ireland from the continent. In Ireland a variety in which the sides are concave emerged (Harbison's sub-type Ballybeg). This modification in shape may be due to contact with axes of the eastern Irish thin-butted series (p. 139).

Flint barbed-and-tanged arrowheads suggest hunting and thumb-shaped flint scrapers could have been used in the preparation of animal skins for curing. It is possible that people of the Western Province had metal awls and tanged daggers. Both types occur in the Knocknague (Kilbannon) hoard, Co. Galway (Harbison, 1968, 53, Fig. 26). The thick-butted axes with which they were associated are of the developed form.

There is no positive evidence for occupation but in view of the presence of Bell Beaker sherds it is possible that it was people of the Western Province that squatted over the Neolithic settlement at Site C, Knockadoon, Lough Gur (Ó Ríordáin 1954, especially pp. 340–1, 377–8; Simpson 1971, 135). Perhaps the activity, very likely seasonal, associated with hearths at Rockbarton, Co. Limerick (Mitchell and Ó Ríordáin 1942), Gortcorbies, Co. Derry (May 1950) and the pre-barrow phase at Ballingoola, Co. Limerick (MacDermott 1949) might be assigned to the Western Province.

Origin and Chronology

The wedge-shaped tombs provide the best evidence for the origin of the Western Province. Prototypes for these tombs can be cited in Brittany, the *allées couvertes* (L'Helgouach 1965, 259–300). About ninety such tombs are known, they occur singly but their siting varies. The chamber is rectangular, sometimes there is an ante-chamber. Outer-walling is also known. The entrance to the vast majority of examples faces to the east of a north–south line. The burial rite is not well known, but it appears to be inhumation. The grave goods include pottery, stone and flint artifacts. The pottery consists of Bell Beakers, flowerpot-shaped vessels, and round-bottomed vessels that had evolved out of the French Neolithic Chassey Ware. The stone objects consist of polished axes, archers' wrist-guards and perforated pendants. Amongst the flints, blades, scrapers, and arrowheads (including the barbed-and-tanged variety) have turned up. Metal is very rare but a tanged 'west European' dagger is known from two sites and a 'Cypriot' dagger from a third. It may be that the 'culture' of these tombs is hybrid, a mixture of older megalithic traditions and new Beaker traditions. According to L'Helgouach the tombs date to the centuries immediately before 2000 B.C.

Discussion

It is the wedge-shaped tomb that is the main factor in the Western Province but due to the virtual absence of metal from excavated tombs it is not possible to link directly the tombs and metal types. However, the concentration of tombs in Munster and the fact that those thick-butted axes which resemble the continental form are numerous in that province (p. 119) suggests that both may be part of the same cultural assemblage. If so it was they who initiated the exploitation of the copper ores of Munster, especially the deposits in Cork and Kerry. They used sulphite ores of copper alloyed with arsenic (Case 1966, 149). There is no information available about their workshops or their method of casting. The thick-butted axeheads were probably cast in open moulds and then finished off by hammering and smoothing. But not one stone mould is known and this contrasts with the evidence available for the thin-butted axeheads (p. 139). Associated finds of thick-butted axes and copper cake from Monastery, Co. Wicklow and Carrickshedoge, Co. Wexford may have been founders' hoards. At Knocksarnet, Co. Kerry a thin-butted axehead was found with a copper cake (Harbison 1968, 44, 55, 53). Gold may also have been used. A trapezoidal-shaped gold plaque decorated with herring-bone pattern was found on a skeleton, with other plates and possibly a small disc, in a small cave at Carrig-a-Crump, near Castle Martyr, Co. Cork (Armstrong 1933, 92 No. 398; Crofton Croker 1854, 143). The sun-discs have mainly an Atlantic distribution, from Wexford around to Donegal (Fig. 52, left; also Fig. 51, 2–3). Similar discs are known in Iberia (MacWhite 1951, 50; Taylor 1968, 261) but they also have Beaker associations in Britain (D. L. Clarke 1970, 63, 70, 94–5, 97). An immediate continental background for these in the north-west part of the North European Plain can also be suggested (Butler 1963, 167–73, 187–90). It is, therefore, possible that the discs were first introduced into the Eastern Province (p. 131).

The tombs are considered to be an introduced type from western France. Their builders occupied lighter upland soils that would have been more suited to pasture than to tillage (p. 119). Indeed, it was probably the good grazing especially over the winter and spring months that attracted them to one of their chosen areas, the Burren of Co. Clare, which they occupied intensively. It was herds of domestic animals, especially cattle, that formed the basis of their economy and provided meat for food and skins for clothes. The presence of barbed-and-tanged arrowheads shows that hunting was practised.

The distribution of the tombs suggests that from primary settlement areas in Munster, especially the peninsulas of Beare, Ballinskelligs and Dingle, these pastoralists and possibly metallurgists spread up along the west coast and then across Ulster. The Leinster tombs are an extension of this spread. It is of interest to note that the wedge-tomb builders had already spread to the east by an early date in the Early Bronze Age. At least one site, the tomb at Kilmashogue, Co. Dublin (Kilbride Jones

1954, esp. pp. 465–6), was used by Bowl Food Vessel people as a cemetery mound, so its primary use must have been over by then.

The cultural context of the tombs is difficult to define. Fine Beaker pottery has been found in wedge-tombs but mainly in the northern part of the country. This includes Bell Beaker, the 'international' form, but also Beakers of British origin. In Munster about half a dozen tombs have been excavated but only two, those at Lough Gur and Labbacallee, produced fine Beaker Ware. The majority produced no grave goods whatsoever. If there was a cultural movement into Ireland and if this came from Brittany, an area where 'wedge'-tombs and broad-butted axeheads are found, other elements should be expected, especially stone alignments and standing stones (Giot 1960, 115–27).

Alignments, standing stones (*gallâin*) and stone circles are known in Munster, and in Cork and Kerry there is a distinctive group of stone circles (Ó Nualláin 1971). The stones are usually free-standing and one of them is recumbent. The entrance is opposite this stone. The size of the circle varies from about 2·50 m (8 ft 3 in) in diameter and consisting of five stones to 17 m (55 ft 10 in) in diameter and fifteen stones (Plate 10b). In two of the circles excavated by Fahy (1959, 1962) each had a small central pit that contained a cremation burial in a flat-based pottery vessel. Some circles have a small monument, a boulder dolmen or cist, in the centre. As yet, however, research is not sufficiently advanced to establish the cultural context of these three types of monuments (Pl. 10b).

It is not known for how long the Early Bronze Age of the Western Province flourished but it may have gone on for several centuries. This is suggested by the virtual absence of Food Vessels, and the later Encrusted and Cordoned Urns, from Munster and their scarcity in Connacht (see distribution maps by Fox 1952. Pls IV, V, VIII). A double-piece stone mould for casting a ribbed kite-shaped spearhead was found in the cairn mass of the Moylisha wedge-grave, Co. Wicklow (Ó h-Iceadha 1946, 125–6). The excavator considered that the mould was in a primary position. But in view of the strength of the Eastern Beaker, Food Vessel and the Urn 'cultures' it is unlikely that wedge-shaped tombs were being built in the east of Ireland as late as the latter half of the second millennium B.C.

The Beginnings of the Eastern Province

This province was established and sustained by waves of new influence which in some, if not all, cases must have been due to the arrival of people from Britain. These new groups had a common trait, they practised the rite of single-grave burial and from the beginning they may have had a knowledge of metal-working. For the early part of the Bronze Age there is a mass of material for study but this has not yet been fully disentangled or placed in strict chronological order. On its own the pottery evidence suggests that there could have been at least as many as three principal movements – Beaker, Food Vessel and Urns. But the whole process of folk movements, borrowings and native innovation may have been complex and the various people represented by their pottery need not all have arrived in strict chronological succession. Indeed, the complex nature of the problem can be summed up in ApSimon's words:

> from the moment that the first Bell Beaker voyager steps from his skin boat . . . we are faced with diverse societies with quite distinct material culture. Not only is there distinction to be made between native 'neolithic' and immigrant 'Bronze Age', but the Bronze Age groups themselves show remarkable diversity. . . .
>
> (ApSimon 1969b, 33)

Single-grave burial makes its appearance in more than one way. One group of such burials concentrates in southern Leinster counties. The main characteristic of this group is a megalithic cist under a round mound, and the unburnt remains were accompanied by grave-goods (p. 81). Objects similar to the grave-goods form some of the southern Leinster burials. Goodland bowls and mushroom-headed pins have been found with coarse Beaker pottery in the communal burial in a rock cavity at Cahirguillamore, Co. Limerick (p. 127). There was also a distinctive movement of Beaker people into the eastern part of Ireland. Meath appears to have been particularly affected. The people used the pan-European Bell Beaker but they also had Beakers of British type, e.g. Clarke's Northern and Southern British groups (long-necked ('A') and short-necked ('C') Beakers: Clarke 1970; Piggott 1963). In Britain Beaker people were physically different from the preceding Neolithic inhabitants; they had broad heads, they were taller and they were more heavily built (Childe 1940, 91). Their Single Burials consisted of either a crouched inhumation in a cist under a round mound or simple pit cremations in a 'henge' monument. They introduced fine and coarse types of pottery and under Beaker influence Neolithic pottery altered in south-eastern England, e.g. Mortlake Ware.

There are different Beaker groupings in Britain but it is not clear from which of these groups the strongest influence came. It may have been mixed, at least a mixed assemblage occurs on Dalkey Island (Liversage 1968, 154–7; see also Harbison 1973, 97). The new arrivals pushed in to the primary area of Passage Grave settlement and also into the eastern half of the Court Cairn province.

Enclosures

The enclosures appear to have had multiple uses – for occupation, for burial, and for ritual practices of an unknown nature. They consist of a circular area that was delimited by either an earthen bank, a bank and ditch, or by stones (a stone circle). Some of the earthen enclosures are very massive (Plate 11). At the 'Giant's Ring', Ballynahatty, Co. Down the bank is 18·30 m–21 m (60–70 ft) wide at the base and 3·65 m (12 ft) in average height. The area enclosed is 183 m (600 ft) (Plate 11a; see *Archaeological Survey Co. Down* (1966), 89–91). But much smaller structures occur. At the Longstone Rath, Furness, Co. Kildare the enclosed area is 58 m (190 ft) in diameter. The bank is 3 m (10 ft) in height and the ditch is 1·50 m (5 ft) deep (Macalister, Armstrong and Praeger 1913). There are also structural differences. For instance at Monknewtown (Sweetman 1971) and Ballynahatty the material for the bank was scraped up from the interior. An internal ditch occurs at Dun Ruadh, Co. Tyrone (cf. Evans 1966, 201), Micknanstown and Mullaghteelin both in Co. Meath (Hartnett 1957, 263–5). At Furness there is an external ditch. The position of the entrance is hard to define but a single entrance appears to have been fairly standard.

Internal features are also known but knowledge of these is meagre as only one site, Monknewtown, has been fairly fully excavated. There, various features occurred. One of these was a wooden house (p. 129) but the most common feature was burials. Thirteen came to light and in all cases the burial rite was cremation. One burial, in a pottery vessel of Carrowkeel type, was seemingly placed unprotected against the base of the bank. Another burial was in the centre of a small barrow and the cremated bones were in a small flat-bottomed pottery vessel. This feature might be related to the 'foundation trenches' which have been found surrounding Beaker graves under mounds on the continent (Lanting, Mook and van der Waals 1973, 47). The remaining eleven burials were in pits and in two instances the pits were lined with stones to give a cist-like structure. One pit burial was in a coarse, flat-based pottery vessel but with the other ten the cremations were placed directly in the pit. Three of the burials were marked by low upright stones each of which was about 50 cm in height (Sweetman 1971).

There is a standing stone in the centre of Furness. This is 6·40 m (21 ft) in height and it weighs twelve tons. This stone marked the position of a subrectangular cist about 2·45 m (8 ft) in length. The cist contained the cremated remains of at least two adults. These were accompanied by sherds of coarse undecorated pottery, a flat stone bead, a fragmentary stone archer's wrist-guard and a worked flint.

There is no up-to-date list of stone circles but they are a fairly common monument (see also p. 123). They range in form and in size. Most consist of spaced free-standing stones but at Grange, Co. Limerick (Site B) the stones were placed side-by-side. They were supported on the outside by an earthen bank through which there was a well defined entrance (Fig. 45, see Ó Ríordáin 1951). Some circles have external features. An outlying stone occurs at the 'Pipers Stones', Athgreany, Co. Wicklow (Price 1934, 3) and there are two outliers at Ballynoe, Co. Down (*Archaeological Survey, Co. Down* (1966) 87–9). Alignments leading up to a circle or circles are also known, and these are a particular feature of the mid-Ulster stone circles (see p. 128).

At least two stone circles, New Grange and Grange, Co. Limerick can be associated with the Eastern Beaker Province. The New Grange circle, which is free-standing, surrounds the Passage Grave. It is 103·60 m (340 ft) in diameter. Only twelve stones (or parts of stones) now remain but if the spacing was maintained there may originally have been thirty-five stones. Some of the stones are huge and measure up to 2·50 m in height above the present surface (C. O'Kelly 1967, 68–9). On the southern and south-eastern sides, between the circle and the Passage Grave mounted Professor O'Kelly's

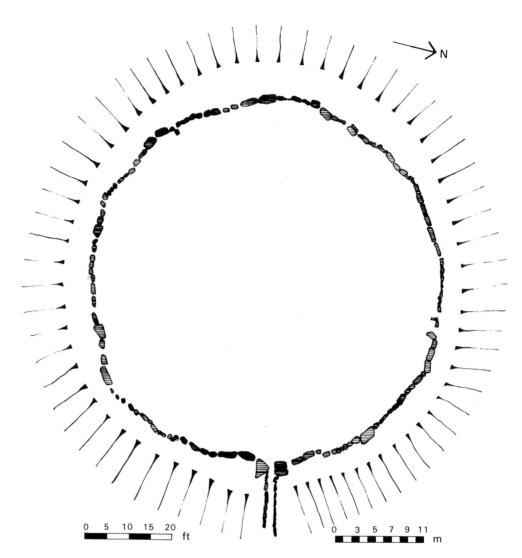

Figure 45 Stone circle, Grange, Co. Limerick (after Ó Ríordáin 1951).

excavations have produced evidence for considerable settlement by Beaker people. The material culture consists of a variety of flint scrapers, lozenge, triangular and hollow-based arrowheads, *petit tranchet* derivative arrowheads, discoidal knives and fabricators. The Beaker pottery appears to belong to D. L. Clarke's (1970, 84ff.) Middle Rhine variety and amongst the sherds are the remains of two polypod bowls (O'Kelly 1966, 98; 1973, 144). Bowls of this type occur commonly in eastern European Beaker assemblages, especially in Saxo-Thuringia and in the Middle Rhine area (Clarke 1970, 90). The type is known in Britain (Manby 1969) and it probably reached that land with other objects from the Rhineland Beaker cultures.

The embanked stone circle at Grange is 65·60 m (*c.* 215 ft) in overall diameter (Ó Ríordáin 1951). The finds consisted of Beaker, Food Vessel and some Neolithic pottery. Not less than six and perhaps as many as twelve Beakers were represented. Both Bell and Necked Beakers occur but it was only possible to reconstruct one vessel. This is a southern British (long-necked) Beaker. Flint artifacts include thumb-shaped scrapers, and transverse, hollow-based and barbed-and-tanged arrowheads. Bronze, though rare, was also represented. Part of a bracelet and a dagger sheath mounting may be noted but these could be secondary. There was no evidence of formal burial or of occupation. Features resembling the barrow or 'foundation trench' at Monknewtown have been discovered.

A free-standing stone circle, 21·35 m (*c.* 70 ft) in diameter at Castle Mahon, Co. Down, may also have been erected at an early stage in the Metal Age (Collins 1956).

A reinterpretation of the Millin Bay Passage Grave (Collins and Waterman 1955) suggests that the free-standing stone circle ('The Outer Stone Setting') is, like that at New Grange, an added feature and, as is also the case at New Grange, cruder and more massive stones were used by the circle builders than were used by the Passage Grave builders for the kerb of the tomb. It is also very likely that the nine cists were associated with the circle. Except for one example the others were grouped along the eastern half of the site. The burials consisted of a pit lined with stones. Four contained cremations; the remainder were empty. This form of cist and the associated rite of cremation burial can be paralleled at Monknewtown.

Another Co. Down site, Ballynoe, may have a similar history (Collins and Waterman 1955, 46–8; *Archaeological Survey, Co. Down* (1966) 87–9). The primary monument may have been a Passage Grave. Later a stone circle with outliers was built. Within the circle the Passage Grave mound occupied an eccentric position, as is to some extent the situation at New Grange.

A 'sepulchral mound' near Temple Patrick, Co. Antrim, possibly one of the Moyadam Passage Graves, was surrounded by a fosse and a free-standing stone circle (Herity 1974, Fig. 14 with p. 222).

In this connection it may also be recalled that some of the cremation burials at wedge-tomb, Baurnadomeeny, Co. Tipperary resemble those from Monknewtown and Millin Bay (O'Kelly 1960). At least burials 6, 18, 19 and 20 are secondary. O'Kelly, however, has argued that the kerb is a primary feature.

Cremation was the principal burial rite. The remains had been deposited in pits that were dug into the sub-soil. Sometimes the pits were lined with stones to form cists (p. 125, Monknewtown, Millin Bay). Ring-barrows, such as the examples at Rathjordan and Ballingoola, Co. Limerick and Moneen, Co. Cork, may also have been built (cf. Ó Ríordáin 1947a and 1948; MacDermott 1949; O'Kelly 1952a, 140–9). At Cahirguillamore, Co. Limerick at least fourteen people were buried in a 'chamber' that was naturally formed from a large boulder resting at an angle against a rock face.

The rite was inhumation and what appears to have been the final burial was crouched. This was outside the entrance. Finds included Goodland bowls, coarse Beaker pottery, mushroom-headed and other types of pins, and stone beads (Hunt 1967). The finds from this burial show that it is of Beaker date and the Goodland bowls and mushroom-headed pins in particular link it to the Leinster megalithic cist burials (p. 81). The Cahirguillamore burial has parallels in Britain. Inhumation burials were found in a rock-shelter at Church Dale, Derbyshire. These were accompanied by a *petit tranchet* derivative arrowhead and Peterborough pottery (*P.P.S.*, 19 (1953), 229–30). A small cave at Gop, Flintshire contained the inhumed remains of fourteen individuals. Grave-goods included Peterborough Ware, two jet sliders (cf. McInnes 1968), a discoidal flint knife and a 'Beaker dagger' (Daniel 1950, 46, 142, 195).

Apparently Beaker people of the Eastern Province also erected single standing stones. Excavation has taken place at five of these monuments. These are Drumnahare and Carrownacaw, Co. Down, Punchestown and Furness, Co. Kildare and Site C, Brugh na Bóinne, Co. Meath (Collins 1957b; Leask 1937; Macalister, Armstrong and Praeger 1913, 354; Shee and Evans 1965). There was a scatter of cremated bone at the base of the Drumnahare stone while close to Carrownacaw there was a scatter of flints, including *petit tranchet* derivative arrowheads. The latter stone stood just outside a ring ditch. Both the Punchestown and Furness stones were erected contiguous to cists and the Furness cist is of Beaker date (p. 125).

There is a distinctive group of free-standing stone circles, alignments and cairns in mid-Ulster. At Neaghmore, Co. Tyrone the combination of these types forms an impressive group of monuments (May 1953; Pilcher 1969; Smith, Pearson and Pilcher 1970, 292, see also Davies 1939a and Waterman 1964). At present it is not possible to place these monuments in their precise cultural context. Radiocarbon (C14) determinations for activity at Beaghmore ranges over the period $1605 \pm 45 - 775 \pm 55$ B.C.

Economy and some other aspects of the Group

Animal bones from New Grange show that grazing played an important part in the economy of the people. Ninety-eight per cent of the bones come from domestic animals. Cattle and pigs were the most important food animals. Sheep/goat only played a minor part in the economy. The inhabitants had dogs and as some of these were old at death they may have been kept for guarding or hunting. Horse-bones were also found and it has been tentatively concluded that these, too, were from domestic animals. The horses were small, about 120–8 cm in height at the withers. Cows reached a height of 120–30 cm at the shoulder and at least one bull was about 137 cm in height. It appears that most of the cattle were killed between the ages of two and three years. It therefore appears that cattle primarily served as beef-producing animals and that secondary uses such as milk or traction were of less importance. Pigs were slaughtered after reaching the age of maturity (van Wijngaarden–Bakker 1974).

Occupation at Ballynagilly, Co. Tyrone coincided with forest clearance. There mixed farming may have been practised (ApSimon 1969b, 35).

Evidence for archery, probably used in hunting, is provided by flint arrowheads, barbed-and-tanged, hollow-based and triangular, and by stone wrist-guards (Fig. 46, 6). These artifacts are common to Beaker assemblages on the continent (for wrist-guards see Sangmeister, 1964; summary of Atkinson's unpublished classification of British wrist-guards in Clarke 1970, 570).

The skins of animals caught could have been cured and the leather used in the manufacture of garments and shoes. During the initial dressing of the skins flint scrapers could have been used. At the manufacturing stage awls and possibly 'daggers' were used (Fig. 44, 1, 2; Fig. 47, 6). Both awls and tanged daggers have Beaker associations on the continent and in Britain (Harbison 1967; Thomas 1968 (awls), Harbison 1969a, 7, 8, 21–3, 'Knocknague type' has an unperforated tang; 'Listack type' has holes in the tang; Piggott 1963, 73–4, 75 (daggers)). It is also possible that the round-butted riveted dagger was also introduced into Ireland at this time (Clarke 1970, 448 for association with Beakers in Britain). Cloaks may have been fastened with V-perforated buttons (see p. 144). These buttons are also a common Beaker type in Britain and on the continent (cf. Arnal 1973 with references). They have an earlier origin in Globular Amphorae and Corded Ware contexts (Piggott 1963, 78).

Occupation took place within the enclosure at Monknewtown and adjacent to the stone circle at New Grange. Rectangular houses up to 20 m long may have stood at New Grange. A wooden house stood at Monknewtown. The Monknewtown house was built in a hollowed-out area. It was trapezoidal in shape and there was a hearth in the centre. There is also evidence for occupation on Dalkey Island, Co. Dublin (Liversage 1968, 164–5) and at Ballynagilly, Co. Tyrone (ApSimon 1969, 35). The remains of houses have not been found at either place. Bell and Necked Beakers were found in the Dalkey settlement. The Ballynagilly Beakers have affinities with Clarke's Northern (British) Middle Rhine group. Site D, Knockadoon, may also have been occupied by Beaker people from the east of Ireland. At that site vessels of Clarke's Wessex/Middle Rhine and Northern (British) Middle Rhine were represented. The wooden house may have been oval in shape (Simpson 1971, 135, Fig. 23, A; Ó Ríordáin 1954, 384–413). The occupation sites show that there was a wide range of Beaker pottery in use. The main divisions of the Beaker wares are represented and within these there are sub-groups which differ in shape and in the range of decorative styles. Coarse Beaker was also present. Vessels of this class, which were probably used for domestic purposes, are usually larger than the fine Beakers. They have flat bases and the sides may be slightly curved or straight. Sometimes there are cordons, or ridges, under the rims. Externally the surface may be decorated with incised lines; occasionally other designs, such as rustication were used (Liversage 1968, esp. pp. 154–7; Case 1961, 206–7, Rockbarton pots).

Flint artifacts were also common. In addition to barbed-and-tanged and hollow-

129

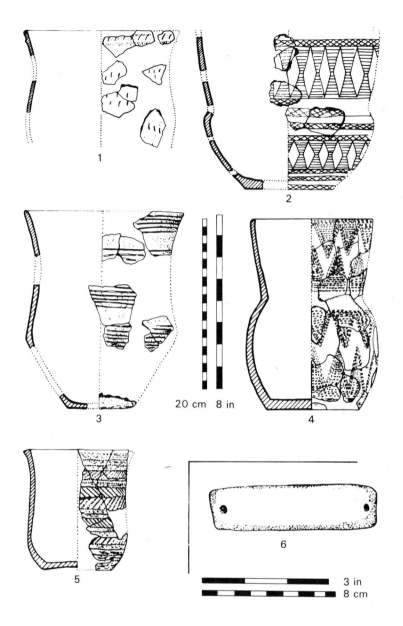

Figure 46 Fine Beaker Ware: 1, 3, 5 Bell Beaker, Dalkey Island, Co. Dublin; 2, 4 Necked Beaker, Dalkey and Grange, Co. Limerick; 6 archer's wrist-guard, stone, Corren, Co. Armagh (4 after O Ríordáin 1951, Fig. 5; 1–3, 5 after Liversage 1968, p. 53 (Fig. 9), p. 71 (Fig. 12), p. 51 (Fig. 8), p. 61 (Fig. 9); 6 after Wilde 1857, Fig. 70: 69). Objects in N.M.I.

based arrowheads, *petit tranchet* derivative 'arrowheads' and discoidal flint knives (O'Kelly 1966, 98; 1973, 144) were also in use.

For personal adornment gold basket-shaped earrings both short (Fig. 51, 4, 5) and long varieties and sub-rectangular plaques should have been current (Armstrong 1933, Nos 348–50, 392–4). A sub-rectangular plaque from Co. Cavan (Fig. 51, 6) may have been found with parts of a gold object that Case has identified as being the remains of at least one diadem of a type known from north-western Iberia and dating from the beginning of the Metal Age (Case 1966, 172 f.n. 29). Sun-discs (p. 122) may also have been worn in the Eastern Province (Fig. 51, 2–3). Gold discs of unknown type were found in a gold-bound box with two stone archers' wrist-guards and jet beads in a bog at Corren, Co. Armagh (Wilde 1857, 89). The geometric decoration found on lunulae can be derived from Beaker pottery (Taylor 1970). Other evidence, however, suggests that lunulae were current at a slightly later date (p. 142). The Early Metal Age gold ornaments were made by beating out ingots into thin sheets. The sheets were then trimmed to shape and decorated usually with linear designs. The designs were normally incised but on occasions faint repoussé work was used.

Origin and Chronology

From the lands around the mouth of the Rhine Beaker people spread to Britain and later to Ireland. The earliest incursion could have taken place by 2000 B.C. and the material from New Grange with its ultimate Middle Rhine background should be early (three C14 determinations centre on 2000 B.C., O'Kelly 1972; the determinations from Ballynagilly are somewhat similar: Smith, Pearson and Pilcher 1971). Apart from pottery, other elements of the Eastern Beaker Province have an origin in Britain. In western and northern Britain stone circles of various forms are known (Atkinson, Piggott and Sandars 1951, Fig. 29; Grimes 1963, for Wales). The earthen enclosures show a resemblance to the 'henge' monuments.

At present it is not known where the primary settlement took place. Indeed it is likely that there was more than one movement, so different areas would have been affected and these could have been any place from Antrim in the north-east to Wexford in the south-east. However, it does appear that the Boyne Valley was an area of early settlement. The newcomers expanded inland and in the south-west they penetrated at least as far as Lough Gur in Co. Limerick. It is not possible to gauge the duration of the Beaker stage in eastern Ireland but in view of the achievements of the people it must at least have lasted for more than a century.

Discussion

The movement, or movements, from Britain to Ireland by Beaker people was an event, or events, of considerable importance. There is the possibility that they, too, introduced metal-working. Cushion stones, which could have been used as hammers

131

by metal craftsmen, are known (Butler and van der Waals 1966, 72, Fig. 17 bottom). A thin-butted copper or bronze axehead was found on the edge of the Beaker settlement at New Grange (O'Kelly 1970b, 27) but it has not been established that it was used by the Beaker people. An axehead of similar type, as well as some copper awls, were found on Dalkey Island (Liversage 1968, 113, 91). These artifacts were not found in a closed context but, nevertheless, it is relevant to remark that Beaker is the pre-dominant Early Bronze Age pottery from that site. The Beaker people may have used and made sheet-gold ornaments, at least earrings and discs.

As yet very little data is available about their occupation sites and economy. Ritual practices may have taken place within the enclosures and they were the first people to practise widely the rite of single grave burial in cists or pits. The enclosures are of further importance as they show that these new Beaker people came in strength. Due to their size the Monknewtown earthwork or the New Grange stone circle could not have been built by a small trading or raiding band. A sufficient number of people must have arrived to lay the basis of a consolidated settlement and to dominate the existing inhabitants. Of particular interest is the fact that the newcomers pushed right into the heartlands of the Passage Grave settlement. This is especially noticeable in Meath. Within the Brugh na Bóinne Passage Grave cemetery they may have erected five or six enclosures – the New Grange stone circle, a possible stone circle north-east of Dowth ('Cloghalea') and four earthen enclosures (Monknewtown, Dowth (Site Q), Site 'A' and an enclosure to the south-west of it). In the Fourknocks area there is an enclosure at Micknanstown while earthworks at Heathtown and Mullaghtelin may be related (Hartnett 1957, 263–5). Close to Sliabh na Caillighe there is a stone circle at Ballinvally and Beaker people also squatted for a while at Knowth. Outside Meath there is further evidence for the domination of the Passage Grave people. In Co. Down the Millin Bay and possible Ballynoe Passage Graves were, so to speak, taken over and the megalithic tomb within the Giant's Ring at Ballynahatty is a form of Passage Grave. A pottery vessel of Carrowkeel type accompanied a cremation at Monknewtown (Sweetman 1971, 138, Pl. 24a). As the new eastern Beaker culture was becoming dominant it is likely that it assimilated the Passage Grave builders and other Neolithic groups. Thus, the foundations were laid for the establishment of the Eastern Province of the Early Bronze Age.

CHAPTER SIX

Food Vessel People: Consolidation of the Single Grave Culture

Background

Some time after 2000 B.C. an alteration in the northern English Beaker cultures took place. This involved the modification of some of the existing types, especially the fine pottery, but also the acquisition of new types from abroad. In the emerging culture the native element consists of Food Vessels, mainly vase-shaped, flat round-butted riveted metal daggers, metal awls, metal earrings, jet buttons with V-shaped perforation, stone battle axes and flint artifacts (Simpson 1968, for Food Vessel associations). The burial ritual and the art is also Beaker-derived. The foreign element consists of metal objects – thin-butted flat axeheads, halberds, bar and ribbed bracelets or armlets, and possibly band armlets although these could be derived from the Beaker culture. The industry was based on single-piece stone moulds for casting and most of the artifacts cast were made from bronze (Britton 1963, 263–84, Migdale-Marnoch Tradition; Coles 1968–9). The origin of the foreign types can be traced back to the central European Early Bronze Age cultures but they appear to have reached northern Britain from north-west Europe. The Food Vessel 'culture' can thus be described as a heavily industrialized and provincialized Beaker society in north Britain.

In Ireland the Food Vessel people lived mainly in the north-east and east of the country. Limited settlement took place in parts of Connacht but Munster did not become a popular area for settlement (Fox 1952, Pl. IV; Simpson 1968, Fig. 48 for distribution).

As will be shown, there are two types of Food Vessel, Bowl and Vase. These were treated independently by ApSimon (1969b, 35–44). He isolated an Irish Bowl culture as distinctive from his Vase group which had Urn affinities.

Burials

These were placed in a pit. Sometimes the pit was lined with stones which were set on edge, usually a longer stone on each side and shorter stone at each end. This structure, which is termed a cist, was roofed with a capstone (Fig. 47). On rare occasions the under-side of the capstone was decorated, i.e. Ballinvally, Co. Meath (Shee 1972, 231; also Hartnett 1950, 194–7; Morris 1929, 114, Hempstown and Moylough respectively). By and large, the burials consist of the remains of one individual. Subsequent burial in a cist is rare. The rites of cremation and inhumation were

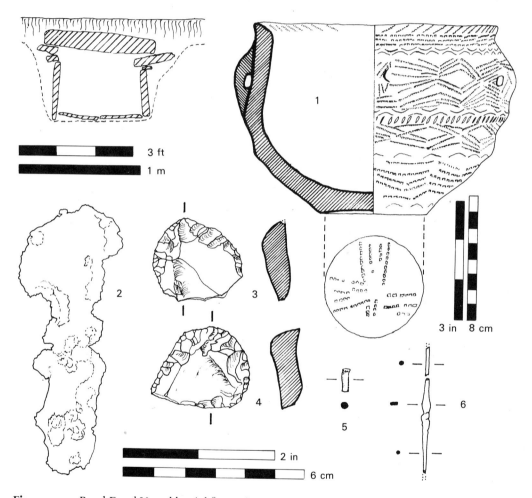

Figure 47 Bowl Food Vessel burial from cist at Carrickinab, Co. Down 1 Bowl Food Vessel; 2 copper or bronze round-butted riveted knife-dagger; 3–4 flint round scrapers; 5 rivet; 6 copper or bronze awl (after Collins and Evans 1968).

practised. The inhumed burials were placed in a crouched position. Grave-goods were often placed in the grave. Prominent amongst these were pottery vessels called Food Vessels.

There are two main shapes of Food Vessels, bowl-shaped and vase-shaped (cf. ApSimon 1958; Simpson 1965 and 1968). The bowl is a squat vessel and there are two principal forms, ridged and smooth (Fig. 47, 1). Ridged bowls are decorated with lozenge and chevron patterns, while panels, vertical lines or grooves and repeated horizontal patterns are the designs that are usually found on smooth bowls. The place of origin of the Bowl Food Vessel has not been conclusively established but the decoration (including that on the base), the technique of its application and the common burial rite where the bowl was placed in front of the face of the crouched burial strongly suggests that the Bowl Food Vessel group developed out of Beakers in northern Britain (Waddell 1974, 35).

Vase Food Vessels consist of a body and neck (Fig. 48, 1). Decoration occurs, but sometimes this is confined to the upper part of the vessel. Some examples have decoration on the base. The motifs include herring-bone and 'maggot' patterns, lozenges, triangles and panels of vertical and horizontal lines. Incision was the predominant technique used in applying the decoration. Vase Food Vessels also developed out of Beakers, probably in north-east England. In Ireland local versions emerged, such as Type E of Abercromby (1912, 127).

Bowl Food Vessels accompanied both cremations and inhumations in roughly equal proportions. The majority of Vase-shaped Food Vessels occur with cremations (ApSimon 1969a, 36). Food Vessel burials have been found both singly and in cemeteries (Fig. 52, right). Two types of cemeteries are known, flat and mound, and close to fifty examples of each have been recorded (Waddell 1970, 100). In the flat cemeteries the graves do not appear to have been grouped in any order. There are two forms of mound cemeteries. In one the mound was specially constructed; in the other an existing mound, usually a Passage Grave, was utilized. It appears that the specially built mounds were the work of the Bowl Food Vessel people. They were constructed on hilltops and they were circular in shape (Fig. 49). Their size and the number of burials that they covered varied. Some mounds were delimited by a kerb and internal features such as rings of stones or U-shaped stone settings have occasionally been placed on the old ground surface. Some of the cemetery mounds have a predominant central burial which takes the form of a massive cist. Frequently a number of burials occur on the old ground surface and this evidence suggests that all of these were inserted at the time that the mound was constructed. Often the burials are grouped in one segment of the area, as at Mount Stewart, Co. Down (Evans and Megaw 1937).

Cemetery mounds are known from the Food Vessel areas of Britain such as Yorkshire. These British mounds could have had their forerunners in Beaker burial mounds (Savory 1972, Fig. 1). It is likely that the Irish cemetery mounds have their origin in Britain; nevertheless, there may have been some native influence, especially from the Passage Graves. At least a hilltop setting, a round-mound and a kerb were

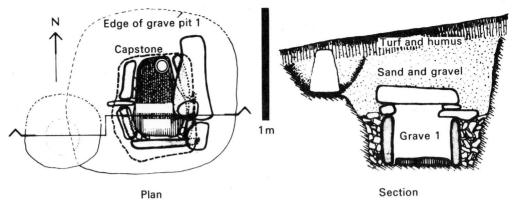

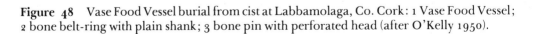

Figure 48 Vase Food Vessel burial from cist at Labbamolaga, Co. Cork: 1 Vase Food Vessel; 2 bone belt-ring with plain shank; 3 bone pin with perforated head (after O'Kelly 1950).

Passage Grave features. The dummy entrance at Lyles Hill, Co. Antrim may also be a megalithic feature. However, there is no need to link the decorated sill stone from that 'entrance' exclusively with Passage Graves despite its central groove or 'line' (cf. New Grange, Knowth). The motifs can be paralleled in the art of the lunulae and flat axes. Its more immediate background should then be found in the decorated cist stones in Scotland, especially those in the Crinan area of Argyll (cf. Simpson and Thawley 1972, 95). Pit burials were used by Beaker people of the Eastern Province and these people also grouped their burials to one side of the site. The rite of crouched inhumation burial could also have been introduced from British Beaker cultures although in Ireland this rite was practised in pre-Food Vessel times as the burials from Cahirguillamore, Site C Lough Gur and some of the Leinster megalithic cists show (p. 81).

Apart from formal burial the Food Vessel people probably practised other forms of ritual. Earthen enclosures and stone circles may have continued to be used. Stone battle axes, decorated flat axes (p. 139) and halberds (Fig. 55, 1) could have been used on ceremonial occasions. Halberds have been found over large parts of Europe but about 40 per cent of the total come from Ireland (Coffey 1908–9; Ó Ríordáin 1937; Harbison 1969a, 35–55). The Irish halberds were derived from central Europe and Ó Ríordáin's Type IV is the primary type. The other Ó Ríordáin types represent insular modification (Butler 1963, 11–26, see also Harbison 1969a, 37–8, 48–55; Case 1966, 152–3).

The natural surfaces of rocks or boulders may have been decorated for ritual purposes but it has not been exclusively established that this was the work of Food Vessel people (Fig. 50). The designs were pocked and the principal motifs include 'cup and rings', labyrinth patterns and 'field' patterns (MacWhite 1946; Ó Ríordáin 1953, 71; Simpson and Thawley 1972; Shee 1972; Herity 1974, 108–9). In Ireland the heaviest concentration is in west Cork and south Kerry and on this evidence, together with the similarity of motifs, MacWhite argued that rock art was introduced from north-western Spain and northern Portugal, hence his term 'Galician Art' (Buhigas 1935). However, apart from the Cork–Kerry concentrations the distribution of rock art in Ireland and Britain coincides with the distribution of Food Vessels (Fig. 54, right).

Technology and Economy

The use of stone for artifact manufacture may have continued in a limited way. Stone axes and hollow-based flint arrowheads have been found in Food Vessel contexts (Simpson 1968, 205; B. Raftery 1969, 26). But the hundreds of metal artifacts that have come to light is a clear indication that large-scale exploitation of ores took place. Metalsmiths of the Eastern Province may have been drawing on the Cork and Kerry deposits, but copper may also have been won from deposits in other parts of the

137

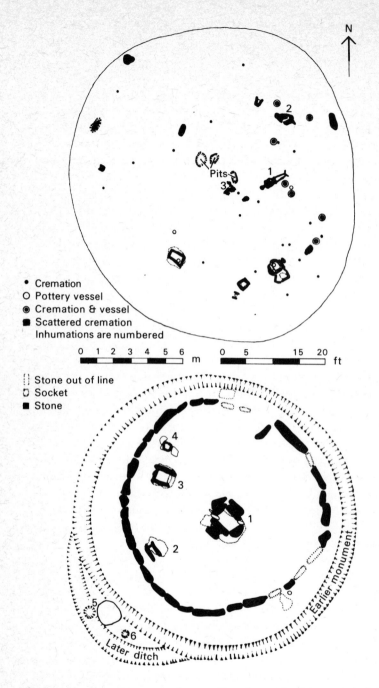

- • Cremation
- ○ Pottery vessel
- ◉ Cremation & vessel
- ■ Scattered cremation
  Inhumations are numbered

⸠⸡ Stone out of line
◌ Socket
■ Stone

Figure 49 Cemetery mounds: top Knockast, Co. Westmeath (after Hencken and Movius 1934); bottom Moneen, Co. Cork (after O'Kelly 1952a).

country. There is no evidence for centres of artifact production, for the manner of distribution of the finished products, or the general organization of the industry. Positive evidence for casting is provided by the presence of stone moulds for thin-butted axes (Fig. 53 and 54, left).

The moulds are shaped blocks of stone that have flat faces, sides and ends (Fig. 53). The surfaces of some of the moulds, such as that from Doonour, Co. Cork, were shaped by percussion. O'Kelly (1969a, 117) has suggested that a pointed chisel or a mallet were used as implements in this work. The matrix was then carved out by using a chisel or a tracer; cuts made by the tool are clearly visible on the Doonour mould. When in use for casting, the mould was levelled so as to make certain that the molten metal was evenly distributed. The matrices were not covered by a lid so the upper surface would have been rough and uneven but the bottom surface would have been smooth. In fact, the objects cast would only have been roughouts for axes which would then have to be forged by hammering, grinding and polishing (O'Kelly 1969a, 123–4). Therefore, the depth of the metal poured in, just as much as the shape of the matrix, could determine the final size of the axe. Of course, if deep roughouts were to be spread out they would have required considerable post-casting treatment.

About 1200 thin-butted axeheads are known. Variations in shape occur (Fig. 55, 3–9 – the Killaha and Ballyvalley types of Harbison 1969a, 24–55). Matrices for casting both forms are found on the same mould as O'Kelly has pointed out and the cast roughouts could subsequently be altered due to hammering (O'Kelly 1969a, 123; 1970b, 28). Many axeheads of the thin-butted variety are decorated, usually with geometric designs. The leading motifs are herringbone and cable designs, lozenges, vertical and oblique strokes, triangles and chevrons. Good prototypes for thin-butted axes are known from Saxo-Thuringia (Case 1966, 150). They reached Ireland by way of north Britain (Britton 1963, 270–1; Britton, in Allen, Britton and Coghlan 1970, 73–4; Coles 1968–9, 5–26).

Round-butted daggers with flat blades were also used and they have been found in burials. These were attached to the haft by rivets (Fig. 47, 2). Such daggers are another Beaker contribution to the Food Vessel 'cultures'. In Britain they are usually found with Southern (long-necked) Beakers. The primary form, of Early Bronze Age central European derivation, has a triangular-shaped blade. In Britain sub-varieties emerged. Some of these have tongue-shaped blades (Piggott 1963, 82–4). The primary and developed forms are also known in Ireland (Harbison 1969a, 8–10, 23 'Type Corkey').

No moulds for casting daggers have been found and this also applies to halberds (p. 137). It is, therefore, likely that objects were cast in some other material, such as sand.

Grain impressions on Food Vessels show that the Bowl people cultivated wheat and barley (Hartnett 1957, 258–9; Waddell 1970, 119). Vase Food Vessel people also cultivated naked barley (Evans 1953, 49). The grain was ground on saddle-querns (O'Kelly 1952b, 130; Raftery 1960a, 84).

Bowl Food Vessel people probably used two rectangular structures on Coney

139

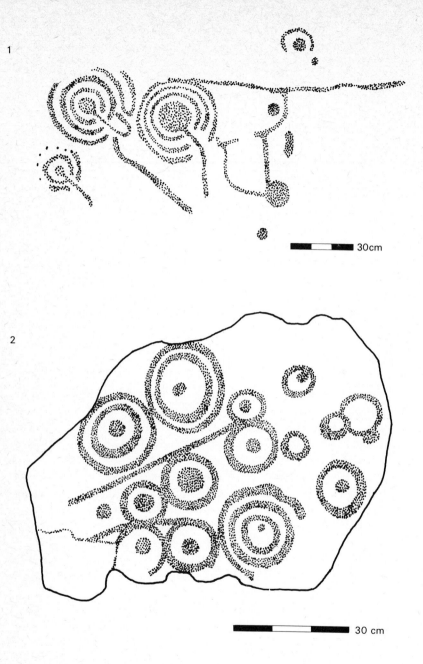

Figure 50 Rock art, Derrynablaha, Co. Kerry, after Anati 1963, Figs 3 (central part of rock No. 2 is No. 1 in this illustration) and 5 (rock No. 6 is No. 2 in this illustration).

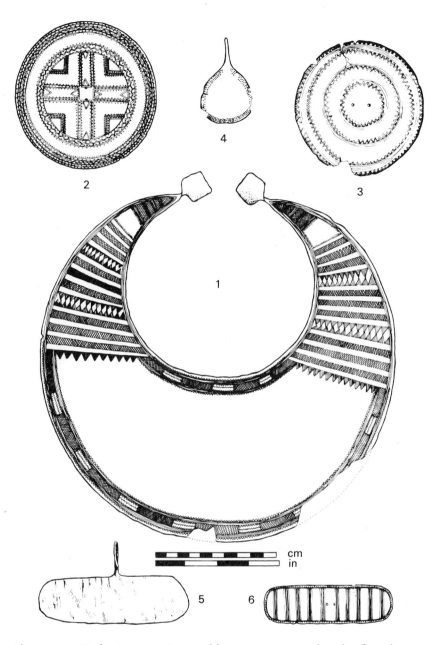

Figure 51 Early Bronze Age gold ornaments: 1 lunula found near Athlone, Co. Roscommon (N.M.I. W.5); 2 disc from Tedavanet, Co. Monaghan (N.M.I. 1872: 34); 3 disc from Ballyvourney, Co. Cork (N.M.I.S.A. 1913: 128); 4 earring from Deehommed, Co. Down (N.M.I. 1876: 18); 5 basket-shaped earring, Ireland (N.M.I. W. 74); 6 'plaque', Co. Cavan (N.M.I. W. 76).

141

Island, Lough Neagh. One structure measured about 2·75 m (9 ft) in width by 6·10 m (20 ft) in length. The walls were probably made from sods. Internally, there was a hearth close to one of the walls. The walls of the other structure were probably made from posts. This building was also 2·75 m (9 ft) in width and over 3·35 m (11 ft) in length (Addyman 1965, 84).

Occupation by Bowl Food Vessel people also took place at Beaghmore, Co. Tyrone and at Dalkey Island, Co. Dublin (Liversage 1968, 157) but no evidence for houses has been found at either site.

Evidence for trade and travel is slight. A wooden trackway from Corlona bog, Co. Leitrim, which was made from longitudinal planks supported by piles, may date from this time. It has an old radiocarbon (C14) determination of 1440±170 B.C. (Tohall, de Vries and van Zeist 1955; Herity 1973, 12).

Personal Adornment and Dress

The most outstanding personal ornament of the Early Bronze Age is the sheet-gold lunula (Fig. 51, 1). When not in use, lunulae may have been kept in wooden cases such as the example from near Newtown, Crossdoney, Co. Cavan (Armstrong, 1933, 10,

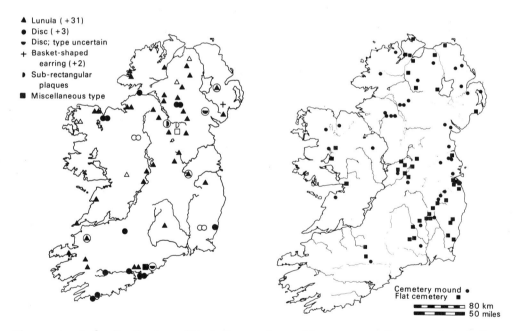

Figure 52 Left: distribution of Early Bronze Age gold ornaments. Open symbols indicate that only the country in which the ornament was found is known. Enclosed symbols indicate associated finds. Right: distribution of cemetery mounds and flat cemeteries (based on Waddell 1970).

Fig. 4). In Ireland nearly all examples are decorated. This is usually confined to one side of the body and even there it is limited to specific areas, towards each end along the edges. There are faint traces of repoussé work on some of the lunulae but on the whole the ornament is engraved or incised. The motifs tend to be geometric and consist of lozenges, triangles, chevrons, criss-cross hatching and bands of these. Over sixty gold lunulae are known from Ireland (Fig. 52, left), five or six from Scotland, one from Wales and four from Cornwall (Taylor 1968, 1970). Gold lunulae also occur in small numbers on the continent.

No lunula has definitely been found in association with other types of objects in Ireland or Britain. However, circumstantial evidence clearly places them within the Early Metal Age. A number of the decorative motifs also occur on flat axeheads, and on Beakers and Food Vessels. Craw has demonstrated that the positioning of the decoration and the motifs on the Irish 'classically' decorated lunulae recalls the spacer-plate jet necklaces, and jet necklaces and lunulae have a complementary distribution (Craw 1928–9, Fig. 8). Following up Craw's theory, Clark (1932, 40–1) showed that the combined lunula–jet necklace distribution coincides with that of Food Vessels and the majority of jet necklace associations are with Food Vessels.

The origin of the lunula has not been definitely established. However, crescentic

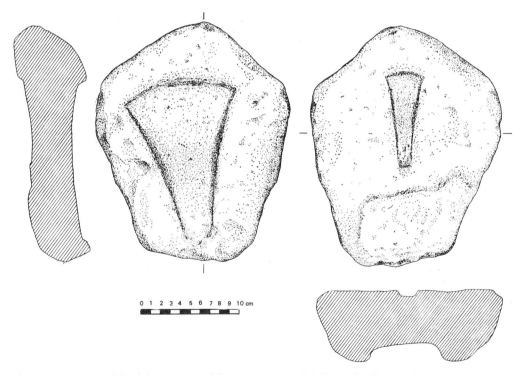

0 1 2 3 4 5 6 7 8 9 10 cm

Figure 53   Open (single) stone mould, Lyre, Co. Cork (after O'Kelly 1970b).

143

neck ornaments in different media were a feature of Early Metal Age Europe. These include copper collars on the continent (Butler 1963, 180–5, 186), amber necklaces in Wessex (Piggott 1938, 80–1) and, as has already been mentioned, jet necklaces in Scotland.

The lunula could be the Irish version of the north European collars, although Butler favours an origin in Iberia. Crescentic metal neck ornaments that have been found outside Ireland are fairly plain. The less elaborately decorated lunulae should be the earliest, and the ornate pieces, Taylor's Classical lunula, an Irish elaboration.

Jet necklaces with spacer beads are rare in Ireland (Jope 1951) but Bowl Food Vessel people had necklaces made from disc-shaped jet beads (Coffey 1895, Oldbridge, Co. Meath). They also had bronze bracelets with tapering overlapping ends (Lalor 1879–82, Luggacurren, Co. Laois) and boar's tusks also appear to have been worn as ornaments (cf. Waddell 1970, 127).

There is no positive evidence for dress but flint plano-convex 'knives' (Hartnett 1952, 160) and round scrapers and metal awls may have been used in the preparation of animal skins. Bowl Food Vessel people could have fastened garments with conical V-perforated buttons (*P.P.S.*, 26 (1960), 341, Mound of the Hostages, Tara). Vase Food Vessel people had bone pins and in addition the Labbamolaga burial also produced a bone belt-ring with plain shank (Fig. 48, 2). Such belt-rings have been found in Beaker assemblages in Britain. The belts may have been used to fasten a wrap-around garment (D. L. Clarke 1970, 113–14, 262, 263, 571–2).

Origin and Chronology

As has already been suggested, the Bowl Food Vessel could have originated in northern Britain in a Beaker milieu. The components of the Bowl group – crouched inhumation burial in a short cist accompanied by an upright pottery vessel, round mound, V-perforated buttons, boar's tusks, metal awls, round-butted riveted daggers and a number of the art motifs – are known from British Beaker assemblages (D. L. Clarke 1970, 438–49). Already in northern Britain additions of metal types (thin-butted axes and bracelets) to the basic Beaker repertoire took place from the continent. At present the evidence suggests that the Bowl Food Vessel group followed on and replaced the eastern Irish Beaker phase. For this event a date of about 1800 B.C. can be suggested.

Vase Food Vessels originated out of Necked Beakers in northern Britain, but it is difficult to know when the type was introduced into Ireland. However, it appears to have been later than the Bowl variety. At Labbamolaga, Co. Cork, a Vase was primary to an Urn but there are a number of associations with Urns, e.g. Corkragh, Co. Tyrone (Evans and Paterson 1939) or with objects contemporary with Urns such as the grooved dagger from Topped Mountain, Co. Fermanagh (Plunkett and Coffey

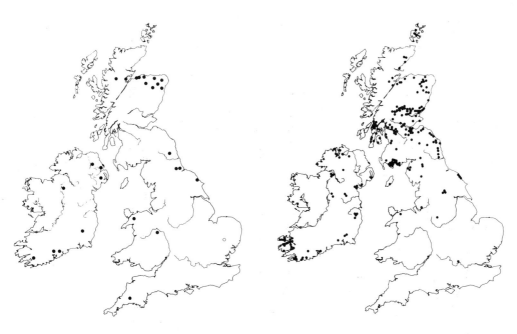

Figure 54 Left: find-places of open (single) stone moulds in Ireland and Britain. Open symbols indicate that only the county in which the mould was found is known. Right: distribution of rock art in Ireland and Britain (based on Simpson and Thawley 1972, Fig. 4).

1896–8). The Vase seems to have more in common with Urn groups than it has with Bowl Food Vessels.

Discussion

Bowl Food Vessel people were more numerous than Vase Food Vessel people and their occupation was of greater significance. In the main they had round skulls with a vertical forehead and generally narrow noses. The stature varied but a number of individuals were tall, in some cases up to 1·80 m (c. 6 ft) in height (Martin 1935, 92–104). The Bowl people lived in wooden houses. They were farmers and they grew wheat and barley. For cutting down trees and for carpentry bronze axes with thin butts were employed, but occasionally polished stone axes were also used. Round-butted riveted daggers were also used. Metal awls and flint scrapers could have been used in the making of leather garments. Garments were fastened with buttons. Personal ornaments included jet necklaces, bronze bracelets and very likely lunulae. Ceremony and ritual was significant. Halberds could have been used on such occasions and burials were carried out according to well prescribed rites.

We know less about the Vase Food Vessel people. Seemingly they were also farmers,

145

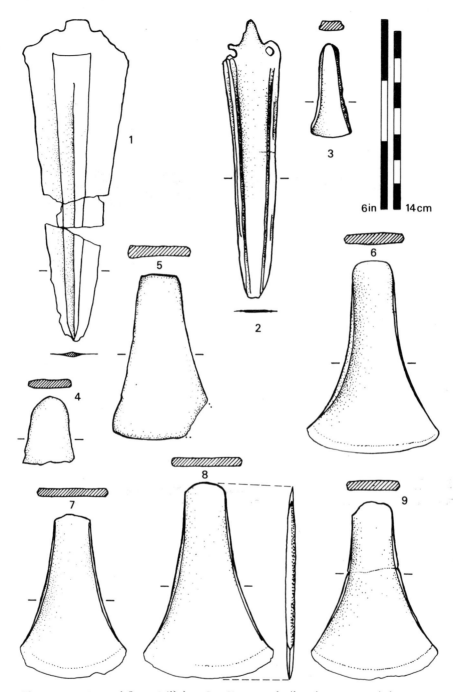

Figure 55 Hoard from Killaha, Co. Kerry: 1 halberd; 2 grooved dagger; 3–9 thin-butted axeheads (after Harbison 1969a, Figs 24–5).

146

at least there is evidence that they grew barley. They buried their dead in cists but unlike the Bowl people they did not build cemetery mounds; they much preferred the isolated Single Burial. They may also have used the same type of artifacts but the plano-convex flint knife is more common to the Vase than to the Bowl people. Garments were probably fastened with bone pins.

It is hard to determine how much contact existed between both Food Vessel groups. At least both groups shared the same part of the country and occasionally the Vase Food Vessel people used an already constructed cemetery mound for burial, such as Lyles Hill (Evans 1953). Both groups had other features in common. For instance each buried their dead in cists or in pits.

Metal production was an important aspect of the Food Vessel people and some of the produce, such as lunulae, were amongst the finest artifacts produced in Early Bronze Age Europe. Lunulae, halberds, and decorated flat axes (Taylor 1970; Butler 1963, Maps 1 and 2) were exported and it is likely that Irish Food Vessel craftsmen made a contribution to the beginnings of a metal industry in northern Europe (cf. Butler 1963, especially p. 202).

CHAPTER SEVEN

Urn People: Further Arrivals and New Developments

Background

As has been shown (p. 133) Food Vessels represent the final development of Beakers in the north of Britain. But parallel developments were taking place in the south of England. In the south an altered form of pottery vessel also emerged. This is the Collared or Overhanging Rim Urn. In the genesis of the Collared Urn, Fengate Ware, a form of English domestic ware of the Beaker Period, was an important constituent but there was also a direct contribution from fine Beaker Wares (Longworth 1961). The Collared Urn people used existing Beaker mounds for burial but they also constructed their own burial mounds. Like their Beaker forerunners the Collared Urn people practised the rite of single grave burial. Sometimes the Urn accompanied an inhumation but much more frequently a cremation. However, an important change in the burial rite took place. When an Urn was present in a cremation grave this no longer accompanied the burial but instead it was inverted over the cremation and thus became a container for the deposit. This custom may have derived from the Rhine-mouth region (Kavanagh 1973, 525).

Apart from the Urn many other Beaker features continued: V-perforated jet buttons, bronze awls, sheet-gold work, and possibly barbed-and-tanged flint arrowheads, stone hones, ring pendants and bronze knives (cf. Piggott 1938). In the south, as also in the north of England (p. 133), the Beaker inheritance is only a part, admittedly the dominant part, of the emerging Collared Urn 'culture'. Influences from the vigorous central European Early Bronze Age cultures such as Aunjetitz, Straubing and Rhône extended westwards by way of Brittany. This led to the augmentation of the types that were available to the Urn people from their Beaker inheritance. The new types include bronze daggers with triangular-shaped blade and grooving parallel to the edges (the Bush Barrow Group), daggers with ogival blades (Camerton-Snowshill Group) (ApSimon 1954), cast-flanged axeheads, crutch-

148

headed, bulb-headed and trefoil-headed pins and halberd pendants (Piggott 1938). The technique of alloying copper with tin to produce bronze was probably also introduced from central Europe (Britton 1961). Cast-flanged axeheads suggest the use of double moulds for casting. There were also contributions from other areas. Segmented faience beads are of eastern Mediterranean, more specifically Egyptian, origin (Stone and Thomas 1956, 37–53). Gold-mounted amber discs, the bone mounts from the Bush Barrow sceptre and the gold cup from Rillaton may reflect Aegean influence but possibly indirectly through central Europe. Amber may have been imported from the west Baltic area, although in this connection it should be noted that amber, naturally derived from across the North Sea, can today be collected on the coast of East Anglia (Coles and Taylor 1971, 11). Innovation in metal types took place. The earliest spearheads of the native series, really a tanged dagger, emerged (Greenwell and Brewis 1909, Class 1). Subsequent developments, firstly with the addition of a loose ferrule, led to the emergence of an authentic socketed spearhead but with a solid blade (Class 3 or end-looped spearheads).

Knowledge is scant of the wider economic aspects and house sites of the Collared Urn people but some 'rich' burials containing gold suggest that wealthy or prominent families existed, especially in the Wessex area (Piggott 1938, the 'Wessex Culture'; Annable and Simpson 1964, 21–8; Moore and Rowlands 1972, 9–13). Rich burials with gold objects and battle axes already existed in southern England during the Beaker period (cf. D. L. Clarke 1970, 448). This and other evidence, such as the large 'henge' monuments, show that Wessex was an area of considerable importance during the Beaker period. By and large the Collared Urn 'culture' of southern England is based on Beaker forerunners but with new metal types and techniques reaching it from north-western France and ultimately from the central European Bronze Age cultures. Thus, at the beginning of the Bronze Age two contemporary provinces emerged, one in the north and one in the south.

From the south of Britain the Collared Urn 'culture' expanded northwards, e.g. Anglesey (Lynch 1970, 128, 142–5; 1971, 24, 26), Yorkshire (Elgee 1949, 95–101) and southern Scotland (Childe and Waterston 1941–2, 87–8, Anderson 1941–2). In northern Britain the Collared Urn continued in use but modified or developed versions emerged. In one form the collar was suppressed and instead the body was surrounded by cordons. Another new form, the Encrusted Urn, has applied ornament resembling that already known from Grooved Ware. The development of the Encrusted Urn is due to strong influence from the Vase-shaped Food Vessel. The use of Food Vessels continued but a change in shape and function took place. The vessel became larger (the Enlarged Food Vessel) and in some burials it was inverted over a cremation burial. In other burials an Enlarged Food Vessel was put in the grave alongside an Urn. Pygmy Cups have also been placed in graves with all forms of Urns as accessories. But, like the Collared Urns, Pygmy Cups were modified in the 'Highland Zone'. The biconical form became the leading type (Rynne 1963c, Fig. 5 for distribution) but less popular forms also emerged (Longworth 1966a, cups with

149

contracted mouth). Grave-goods include small bronze blades, Class 1 razors, segmented and quoit-shaped faience beads, bone and bronze pins, stone battle axes and daggers. Hoards of bronze objects also occur, e.g. Ebnal, Shropshire (Cowen and Burgess 1972).

The Collared Urn 'culture' extended to the Food Vessel province in the north of Britain but it also revitalized itself by absorbing, no doubt, Food Vessel stock and some of their traits as the Encrusted Urn shows. New forms such as the Cordoned Urn or the quoit-shaped faience bead were developed. This expansive 'culture' then expanded further, across the sea to Ireland. This must have been a movement or movements of people as nearly all the components of the north British Urn 'culture' appeared in Ireland, not only the pottery (Collared, Cordoned and Encrusted Urns, Enlarged Food Vessels and Pygmy Cups) but also other elements of the 'culture' (perforated-headed and crutch-headed pins (in bone), stone battle axes, stone hones, flanged axeheads, trunnion chisels, Class 1 razors and possibly faience and amber beads). It is not known if the different types of Urn arrived in a chronological sequence or if an already mixed pottery assemblage came. Whether they came singly, i.e. a group of people using Collared Urns exclusively, or collectively, the Urn people came to Ireland from north Britain, probably from south-west Scotland rather than north Wales. At least this is suggested by the concentration of urns in north-east Ireland (see Fox 1952, Pls V and VIII for distribution maps of Encrusted and Cordoned Urns). Miss Lynch (1971, 80) has, however, drawn attention to a small group of Irish Urns, all from south Leinster, that may have been derived from Anglesey. The Urn people mainly settled in the north-east and east of Ireland with extensions into Munster and to Connaught. In other words, in Ireland, as they had done previously in north Britain, the Urn people took over the territory of the Food Vessel people. Their settlement brought about technological, industrial and possibly ritual changes and these alterations laid the foundations for developments that were to take place during the ensuing centuries.

Burials

The Urn people buried their dead singly. The burial rite was cremation. The Urn was inverted over the remains. Sometimes grave-goods were included. Often a small vessel, a Pygmy Cup or an Enlarged Food Vessel, accompanied the Urn in the grave. The small vessel might have been placed within the Urn or it might have been placed alongside it. Other grave-goods included bronze daggers, stone battle axes and Class 1 razors (Fig. 56). The majority of burials were in pits. Cists were more rare than during the Food Vessel phase. When a cist was constructed this was usually a badly-built structure. Urn burials occur in isolation and in cemeteries. The Urn people used the same cemeteries, both flat and mound, that had been used by the Food Vessel people but they also initiated cemeteries, both flat and mound, of their own.

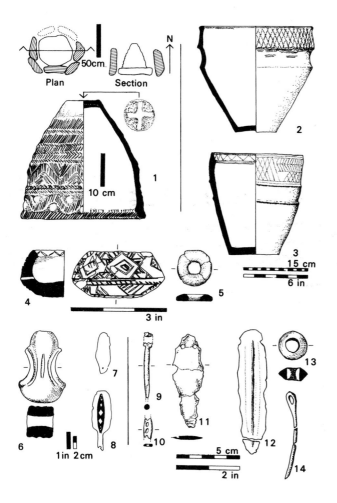

Figure 56 Urns and associated finds: 1 Encrusted Urn, Maganey, Co. Kildare (after Prendergast 1962); 2 Collared Urn, Turnabarson, Co. Tyrone (U.M. 369: 1921); 3 Cordoned Urn, Donaghmore, Co. Tyrone (U.M. 1911: 326. Nos 2–3 after ApSimon 1969a, Fig. 8); 4 and 5 biconical Pygmy Cup and quoit-shaped faience bead, found with an Urn which no longer survives, Knockboy, Co. Antrim (after Rynne 1964a, Fig. 1 A–B); 6 stone battle-axe, Bann type, Laheen, Co. Donegal (after A. B. Ó Ríordáin 1967, Fig. 2c, N.M.I. 1964: 221); 7 Class 1a razor, Barrow II, Carrowjames, Co. Mayo; 8 Class 1b razor, Poolacorragune, Co. Galway (N.M.I. 1935: 879) (Nos 7 and 8 after C. M. Piggott 1946, Figs 5: 19 and 4: 17); 9–11 grave-goods from cremation burial at Rahinashurock, Co. Westmeath; 9 bone crutch-headed pin; 10 perforated bone object; 11 bronze riveted blade (after Danaher 1965, N.M.I. 1963: 37–9); 12–14 grave-goods from cremation burial under Cordoned Urn (Urn 2) at Harristown, Co. Waterford; 12 bronze blade; 13 quoit-shaped faience bead; 14 bone pin with perforated head (after J. Hawkes 1941, Fig. 5: 4).

Scarawalsh, Co. Wexford (Rynne 1966) and Clonshannon, Co. Wicklow (Mahr and Price 1932) can be cited as examples of flat cemeteries.

While some of the mounds were constructed to cover a single burial, e.g. Lissard (Ó Ríordáin 1936), others covered more than one burial, e.g. Carrowjames (Raftery 1938–9, 1940–1), and furthermore at Carrowjames there was a cemetery of mounds. At least two main forms of mound were constructed and these can be termed bowl-barrows and ring-barrows (cf. Grinsell 1941, 75–90 for typology of Wessex barrows; Ashbee 1960; for Ireland, Ó Ríordáin 1953, 79).

All the pottery types have their forerunners in Britain. The Collared Urn, the earliest form, has a flat-topped rim which may expand slightly or there may be an internal bevel. A cavity surrounds the vessel about a quarter of the way down. Above this the neck has the appearance of a collar. Decoration is mainly confined to the collar or to the top of the rim. A 'net' pattern of cord impressions is a common design (Fig. 56). Associated objects include bronze daggers with slightly rounded butt and straight sides to the blade, stone battle axes, flint barbed-and-tanged arrowheads and plano-convex knives, and ring-headed bone pins (cf. ApSimon 1969b, 46, 64).

The evolved form, Cordoned Urns, are similar in ware, ornament and some in shape to Collared Urns (Fig. 56). Associations include a stone hone, axehead and battle-axe, flint thumb-scraper and plano-convex knife, quoit-shaped faience bead, bone pin with perforated head and Pygmy Cups (Ó Ríordáin 1967, 42–3; ApSimon 1969b, 64–5). But the most common associated artifact is a small bronze blade that has been termed a razor knife if the blade has a short, broad tang and one or two rivet holes (Class 1a) or a razor if the blade has a long narrow tang (Class 1b) (Binchy 1967; Butler and Smith 1956; Piggott 1946, 122–6; see Fig. 56). Razor knives may have developed out of small blades that were in use during the Beaker and Food Vessel periods. The origin of the Class 1b razor is difficult to determine. Continental Tumulus Culture razors have been cited as prototypes.

The Encrusted Urn is vase-shaped (Fig. 56, Plate 12b). The applied ornament consists of ribs, usually occurring as zig-zags or chevrons, knobs and rosettes. Incised ornament is also found. Designs include bands of oblique lines and 'net' patterns (Kavanagh 1973).

As previously pointed out, Vase Food Vessels were in use. There were also Enlarged Food Vessels. These resemble the Vase-shaped Food Vessel. The pot, usually divided into neck and body, is often decorated with incised lines. Association with Encrusted Urns and Enlarged Food Vessels are limited. They mainly consist of plano-convex flint knives.

The main form of Pygmy Cup is biconical (Rynne 1963c. See Fig. 56). A limited number of other forms are also known. These include cups with openwork body, cups with concave neck and cups with contracted mouth (for the latter see Longworth 1966a).

Other forms of ritual may also have been practised. A new type of stone 'battle axe' or mace-head, the Bann type (Fig. 56), was now current (cf. Ó Ríordáin 1967, 42, 43;

Frazer 1889–91). Bann type battle axes have affinities with the Scottish Crichie and Scotsburn groups. These groups seem to be a north British variant of southern British battle axes, especially the Snowshill group (Roe 1966). The bone cylinders from Burial 6 at Knockast, Co. Westmeath (Hencken and Movius 1934, 237, 252, Fig. 2a) may be compared with the mounts for a wooden mace-head shaft from the Bush Barrow, Wiltshire (Piggott 1938, Fig. 3: 7). Decorated axeheads may also have been used on ceremonial occasions. At least one such axe, from Brockagh, Co. Kildare, was kept in a skin sheath (p. 158; see Fig. 59).

Technology and Economy

Like their Food Vessel forerunners, the smiths were probably itinerant. But they were more skilled. They used stone moulds but these were now two-piece. In these moulds the matrix was cut to half the depth of the object to be cast in each piece or valve. When in use both halves were fitted neatly together. As such these were closed moulds and for the first time Irish smiths could cast socketed objects. In this connection it may be noted that on a mould from Lough Gur for casting a small pointed blade and an end-looped spear-head there is a short notch on each side at the base of the blade. As Evans suggested, these notches must have been intended to keep the core in its proper position (Evans 1881, 435, Fig. 523). An important hoard of moulds dating from this period was found in the vicinity of Omagh, Co. Tyrone (Coffey, 1907a). They were for casting tanged spear-heads, rapier-bladed spear-heads with peg-holes in the socket, and in some instances with loops near the top of the socket, triangular-shaped blades with midribs (daggers?), trunnion chisel, flat strips and a narrow bar (Fig. 57–8). Stone hones were also in use.

The bronze flanged axehead is the most common tool (Fig. 59). Over three hundred examples are known and the majority of these are decorated (Harbison 1969b, 79–80, Type Derryniggin). Trunnion chisels were also in use, there are matrices on the Omagh and Inch Island moulds (Coghlan and Raftery 1961, 234, Fig. 22).

Spear-heads were coming into use, but only in limited numbers. A few examples of the earliest insular form, the tanged variety, are known (Harbison 1967, 97) and the Omagh moulds show that this type was cast in Ireland. The typologically advanced end-looped spear-head (Class III) is fairly common. It appears that this Class developed along the northern fringes of the original Collared Urn territory (Cowen and Burgess 1972, Fig. 6: 4). Daggers with a triangular-shaped blade, which sometimes has grooves parallel to the edges and either a straight or slightly rounded butt, were in use (Harbison 1969a, 10, 11, Topped Mountain and Dunshaughlin Types; see Fig. 60, 1). Daggers of these forms, central European in origin, were used by Urn People in Britain. Both forms occur side by side in the Bush Barrow grave (Piggott 1938, Fig. 3: 1–2, see also ApSimon 1954). Daggers with a slightly rounded butt that has three rivet holes and a blade with straight sides and a slight midrib have been found in association with Urns (Harbison 1969a, 17–18, Nos 101a, 119, 142a).

153

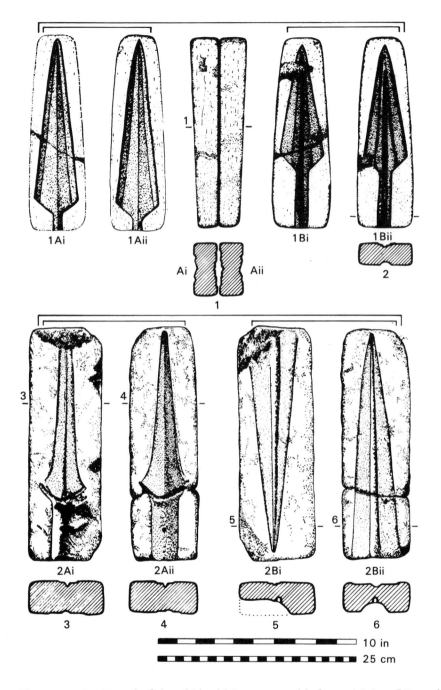

Figures 57–8 Hoard of closed (double) stone moulds from vicinity of Omagh, Co. Tyrone (N.M.I. 1956: 416–24).

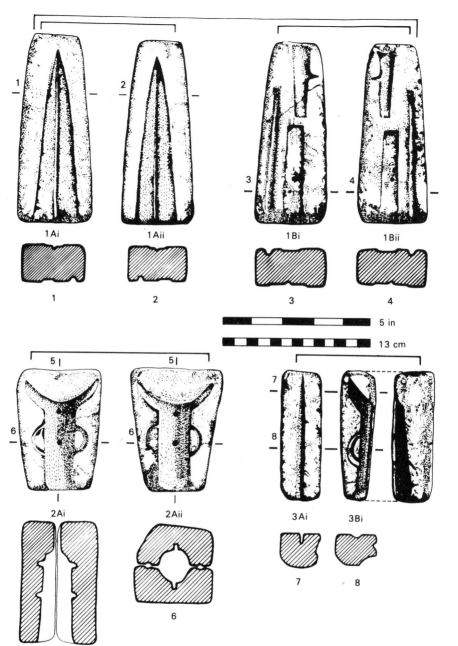

1Ai   1Aii   1Bi   1Bii

1   2   3   4

5 in

13 cm

5| 5| 7   8

6   6   8

2Ai   2Aii   3Ai   3Bi

5   6   7   8

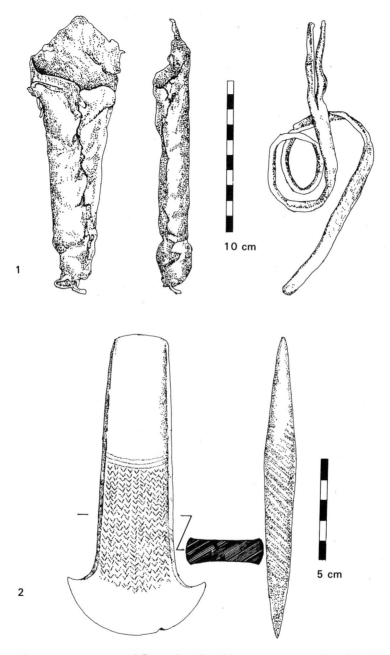

Figure 59 Decorated flanged axehead (Derryniggin type) and leather sheath, Brockagh, Co. Kildare (after Rynne 1961–3, Pls 2–3).

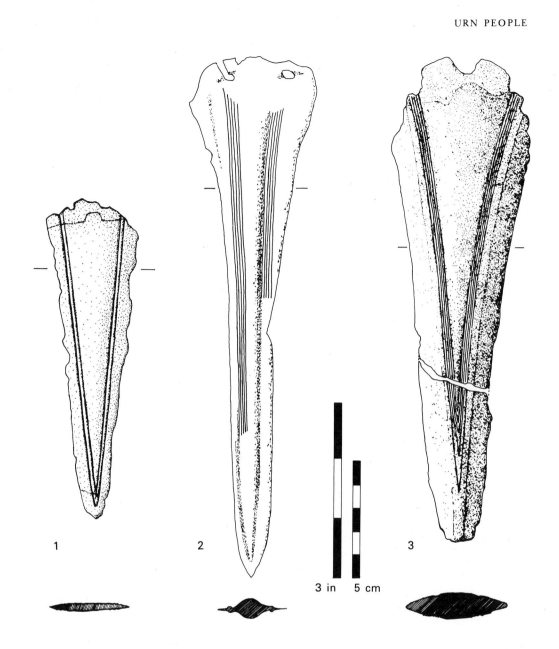

Figure 60   Daggers: 1 triangular grooved form. Topped Mountain, Co. Fermanagh; 2, 3 ogival daggers, 2 Offaly Type, Co. Offaly (U.M. 185:1913), 3 Kiltale Type, Kiltale, Co. Meath (N.M.I. W.44). (After Harbison 1969a, Pl. 2:43, Pl. 3. 55, 60.)

The origin of this group is not clear. There are a number of unassociated finds of ogival daggers (Harbison 1969a, 12–13, Offaly (with midrib) and Kiltale Types. See Fig. 60, 2–3). Ogival daggers (Camerton-Snowshill Group) occur in Urn contexts in Britain. Their origin goes back to the Sögel cultures of Jutland and north-western Germany (Burgess 1974, 190).

A settlement that consisted of at least two circular wooden houses, pits and other features at Meadowlands, Downpatrick, Co. Down has been attributed to the Cordoned Urn people (Pollock and Waterman 1964). However, Simpson (1971, 135) considers that the pottery is Beaker ware.

Occasionally sherds of Urns turn up on occupation sites of another period, e.g. Coney Island, Co. Armagh (Addyman 1965, 87), but there were no structures or features of the Urn period.

During this period naked barley seems to have been the predominant cereal grown (Jessen and Helbaek 1944, 20–1).

Personal Adornment and Dress

Slight attention appears to have been paid to personal adornment. The composite necklaces from the Mound of the Hostages, Tara and Cruttenclough, Co. Kilkenny may date to this period (Ó Riordáin 1955; Wilde 1862, 37, 42 and Armstrong 1933, 41, 90). The Tara necklace, which was around the neck of a male adolescent who was buried in a pit, consisted of a biconical jet bead, four amber beads, eight copper or bronze tubular beads and four segmented faience beads. The find circumstances of the Cruttenclough necklace are not known. It consists of fourteen amber beads, seven biconical gold beads and seven tubular gold beads. Amber and segmented faience beads are known from Urn graves in Britain. Tubular bronze beads appear to have had a long life in Britain. They are known from Beaker (Clarke 1970, 439), possibly Food Vessel (Britton 1963, 271), and Urn (Butler and Smith 1956, 33) contexts. It is not possible to be precise about the date of these necklaces but their overall composition suggests an Urn rather than a Food Vessel context.

There is circumstantial evidence for dress. The Urn people had flint thumb-scrapers, plano-convex flint knives and bronze awls (cf. Binchy 1967, 56: 20; May 1947, c. 173; ApSimon 1969b, 63, No. 9; Rynne 1963b). The discovery of a decorated flanged axehead at Brockagh, Co. Kildare in a sheath of raw hide which was stitched up the front with a thong shows that the Urn people worked skins and made leather (Rynne 1961–3, 459; see Fig. 59).

Two types of bone pins, perforated-headed and crutch-headed, were current and may have been used in fastening garments (Knowles 1889a, 110; Binchy 1967, 56: 20; Hawkes 1941, 140; Rynne 1961a; Danaher 1965; see Fig. 56). These pins are copies of the bronze pins of the Collared Urn culture, especially from the rich Wessex graves.

A bone belt-fastener (?) was found in a cemetery mound at Killicarney, Co. Cavan. Wakeman (1879–82, 193) stated that the object was found with a Bowl-shaped

158

Food Vessel but the context of this type of belt-fastener in Britain is Urn (Piggott 1938, Fig. 3: 3; Childe and Waterston, 1941–2, 87–8, Fig. 4). Killicarney was dug through by workmen building a railway. Some of the graves contained Urns and their contents could have got mixed up. Furthermore Wakeman wrote up the site at secondhand.

Ensuing developments

As the Urn 'culture' was maturing, developments, especially technological and typological, were taking place. The smiths were still using the same form of double-piece stone mould but bronzes that were more complicated to cast were being produced, for instance a spear-head with the socket extending into the blade. About forty-four moulds from this developed stage have been found and recorded within recent centuries and amongst these is the hoard from Killymaddy, Co. Antrim (Coffey 1912b, 83–5; see Fig. 61. See also Figs 62, 63 and 64). The mould evidence and the artifacts show that large-scale metal production was going on but the absence of associated finds (other than the mould hoards) makes deductions difficult. Furthermore, none of the metal types – dirks or rapiers, spear-heads and palstaves, or palstave-type axes – have been comprehensively studied.

Two larger forms of dagger were now coming into use in Britain and in Ireland; these are dirks and rapiers (conventionally a rapier if over 35 cm) of Burgess's Group I and Group II (Burgess, 1968b, 7–12); Group I dirks have a ribbed and/or grooved blade. The edges are usually bevelled. The rhomboid-shaped hafting plate has two rivet holes. Weapons of Group I were included by Harbison (1969a) under daggers, 'Type Antrim' and most of 'Hill of Allen Type'. Moulds, with a matrix on each face, for casting Group I dirks (rapiers) have been found at Inchnagree, Co. Cork, and Broughshane, Co. Antrim (Evans, 1881, 433, Fig. 519. Incidentally, the 'matrices' which Evans refers to on the back of this mould are not genuine.)

The blade of a Group II dirk or rapier has a lozenge-shaped cross-section (Harbison, 1969a, 13–14, Type Antrim and most of Hill of Allen Type). There are two rivet-holes in the trapeze-shaped butt. The Killymaddy moulds (Fig. 61) show that Group II dirks were made in Ireland.

The typological evidence indicates that the manufacture of Group I dirks started at a time when ogival daggers were still in use. Their origin appears to be due to influence from continental dirks and rapiers inspiring insular dagger manufacturers. As Burgess has pointed out, the immediate source of influence was probably the Tréboul stage of the Breton Bronze Age (Briard 1965, 79ff.). But the continental influence is more obvious on the dirks of Group II. The use of dirks of Groups I and II continued down to the eleventh–twelfth centuries. At least in Britain examples of Group I rapiers formed part of the Glentrool (Kirkcudbright) and Swaffham (Norfolk) hoards (Burgess 1968a, 7, 24, 25).

The bronze-hilted rapier from Kanturk, Co. Cork and possibly also the bronze-hilted dagger from Drummond Lough, Co. Armagh (Harbison 1969a, 14–15, 26)

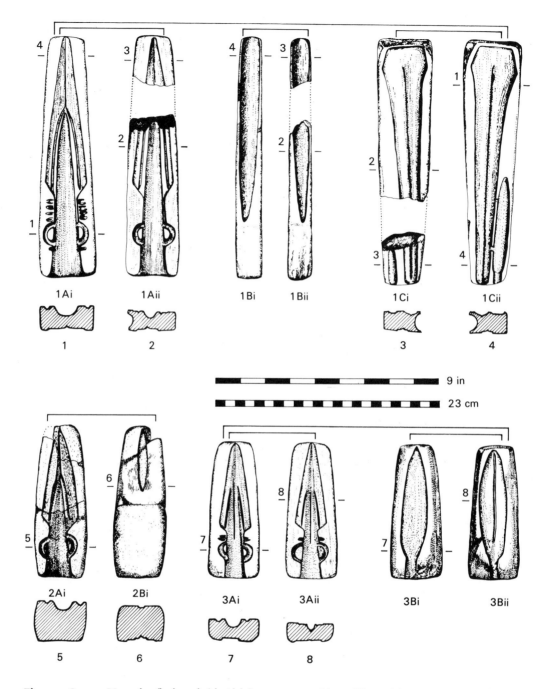

Figures 61–2 Hoard of closed (double) stone moulds, Killymaddy, Co. Antrim (after Coghlan and Raftery 1961, Figs 17–19, 34, 39, 41, N.M.I. 1911: 85).

160

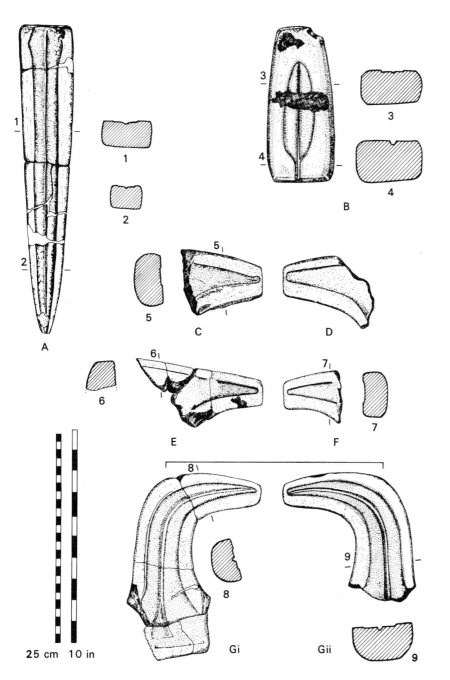

1

2

A

3

4

B

5

C

D

6

E

7

F

8

Gi

9

Gii

25 cm   10 in

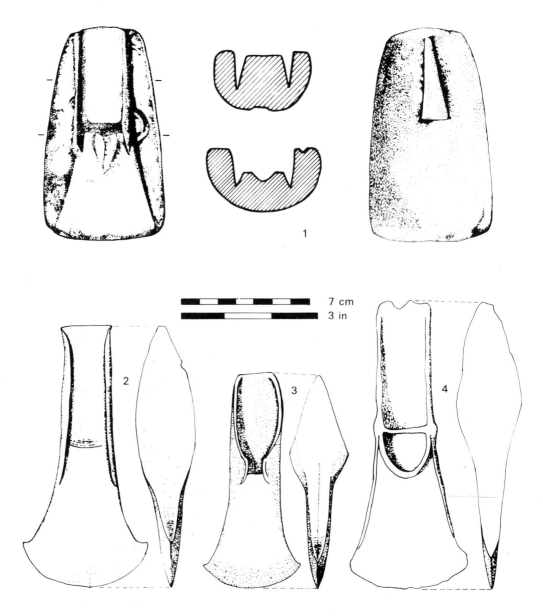

Figure 63 1 Closed (double) stone mould, Ireland (N.M.I. P. 438) (after Coghlan and Raftery 1961, Fig. 13); 2 haft-flanged axehead, Doagh Glebe, Co. Fermanagh; 3 wing-flanged axehead, Killamonagh, Co. Sligo (both N.M.I. 1913: 21; 1897: 10); 4 shield pattern palstave, Ireland (N.M.I. W. 600).

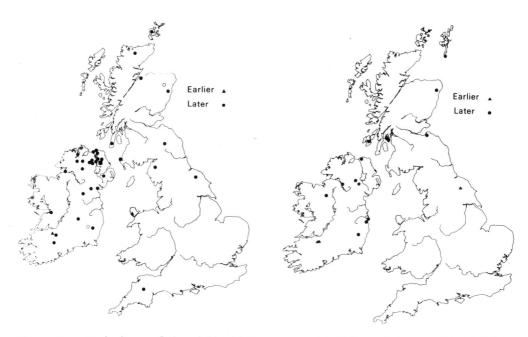

Figure 64 Find-places of closed (double) stone moulds (left) and clay moulds (right) in Ireland and Britain. Open symbols indicate that only the county in which the mould was found is known. In the map of stone moulds (left) symbols enclosed by a circle indicate a hoard of moulds. Symbol enclosed by a square indicates Ballymena, Co. Antrim. The find-place of eight moulds is given as Ballymena but this is probably due to activities of collectors.

very likely date from this time. Rapiers found in Tréboul contexts in Brittany can be cited as a parallel (Briard 1965, 86–91, Fig. 26: 3 and Fig. 27).

Three varieties of spear-heads were in use. All have loops and they represent further insular development. The principal type was the spear-head with ribbed kite-shaped blade and loops on the socket (Fig. 65, 1). This is predominantly an Irish type (provisional distribution in Mitchell, O'Leary and Raftery 1941, Fig. 1). Spear-heads with leaf-shaped blade and loops at the base (Fig. 65, 2) were also current (Greenwell and Brewis 1909, Class IVb). A stone mould (unlocalized) for casting such spear-heads is known (Coghlan and Raftery 1961, 238, Fig. 32). A small number of spear-heads with leaf-shaped blades and loops on the socket were in use (Greenwell and Brewis, 1909, Class IVa). Class IV spear-heads are in the main a southern English type. However, half of a double-piece stone mould for casting such spear-heads was found at Ballyshannon, Co. Donegal (Coghlan and Raftery 1961, 234, No. 21, Fig. 21). There is one associated find. This is with a broad-bladed palstave, from an unrecorded find-place in Co. Westmeath (Pegge 1789).

Axe development was also taking place. In Ireland, and also in Britain, a type of axe in which the flanges are confined to the hafting part and which occasionally may have

163

a stopridge emerged, the 'haft-flanged axe' of M.A. Smith (1959, 171–3; see Fig. 63, 2). Palstaves were also in use but these did not become a common tool in Ireland or even in northern Britain. A palstave has a definite stopridge, high flanges that do not extend beyond the stopridge and a wide cutting edge. Several forms and regional varieties of palstave exist.

In Britain Class 1b razors were in use down to at least the twelfth century (cf. Smith 1959, 147; Eogan 1962, 53). Matrices on a number of moulds, e.g. Killymaddy and Inchnagree, were for casting blades that Binchy (1967, Fig. 4) considered as razors. If so the blades cast would have had tangs and therefore would have been more appropriate to Class 1b razors than to Class 1a. On the other hand the object cast may have been a double-edged tanged knife of a similar type to that found in the Glentrool hoard, Kirkcudbrightshire (Coles 1963–4, 153, No. 6, Fig. 16) or the Monkswood hoard from Somerset (*Inventaria Archaeologia*, G. B., 42: 21).

Origin and Chronology

The origin of the Irish Urn 'culture' is not in doubt; it came from northern Britain and possibly immediately from south-west Scotland. But the time of arrival is not clear. As has been pointed out, the Collared Urn 'culture' emerged out of Beaker (or Beaker influenced) assemblages in southern England at about the same time that the Food Vessel was developing, also out of Beaker, in northern England. The Urn culture expanded to the north of Britain, and then to Ireland. At a guess it is unlikely that the Urn people reached Ireland before the seventeenth century; it might be much later. There is clear evidence for the unabated continuation of the industry, subject to slight modification (e.g. dirks), until the twelfth century when large-scale industrial changes took place. Despite the eleventh–twelfth century changes the Urn 'culture' tradition continued on in its metal types (rapiers, looped spear-heads, wing-flanged axes) down to the eighth century. But with the pottery and the burials the story is not so clear-cut. None of the developed metal types (dirks, looped spears, axes or palstaves) has been found associated with Urns in either Ireland or Britain (Burgess 1969a). Class 1b razors have been found with Urns and that type of razor continued in use at least down to the twelfth century (above). In addition matrices for casting small, tanged blades have been found on moulds that were used for casting the developed metal types. If these matrices were for casting Class 1b razors, and not tanged double-edged knives, this would provide a strong hint that Urn burial could have continued down until at least the twelfth century or so. At present it is not possible to say when the Urn 'culture' terminated. The typological tradition survived to about the eighth century. The burial rite may, however, have changed several centuries before then.

Discussion

The Urn period was a vigorous, innovating and receptive stage of the Bronze Age. The

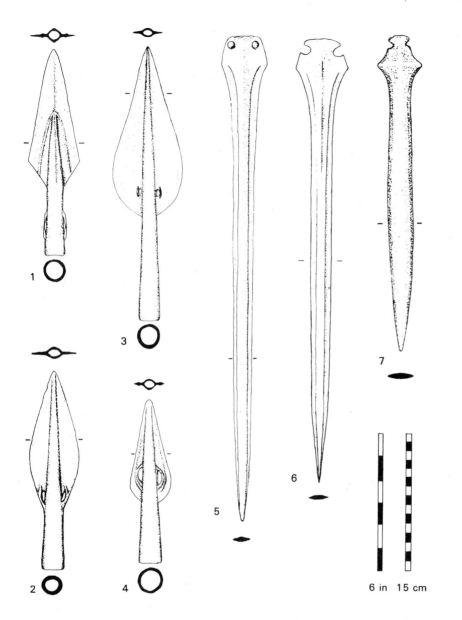

Figure 65 Spear-heads: 1 ribbed kite-shape with loops on the socket, Ballyhaw, Co. Westmeath (N.M.I. 1934: 436); 2 base-looped, Moatstown, Co. Kildare (N.M.I. 1929: 1152); 3 protected loops in the blade, Finea, Co. Westmeath (N.M.I. 1934: 485); 4 lunate-shaped openings in the blade, Ireland (N.M.I. W. 30).
Rapiers: 5 Group III, Toberbane, Co. Kerry (N.M.I. 1934: 5836); 6 Group IV, Killeshandra, Co. Cavan (N.M.I. W. 106); 7 Cutts Class, Murhaun, Co. Leitrim (N.M.I. 1966: 26).

presence of a new burial rite, new techniques, and new artifacts suggest that there was a migration to Ireland and that a new culture emerged. It is not clear what happened to Food Vessel societies. This problem will only be solved when a more comprehensive knowledge emerges of the chronology and cultural status of those societies. There is stratigraphical evidence to show that Food Vessels were primary to Urns, e.g. Labbamolaga, Co. Cork (Food Vessel and Encrusted Urn, O'Kelly 1950) and Moneen in the same county (identifiable Food Vessel was in the Vase tradition, O'Kelly 1952a, 154). A number of associated finds provide evidence for Vase Food Vessel–Urn contemporaneity. A cist at Corkragh, Co. Tyrone contained an Encrusted Urn, a Vase Food Vessel, a small vessel identified as a Cordoned Urn or a Vase Food Vessel, a Pygmy Cup and fragments of a fifth vessel (Evans and Paterson 1939). In a cist at Tullywinny, Co. Armagh an Encrusted Urn covered a Vase Food Vessel (Collins 1965b, 71). At Topped Mountain, Co. Fermanagh, a grooved triangular dagger with ribbed gold pommel binding was found with a Vase Food Vessel of Type E (p. 144), while at Ballyduff, Co. Wexford a segmented faience bead was found with a Vase Food Vessel (Hartnett and Prendergast 1953, 49–57). It is interesting to note that the unequivocal association of Urn material and Food Vessel is confined to the Vase type of Food Vessel; it is likely that the Bowl type had already gone out of use.

There is slight evidence for overlap on the industrial side. The dagger from the Killaha hoard, Co. Kerry is related to the Topped Mountain type. Therefore it would seem that this hoard with its thin-butted axehead and halberd was deposited after the arrival of the Urn people (Fig. 55). A thin-butted and a flanged axehead (Derryniggin type) were found together at Bandon, Co. Cork (Harbison 1969b, Fig. 1: D).

The Urn people had a ritual associated with the dead and a well organized metal industry. Mace-heads (battle axes) and a few flint artifacts show that they also had craftsmen who were capable of working in stone. Leather- (p. 158) and bone-working were also practised. Otherwise our knowledge of Urn society is meagre. With the possible exception of the beads from Cruttenclough (p. 158) there is no evidence for the use of gold. Neither are there rich burials, the nearest being the burials from the Hill of Rath, Co. Louth (bone pin with perforated head, bronze razor (1a), flint thumb-shaped scraper, stone hone and a Cordoned Urn, Binchy 1967, 56, No. 20), Burial XVI, Mound of the Hostages, Tara (Collared Urn, Food Vessel, stone mace-head (battle axe) and bronze dagger, Ó Ríordáin 1967, 42) and Harristown, Co. Waterford (Cordoned Urn, bronze razor (1a), bone pin with perforated head and a quoit-shaped faience bead, Hawkes 1941, 141, Urn II). Hoards are even rarer. The only definite one where objects of different types have been found together is the hoard from Derryniggin, Co. Leitrim (Ó Ríordáin 1958).

Although there is a hint of sub-assemblages, razor-knives or razors with Cordoned Urns for instance, yet there is no positive proof for the existence of separate Urn communities in Ireland. It is, therefore, more likely that a mixed Urn assemblage got to Ireland.

166

CHAPTER EIGHT

Industrial Changes Late Second–Early First Millennia

Background

In common with most of Europe an alteration took place in the Bronze Age industries of Ireland around 1200 B.C. But the Irish and other European changes are only part of a series of wide transformations, not necessarily directly related, that affected practically the whole of the Old World. In many ways these changes repeat the events of a thousand years previously. It was a time of collapse in the 'civilized' regions but of progress in the 'barbarian' regions. But now over large tracts of western Asia and the Aegean there was a finality, for it was at this time that the Bronze Age came to a disastrous end. Practically the whole of the civilizations of the Near and Middle East which were centuries in the making collapsed (e.g. Troy, Blegen 1963; Boghazköy, Gurney 1954; Palestine, Kenyon 1960; Mycenae, Desborough 1964, Taylour 1964). Thus, around 1200 B.C. the pattern of civilization throughout eastern Mediterranean and Aegean lands changed and from the material culture point of view this is the time that the Late Bronze Age terminated and the Iron Age began.

If the story is one of gloom, destruction and collapse of civilizations in western Asiatic and Aegean lands the contrary is the case in barbarian Europe where immense industrial, technological and economic advances were taking place; changes involving burial practices were also happening. Evidence for industrial expansion is clearly demonstrated in the ore-rich areas of the Carpathians and the Alps. Deep mining was being practised (Childe 1948, 189) and large founders' hoards, especially from Transylvania (Rusu 1963, 177–89), demonstrate the abundance of metal. In north Alpine Europe, and especially in Upper Bavaria, the first big changes start in the course of the thirteenth century, Bronze Age D, and by the twelfth century the 'Urnfield' period, with its new burial rite and technological and industrial accomplishments, had commenced (Müller-Karpe 1959, 144–60).

But it is events that were taking place outside the western and northern perimeters of the central European Late Bronze Age that are of immediate concern and in this connection the relevant areas are France, the west Baltic region and more especially southern Britain. During the earlier part of the second half of the second millennium B.C. changes in the southern English Urn 'culture' were beginning to take place. This is shown in the metal types, dirks of Groups I and II, base-looped spear-heads and palstaves, but changes in the pottery types also took place. Indeed, most of the pottery types of the Deverel-Rimbury 'culture', as well as the burial rite of cremation in flat cemeteries and occasionally in mounds, continue the Urn tradition (Burgess 1974, 214–18; Calkin 1962). The Deverel-Rimbury people were large-scale farmers and they had protected farmsteads, field systems, cattle enclosures and trackways. But into their 'territory' and adjoining areas, especially Somerset, during the twelfth century new bronze types were introduced and the combination of old (native) and new (foreign) form an industry that has been termed the 'ornament horizon' by M. A. Smith (1959) and the 'Taunton/Barton Bendish Phase' by J. J. Butler (1963, 218–23). The industry's native element consists of rapiers (the more developed forms, Groups III and IV, Burgess 1968b, 12–15), base-looped spear-heads and palstaves. The foreign element consists of bronze tools and ornaments 'representing usages of adornment and dress hitherto unknown among the population of southern England' (Smith 1959, 154). These are non-socketed sickles, socketed hammers and punches, socketed axes, narrow-bladed palstaves (Rowlands 1971, 194, 195), plain, coiled and ribbed bracelets, doubled and hooked bracelets, incised decorated arm-rings (Rowlands 1971), plain, coiled and ribbed finger-rings, pins (Hawkes 1942), Class II razors and possibly the saw and 'flesh-hook'. The ultimate place of origin of a number of the foreign types goes back to the Middle Bronze Age (Tumulus culture) of north Alpine Europe but the immediate background is the west Baltic area (southern Scandinavia and northern Germany) and France. The narrow-bladed palstaves, pins and Class II razors and the incised decorated arm-rings are of French origin. The socketed axe, at least the plain and ribbed bracelets, the finger-rings and tores are of west Baltic origin. It is difficult to know whether the sickles, hammers, punches and twisted bracelets have an immediate background in the north of Europe or in France. Development also took place and objects such as Sussex loops (based on the doubled and hooked bracelet) and quoit-headed pins (based on the Tumulus culture wheel-headed pins) provide evidence for it. A number of the bronzes are often found together in hoards. When so found they are usually in a damaged or worn condition.

In Ireland an altered metal industry with improved techniques became established and in its formation the 'ornament horizon'/Taunton industry played an important part. The new industry, elsewhere called the 'Bishopsland Phase' (Eogan 1964, 272–88), is also characterized by the introduction of tools and ornaments, but above all by native adaption and the widespread use of gold for ornaments.

But despite these changes the tradition of the Urn 'cultures' continued, even though typological changes took place. The wing-flanged axeheads (Fig. 63, 3) represent a typological advancement on the haft-flanged axe. The flanges were lengthened and bent inwards at about mid-point on the axehead so as to afford a better grip for hafting purposes (Smith 1959, 172). Broad-bladed palstaves (p. 164) were still in use; an example with trident decoration is stated to have been found with other objects at Annesborough, Co. Armagh (Coffey and Armstrong 1914; see Fig. 69). Palstaves with a medium blade splay and a V-shaped swelling on each face (Fig. 69, 2) were also in use.

While the Irish evidence is inconclusive, nevertheless it is likely that ribbed kite-shaped and base-looped spear-heads (Smith 1959, 178–80; Coles 1963–4, 153, Glentrool hoard; see Fig. 65, 1, 2) and rapiers were the weapon types that were current. There was a change in the form of the rapier. The trapeze-shaped butt is now well developed and the blade has a triple arris (Fig. 65, 5; Group III of Burgess 1968b, 12–13). Typologically Burgess has considered Group III rapiers as the product of the crowding on to a narrower blade the central ridge and bevel lines that are found on blades of Group II rapiers. However, their origin may not be solely due to typological progression, for as Burgess has noted, rapiers with triple arris are fairly common in north-western France. In the words of Burgess (1968b, 12–13) rapiers of Group III represent 'the ultimate achievement of Irish–British dirk and rapier manufacturers from the point of view of length and refinement . . . they include . . . the longest and most elegant rapiers from these Islands, such as the magnificent example from Lissane, Co. Derry'.

Rapiers of Group IV were probably also coming into use (Burgess 1968b, 14–15, 25–6). Rapiers of this group have notched butts and the cross-section of the blade is flat (Fig. 65, 6). In comparison to rapiers of the previous group Group IV rapiers are inelegant and they display a fall-off in design.

Technology and Economy

The casting achievements of the bronze-smith rose to a new height during this stage. These include the elegant rapier from Lissane, Co. Derry. This piece is 79·7 cm long and has been described as the 'longest rapier . . . in Western Europe' (Coffey 1913, 58), and 'a remarkable tour de force of bronze casting' (Trump 1962, 87). The finishing-off of artifacts was of equal importance and in this connection the completion of the magnificent flange-twisted bar torcs, such as those from Tara, was an outstanding accomplishment (p. 176).

There is no specific evidence for copper mining or for collecting gold. The smiths must have been melting down used artifacts, at least in bronze, but the Towednack hoard from Cornwall (Eogan 1967a, 144–5) suggests that its contents might have been bartered for tin which was known to have occurred in that area. Gold was also available in quantity and the smiths may have commenced alloying it with copper, possibly to improve its colour (Hawkes 1962, 35–6). Solder was used for the first time (Eogan 1964, 281).

There is no positive evidence available for the casting of gold but the ornaments were probably finished off by hammering from a cast nugget. For the bronze implements there is some evidence to suggest that they were being cast both in double-piece stone moulds and in clay moulds. Indeed, it was probably at this time that the use of clay moulds for casting was becoming widespread. While material other than stone may have been used for casting from the beginning of the Bronze Age yet the cord moulding around the necks of the socketed axehead and hammers from the Bishopsland hoard (Fig. 68, 2–4) probably provides the earliest definite evidence for casting from clay moulds. As Hodges (1956, 47) has pointed out it would be difficult to produce that sort of moulding if the objects were cast in a stone mould.

As was the case during preceding stages of the Bronze Age (see p. 153) artifacts were probably made at several centres throughout the country. Double-piece stone moulds were still used, such as an unprovenanced mould for casting a Group III rapier (Coghlan and Raftery 1961, 240, Fig. 36). Theoretically, it was possible for smiths who were using stone moulds to be itinerant. But there is evidence for sedentary centres of bronze casting at Knockadoon, Lough Gur, Co. Limerick. At Site D a hut, 5 m (17 ft) by about 3 m (10 ft) across, was used as a workshop and at Site F the structure tended to be rectangular and it measured 8·25 m (27 ft) by 6·30 m (21 ft) (Fig. 66). In both instances the lower part of the wall was constructed from stones and the upper part from perishable material such as sods. At both sites the craftsmen used clay moulds, but there is also slight evidence for the use of stone moulds. Fragments of clay crucibles were found at Site D (Ó Ríordáin 1954, esp. pp. 384–5, 400–1, 415ff.). Objects cast on these sites include spear-heads with loops on the socket, palstaves and rapiers, possibly of Burgess's Group IV (Fig. 67).

Clay moulds were double-piece and in the manufacture of each valve two principal layers were used. The outer layer was made of fairly coarse clay. On top of this a layer of fine clay was spread. When the clay was still soft a pattern was pressed into the inner layer for half its depth so as to form an impression. The same process was repeated for the other half of the mould. Between the edge of the impression and the edge of the valve each half had either corresponding depressions or projections. When both valves were placed together the projections on one would fit into the depressions on the other. This would ensure perfect matching of both parts at the time of casting. If the object to be cast required rivet holes further projections were left at the relevant points. Especially in long moulds, a straight rod of wood was incorporated in the outer layer for strengthening purposes. After drying the pattern was removed and the mould was trimmed. Then the two valves were fitted together and they were enclosed in an outer casing. This was also of clay but it was usually much coarser than that forming the inner layers. The whole was then baked. In order to facilitate pouring, a 'gate' or a funnel was created at one end. This usually consisted of an extension of either the middle layer or the outer casing but more elaborate gates could have been used such as those visualized by Curle (1932–3, cf. Fig. 41) for moulds found at Jarlshof, Shetland. For the casting of socketed objects it was necessary to insert a core. This was also made from clay and it was held in position below the gate (Liversage

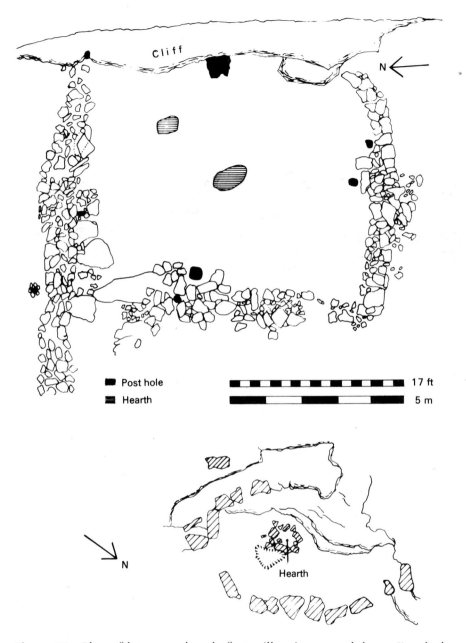

Figure 66 Plan of late second–early first millennia B.C. workshops, Knockadoon, Lough Gur, Co. Limerick. Top: Site F. Bottom: Site D ('House I') (both after Ó Ríordáin 1954, Pls 50 and 41).

171

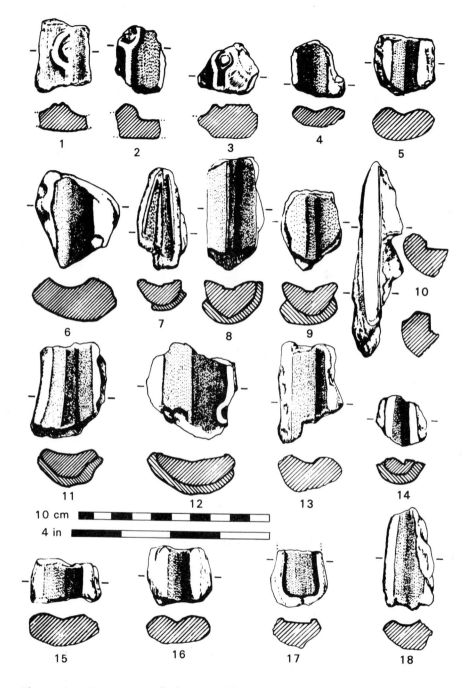

Figure 67 Fragments of clay moulds from Site F, Knockadoon, Lough Gur (after Ó Ríordáin 1954, Fig. 46).

1968, 149, Fig. 7). Ducts were left so as to let the metal run into the cavity. When the metal had cooled the mould was broken to extract the rough casting. This was then trimmed and its surface was smoothed down and beaten so as to make the metal harder.

A wide range of bronze and gold artifacts were manufactured. In addition to weapons (p. 169) a variety of tools were being used. The common axe type was the wing-flanged axehead (Fig. 63, 3) which was a product of the north British and Irish industries (Smith 1959, Map 4b). Broad-bladed palstaves and palstaves with a medium blade splay had limited use (Fig. 69, 2, Fig. 68, 1). But a novel form of axehead, the socketed variety, was introduced. The homeland of this type is in northern Germany, the *Hademarschen type* (Butler 1963, 75–9; Smith 1959, 150, 171). Socketed hammers, saw, graver or narrow-tanged chisel, flat chisel, trunnion chisel, anvil and vice or clamp were also in use (Fig. 68). Apart from the trunnion chisel, which was current at the beginning of the Urn period (p. 153), the other types were introduced. Nearly all can be paralleled in 'ornament horizon'–Taunton phase contexts (see relevant sections of Butler 1963; Smith 1959).

It is during this stage of the Bronze Age that a range of craftsmen's tools are first found in a hoard. This is the hoard from Bishopsland, Co. Kildare (Fig. 68). The Bishopsland hoard, together with the Lough Gur workshops, provide good evidence for the presence of professional craftsmen. However, not all the tools discussed above need belong exclusively to professionals. The axes, both socketed and those belonging to the palstave family, can be considered mundane implements that could have been used by a specialist craftsman but also by the farmer for cutting down and chopping wood. The hammer could have been common to both the carpenter and to the bronze-smith. The saw, the flat chisel and the axes are woodworking implements but it would be more appropriate to consider the punch, the narrow-tanged chisel, the trunnion chisel, the anvil and the vice as metal-working implements.

There may also have been an improvement in farming practices. For the first time there is positive proof for the use of the bronze sickle. The Bishopsland example has an elongated hafting knob. Non-socketed sickles with knobs are a feature of the Tumulus cultures (Torbrügge 1959, 84). From southern Germany the type spread northwards to southern Scandinavia (Kersten 1936, 91) and westwards across France (Sandars 1957, 109, 114, 150). In Britain knobbed sickles were only used in the south (Fox 1941, 148, Fig. 5).

Palstaves, wing-flanged axes and the new socketed axeheads may also have been part of the farmers' equipment.

Personal Adornment

Bronze depilatory tweezers were current (Fig. 68, 17) and a range of personal ornaments, nearly all made from gold, came into use. The ornaments consist of earrings, neck ornaments (bronze torcs, gold bar torcs and possibly ribbon torcs,

173

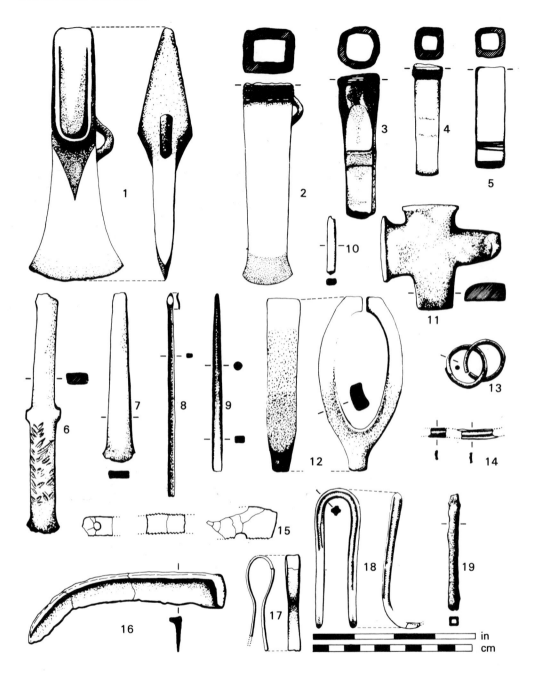

Figure 68 Hoards of bronze artifacts from Bishopsland, Co. Kildare (N.M.I. 1942: 1750–71; 1944: 148–9).

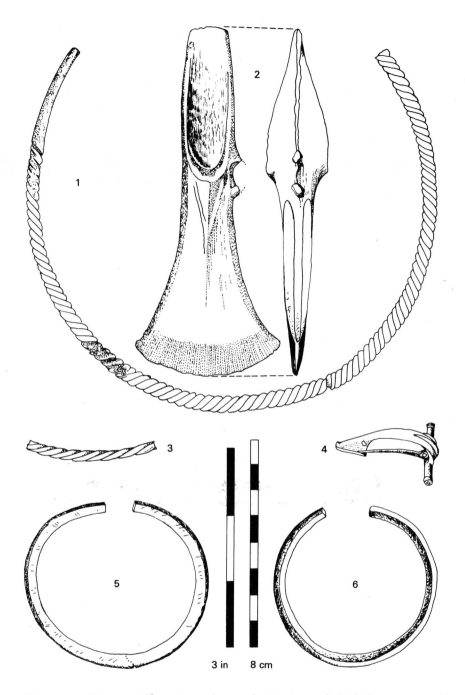

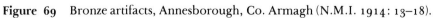

Figure 69 Bronze artifacts, Annesborough, Co. Armagh (N.M.I. 1914: 13–18).

175

penannular rings with unexpanded terminals, composite rings), bracelets (broad ribbed and narrow ribbed with closely-set ends, penannular with solid body usually with rounded cross-section and unexpanded terminals, penannular with twisted body and unexpanded terminals), 'tress-rings', spiral rings and pins with undecorated disc-shaped heads and loops on the stem (Figs 68, 13–14; 69, 1, 5–6; 70).

The earrings have twisted bodies, either bar- or flange-twisted. The bar-twisting technique is fairly widespread but in Hawkes's view (1961) the flange-twisting technique was developed in Ireland and western Europe to imitate the more complicated eastern Mediterranean strip-twist technique. According to Hawkes the earrings originated in the Palestinian–Cypriot area. However, larger gold objects that resemble earrings are known from the Carpathian region where they can be dated to about the thirteenth century B.C. (Mozsolics 1973, 206, Taf. 92). Perhaps the bar earrings in the Lanrivoaré hoard, Brittany (Hawkes 1961, 472, Pl. 2) might then represent a stage on the westward diffusion of twisted rings from the Carpathians. This hoard also had the remains of a gold plaque of central European type.

Bronze torcs are common in 'ornament horizon' contexts and in the west Baltic area (Smith 1959, 141; Butler 1963, 137–40, Map 11; Kersten 1936, Abb. 2: 2). Gold bar torcs with recurved terminals are amongst the most elaborate types of ornament found in Bronze Age Europe (Eogan 1967a). About ninety are known and they are concentrated in Ireland and southern Britain with a scatter in France (Fig. 71, left). As was the case with the earrings the techniques of bar-twisting and flange-twisting were used in their manufacture. Bar torcs emerged in either Ireland or southern Britain. They might even have been developed by Irish smiths as elaborate versions of the bronze torcs. Powell has, however, pointed out that possible prototypes exist in central European Early Bronze Age contexts, for instance the multiple-stranded gold arm-ring from Barca, Slovakia (Powell 1966, 146–7). It is usual to consider ribbon torcs as part of this phase but their dating is not secure (Eogan 1964, 280). The bracelets of all forms can be paralleled in 'ornament horizon'–Taunton phase contexts. On the continent ribbed bracelets occur chiefly in Denmark and north-western Germany but penannular bracelets have a wide distribution in Tumulus culture and Period III contexts (see relevant sections in Butler 1963; Smith 1959). The spiral ring can likewise be paralleled in 'ornament horizon' contexts. The disc-headed pin with loop on stem has been found in an equivalent British context. Its continental background is northern Germany where the type has been found in Period III contexts (Butler 1963, 148, Map 12).

Miscellaneous objects include a 'flesh-fork' (Fig. 68, 18). Again this type of object was in use in England shortly before 1000 B.C. (Briscoe and Furness 1955). There are early Urnfield associations on the continent (Kytlicova 1955, 62, 74, Obr. 6). There is no positive evidence for the use of pottery at this time. It has been stated that the ribbed bracelet and other objects from Dysart, Co. Westmeath were found with pottery but the vessel has not survived (Armstrong 1933, 44). Sherds of coarse flat-based ware

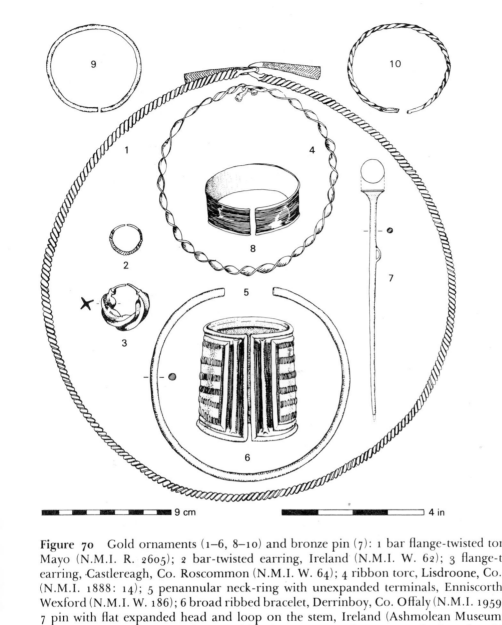

Figure 70 Gold ornaments (1–6, 8–10) and bronze pin (7): 1 bar flange-twisted torc, Co. Mayo (N.M.I. R. 2605); 2 bar-twisted earring, Ireland (N.M.I. W. 62); 3 flange-twisted earring, ·Castlereagh, Co. Roscommon (N.M.I. W. 64); 4 ribbon torc, Lisdroone, Co. Mayo (N.M.I. 1888: 14); 5 penannular neck-ring with unexpanded terminals, Enniscorthy, Co. Wexford (N.M.I. W. 186); 6 broad ribbed bracelet, Derrinboy, Co. Offaly (N.M.I. 1959: 693); 7 pin with flat expanded head and loop on the stem, Ireland (Ashmolean Museum 1927: 2853); 8 'tress-ring', St John's, Co. Kildare (N.M.I. W. 279); 9 penannular bracelet with solid body of rounded cross-section and unexpanded terminals; 10 penannular bracelet with twisted body and unexpanded terminals, both St John's, Co. Kildare (N.M.I. W. 90, 171).

Figure 71 Left: find-places of gold bar torcs. Right: find-places of 'lock-rings'. Open symbols indicate that only the county in which the ornament was found is known. Enclosed symbols indicate that more than two ornaments have been found together.

have been found on Sites D and F at Lough Gur (p. 170), but the evidence is not sufficient to establish whether the craftsmen used pottery.

Hoards

The practice of depositing hoards was revived. About eleven hoards can be assigned to the period: Bishopsland, Annesborough, Cappeen, Derrinboy, Enniscorthy, Tipper (Naas), St John's, Skelly (Eogan 1964, Appendix, Nos 40, 6, 19, 57, 80, 42, 43 and 71), Trimblestown (*Dublin Penny Journal*, I (1833), 413–14), Dysart (Armstrong 1933, 44), Co. Westmeath (Pegge 1789) and possibly Downpatrick hoards (Eogan 1964, Appendix, Nos 26–7). If gold ribbon torcs belong to this period then the hoards from Ballylumford, Largatreany, Inishowen and Derravonna (Eogan 1964, 280 and references) should also have been deposited at this time. The chronological status of the Vesnoy hoard is difficult to fix (Eogan 1964, Appendix, No. 63). It is also not possible to say whether the hoard of three ribbed kite-shaped spear-heads from Tattenamona (Evans and Mitchell 1954) and the haft- and wing-flanged axes from

Doagh Glebe (Armstrong 1916–17, 514) were deposited at this time or during the preceding stage.

In the eleven hoards that definitely belong to this period all contain ornaments, except that from Co. Westmeath which has a spear-head and a palstave. There is also a palstave in the Annesborough and Bishopsland hoards. In Annesborough the other pieces are ornaments. Tools predominate in Bishopsland but there are a couple of fragments of ornaments. The tools could have belonged to different types of craftsmen; the metal-worker predominates but the carpenter and the agricultural worker are also represented. The Dysart ribbed bracelet was associated with a pottery vessel and a copper cake. The other seven hoards consist of ornaments, gold ornaments in the vast majority of instances. Some of the ornament hoards (e.g. Cappeen) contain unfinished pieces suggesting that these might have also been the property of a craftsman and were probably buried at a time of trouble, others just the personal possessions of an individual (e.g. St John's) that were also hidden away during times of danger. But various interpretations for the reasons for depositing hoards can be put forward. It has been suggested that as burials are absent perhaps the hoards should be looked on as 'graveless grave goods' (Eogan 1964, 285). Instead of placing objects in a grave they were committed to the earth but unaccompanied by a body.

Origin and Chronology

In discussing origins and chronology one must rely exclusively on the evidence provided by the metal types. When one considers the origin of the individual types that are believed to have been current during the twelfth and immediately succeeding centuries we find that a number represent continuity from an earlier stage of the Bronze Age but that others were new. The older types were represented by looped spear-heads, rapiers, palstaves, haft-flanged or wing-flanged axes and the trunnion chisel. But even with these development took place. The rapiers then current were not the same as those that were in use in the preceding centuries. Regarding the prototypes of introduced types we find that nearly all of these occur in one area, southern England, and to be even more specific most of the proposed prototypes occur in 'ornament horizon', or Taunton phase, contexts. Amongst comparative pieces occurring in actual 'ornament horizon'/Taunton phase contexts one can mention double-looped palstaves, socketed axe of Hademarschen type, socketed hammer, flat chisel, non-socketed sickle, bronze torc, broad and narrow ribbed bracelets, penannular bracelets with irregular or rounded cross-section, twisted bracelets, spiral rings, and small ribbed rings. Although not occurring in an 'ornament horizon' context, flesh-hooks and saws were in use in southern Britain about the same time. A number of 'ornament horizon' objects can be derived from the west Baltic area (p. 168) – socketed axeheads, broad and narrow ribbed bracelets, and possibly bronze torcs. Some of the other types could be of west-central European

179

origin. With some 'ornament horizon' objects, such as non-socketed sickles and twisted bracelets, it is difficult to know whether they come from the west Baltic area or from France. Regarding objects not paralleled in 'ornament horizon' contexts pins with flat, disc-shaped heads and loops on the socket are of north German type, the anvil could have a French background, while an eastern Mediterranean background can be suggested for at least the flange-twisted earrings and possibly the composite neck-ring.

Bar torcs with recurved terminals represent a group of objects that developed in Ireland or southern Britain. Objects such as the penannular neck-rings with unexpanded terminals and tress-rings can be considered as Irish inventions.

From the evidence to hand it is clear that the industry of the twelfth and immediately succeeding centuries owes its origin to the acquisition of individual types from a variety of industrial areas – the west Baltic, the east Mediterranean, west-central Europe, but especially the south of England where many objects of diverse origin had previously been brought together in the 'ornament horizon'/Taunton industry. That industry acted as a source of diffusion of continental types to Ireland.

The 'ornament horizon'/Taunton industry can be dated fairly accurately. The forerunners of the metal types can be paralleled in northern Europe in contexts that date from Period II to Period IV. But as Butler has emphasized, it was only during Period III that all the types were in simultaneous use (Butler 1963, esp. p. 219). On the current dating of Period III (Randsborg 1968, esp. pp. 131–8, with Müller-Karpe 1959, 144ff., and Sandars 1971, for dating of Bronze Age D) one can suggest that the 'ornament horizon'/Taunton phase started shortly after 1200 B.C. Corroboratory dating is provided by the Elpe and Ommerschons hoards in the Netherlands (Butler 1963, 68–9 and 157). It is also to around this time that the relevant French material dates, e.g. hoard from Porcieu-Amblagnieu (Déchelette 1924, Fig. 49; Sandars 1957, 114 for dating).

The arrival of Early Urnfield metal types in England towards 1000 B.C. (Burgess 1968c, 3–9) marks the beginning of the end of the 'ornament horizon' industry. One of the latest hoards to be deposited is that from Blackrock, Sussex (Piggott 1949). This hoard has a bracelet with terminals in the form of kidney-shaped swellings, a mock *Nierenringe*. As M. A. Smith (1959, 160) has pointed out, *Nierenringen* are a north European Period IV type, as is shown by the associated finds from Rethwich, Lower Saxony (Jacob-Friesen 1963, Abb. 298) and Bargeroosterveld, Netherlands (Butler 1963, 69–70).

It is possible that the Irish industry got under way shortly after the establishment of the 'ornament horizon'. It is not clear when the industry ended. At present the material available does not provide concrete evidence, and even if such objects as the 'flesh-hook' in the Bishopsland hoard has an Early Urnfield background this still need not mean a date much later than 1000 B.C. As will be shown, the next major change in the Irish industry took place during the eighth century and the industry at present under review contributed to the industry of the eighth century and later. For instance both industries used clay moulds for casting, the composition of a number of the hoards of both periods is similar and the gold bracelets with solid evenly expanded terminals of the eighth century and later can be explained as a typological development out of bracelets with expanded terminals. It may be that the industry that was established during the twelfth century continued on and received new types until finally swamped by the great industrial revolution that commenced during the eighth century.

It is not certain if the novel metal types document the arrival of new people or if it was due to trade or commercial contacts. In discussing the 'ornament horizon' M. A. Smith concluded that that industry owes much to types that were 'selectively adopted from different areas on the continent', but as only a limited number of the types found in the relevant areas on the continent occur in Britain, Miss Smith ruled out the arrival of immigrants. But Butler rightly points out that the 'ornament horizon'/Taunton industry is something more than a casual importation of metal types, for there was also a transfer of techniques. So from the industrial point of view there must have been concentrated effort. It might also be recorded that 'ornament horizon' material was associated with inhumation burials at Ramsgate and Hanley Cross (Smith 1959, 162). This contrasts with the cremation rite of the Deverel–Rimbury cultures.

In Ireland the evidence available need not cause one to postulate the arrival of immigrant bands, perhaps some craftsmen. It has already been remarked that Bishopsland is on the Wicklow–Kildare border and nearly all the other hoards have been found in Leinster, so perhaps exploiters were involved, Wicklow gold being the objective. The other point is the chronological context of the time. As has been stated at the beginning of this chapter the decades around 1200 were a time of tremendous change in various areas of Europe and western Asia and indeed this involved folk movements. But there is a universality about the metal types. Some of the individual types in the Bishopsland hoard, for instance Hademarschen axes, can be paralleled in northern Europe, but others can be compared to pieces (especially small tools) that form part of the hoards of the Late Mycenaean-Late Cypriot periods, not proved later than Late Helladic IIIB (cf. Desborough 1963, 48; Catling 1964, 278–98). At least when it comes to metal types there were a number of international forms; there was a sort of international pool into which Ireland was drawn.

Discussion

During the twelfth or eleventh centuries B.C. a new industrial and technological stage of the Bronze Age emerged. The components of this industry are in part native and in part foreign but in addition developments, both typologically and technologically, took place. And when some of the creations of the craftsmen, such as the bronze rapier from Lissane, the gold ribbed bracelets from Derrinboy, or the gold torcs from Tara (Plate 12a), are taken into consideration it is hardly an exaggeration to say that the craftsmen of this stage of the Bronze Age were producing some of the most superb specimens of metalwork in contemporary Europe. Specialist craftsmen were operating, and at least at Lough Gur they worked from fixed centres. Furthermore, it can now be stated positively that for the first time smiths were using clay moulds for casting. But there were other technological advances. From this point of view the broad ribbed bracelets are of considerable importance because they provide the earliest evidence for the use of distinctive repoussé work in Ireland. The repoussé technique consists of the beating or pushing out from the back on a sheet of metal ridges, bosses, or other ornamental features. Faint repoussé work was practised by the Irish goldsmiths at the beginning of the Metal Age (see p. 143 above) so perhaps the repoussé work at this period represents internal development but there is the possibility that it was also a borrowed technique.

As has been previously mentioned, bar twisting was introduced at around the same time from different sources, especially the west Baltic area and the east Mediterranean area. Flange twisting (p. 176) was a technique devised to reproduce the elaborate east Mediterranean 'strip-twist', a technique that the west European smith failed to master. But even so, the manufacture of such objects as bar torcs presupposes considerable skill and technical ability. In addition the evidence of so much gold work is a reflection of the material wealth of the period. Perhaps hoards also reflect this new material wealth and a change in the organization of the metal industry. But they might also give some hint as to the belief of the people in an afterlife (see p. 179).

What is probably one of the most interesting features about the stage is the evidence that is shown for innovation and adaption. This is clearly demonstrated by a number of the metal types. Very few of these are straightforward copies of their prototypes; most can be described as insular renderings of external prototypes and in this adaptation sometimes a complete new type was created.

This new industry was probably also an exporter. Some of the bar torcs that have been found in Britain were probably manufactured in Ireland and the gold for the others very likely came from Ireland.

While we have considerable knowledge about the artifacts and techniques of the period we have none at all about domestic sites and burial rites. We do not know if the rite of Urn burial was still being practised, but if it was artifacts were no longer being placed with the Urn in the grave. As has been argued above the razor evidence may suggest that Urn burials continued down towards the end of the second millennium. Around the twelfth century the practice of depositing hoards became fashionable (p. 178). The causes of deposition are not known but could they coincide with ritual changes, part of which would have been the abandonment of Urn burial and its replacement by 'graveless grave goods'?

Augmentations, tenth–ninth centuries

From the latter part of the eleventh century new continental influences were affecting southern Britain (Burgess 1968c, 3–9, his 'Penard phase'). The novel bronzes that initiated this phase have their continental homeland in various areas, viz. central Europe (especially during the Hallstatt A2 stage), northern Europe of Period IVa and Atlantic Europe. Others have a continental background that is too wide to allow the precise place of origin to be determined. Amongst the new bronze artifacts were swords of the Erbenheim and Hemigkofen types (Cowen 1951), tanged recurved knife, barbed-and-tanged arrowheads and pointed spear-shaft butts. In addition to the arrival of new types development and experimentation took place. 'Indigenous development influenced by exotic fashions' produced swords of the Ballintober type (Irish Class 1) while straightforward indigenous development, or invention, produced cylinder-socketed sickles, rapiers of Trump's Lisburn Class (a class within Burgess's Group IV), base-looped spear-heads with straight-based blades and 'transitional' palstaves.

From about 1000 B.C. novel bronze types also appear in Ireland. These include sickles with cylinder-shaped socket (Fig. 75, 5; Fox 1939a) and the first swords, Class 1 (Eogan 1965, 5–9). These swords have a sub-rectangular hilt-tang with four rivet-holes set in pairs. The leaf-shaped blade has a lozenge-shaped cross-section (Fig. 72, 1). The origin of these swords is complex but Burgess (1974, 295, 318 f.n. 270) considers them as a modified version of the continental rod-tanged swords. A distinctive form of rapier, the Cutts Class, emerged (Burgess 1968b, 14; Trump 1962, 92–3. See Fig. 65, 7).

The influences from the continent that reached Britain about 1000 B.C. were forerunners of greater changes that followed. During the tenth century large-scale industrial alterations took place in north-western France and south-eastern England: the Wilburton/Saint-Brieuc-des-Iffs phase (Burgess 1968c, 9–17, 36–7, Fig. 8; Briard 1965, 175, 98). A feature of this industry is the practice of depositing massive hoards that contained a large proportion of metal. Weapons (swords and spear-heads) are a common component of these hoards but tools, especially socketed axeheads, are also prominent. In the north of Britain conservative industries survived, the Wallington complex in northern England and the Poldar phase in Scotland (Burgess 1968a, 7ff.; 1968c, 13–14; Coles 1959–60, 20–5, 53).

Influences from the Wilburton complex reached Ireland (Eogan 1964, 288–93, the Roscommon phase). The new types consist of the earliest flange-hilted swords, Classes 2 and 3, tongue-shaped chapes (Eogan 1965, 9–10, 169), cylindrical-shaped butts for spear-heads (Eogan 1964, 290) and possibly spear-heads with lunate-shaped openings in the blade (Evans 1933, 197–200; see Fig. 72, 2–3). But older traditions continued. It is likely that Group IV rapiers were still current and it may have been at this time that spear-heads with protected openings in the blade were in use (Evans 1933, 196–7; see Fig. 65, 3). A developed form of the socketed axe of Hademarschen type with broad low collar around the neck and body of rectangular cross-section may have been in use at this time (Eogan 1964, 290; Burgess 1968a, 15).

As has been shown there was a considerable influx of new metal types and an improvement in technology during the eleventh–twelfth centuries but knowledge

183

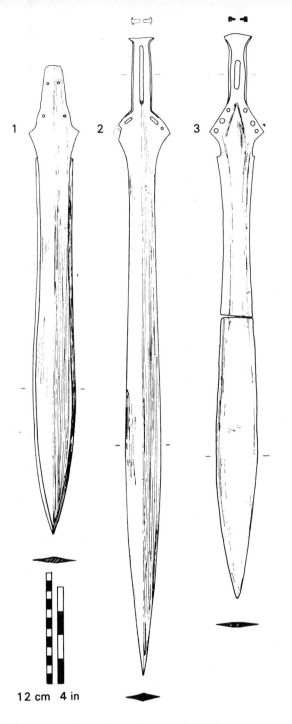

Figure 72 Late Bronze Age swords, Classes 1–3: 1 Class 1, Athlone, Co. Westmeath (N.M.I. W. 42); 2 Class 2, Toome, Co. Antrim (N.M.I. W. 1); 3 Class 3, Carnstroan, Co. Antrim (N.M.I. SA. 1927: 929).

184

concerning ninth–tenth-century events is vague. There was a limited contribution from the Wilburton complex, the most significant aspect of which was the arrival of the first flange-hilted swords. The Irish industry of this period had more in common with the north British industry. There is no indication for significant change in the organization of the metal industry. The absence of associated finds of native types for the whole of the period that extends back to the beginning of the Urn period makes it difficult to know what artifacts were in contemporary usage. It should be noted that metal types that come into use at the time of the introduction of Urn burial, and their descendants, were not generally placed in hoards. When one finds hoards during these centuries (e.g. Bishopsland, Cappeen) they were introduced types. The evidence available suggests that the ninth century was a time of recession but simultaneously a time of adjustment between two active industrial phases.

CHAPTER NINE

Final Bronze Age Society

Background

The eighth century and the beginning of the seventh was again a time of change throughout the Old World. Two major events, the Assyrian conquest of Syria and Palestine and the ravages of the Cimmerians in Asia Minor, brought considerable upheaval to western Asia (cf. Hencken 1968, .597–8). In central Europe the Late Bronze Age (Hallstatt B) was ending and the first phase of the Iron Age (Hallstatt C) was commencing (Müller-Karpe 1959; Kossack 1959). In north-western France and south-eastern England the Wilburton/Saint-Brieuc-des-Iffs industry was being replaced by the Carp's Tongue Sword Complex (Evans 1930; Savory 1948; Burgess 1968c, 17ff.; 1974, 210). Like its predecessor this industry is characterized by large founders' hoards and its leading metal types are carp's tongue swords, an insular form of the flange-hilted sword with leaf-shaped blade (the Ewart Park type), bag-shaped chapes, plain leaf-shaped spear-heads, hog's back knives, triangular perforated knives, bugle-shaped objects, winged axes and socketed gouges. The carp's tongue sword industry had a Late Urnfield background (i.e. winged axes) but it represents regional development on both sides of the English Channel. Outside the kernel carp's tongue sword area of Britain industries were influenced by the 'carp's tongue sword complex' and the Late Urnfield period.

Ireland, too, but in its own way, participated in these eighth–seventh-century changes. There was a tremendous increase in the amount of metal available. This is shown by the vast number of individual types current. But other economic and technological changes took place. There was also a break in the pattern of external connections. Influences were now reaching Ireland from areas other than Britain and regional industries were emerging.

Farming and hunting

Domestic animals, especially cattle, were kept and grain was grown. The inhabitants of Ballinderry No. 2 kept cattle, sheep, pigs and goats (Hencken 1942, 21). Amongst the animal bones at Knocknalappa cattle again predominated but pigs and sheep were represented. Dogs were also kept (Raftery 1942a, 68–9). Bronze rattle-pendants or jangles (Fig. 82, 8) would have been suspended from a bridle-bit or other piece of harness-trapping as at Svartap, Sweden (Sprockhoff 1956, 1, Abb. 56: 9). Rattle-pendants are also known from 'carp's tongue sword' assemblages (Thrane 1958, 221–7). Some of the perforated bone objects from Ballinderry No. 2 and the 'toggle' from Knocknalappa (Hencken 1942, 15, Fig. 5; 667; Raftery 1942a, 57, Fig. 3: 5) may have been horse-trappings. An ornament from a hoard at Cromaghs, Co. Antrim is made from horse hair (Coffey 1906, 123, see Plate 14a). It is possible that the horse was used for traction purposes. Wooden block wheels which revolved on an axle are known. These would have been from carts. One such wheel, from Doogarymore, Co. Roscommon, has a radiocarbon determination of 450 ± 35 years B.C. (Lucas 1972). Such carts might have been in use during this final phase of the Bronze Age.

Saddle-querns, which have been found on nearly every occupation site, provide evidence for the growing of grain (Fig. 73, 1). The grain was reaped with bronze socketed sickles (Fox 1939a). There are two groups. Group I (Fig. 73, 6), the laterally socketed sickles, developed in south-eastern England out of the open-socketed sickle (p. 183). Sickles of Group II are socketed vertically. According to Fox these sickles were derived in Britain from the socketed knife. If so their initial date must be later than the sickles of Group I (Fig. 73, 7; Fig. 76, left, for distribution).

The inhabitants of Ballinderry No. 2 hunted the red deer and they also practised fowling but to a very limited extent. Wooden traps, 'thread-traps', are known from Ireland and one of these, from Drumacaladerry, Co. Donegal, was found at a level in a bog that might suggest that it could have been in use during the Late Bronze Age (Clark 1952, 53). In Ireland 'thread-traps' continued in use into the Early Christian period. On the base of one of the High Crosses at Clonmacnois, Co. Offaly a figure scene shows a deer caught in such a trap (Clark 1952, 51, 53).

Occupation sites and centres of artifact production

About six occupation sites can be assigned to an eighth-century or a later date. Ballinderry (No. 2) and apparently also Knocknalappa were domestic sites, probably the homestead of a family, and it is also of interest to note that occupation took place on the damp edge of a lake. Dalkey, Lough Eskragh, Rathgall and Rathtinaun were domestic and industrial sites, like Sites D and F, Lough Gur (see p. 170), but unfortunately it is only at Rathgall that evidence for a building came to light and this may have been used exclusively for industrial purposes. On the industrial sites the

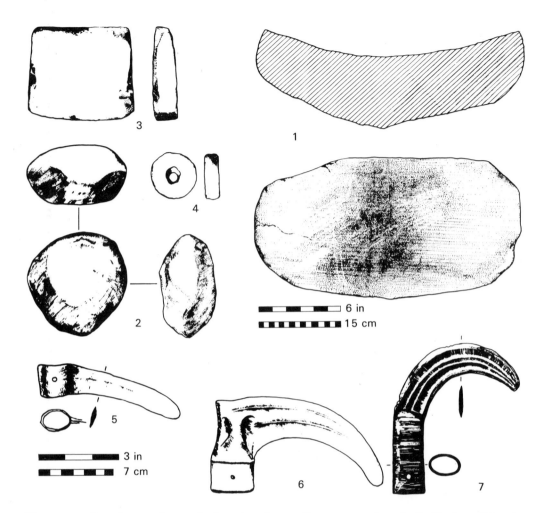

Figure 73   Late Bronze Age agricultural tools: 1–4 from occupation site Ballinderry (No. 2), Co. Offaly, 1 saddle-quern stone, 2 rubbing-stone possibly from a saddle-quern, 3 whetstone, 4 spindle-whorl (after Hencken 1942, Fig. 6, Nos 418, 472, 230, 668, material in N.M.I.); 5–7 socketed sickles, 5 open-socketed, Lawrencetown, Co. Meath (N.M.I. 1925 : 12). Group I (sickle socketed laterally), Co. Westmeath (N.M.I. W. 6), Group II (sickle socketed vertically), Athlone, Co. Westmeath (B.M. 1862, 12–9. 3).

smiths used clay moulds for casting. The manner of preparation and use of such moulds has already been described (see p. 170).

The Late Bronze Age occupation layer (which was underneath a crannóg of Early Christian date) at Ballinderry, Co. Offaly extended over a somewhat kidney-shaped area around 50 m long by 28 m in width but it was not an artificial island (Hencken 1942, 6–29). There were two groups of structural remains. A group at the eastern end

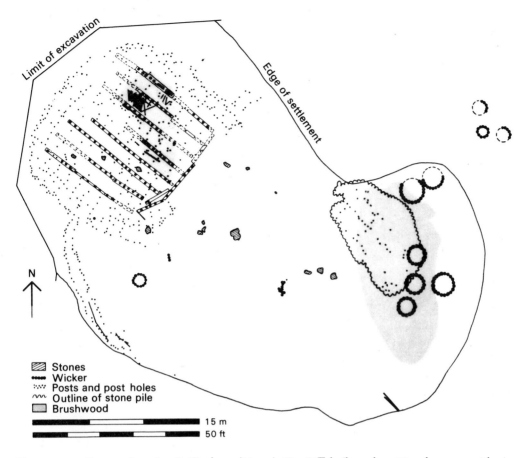

Figure 74   Occupation site, Ballinderry (No. 2), Co. Offaly (based on Hencken 1942, Pl. 2).

consisted of nine wicker structures of uncertain use. These varied in internal diameter from 1 m to 2·17 m. Near the eastern end there was a well laid layer of brushwood that measured 12·30 m by 8·20 m. Part of this was covered by a pile of stones. At the western end an area 12 m by 12 m was covered with oak planks that were placed parallel to each other. Each plank had a row of squarish holes. Hencken suggested that this may have been part of a wicker or wattle-and-daub house but as the 'aisles' between the foundation planks were only about 1·50 m wide it would not have been an easy house to move around in. The house was surrounded by light posts and a double row of posts extended southward for about 14 m. To the south of the house there was another wicker 'hut' or hearth (Fig. 74). The site produced a variety of finds in bronze, stone, wood, pottery, amber, lignite and shale, bone and antler, and leather. Seemingly the inhabitants were a self-contained economic group that kept domestic animals, grew grain and spun thread.

189

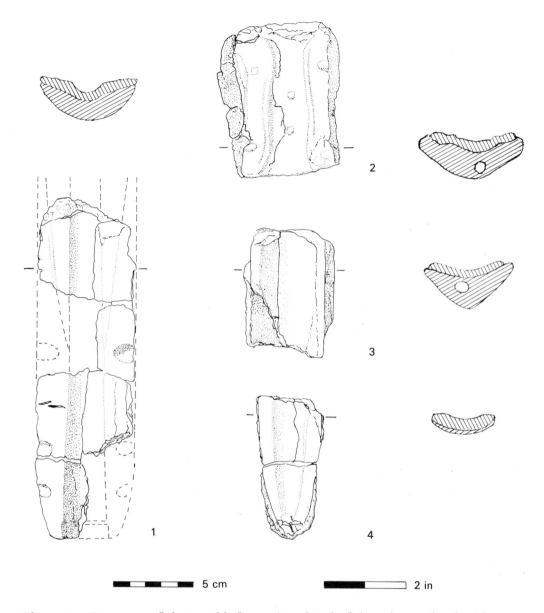

Figure 75 Fragments of clay moulds for casting plain leaf-shaped spear-heads with peg-holes in the socket (1) and Class 4 swords (2–4). 1, 2, 4, Whitepark Bay, Co. Antrim (U.M. 654. 30 (No. 1), 534. 30, Nos 2, 4); 3 Lough Eskragh, Co. Tyrone (County Museum, Armagh).

A bronze-smith's workshop must have stood on Dalkey Island, but unfortunately the excavation did not reveal any structural features. However, there is ample evidence for casting from clay moulds (Liversage 1968, esp. pp. 147–50, 184, 186).

Knocknalappa, Co. Clare was a sort of artificial island that was constructed by the laying down of a thick layer of peat over the natural marl (Raftery 1942a). On top of this there was a layer of stones. The occupation area was oval in shape. It measured nearly 60 m long by a little over 30 m wide and it was delimited by piles that averaged from 3 cm to 15 cm in diameter. On the northern and eastern sides stones were thrown down to strengthen the piles. No evidence of houses came to light, and the excavator doubted if it was ever inhabited. The structural layers yielded finds. These included the bottom stone of a saddle-quern, sherds of pottery ('Flat-rimmed ware'), amber beads, sunflower pin, lignite bracelet, small bronze ring and bone spindle whorl.

In the autumn of 1959, when the level of Lough Eskragh, Co. Tyrone was lowered, three main areas, where seemingly structures stood, came to light. Piles occurred at all areas, but apart from noting the areas of structures and collecting surface finds, large-scale investigation has not been carried out (Collins and Seaby 1960).

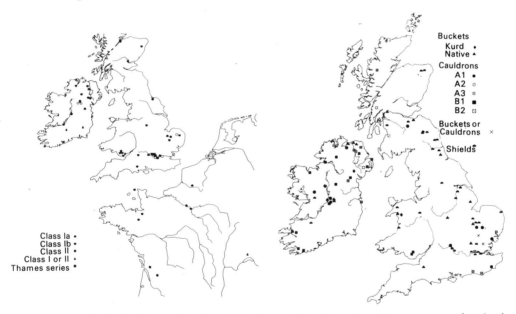

Figure 76 Left: find-places of socketed bronze sickles (based on Fox 1939a and Briard 1964). In addition an open-socketed sickle has been found at Arganil, Portugal (*Zephyrus* 8 (1957), 135–45). Open symbols indicate that only the county in which the sickle was found is known.
Right: find-places of bronze vessels (buckets and cauldrons) and bronze shields in Ireland and Britain. Open symbols indicate that only the county in which the object was found is known (based on Hawkes and Smith 1957 and Coles 1962).

191

At Site A there were three separate areas of piling. One area, almost circular and about 10 m in diameter, consisted of horizontally laid timbers and brushwood. This was delimited on the eastern side by piles. A saddle-quern was found near the interior and close by there were two dug-out canoes. Closer and parallel to the shore of the lough there were two other areas of piling. In the southerly area the piles were arranged in a somewhat circular fashion and at one point along the edge a saddle-quern stone turned up. In the northerly area the piles were set in a more random manner. Eleven saddle-quern stones were found amongst them.

Site B consisted of a small area of piles. There were two heaps of charcoal and a large stone that had apparently been hammered on. Nearby there were a number of fragments of clay moulds. Collins and Seaby have suggested that this was probably a bronze-smith's workshop.

Site C consisted of two small low mounds which were surrounded by double or treble rings of piles.

Of the three sites it is only possible to assign a definite date to one of them, Site B. There the mould fragments, especially those for Class 4 swords, establish that workshop activity was going on there around the eighth century or subsequently. As rotary querns were replacing saddle-querns during the Iron Age (see p. 233 below) it could be assumed that Site A is pre-Iron Age in date but there is no proof that it is contemporary with Site B. There is no dating evidence at all for Site C. It is not clear whether these sites are artificially constructed islands (crannógs) or whether they were lakeside settlements like Ballinderry. If the latter is the case then the lake must have been considerably smaller during the Late Bronze Age.

Current excavations are providing evidence for extensive activity at Rathgall, Co. Wicklow. Amongst the features revealed was a wooden structure of uncertain shape. This appears to have been a bronze-smith's workshop (Raftery 1970, 1971, 3). In a black 'occupation' layer in and around the building dozens of fragments of clay moulds for casting swords, spear-heads and other objects turned up. The layer also yielded a socketed axehead, lumps of waste bronze and a couple of ingots. Although not directly associated with the occupation material, a saddle-quern, a bronze socketed gouge and a bronze 'toggle' were found. An open-air hearth (or hearths) was located outside the house.

The occupation site at Rathtinaun, Lough Gara, Co. Sligo consisted of a foundation of brushwood and peat which was laid down in the shallow water of a swamp (unpublished, brief note in COWA Survey – Area I – British Isles, No. I, 1958). There were wooden piles around the edge. A number of hearths turned up but no evidence for houses came to light. The hearths were surrounded by woven twigs which were plastered, giving a basket-like appearance. Some plain domestic pottery was re-covered (see p. 204) and a number of fragments of clay moulds were also found. A hoard of ornaments was discovered beside the occupation site (Eogan 1964, 347, No. 67).

Several objects that date from the final phase of the Bronze Age are recorded as having been found on a crannóg in Loughnaglack and another crannóg in Monalty Lough, south Co. Monaghan (*J.R.S.A.I.*, 98 (1968), 106ff.).

Occupation may also have taken place in natural caves. Coffey (1912b, 86) records the discovery of amber beads, a bronze sickle and other Bronze Age objects of unknown type in a cave at Whitechurch, Co. Waterford and a couple of bronze artifacts were also found in Kilgreany Cave (Movius 1935a, 277).

In addition to Dalkey Island, Lough Eskragh, Rathgall and Rathtinaun, clay mould fragments have been found at other sites, namely Whitepark Bay, Co. Antrim, Old Connaught, Co. Dublin and Bohovny, Co. Fermanagh (Eogan 1965, 176–8) and although no evidence has come to light it may be assumed that a manufacturing site was in operation at those places. There is a record of the discovery of part of a (?clay) sword mould on the 'surface of an ancient crannóg associated with rude huts which were. found at a depth of 21 feet (6·40 m) underneath peat' (Eogan 1965, 178). Although not specifically stated in the original report it is likely that the mould fragment was found in Co. Fermanagh; one might ask could it have been one of the Bohovny moulds (cf. Fig. 75)?

During this final stage of the Late Bronze Age the use of stone moulds had virtually ceased. Only a couple of examples are known (Ballydaw, Co. Kilkenny and Ireland; Coghlan and Raftery 1961, 231, Figs 15 and 16). The axes cast in those moulds would not have been the common bag-shaped axe but the more unusual form with vertical rib decoration on each face. The moulds may have been introduced from Britain (cf. Hodges 1954, 78) and not a continuation from the industries of the Urn 'cultures'.

Tools and Weapons

Hundreds of socketed axeheads can be assigned to this stage. The overwhelming number of axes belong to a distinctive variety, the so-called 'bag-shaped' type. Axes of this type have an oval or sometimes a circular mouth, a body of oval cross-section and a widely splayed blade that is almost semicircular in shape (Fig. 77, 3). Bag-shaped axeheads may be a modified version of certain north German axeheads (Butler 1960, 111–12).

Other socketed axeheads that were current at this time, but in much smaller numbers, were faceted axeheads, with a body that was either of octagonal or hexagonal cross-section (Fig. 77, 2) and axeheads with body of rectangular cross-section and plain vertical ribs on each face (Fig. 77, 4). Plain ribbed axeheads occur frequently in Britain.

Awls, anvils, socketed hammers, including examples with expanded T-shaped head, trunnion chisels, tanged chisels, socketed chisels and socketed gouges (Fig. 77, 5–18) were current. Chisels provide the greatest variety of forms (Eogan 1964, 296–8). In the tanged variety there are two sub-types. In one the blade is kite-shaped (Class 1). This is probably the primary type and is known on the continent. The other variety, whose blade has concave sides, is probably a development (Class 2) (see Roth 1974,

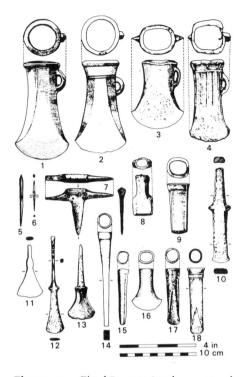

Figure 77 Final Bronze Age bronze tools: 1–4 socketed axeheads, 1 octagonal cross-section, Trillick, Co. Tyrone (Ashmolean Museum 1927: 2917); 2 hexagonal cross-section, Mountrivers hoards, Co. Cork (N.M.I. 1908: 11); 3 bag-shaped socketed axehead, Glenstal, Co. Limerick (N.M.I. 1901: 47); 4 rectangular cross-section and vertical ribs on each face, Crevilly-valley, Co. Antrim (B.M. W.G. 1586); 5 and 6 bronze awls, Killeavy hoard, Co. Armagh and Ballinderry No. 2 (N.M.I.) respectively; 7 anvil, Lusmagh, Co. Offaly (B.M. 1883. 2–18, 19); 8 socketed hammerhead with expanded head, Lusmagh, Co. Offaly (B.M. 1883. 2–18. 20); 9 socketed hammerhead with unexpanded head, Trillick, Co. Tyrone (Ashmolean Museum 1927: 2918); 10–13 tanged chisels: 10 trunnion chisel, Lusmagh, Co. Offaly (B.M. 1883. 2–18. 23); 11 kite-shaped blade, Booltiaghadine, Co. Clare (N.M.I. 1942: 764); 12 lateral projection and blade with concave sides, Lusmagh, Co. Offaly (B.M. 1883. 2–18. 24); 13 collar and blade with concave sides, Crevilly-valley, Co. Antrim (B.M. W.G. 158); 14 long-socketed sickle, Ross, Co. Tipperary (N.M.I. S.A. 1927: 1); 15 short square socket, Grange, Co. Kildare (U.M.A.E. Cambridge. M.C. 99. 246. 2); 16 short rounded socket, Ireland (N.M.I. W. 510); 17–18 Class 1 (plain) and Class 2 (moulded) socketed gouges from Crevilly-valley, Co. Antrim (B.M. W.G. 1589) and Bootown, Co. Antrim (N.M.I. 1929: 1528).

but with different classification). There are three varieties of the socketed chisel. One has a long stem (Fig. 77, 14). In the other two varieties the stems are short: one has a socket of square cross-section (Fig. 77, 15), in the other the socket is of rounded cross-section (Fig. 77, 16). Socketed gouges may be plain (Class 1; Fig. 77, 17) or decorated with a moulding, or mouldings, around the mouth (Class 2; Fig. 77, 18). In Britain they came into use during the 'Wilburton' stage (MacWhite 1944b). Their origin may go back to eastern Europe (Eogan 1966).

Although placed in this category it is not certain that knives were exclusively used as tools. They would have been useful as household artifacts, such as in cutting up meat, the preparation of skins or even in wood-working, but they would equally have served as weapons. All the knives of the final phase of the Bronze Age are two-edged. They can be divided into two main groups, tanged (Fig. 78, 1) and socketed.

Tanged knives as such were in use in Britain during the 'ornament horizon' (cf. *Inventaria Archaeologia*, G.B., 42:21) and subsequently during the 'Wilburton' phase (Britton 1960, 281) but they were also common in Britain and in France during the 'carp's tongue sword complex' or an equivalent stage (cf. Eogan 1964, 296).

There are four varieties of socketed knives (Hodges 1956, 38; see also Eogan 1964, 296). In the Thorndon type (Fig. 78, 2) the junction between the socket and the blade forms a straight line and the blade is normally parallel-sided. These knives are the west European counterpart to the one-edged knives of the Urnfield period (Sandars 1957, 280–1). They occur in 'carp's tongue complex' assemblages. The Dungiven type seems to represent insular development. There is a U- or V-shaped notch in the junction between the socket and the leaf-shaped blade (Fig. 78, 3). Knives of the Kells type have a socket that tapers slightly towards the blade which is triangular in shape (Fig. 78, 4). The fourth variety has a curved blade, and may have originated on the continent (Eogan 1967a, 135).

Spear-heads of the old insular looped variety were current but in view of the rarity of their occurrence in hoards it would seem that their numbers were few. The common spear-head was the plain form with leaf-shaped blade and peg-holes in the socket (Fig. 78, 6–7). This type of spear-head was in use on the continent from the Early Bronze Age (cf. G. Jacob-Friesen 1967, 89ff.) and it may also have arrived in Britain at that time (Britton 1963, 289).

The type of sword (Fig. 78, 11) now in use is what has been termed Class 4 (Eogan 1965, 10–13). These swords are equivalent to the English Ewart Park type. They originated in the south-east of England, their prototypes being the broad V-butted swords of the Wilburton complex. The scabbards in which these swords were carried were tipped with chapes (Fig. 78, 8–9) that had a body of lozenge-shaped cross-section and an expanded foot, Class 2 (Eogan 1965, 169). Bag-shaped chapes (Fig. 78, 10) were also used (Class 3, Eogan 1965, 169). Both varieties of chapes can be paralleled in Britain in 'carp's tongue sword complex', or an equivalent industry.

In contrast to Britain (Coles 1962, 187–90) bronze shields are very rare in Ireland, only two examples, those from Lough Gur, Co. Limerick and Athenry, Co. Galway being known. However, shields of organic material were probably in fairly common usage. From experiments carried out, Dr John Coles has demonstrated the efficiency of such shields as items of defence. Five shields of organic material are known from Ireland. All are single finds and each is distinguished by having a series of ribs which are interrupted by either a V- or U-shaped notch (Coles 1962, esp. p. 186). One shield,

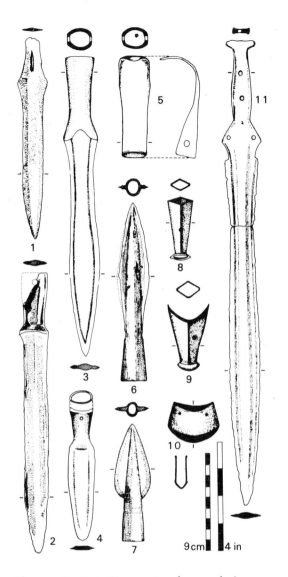

Figure 78 Late Bronze Age bronze knives, spear-heads, chapes and sword: 1–5, knives, 1 tanged, Derryhale, Co. Armagh (N.M.I. 1906: 106); 2 Thorndon type, Boa Island, Co. Fermanagh (Ashmolean Museum, 1927: 2910); 3 Dungiven type, Kilmore, Co. Galway (N.M.I. 1930: 223); 4 Kells type, Co. Armagh (Co. Museum, Armagh, 98. 1935); 5 curved blade, Knockmaon, Co. Waterford (N.M.I. P. 1948: 148); 6 socketed spear-head with peg-holes and narrow blade, Blackhills, Co. Laois (N.M.I. 1962: 58); 7 socketed spear-head with peg-holes and wider blade, Kinnegoe, Co. Armagh (N.M.I. 1906: 52); 8 scabbard chape, Class 2, Sruhagh, Co. Cavan (N.M.I. R. 1580); 9 Class 2 chape, Ireland (N.M.I. 1881: 218); 10 scabbard chape, Class 3, Ireland (N.M.I. 1872: 11); 11 sword, Class 4, Blackhills, Co. Laois (N.M.I. 1962: 57).

from Clonbrin, Co. Longford, is made from leather; the others are made from a single slab of wood. Two of these, Annandale, Co. Leitrim and Cloonlara, Co. Mayo, are probably shields proper but the two other wooden examples, Churchfield, Co. Mayo and Kilmahamogue, Co. Antrim are models for the making of leather shields. A sheet of wet leather would be pressed around the boss and into the grooves (p. 218). It may be noted that the Clonbrin leather shield and the two wooden models (or 'moulds') have V-shaped notches; the wooden shields have U-shaped notches (Plates 13a and b).

According to recent research (Coles 1962, esp. pp. 157–62 and references therein; also Gräslund 1967) notched shields originated in the eastern Mediterranean area. The V-notched shield reached Ireland by way of Spain but it has been assumed that the type also got to northern Europe where the V-notch was transformed into a U-shaped notch. It would have been from that area that the Irish U-notched shields came.

Personal Adornment and Dress

In addition to toilet articles, depilatory tweezers and tanged bifid razors (Class II of C. M. Piggott 1946; see Fig. 82, 9, also p. 168), a wide range of personal ornaments was worn. These include ornaments of non-metallic material such as jet or lignite rings that may have served as bracelets or as armlets, the multiple-stranded necklace of 500 amber beads from Derrybrien, Co. Galway (Plate 14b; Prendergast 1960b, 61–3) or the single-stranded necklace of 421 beads from Kurin, Co. Derry (Flanagan 1960, 61–3). Although used during an earlier stage of the Bronze Age (p. 158) it is only from the eighth century onwards that amber occurs plentifully (MacWhite 1944a).

Apart from a few examples, the metal ornaments were made from gold. Neck ornaments are again well represented. The most outstanding neck ornament is the gold gorget (Fig. 79, 2). Gorgets do not occur outside Ireland and even in Ireland their distribution is limited, mainly to north Munster (Eogan 1964, Fig. 19). Their origin is uncertain but north German prototypes have been suggested.

Another type of gold 'collar' from Ireland has a C-sectioned body and evenly expanded solid, or slightly hollowed, terminals (Fig. 79, 3).

The gold penannular neck-ring with solid body of rounded cross-section and evenly expanded hollow terminals (Fig. 79, 1) probably developed out of the neck-rings with unexpanded terminals of the eleventh–twelfth centuries (p. 176). The fourth type of neck-ring is represented by a single bronze example from Bally-keaghra, Co. Galway (*J.R.S.A.I.*, 92 (1962), 150, p. xvi top). This is also penannular, the solid body is of rounded cross-section and the solid oval terminals are set at an oblique angle to the body. Ornaments with obliquely set terminals were in use in Denmark during Period VI of the Bronze Age (Broholm 1953, 83, Nos 280–2). While of uncertain use the heart-shaped bulla may have been suspended around the neck (Fig. 80, 10).

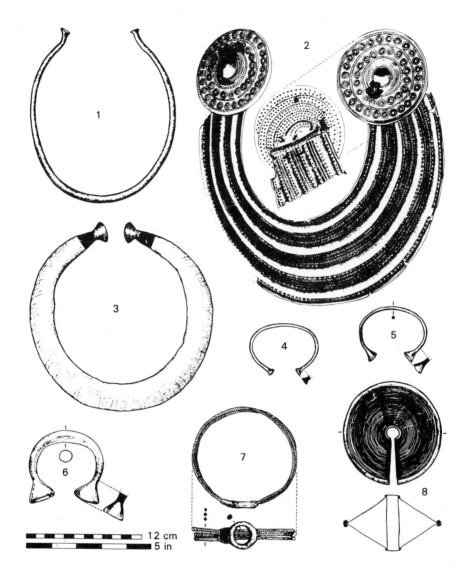

Figure 79 Late Bronze Age personal ornaments, gold except 7 which is bronze: 1 penannular neck-ring with evenly expanded terminals, Mooghaun assemblage, Co. Clare (N.M.I. W. 175); 2 gorget, Borrisnoe, Co. Tipperary (N.M.I. W. 17); 3 'collar'. Mooghaun assemblage, Co. Clare (N.M.I. W. 25); 4 penannular bracelet with expanded solid terminals, Lattoon, Co. Cavan (N.M.I. 1920: 27); 5 penannular bracelet with expanded hollow terminals, Drissoge, Co. Meath (N.M.I. 1953: 3); 6 thick penannular bracelet with expanded hollow terminals, Drissoge, Co. Meath (N.M.I. 1953: 1); 7 penannular bracelet with circle, Ballytegan, Co. Laois (N.M.I. 1967: 11); 8 'lock-ring', Gorteenreagh, Co. Clare (N.M.I. 1948: 236).

198

Several varieties of penannular bracelet were current and nearly all were made of gold. These include bracelets with solid body of rounded cross-section and evenly expanded solid terminals (Fig. 79, 4), probably a development from the bracelets with unexpanded terminals (p. 176), bracelets with body (usually solid) of rounded cross-section and evenly expanded hollow terminals (Fig. 79, 5) and penannular bracelets with body that is normally of rounded or oval cross-section and that has a much greater diameter than the bodies of bracelets of the preceding type. The body, which is usually hollowed, is bent almost to a semi-circular shape and it has evenly expanded hollow terminals that are set at a marked inclination to the plane of the body (Fig. 79, 6). It is likely that bracelets of the two foregoing groups originated in Ireland, an elaboration of the type of bracelet with solid, evenly expanded terminals under the influence of the 'dress-fastener' (Hawkes in Hawkes and Clarke 1963, 226).

Annular bracelets or armlets with circle (Fig. 79, 7) are also known. This is a north European Period V type (Sprockhoff 1953 and 1956, 195–8; for Ireland see J. Raftery 1971, 96–9).

In addition to the neck ornaments and bracelets there are other gold objects that may have served as ornaments. 'Lock-rings', 'hair-rings' and possibly the striated rings and thick penannular rings may have been hair ornaments (Eogan 1969; 1972. See Figs 79, 8; 80, 1–3).

The only piece of textile that can definitely be assigned to this period is from the Cromaghs hoard, Co. Antrim (Coffey 1906, 121–2; Henshall 1950, 135). The piece, which consists of two widths of plain, woven cloth, might have been part of a garment. Coffey suggested that the 'garment' might have simply consisted of a square or oblong piece of cloth that was wrapped round the body below the arms.

The horse-hair objects, also from the Cromaghs hoard (Coffey 1906, 123–4; Henshall 1950, 138–9), are likely, as Miss Henshall has suggested, to have been parts of a belt. The three pieces consist of portion of the body and two end-pieces each of which is attached to part of the body. The body, according to Miss Henshall, has been very evenly woven from single hairs into a 'herring-bone twill with a displacement' and, as a result, the end product is a 'very fine and delicate piece of work'. The ends of the belt were finished off in an ornamental manner with an arrangement of tassels. Each tassel started off as a bunch of horse-hair which was bound round by other horse-hairs. From the bunch hairs were drawn out to form members and each member was in turn subdivided into thinner members which terminated in small knobs. Just above the row of tassels a horizontal band, formed by plain weaving, was attached (Plate 14a).

There is also indirect evidence for dress. As Hawkes points out (in Hawkes and Clarke 1963, 226), the presence of the 'dress-fastener' would indicate that a heavy cloak was worn. In Ireland, apart from one or two exceptions, all 'dress-fasteners' were made from gold. 'Dress-fasteners' (Fig. 80, 4; Fig. 81) are characterized by large, usually evenly expanded, hollowed terminals, the mouths of which are placed horizontally, or almost so, so as to rest on the same plane.

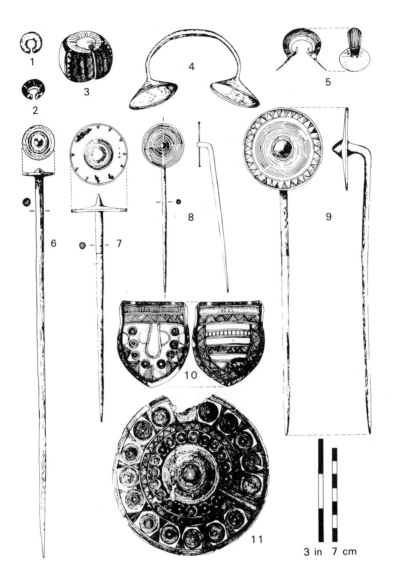

Figure 80   Late Bronze Age personal ornaments, gold except 6–9 which are bronze: 1 hair-ring, Loughmacrory, Co. Cavan (N.M.I. 1897: 17); 2 striated ring, Ireland (N.M.I. R. 4036); 3 thick ring, Ireland (N.M.I. W. 259); 4 dress-fastener, Lattoon, Co. Cavan (N.M.I. 1920: 25); 5 sleeve-fastener, Belfast (Ashmolean 1927: 2937); 6–7 disc-headed pins with straight stem, 6 primary series, Trillick, Co. Tyrone (Ashmolean Museum, 1927: 2925); 7 secondary series Ireland (U.M.A.E. Cambridge 27: 623); 8–9 disc-headed pins with bent stem (sunflower-pins), 8 primary series, Edenderry, Co. Offaly (U.M.A.E. Cambridge, M.C. 99: 198), 9 secondary series, Boolybrien, Co. Clare (N.M.I. 1931: 232); 10 bulla, Bog of Allen, Co. Kildare(?) (N.M.I. W. 265); 11 disc, Lattoon, Co. Cavan (N.M.I. 1920: 28).

There is a group of gold objects of uncertain use which could have served as fasteners for garments, possibly even as 'sleeve-fasteners' (Fig. 80, 5). This type of ornament is exclusively Irish. Other ornaments, the 'dress-fastener' in particular, may have been used as a model (Eogan 1972).

Pins could also have been functional and, while not throwing any light on the garments themselves, the widespread use of pins in Ireland at this time may indicate that a change in fastening methods had taken place. The pins of this period have disc-shaped heads. There are two groups. In one group the head is placed vertically. Both types of Irish pins have forerunners in the west Baltic region (Baudou 1960, 78). In the west Baltic area the decoration on the heads consists of concentric circles around a small central boss. Pins with this type of decoration in Ireland represent a primary form (Fig. 80, 6, 8). Development takes place in Ireland, the central boss becomes larger and in addition to circles surrounding the boss other decorative motifs such as zig-zags, triangles and chevrons are found. This is a secondary form (Fig. 80, 7, 9).

A bronze 'toggle' from Rathgall, Co. Wicklow (B. Raftery 1971, 297) may also have been used in fastening clothes. Bar-toggles are known from the west Baltic area (Baudou 1960, 89–90; Sprockhoff 1956, 1, 232); those with a straight bar are

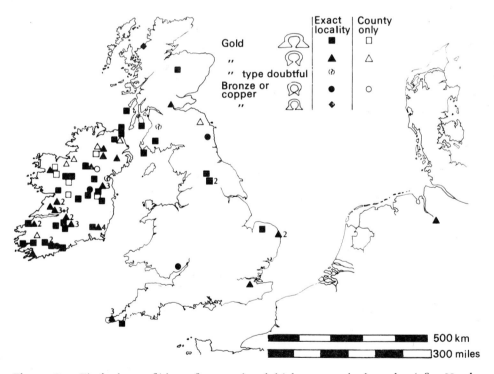

Figure 81 Find-places of 'dress-fasteners' and thick penannular bracelets (after Hawkes and Clarke 1963, Fig. 51). Open symbols indicate that only the county in which the ornament was found is known.

predominantly a Period V type. They are mainly found in Denmark where about one hundred and fifty examples are known (Baudou 1960, 90 (XXVI, B2), Karte 50).

There is a variety of bronze rings but their use is uncertain. Some might be ornaments, the large plain rings for instance could be bracelets, but others might have been parts of horse harness trappings.

Plain rings occur in various sizes (Fig. 82, 1–2). Rings with one or two transverse perforations through the body and rings with lateral buffer-shaped perforated projections (Fig. 82, 3, 6) are probably Irish versions of rings that are found in Britain where they form part of the Late Urnfield 'carp's tongue sword complex' element of the final phase of the Late Bronze Age (cf. Eogan 1964, 309). A ring combination that consists of a small ring threaded on to a larger one (Fig. 82, 4) is also known. Chains, too, occur. An example from Boolybrien, Co. Clare (Fig. 82, 7) consists of triple and double links. Double links also occur as individual finds in hoards (Fig. 82, 5). These can be paralleled in western Europe in Late Urnfield or equivalent contexts (Hawkes in Hawkes and Clarke 1963, 229). Parallels for the Irish chains are known from France (Eogan 1964,309ff.).

Vessels

Vessels of different shape, function and material were current. The most striking are the buckets and cauldrons of sheet bronze.

Wooden vessels. These were carved out of solid wood. Wooden vessels or fragments were found at Ballinderry (No. 2), Co. Offaly but the only distinguishable piece is part of a shallow bowl (Hencken 1942, 17, Fig. 7, bowl No. W. 120). A portion of a wooden bowl was found at the same level as a bag-shaped socketed axehead in Cranberry Bog, Oldtown, Kilcashel, Co. Roscommon, but a distance of about six metres separated both objects (Ó Ríordáin 1938). Hoards from Kilmoyly North, Co. Kerry (Raftery 1940, Fig. 189), Killymoon, Co. Tyrone (J. Raftery 1970b, 170, Pl. 22) and possibly those from Bootown, Co. Antrim and Grange, Co. Kildare (Eogan 1964, 331, 340) were deposited in wooden boxes. The cauldron from Altartate, Co. Monaghan (Mahr 1934) has been compared by Hawkes and Smith (1957, 198) to Hallstatt D cauldrons. Another cauldron, whose find-place is not known, has an everted rim reminiscent of the bronze Class B cauldrons (Hodges 1957, 57, Fig. 6).

Metal vessels. A number of gold bowls and round boxes have been recorded (Wallace 1938, 91–2; Armstrong 1933, 40). Decorative motifs consist of multiple concentric circles and in addition a 'rope' pattern occurs on the boxes.

The bucket was one type of sheet-bronze vessel that was in use during the continental Late Bronze Age (von Merhart 1952). Some examples of the continental Kurd type (the name is derived from a Hungarian find) were imported into Ireland (Hawkes and Smith 1957, 139ff.). Kurd type buckets have sheet-bronze ring carriers

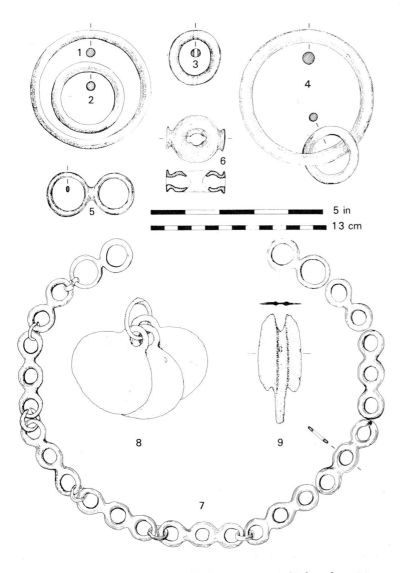

Figure 82   1–2 Plain rings, Trillick, Co. Tyrone (Ashmolean Museum 1927: 2920 (No. 1), 2921 (No. 2); 3 ring with transverse perforations, Bootown, Co. Antrim (N.M.I. 1929: 1534); 4 ring with small ring threaded on to it, Bootown, Co. Antrim (N.M.I. 1929: 1530); 5 double ring, Ireland (N.M.I. 1872: 10); 6 ring with lateral buffer-shaped projections, Glenstal, Limerick (N.M.I. 1901: 49); 7 chain, Boolybrien, Co. Clare (N.M.I. 1931: 221–31); 8 rattle-pendant, Lissanode, Co. Westmeath (private possession); 9 Class 2 razor, Dowris, Co. Offaly (B.M. 1883. 2–18. 14).

which were riveted on to the body and neck of the vessel. The neck is short, the shoulders tend to be rounded and nearly always bear corrugations. The base of the high tub-shaped base is protected by individual angle plates (Fig. 83, left). The introduced buckets were soon successfully copied by local smiths and native versions emerged. These native buckets retain the shape and other structural features of the Kurd type, but have distinctive insular features such as the use of more base plates and above all the use of cast staples, ribbed and/or grooved externally and set on the inside of the ring, to take the handle rings which now fall inwards (Fig. 83, right). Staples of this type were borrowed from the cauldrons (see below).

Leeds (1930, 4–15) divided cauldrons into two main classes – A and B. Both types are round-bottomed and like the buckets they are made from plates of sheet-bronze held together by rivets.

Class A cauldrons are distinguished by a short upright neck that is normally strengthened by corrugations (Fig. 84, 1). The rim is flat-topped and the handle rings are held in place by semi-circular-sectioned tubular holders. On the extent of the elaboration of the ring-staple it is possible to sub-divide Class A cauldrons. In sub-Class A1 the handle rings ride free between their staples and the rim top. Later, bracings across the rim top were added and this culminated in a continuous bracing that distinguishes Class A3. Class A cauldrons occur frequently in Ireland but they are also found in Britain, especially in the south (Fig. 76, right). Hawkes and Smith (1957, 165ff.) and previously Leeds (1930, 26ff.) derived cauldrons from the Mediterranean, but Dr David Coombs (personal communication) prefers a north Alpine European origin, such vessels as that from Skallerup, Denmark (Thrane 1962, Fig. 25) being possible prototypes. In the course of their development Class A cauldrons borrowed features from the buckets. These include the inturning of the rim and rolling it around a wire, possibly the neck corrugation, and in the construction of the body not from one sheet but from a number of riveted sheets of bronze. This is as one would expect for both the native buckets and the cauldrons of Class A must have been manufactured by the same insular craftsmen and the interchange of features (cast staples to the buckets) is, therefore, to be expected (see comments by Hawkes and Smith 1957, 165).

Class B cauldrons (Fig. 84, 2) have a rim that is everted at a slant. The staples are attached to the inner face of the rim. As a result of the method of attachment used, Leeds sub-divided the class into two groups. In sub-Class B1 the staples resemble those of Class A and they are attached by the same method of running-on. In sub-Class B2 the staples were cast as a separate unit and then fixed by some means such as riveting. Class B cauldrons are later than Class A; they have been found in Britain with Hallstatt C material (Hawkes and Smith 1957, 187–9).

Pottery vessels. The ware is coarse, gritty and crumbly. The shape of the vessel may vary. Some have a short neck and this may be upright or everted. Despite the name often used, 'flat-rimmed ware', only occasionally is the rim flat-topped, rims with an

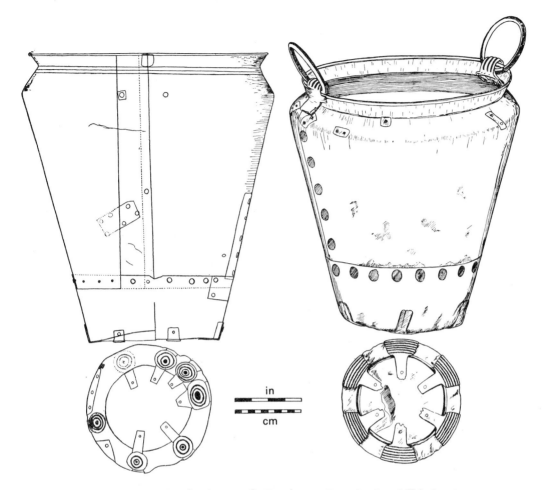

Figure 83   Late Bronze Age buckets. Left: Kurd type, Dowris, Co. Offaly (B.M. 1854. 7–14. 313); right: Native (insular) type (N.M.I. 1898: 114) (after Eogan 1964, Fig. 13).

internal bevel being common (Fig. 85). The pottery comes from occupation sites. The place of origin is not clear. Its shape resembles some late Neolithic wares (p. 119) but the view has been put forward that its homeland may have been north-western Germany (Hencken 1942, 10–12).

Decorative features

Decoration is mainly found on ornaments but it is not exclusively confined to them. Mouldings occur around the neck of Class 2 gouges and on a number of socketed axeheads. Some socketed axes have decoration, consisting of vertical ribs, on the

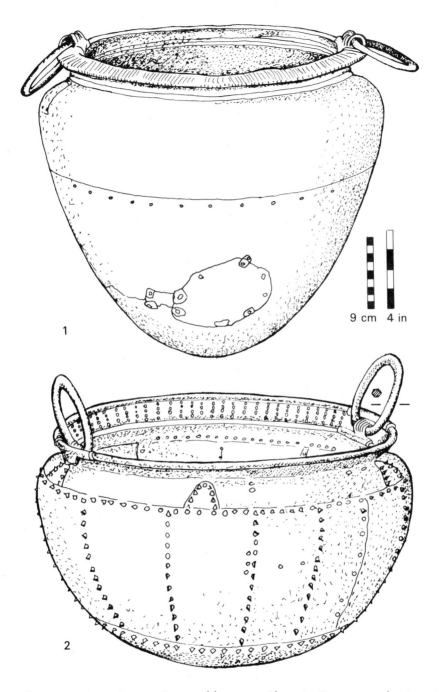

9 cm 4 in

Figure 84 Late Bronze Age cauldrons: 1 Class A, Barnacurragh, Co. Galway (N.M.I. 1932: 6523); 2 Class B, Lisdromturk, Co. Monaghan (N.M.I. 1965: 181).

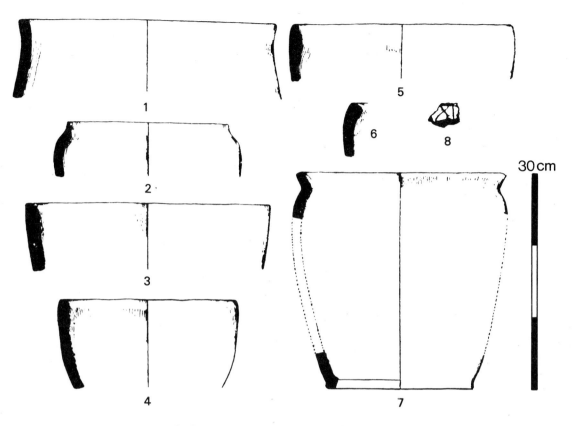

Figure 85 Pottery vessels from occupation site at Ballinderry (No. 2), Co. Offaly (after Hencken 1942, Fig. 2).

faces. Horns were also decorated. This consists of line ornament, which may consist of a group or groups of lines, or single zig-zag motif around the bell end of Class 1 horns. Class 11 horns are decorated with conical spikes and this form of decoration is also found on Class B cauldrons. On the shields, both bronze and leather, the decoration consists of ribs and small bosses. Sometimes small bosses are found on the buckets and cauldrons and on the gorgets, bowls, boxes, bullae, the Lattoon disc and the disc-headed pins. Occasionally multiple concentric circles, as on the secondary series of sunflower pins and on the terminals of the gorgets, are placed around a well defined conical boss. Hatched triangles and a sort of herring-bone pattern also occur. The decoration on the body of the gorget consists of ribs, either plain or in the form of a rope moulding. Longitudinal ribbing is found on the body of the 'sleeve-fasteners' and on the small striated rings, while at the junction with the terminals a diaper pattern occurs and a somewhat similar pattern occurs at the ends of the thick penannular rings. Occasionally 'dress-fasteners' and penannular bracelets have decoration. The principal motif is the hatched triangle. In the application of the ornament two main techniques, repoussé and incision, were used.

Regional groups

For the first time since the beginning of the Metal Age there is definite evidence of regional groups (Eogan 1974b). The most notable of these occurs in Munster. Six metal types are almost exclusively confined to that area. These are bronze shields and Class 11 horns and gold 'lock-rings', gorgets, 'collars', and bowls (Fig. 86, left). None of the gold boxes has a definite recorded find-place but on grounds of manufacture and decoration they appear to have been made by the North Munster School of gold-workers. It is also in the north Munster area that the largest hoards have been found. At Dowris, Co. Offaly, which is at the northern end of the region (cf. Eogan 1964, 344), over 200 bronze objects were found. The Mooghaun assemblage, Co. Clare (Armstrong 1917) contained over 150 gold objects and it is the largest associated find of Bronze Age gold ornaments from northern or western Europe. At least 100 objects, gold and bronze, were discovered in the Bog of Cullen, Co. Limerick (Wallace 1938). It is not possible to estimate the number of objects, probably all gold, that were

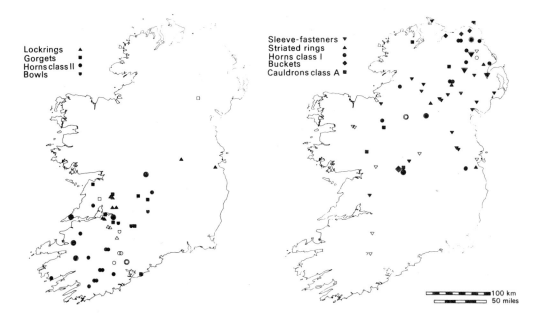

Figure 86 Left: find-places of lock-rings, gorgets, Class II horns and bowls. Right: find-places of sleeve-fasteners, striated rings, Class I horns, buckets, Class A cauldrons. Open symbols indicate that only the county in which the object was found is known. An enclosed symbol indicates that more than two objects of the same type have been found together.

found at Askeaton, Co. Limerick, but it seems to have been large (Eogan 1969, 131). It is clear that in the area of the lower Shannon valley in particular, up to Dowris on its northern periphery, metal was abundant and that it was worked by outstanding craftsmen. The gold objects are prestigious pieces. Therefore it must be assumed that the craftsmen were sustained by 'wealthy' patrons who purchased, or possibly commissioned, the goods, some of which are great works of art. An as yet not understood social order must have existed in north Munster.

It is difficult to explain the origin of this north Munster group. As none of the localized types appear to have forerunners in Ireland they must be based on external prototypes. But it is difficult to cite exact prototypes and those that have been cited range from northern Europe to the Mediterranean (p. 197). There is no definite proof that gold occurs naturally in north Munster and the copper deposits are located in the south of the province. Was there an *entrepôt* in the lower Shannon valley or was there a landfall of immigrants? Or could it be that local families grew in wealth and that they built up contact with foreign parts and that a native school of metal-working grew up under their auspices? There was material wealth in north Munster but did this area also witness the emergence of new religious practices? The horns could have been used on religious or ceremonial occasions and the hoards, especially the great assemblages, might have been deposited as part of a religious ceremony. This north Munster society was not an exclusive one. In addition to their own specific types they also used 'national' types such as 'dress-fasteners'. But for Munster the negative evidence must also be considered. In this regard the scarcity of tools, for instance, is surprising.

Other types have a distribution that is confined to the northern part of the country. The most localized of these are the gold 'sleeve-fasteners' and striated rings which are largely confined to north-east Ulster. Buckets, cauldrons, disc-headed pins, Class 1 horns, gouges, chisels, socketed sickles, socketed axes (especially the variety with vertical ribs on each face), and knives have their main distribution in the northern and eastern part of the country (Fig. 86, right). These types are of Nordic or British origin, so on geographical grounds one would expect that they were introduced first into the north or east.

Religion, Ceremonies, Ritual

Some of the personal ornaments, such as the large 'dress-fastener' from Castlekelly, Co. Roscommon (Armstrong 1933, 68, Nos 155, Pl. XV: 276) and Clones, Co. Monaghan (Wilde 1862, 60, Fig. 593), may have been intended for wear on ceremonial occasions. Gorgets, too, could have been ceremonial trappings as could have been the gold disc from Lattoon, Co. Cavan (Armstrong 1933, 47) and the multi-stranded chain object which was found near the town of Roscommon (Wilde 1861, 576–7, Fig. 487). In northern Germany gold bowls have been considered as cult vessels (Kossinna 1913). The use of sheet-bronze cauldrons and buckets may also have been confined to special occasions. Bronze horns (trumpets) could have had a ceremonial use (MacWhite 1945; Coles 1963, with 1965).

The horns fall into two main groups. In Coles's Class 1 the body is curved, and some are decorated with incised or moulded motifs (Fig. 87, 1–2). Class 11 horns the decoration, when present, consists of conical spikes (Fig. 87, 3–4). Musically the horns are very restricted in their range of notes as Coles has shown. It is only possible to get one note each from the side horns and not more than four from the end-blow horns. Furthermore, the horns are often imperfectly cast. Repairs are frequent, and in the inside the metal is left rough and this would impair the pitch. Few mouthpieces have survived. These could have been made of organic material in addition to metal and their rarity suggests that when the horns were hidden the mouthpieces were removed so as to prevent misuse.

Enigmatic objects, called crotals, are known from the Dowris hoard. Coles (1965) would also include the crotals among objects that were used during ceremonies. Indeed, he would consider both crotals and horns as being part of a Bull Cult', evidence for which he has detected in various parts of western Europe from about 1000 to 700 B.C., the Irish horns being the bull horn translated into metal and the crotals representing the virility of the bull.

A cremation burial in a pit at Rathgall has been assigned by B. Raftery to the Late Bronze Age (1973). Otherwise there is nothing known about the burial practice of the period but perhaps some of the hoards, as has previously been stated (see p. 179 above, originally in Eogan 1964, 311–14), represent in an oblique way burial practices, the personal belongings of the dead man deposited by his successors. It is possible to interpret other hoards as being deposited to fulfil ritual practices. Even some of the hoards containing broken objects are a feature of the north German 'sacrificial' deposits and also of the grave-goods (Hundt 1955, 101). The symbolic destruction of the metal objects might have been part of a wider cult that also involved the destruction of the body (cremation). Some of the large hoards, the Bog of Cullen, Co. Tipperary and Dowris, Co. Offaly (cf. Eogan 1964, Appendix Nos 69, 58) for instance, may have been the remains of a votive deposit, an offering to a deity. Votive deposits are known from the end of the Bronze Age on the continent. In northern Germany there are the *Opferplätzen* and *Opferfunden* (Hundt 1955, 100ff.; see also Stjernquist 1962–3; Jankuhn 1970). The discovery of so many Irish hoards in bogs shows that they were consciously deposited there. It would be difficult to recover objects from a bog so perhaps they were laid down as an offering to a deity with the intention of not being retrieved. As has been mentioned above, the concentration in Munster of non-utilitarian types and large assemblages, especially around the region of the lower Shannon (p. 208), may have been bound up with cult practices. Some river finds may also have been deposited as part of a ritual practice (Torbrügge 1960, and 1970–1 for the deposition of objects in rivers).

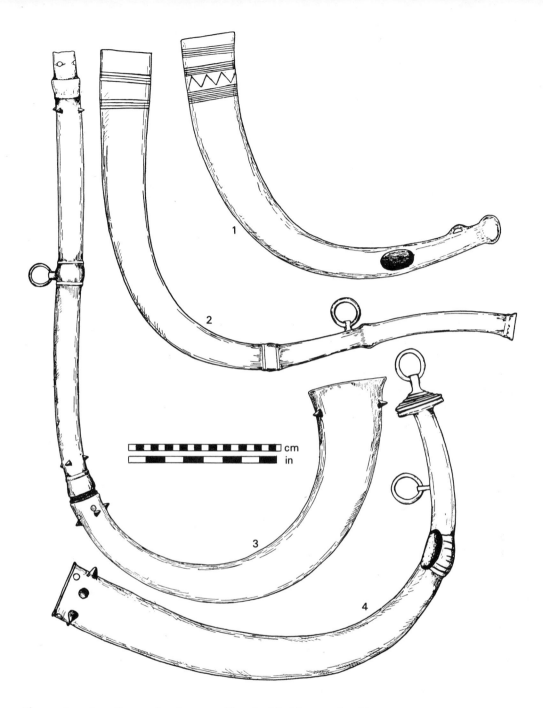

Figure 87 Late Bronze Age horns: 1 Class I, side-blow, Ireland (N.M.I. 1882 : 225); 2 Class I, end-blow, Drumbest, Co. Antrim (N.M.I. 1893 : 17); 3 Class II, end-blow, Clogherclemin, Co. Kerry (N.M.I. 1886 : 37 and 40); 4 Class II, side-blow, Derrynane, Co. Kerry (N.M.I. W. 12), (after Eogan 1964, Fig. 17).

Trade and Transport, External Trade Routes

This was a most important aspect of all periods of the Bronze Age but again evidence is meagre. Dug-out canoes may have provided water transport, while on dry land the horse or the ox may have been used, even yoked in block-wheel carts (p. 187).

It is impossible to say how movement around the country was organized. However, the distribution of certain metal types indicates the approximate position of trade routes out of Ireland. 'Lock-rings' are particularly informative. The distribution of these objects suggests that the area of manufacture was north Munster (Fig. 71, right). From there a route led to the Dublin neighbourhood and then across the sea to north Wales, then over the Pennines and up the Vale of York to Northumberland and finally on to eastern Scotland. It has been postulated that a second route extended from north Munster to the south of England and then across to France (Eogan 1969, esp. pp. 106–10).

The distribution of 'dress-fasteners' and large penannular bracelets with inclined hollow terminals also provides good evidence for trade routes (Fig. 81). Again these appear to have been traded across to north Wales, and over the Pennines and south to East Anglia and finally across the North Sea to Lower Saxony, i.e. Gahlstorf (Hawkes in Hawkes and Clarke 1963, 195ff).

The mould of the Irish type disc-headed pin with bent stem (sunflower pin) with a large central boss from Jarlshof in the Shetlands (Hamilton 1956, Fig. 14, 1) may indicate a route around by the north of Scotland. Irish gold ornaments in the Morvah hoard (Hawkes and Clarke 1963, 231) indicate trade between Ireland and Cornwall. In return Ireland was probably acquiring tin from Cornwall.

Overseas trade implies boats. The only possible evidence for these are the dug-out canoes from Lough Eskragh, Co. Tyrone but such boats would hardly be suitable for high seas. Each boat, or canoe, was originally at least 7·50 m long. Canoe 1 had a maximum beam of 80 cm; in canoe 2 it was 90 cm. The thickness of the hull varied. Both were of oak and were made by the 'dug-out' method. The cross-section tended to be U-shaped with a flat base. In canoe 2 the stern end had been repaired. This involved the hollowing out of that end and the replacement of the solid wood by two transoms of oak which were held in place by a retaining bar and pegs (Collins and Seaby 1960, 27–30).

Origin and Chronology

In discussing these problems one has to rely almost exclusively on the evidence that the metal types provide. On the industrial side new types of far-flung origin appeared. In addition, artifacts of a type that were introduced during the eleventh and twelfth centuries, or modified versions of them, were also in use and with some of these insular modification took place. These include hammers, anvil, 'flesh-fork', tweezers, penannular bracelets with solid evenly expanded terminals, and neck-rings with solid evenly expanded terminals. Of course, it is possible that some of the foregoing types, such as hammers or tweezers, were reintroduced. Saddle-querns could have been in use since Neolithic times and trunnion chisels since the beginning of the Urn culture.

Despite continuity, nevertheless, external influences were of paramount importance. The southern English connection was maintained but there appears to have been fairly close contact with the west Baltic area and to some extent with the Mediterranean area. There may also have been direct contact with western France. At least triple-linked chains, double rings and socketed knives with curved blades have not been found in the south of England.

The *southern English* contribution can be divided into two groups:

1   Modifications of earlier types, i.e. Class 4 swords, short tongue-shaped chapes, socketed sickles, at least the vertically socketed variety, and Class II razors.

2   Types that had recently arrived, or developed, in southern Britain or in north-western France. There are purse-shaped chapes, knives of the Thorndon type, Class 1 tanged chisels, socketed chisels, socketed gouges, Athenry shield, buckets and plain rings. There are also types rarely found in Ireland but which may have come from southern England and include penannular bracelets with coil-ended terminals, rattle-pendants and 'phalerae' (cf. Eogan 1964, 306, 307).

The starting-off point for the southern English influences should have been the 'carp's tongue' province of south-east England and its wider province of north-western France. The Carp's Tongue Sword Complex has an 'Atlantic' component (i.e. the swords themselves) but there is also a Late Urnfield element and, indeed, the Late Urnfield element is strong in Britain well outside the 'carp's tongue' concentration, as is clearly shown in some of the components of hoards such as Welby (Powell 1950) and Heathery Burn (Britton, *Inventaria Archaeologia* G.B. 55, 9th set). From Britain the types could have filtered over by various routes. The Llangwyllog and Ty-Mawr hoards in Anglesey (Lynch 1970, 206–13) with their south British types might mean that Anglesey was an important area of contact.

The *west Baltic element* consists of disc-headed pins (both straight- and bent-stemmed varieties), 'dress-fasteners', bracelets with circle, toggle, horns (at least Class 1) and amber. Possible Nordic derived types are gorgets, bowls, boxes, U-notched shields, rattle pendants, Lattoon disc, concentric ornament and conical spikes. The emphasis on personal ornaments indicates that it closely resembles the contribution that the same area made during the twelfth and eleventh centuries. There is one major difference; during the late second millennium B.C. the Nordic types came by way of the south of Britain, but this was now no longer the case, for around 1000 B.C., first with the Wilburton Complex and then with the Carp's Tongue Sword Complex, the south of Britain became a province, at least on the industrial side, of the west-central European industries and these industries had very little contact with northern Europe. So when Ireland revived her contacts with the west Baltic area (perhaps they were never truly severed) there was no secondary British industry to act as a centre of diffusion. There must now have been fairly direct contact between Ireland and the west Baltic area. At least there is a scarcity of west Baltic types of Period IV/V in any part of Britain and evidence for trade routes across that land is not good. However, if the buttons from the Parc-y-Meirch (Denbighshire) hoard and also the rattle pendants (and this is not certain) are of west Baltic origin then perhaps there might have been a route across to north-east England and on southwards to cross the Pennines leading on to north Wales (cf. Eogan 1969, 108–10).

The prototypes of the Baltic types in Ireland are not concentrated in one limited area. For instance, fibulae of different types are widely distributed in Denmark. The disc-headed pin with straight stem is mainly found in north Jutland and the toggle with straight bar is found in the same area (Baudou 1960, Karte 40 and 50), the armlet with circle principally in Jutland and the Danish islands with outliers to the south in Schleswig-Holstein and as far east as Pomerania (Sprockhoff 1956, II, Karte 42a). Rattle pendants are distributed from Jutland to east Prussia (Thrane 1958, Fig. 3). *Neumärkische Halskragen* possible gorget prototypes) occur in southern Pomerania and the adjoining parts of Poland (Sprockhoff 1956, II, Karte 24).

The presumed *Mediterranean types* are V-notched shields, 'lock-rings' and possibly cauldrons and bullae. The Lattoon disc has been compared to Sardinian shields, and bullae have been found in Phoenician contexts as far west as Spain. The Iberian peninsula probably played a part in the diffusion of these types to Ireland. It is in Iberia that one finds the immediate background to the V-notched shields, although they started off in the eastern Mediterranean area. Conical spikes or rivets and even concentric ornament could theoretically be derived from the Mediterranean. The technique of soldering individual wires together to form a sheet of gold must also have come from the Mediterranean.

Regarding chronology the British prototypes can be dated against Late Urnfield chronology. Conversely the 'lock-rings' in the Saint-Martin-sur-le-Pré hoard were associated with Late Urnfield types and this was also the case in the Heathery Burn deposit (Eogan 1969, 107). The hoards from Morvah, Cornwall (Hawkes and Clarke 1963, Fig. 53) and Walderslade, Kent (Longworth 1966b) consist of Irish ornaments and British ornaments of Late Urnfield type. As the Urnfield cultures were ending around 700 B.C. (Müller-Karpe 1959, 228) the prototypes must have been in use in England during the eighth century. Turning to west Baltic types, the disc-headed pin with straight stem is a Period IV type and some *luren* (possible prototypes for Class I horns) also date from that time. This means that the straight-stemmed disc-headed pin could have arrived in Ireland from say 1000 B.C. But all the other west Baltic types were in use there during Period V, although some could have started in IV. It therefore seems that it was during Period V that the influx from the north of Europe took place. Baudou equates Period V with the Central European Hallstatt B3 of Müller-Karpe. Such an equation would place its beginning at around 800 B.C. (Baudou 1960, 135–7). In the eastern Mediterranean the prototypes of the V-notched shields are considered to have been current from, say, 800. All the evidence, therefore, points to the fact that this period of the Bronze Age started in the course of the eighth century at a time when a number of types converged on Ireland from different areas.

The arrival of new types initiated native development and, indeed, some of the proposed prototypes, such as fibulae for 'dress-fasteners', have not been found in Ireland. Some of the disc-headed pins with bent stem of the primary series could be imports, as are the buckets of Kurd type and possibly triple-linked chains. But the number of actual imports are few and what one has is a variety of types based on foreign prototypes. It is the emergence of naturalized versions that is an important characteristic of the period. The emergence of a secondary series is hard to measure in years. If the two disc-headed pins with bent stem from the Ballytegan hoard belong to the primary series, and they were found with a similar pin but of the secondary series (Raftery 1971, 85–7), this would suggest that the period of experiment and development was rather short. Half a century can be suggested and this was about the time that Hawkes and Smith (1957, 147) reckoned that it took for the 'native' Irish buckets to emerge. While one cannot be completely confident about suggesting absolute dates, it appears that the influx of external types commenced by the beginning of the eighth century and that before the end of that century, possibly by the middle, a new industry had emerged and very soon some of its produce was being exported.

The evidence available indicates that new types, from different sources, were arriving in Ireland simultaneously. It is not possible to say why this happened or the mechanism that brought it about; anyhow, it can hardly be due to chance. As has already been pointed out (p. 186). the eighth century was a time of considerable change in Europe and in certain areas, middle Europe and the Mediterranean in particular, people were on the move. For Ireland, the nearest event of importance was the establishment of the south-eastern English Carp's Tongue Sword Complex and the spread of Late Urnfield bronzes throughout Britain. Greek expansion and Phoenician commercial activities made the Mediterranean a lively place and the Phoenicians had a settlement at Cadiz on the Atlantic coast of southern Spain (Moscati 1968, 230–42). Perhaps the Phoenician trade even extended northwards, or if not there may have been enterprising middle-men. In this connection two points should be remarked on. One is that the main concentration of engravings of V-notched shields is inland from Cadiz; the other is that Professor Hawkes has demonstrated that the boat model from Caergwrle in Flintshire is an imitation of a Phoenician boat (Hawkes 1969, 191).

Regarding the north European types, Hawkes (Hawkes and Clarke 1963, 220) has pointed out that the north Europeans derived a considerable amount of their raw material, copper and gold, from the natural deposits of the Carpathians and the Alps. But there was trouble in central Europe during the eighth century and new people from the east, possibly the 'Cimmerians', may have arrived. It might be that the winning of metal in central Europe was disrupted. This could have caused a scarcity in Nordic lands, and it may have been that the smiths turned to Ireland for alternative supplies. But at this stage it was no longer possible for the bearers of the types to come by southern England because shortly after 1000 that area became a province of the western continental industries, first the Wilburton Complex and second the Carp's Tongue Sword Complex, and contact between southern England and the Nordic world was virtually eliminated. So when contacts between Ireland and the Nordic world were revived the routes went by northern Britain. The shift to northern Britain is clearly demonstrated when we compare the distribution map of gold bar torcs (Fig. 71, left) with the distribution map of 'lock-rings' (Fig. 71, right).

Discussion

Most of our knowledge of the period of the Bronze Age that started in the eighth century is derived from metal types, indeed during this period an industrial and technological revolution took place. The large number of individual types and of hoards clearly shows large-scale production, how abundant metal was, and how prolific the smiths were. That there was a market for these types is a good indication of the wealth of the period and this is further reflected in the lavish use of jewellery. The abundance of metal is also borne out by the number of hoards. For this period there are around eighty-five hoards and although some of these only consist of two objects there are the vast hoards like Dowris, Mooghaun, Bog of Cullen and Askeaton. While it is impossible to say why a particular hoard was deposited (p. 210), yet it is clear that for the first time in Ireland massive hoards appear.

It was a sound economic basis that facilitated the rise of this new industry. Probably the biggest economic factor was the large-scale production of metal but the scarcity of domestic sites makes other economic deductions sketchy. On four occupation sites, Ballinderry, Knocknalappa, Lough Eskragh and Rathgall, saddle-querns were found and further evidence for corn growing is provided by the presence in fair numbers of bronze sickles.

The meagre evidence from Ballinderry and Knocknalappa shows that the inhabitants kept domestic animals. Cattle predominated but pigs, sheep and goats were also kept. At Knocknalappa dog-bones were found. Hunting and fowling was only practised to a very limited extent as is shown from the scarcity of the remains of wild animals and birds. The bones of red deer were found at Ballinderry and if some of the wooden traps (p. 187) date from this period, then this is evidence for deer trapping.

Although it cannot be conclusively established it is very likely that the natural resources of copper and gold were exploited. One workshop where objects were cast is known (Rathgall) and although house plans have not been found the discovery of mould fragments shows that casting took place at Dalkey Island, Rathtinaun, Lough Eskragh, Old Connaught, Bohovny and Whitepark Bay (see p. 192 above). At all of these sites the founder was using clay moulds (for manufacture see p. 193). Clay moulds were the prominent type in use. The almost complete absence of stone moulds in any part of Ireland shows that these had virtually gone out of use.

Not only were the metal craftsmen able to cast new objects but it was also possible for them to repair old pieces and even to cast-on entirely new parts. Although practised in England by smiths of the Wilburton Complex, it is at this stage that the technique of 'casting-on' was mastered in Ireland (Eogan 1965, 5). This technique was used to repair, say, a sword whose hilt had been broken off. It involved the construction of a mould around the object that was to be repaired and extending the matrix beyond the broken end in the shape of the missing portion. The fractured end of the original was often grooved so as to facilitate a bond. The molten metal was poured in and the entirely new part became fused to the old.

It also seems that this was the time when smiths started to use lead as a very definite component in the bronze alloy. Bronze with a high lead content was already being used by southern English smiths during the period of the Wilburton Complex (Smith and Blyn-Stoyle 1959, 193ff.). In the manufacture of objects solder was now commonly used. But probably the greatest achievement of the Irish smiths was their competence in manufacturing large vessels – buckets and cauldrons – from sheet-bronze. In western Europe Irish craftsmen became foremost in sheet-bronze working. Equally significant were their achievements in gold-working. Some of the objects were manufactured from bar-gold, the penannular bracelets with expanded terminals for instance, and these were probably hammered into shape (cf. Maryon 1938, 200–1). Hollow gold-working was also practised. It is, however, in sheet-gold working that one finds the best evidence for the accomplishments of the goldsmiths. In this connection one can instance the gorgets where, amongst other techniques, the skilled use of repoussé work enabled the creation of some of the most outstanding examples of gold ornaments in the Old World. In addition, the skill and ingenuity displayed by the craftsmen in manufacturing from individual wires the face-plates of the lock-rings is without parallel in barbarian Europe of the time and it probably ranks as one of Bronze Age Europe's foremost technical achievements. Twisted wires are also found on bullae where they give a filigree effect (Armstrong 1933, No. 402). In this connection it may be noted that a number of 'hair-rings' were decorated with an inlay, usually of silver solder. This gives the effect of niello (Maryon 1938, 198–9). Another technique was the application of gold leaf over a core or against a backing.

Wood-working was practised. As has been shown, there are a number of wooden vessels that can be assigned to this phase (p. 202). Notched shields, and models for making leather shields, were made from single slabs of wood (p. 197). This evidence, together with the dressing and mortising of the large oak foundation planks of the house at Ballinderry (p. 189), shows that the carpenter, too, was a competent craftsman.

Stone craftsmen were in operation as the presence of saddle-querns shows (p. 187), while leather-workers were capable of producing such large objects as shields out of wooden moulds (see p. 197). Demonstrations carried out by Coles (1962, 175–81) have shown the complicated nature of leather-making. As an animal skin or hide is made up of three layers it was first necessary to remove the outer and inner layers. This was done by a process that involved soaking, kneading and scraping. What was left, the middle layers, was true skin. After further treatment the skin was ready for tanning. Regarding the actual process of making the shield, the leather is first soaked, then placed on a mould, such as Churchfield or Kilmahamogue, and pressed and beaten into the central hollow and into the grooves. After being removed from the mould the shield may have been impregnated with wax so as to harden it and make it water-resistant. The shield from Clonbrin was, then, a perfectly serviceable piece. Tanged chisels could have been leather-workers' tools (Roth 1974).

The piece of cloth from Cromaghs (p. 199) and the spindle-whorls from Ballinderry No. 2 and Knocknalappa (p. 188) show that weavers were operating. The ornaments of horse-hair from Cromaghs are further evidence for the skills of the textile worker. The Cromaghs objects clearly demonstrate the dexterity and expertise of the weaver and show that the arts and crafts of the textile-workers were just as skilful as those of the metal-workers.

Bone and antler were also worked, as were amber and jet (or lignite).

The craftsman had a good range of tools, viz. hammers, chisels, gouges, anvils, and knives. Socketed axeheads could have been used not only for felling trees but for the subsequent working of the timber. The presence of hoards that exclusively contain tools such as Crevilly-valley, Co. Antrim (Raftery 1942b, 130–1), Glastry, Co. Down (*Archaeological Survey, Co. Down*, 1966, 65, Fig. 15:7–9), Crossna, Co. Roscommon (Sprockhoff 1956, I, Abb. 14: 1–5), Ross, Co. Tipperary (Coffey 1907b, 86–9) and Ballinderry, Co. Westmeath (Sprockhoff 1956, I, Abb. 14:6–14) is a clear indication of the presence of specialist craftsmen. These hoards appear to consist of the kit of a carpenter or somebody working organic materials. This indicates that the carpenter must have been an important member of society at this time and that the evidence that we have of wooden objects or wood-working is only a tiny fraction of what existed originally.

The Irish industry became an exporter. 'Lock-rings', 'dress-fasteners' and large penannular bracelets with inclined, evenly expanded terminals were exported to Britain and the bracelets also to the continent.

On the whole it can be said that during the eighth century an industry based on foreign prototypes, but to a lesser extent on new naturalized types, emerged. Its smiths were prolific manufacturers and also innovators; the innovations of the smiths at this time are a most characteristic feature. Indeed, imported prototypes are exceedingly rare; what exists are derivative types that have a characteristic Irish stamp. This was partly achieved by the borrowing and pooling of techniques and features and it is clearly demonstrated on the buckets and cauldrons. In the manufacture of insular buckets the ribbed staple handle attachment was borrowed from the cauldron. On the other hand the insular cauldron has such bucket features as the neck corrugation, the in-bending and rolling around a wire of the rim, the body made from riveted sheets and the altering of the form of the body from a spherical to a high-shouldered shape (Hawkes and Smith 1957, 164–5).

It is clear that from a sound economic foundation based on farming and on native supplies of copper and gold a wealthy society emerged in Ireland during the eighth century. The mundane and aesthetic needs of this society were supplied by skilled craftsmen whose achievements rank with the best in the Europe of the day and whose produce also found a market outside Ireland.

Finally, on the industrial side there is evidence for regional groupings (p. 208). This may be due to influences reaching different parts of Ireland from different sources. Thus the end of the Bronze Age, as was its beginning, may also have been of dual origin.

The End of the Bronze Age

Despite the great technological and industrial achievements of the Dowris phase, this phase was the swan song of the Irish Bronze Age. Towards 700 B.C. the Bronze Age of Middle Europe was being replaced by the first phase of the Iron Age. This is Hallstatt C of Reinecke's terminology (Reinecke 1965; also Kossack 1959).

From their original homeland in the northern foothills of the Alps Hallstatt people spread northwards and westwards and, seemingly, within a fairly short space of time they reached the North Sea coast, as Mariën's investigations at Court-Saint-Etienne in Belgium have shown (Mariën 1958). Very soon Hallstatt C types were arriving in Britain as some of the objects in the Llyn Fawr hoard, Glamorganshire show (Fox 1939b).

In Ireland during the seventh century a way of life that had been established during the eighth century continued. Augmentations to the material culture were taking place from the already established areas of external contact. Cauldrons of Class B (see p. 204) came into use. Seemingly connections, albeit tentative, were kept up with the west Baltic area. The suggested evidence for this is provided by the cup-headed pins (Baudou 1960, 83).

Limited connections with southern Britain survived. There are a few axes of the Sompting type (Burgess 1969b). It was probably by way of southern Britain that the small number of axeheads of Breton type reached this country (Briard 1965, 241–82, Fig. 107 for distribution).

But it is a new form of bronze sword (Fig. 88, 1) and chape that are the chief representatives, albeit stages removed, of the dawning central European Iron Age. These swords, Class 5 of Eogan (1965, 13–15), are a late and insular version of the Gündlingen swords, a type fossil of the Hallstatt C cultures (Cowen 1967).

There are two groups of chapes. One group consists of 'boat-shaped' chapes. The other group consists of winged chapes (Fig. 88, 2–3; Eogan 1965, 170). The bronze bracelet with bulbous terminals and bands of transverse body decoration from Kilmurry, Co. Kerry was probably worn around this time (Eogan 1964, 320). The flesh-fork from Dunaverney, Co. Antrim (British Museum 1953, 32) has been considered as a Hallstatt C import by Powell (Scott and Powell 1969, 125, f.n. 3).

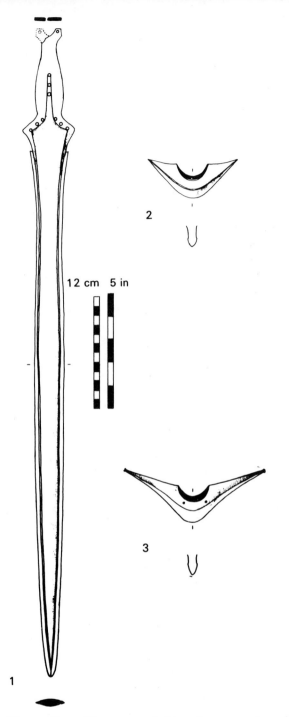

12 cm   5 in

Figure 88 1 Class 5 sword, River Bann near Lough Beg, Toome, Cos Antrim/Derry (U.M. A465: 1975); 2 boat-shaped chape (Class 4a), Keeloge, Co. Galway (N.M.I. W. 286); 3 winged chape (Class 4b), Ireland (N.M.I. P. 744).

The work of Kossack (1959) in particular has placed the Hallstatt C cultures in a secure chronological context. It is now generally agreed that the Hallstatt C cultures were emerging in the decade or so on either side of 725. In view of the close similarity between Court-Saint-Etienne, both in burial and in material, it would seem that those horse-using Hallstatt C people got as far north as Belgium by fairly early in the seventh century. Again a number of the Llyn Fawr objects can be closely paralleled at Court-Saint-Etienne so it would seem that Britain was receiving Hallstatt C types by the middle of the seventh century. It was later that Hallstatt C types reached Ireland, the material is less abundant and the continental element is weak. This is shown by the swords which come at the end of the series according to Cowen (1967, esp. pp. 406–9). Nevertheless, it would appear that Hallstatt C types reached Ireland before the end of the seventh century. The problem of how they arrived has not yet been solved. On the continent well armed cavaliers who were capable of leading and dominating were part of Hallstatt C society but Hallstatt C culture, as the term is understood on the continent, is absent in Britain. It may be that some groups of people, including possibly blacksmiths, crossed over. The sword evidence suggests that the main area of influence was south-east and eastern Britain (Burgess 1968c, Fig. 19). It is this British material that offers the background to the Irish material. But whether this material was initially introduced as a result of the arrival of people, even a small infiltration, or as a result of a continuing process of peaceful contacts, such as trade, is a problem that still remains outstanding. The fact that one finds Class 4 swords modified under the influence of Class 5 swords (Eogan 1965, 12) is an indication that the Late Bronze Age industry continued. How long is not, as yet, known but even if the Hallstatt C elements do not in themselves bring about an alteration yet they are indicative of the New World of the Iron Age that was about to dawn.

CHAPTER TEN

Later Prehistoric Events: The Iron Age and the Celts

Background

At the end of the previous chapter reference was made to the Iron Age. In the general sequence of technological events in Europe the use of iron comes after that of bronze. The period stretching from the late seventh century through the succeeding centuries is one of the more obscure periods in Irish prehistory. It is, however, possible that formative events took place during these centuries. It may even have been the time that Celtic settlement took place. A new technology was probably also introduced but over-use of the term 'Iron Age' can limit a wider appreciation of the period. The first fixed point in the 'Iron Age' is provided by the fine bronze-work decorated in the La Tène style and dating from late in the first millennium B.C. But the outstanding question is what events took place between, say, 600 B.C. and 200 B.C. Was a new culture established and if so was the change brought about by the arrival of new people? The answer may be held by the hill-forts, a western multivallate group and an eastern univallate group (p. 227). Now, attention has already been drawn to the regional distribution of some metal artifacts of the final phase of the Bronze Age (p. 208). At that time a distribution pattern emerged and this pattern continued into the Early Christian period (Eogan 1974b). In view of the distribution patterns it is tempting to suggest that a south-western industrial province with its abundance of gold (Eogan 1964, Fig. 19) might be linked with the occupiers of the multivallate hill-forts while the users of some of the artifacts that have a predominantly north-eastern distribution might be part of the other cultural province that had univallate hill-forts; in other words that people of the final phase of the Bronze Age in two different regions of Ireland took to the building of different forms of large-scale settlement site. At present there is not enough evidence to prove this point. On the other hand there is the possibility that the multivallate and univallate hill-forts document the arrival of new people. As will be argued below, it is possible that there is an assemblage of monuments – promontory forts, stone forts, souterrains – of which the multivallate hill-fort is only a part. Furthermore, the hill-forts lack insular forerunners and their construction was a formidable task. But above all their presence suggests a new, possibly intrusive, society with tribal centres and probably chiefs. This new society had its bronze-smiths but very likely they were joined by the blacksmith.

This chapter mainly consists of a description of the material remains, field monuments and portable antiquities, but an attempt at a historical interpretation of this material is also made. The range of portable antiquities is not large and the majority of these that have survived were made from bronze; indeed it seems that most of the prestige objects were made from bronze. However, iron, unlike bronze, is much more prone to destruction by agencies such as rust, so the objects that are available in collections are probably only a small fraction of the range of tools, weapons and implements that were in use.

In many ways iron is a more useful metal than bronze. The ores are more widely distributed and it was cheaper to produce iron rather than bronze artifacts. However, the smelting of iron ores for metal is a difficult technique to develop and even after attaining competence the objects produced would be soft. Therefore, it was not until the added technique of carburization had been devised for hardening and toughening the forged metal, and thereby producing a keener edge, that the widespread use of iron took place. Carburization involved hammering repeatedly the red-hot bloom in contact with charcoal so as to introduce carbon (Clark 1952, 199).

The knowledge of iron-working seems to have emerged before the middle of the second millennium B.C. In Armenia the Chalybes, a people that were subject to the Hittite kings, were working iron from an early date. As a result the Hittites had a monopoly in iron-working (Clark 1952, 199–200). The collapse of the Hittite confederation about 1200 B.C. may have been a factor that contributed to the spread of the knowledge of iron-working. The use of iron became widespread in central Europe during the latter half of the eighth century, Hallstatt C. It appears that it was the Hallstatt C people who diffused the knowledge of iron-working to western and northern Europe. Objects from the Llyn Fawr hoard, Glamorganshire (Fox 1939b) show that iron artifacts were being made in Britain by 600 B.C. The use of iron became more widespread during the sixth century as the manufacture of daggers indicates (Jope 1961). It is not known when iron-working spread to Ireland. The earliest definite evidence, swords of La Tène type (p. 236), are hardly earlier than the second century B.C. Iron ore occurs in Ireland, an important source being the interbasaltic laterites of Co. Antrim (Scott 1974, 19) but bog-ore could also have been used (Clark 1952, 202).

The beginnings of the later prehistoric events in Ireland coincide with changes in west-central Europe, especially in eastern France and the Rhineland. During the sixth century, mainly in Burgundy and Württemberg, a rich and aristocratic society emerged. This is called Hallstatt D. The chieftains of this society had strongholds and they often buried their dead with considerable pomp in lavishly furnished graves.

Around 500 B.C. violence brought a dislocation in Hallstatt D society (Hawkes 1965, 11; Piggott 1965, 175–207). Soon a resurgence took place, not in the old Hallstatt D territory but north of it in the lands bordering the Saar and Moselle. There richly furnished graves and possibly princely courts re-appear. This is the beginning of the second main phase of the continental Iron Age, the La Tène period. This phase is characterized by innovations and by practical improvements in the material culture. Large semi-urban centres called *oppida* and the use of coinage show that an incipient urban society was emerging.

A distinctive feature of the La Tène people is their art, 'the first conscious art style to be created in Europe north of the Alps' (Powell 1966, 185). This art, or Celtic Art as it is usually called, is largely abstract and motifs such as spirals, lyre pattern and curved lines dominate. In origin Celtic art is a blending of various elements that were borrowed from different sources, Hallstatt, Scythian, Oriental, Greek and Etruscan. By skilful mingling and transformation the La Tène artist created 'a real style, the first great contribution by the barbarians to the European arts, the first great chapter in the everlasting mutual stock-taking of Southern, Northern, and Eastern forces in the life of Europe' (Jacobsthal 1944, 163, see also Megaw 1970; Sandars 1968, 226).

Whatever about earlier cultures it is certainly possible to equate the bearers of the La Tène cultures with the Celts. Initially the Celts consisted of a loose confederation of people around central and west-central Europe but soon they overran large parts of Europe. In Italy they contributed to the downfall of the Etruscan civilization and in 390 they attacked Rome. To the south, they had reached northern Greece by 300 and within the next generation they had established themselves in Asia Minor. There they became known as the Galatians, a people who were later addressed by St Paul in his Epistles. The Celts also spread westwards across France and on to Britain and Ireland. But from 240 B.C. the contraction of Celtic power started. In that year they were defeated in Asia Minor and in 225 they suffered a crushing blow at the hands of the Romans at Telamon. Eventually the Romans dominated them north of the Alps and in most of Britain after A.D. 43 (on the Celts see Powell 1958; Filip 1960; Chadwick 1970).

Occupation Sites

Probably the most common site was the single protected farmstead. These are termed crannógs and ring-forts.

A crannóg is an artificial island that was built in a lake or marsh. The first phase of Lagore, Co. Meath, which was constructed from alternating layers of peat and brushwood, may have been built during the prehistoric Iron Age (Hencken 1950, 6). At Lisnacrogher, Co. Antrim, Wakeman observed large quantities of timber and 'encircling stakes, and wickerwork'. Some of the beams had mortices (Wakeman 1883, 377). It has not been established conclusively that the range of metal objects that were found in Lisnacrogher bog actually came from the structure. These include bronze scabbard plates, iron swords, an iron spear-head and eight bronze spear-butts. If these objects came from a crannóg then it must have been the home of either a 'war-lord' or an artificer. The origin of crannógs is as yet unsolved but lake-side settlements, even artificial islands of a sort, were occupied during the final phase of the Late Bronze Age (pp. 187–92).

The term ring-fort is being used as a generic name for a dryland protected homestead where a farmer and his family lived and where he may also have housed some of his domestic animals. Usually a ring-fort consists of a circular area of varying size (about 25 m is average diameter) that is surrounded by single or multiple banks and ditches which normally occur outside the banks. A causeway interrupts these and this provides an entrance to the interior. The entrance was closed by a gate. A structure (usually a central round house) or structures stood within. The material used in the building of the banks is normally determined by local geology. In the earthen forts the banks consist of material thrown up from the ditches. In the stone forts the central area is enclosed by a wall which was generally built from surface collected stones and not material dug from a ditch. It is usual for ring-forts to occur in isolation. Conjoined examples, are, however, known, such as the Forradh and Teach Cormaic at Tara (Fig. 90). At Cush in Co. Limerick there are groups of forts (Fig. 89). Ring-forts, with crannógs, continued to be lived in and constructed throughout the Early Christian period and their use even extended well into mediaeval times (for a comprehensive account of ring-forts, see Westropp 1901).

Although the term ring-fort is being used this must not be taken as implying that the sites were strongholds of a military nature. Strictly speaking the term is not a correct one but it is being retained pending an agreed name. Colloquially ring-forts are known under a variety of names, *lios*, *rath*, *dún*, *caiseal*, *cathair*, and *daingean*. Originally some of these terms meant parts of the homestead. *Lios* was the open space in the centre, while *rath* meant the surrounding bank and ditch. *Caiseal* and *cathair* are terms applied to the stone forts and the terms *dún* and *daingean* seem to have been reserved for the more heavily fortified structures (cf. O'Kelly 1970a, 50–1).

Probably between 30,000 and 40,000 ring-forts were erected over a period of at least 1500 years, although of course it cannot be stated how many of these were erected during the Iron Age. There is, however, positive evidence that a number were erected and used during the prehistoric Iron Age. Earthen forts include Ráth na Seanaid (Rath of the Synods), Tara (Ó Ríordáin 1960, 21–2), Cush, Co. Limerick (Ó Ríordáin 1940), Feerwore, Co. Galway (Raftery 1944b) and Lugg, Co. Dublin (Kilbride-Jones 1950).

Although there is no evidence from excavation some of the stone forts, especially those of the southern and western seaboard, may also have been built during the Iron Age (for accounts of stone forts see Westropp 1897, 1901). A good example is the fort at Staigue, Co. Kerry (Plate 15b). This is 27 m in diameter. The wall is battered, it rises to a height of 5.50 m and it is 4 m wide. Internally there is a series of steps, elaborately constructed, leading on to terraces. There is a ditch on the outside.

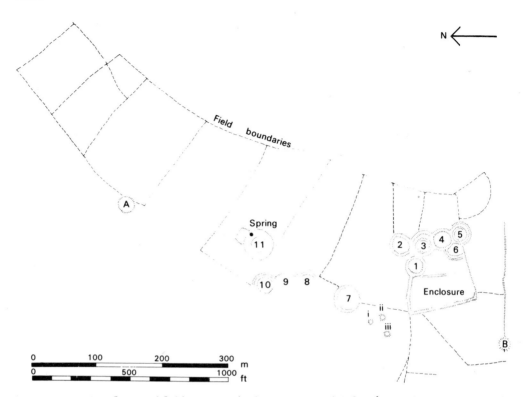

Figure 89 Ring-forts and field systems, Cush, Co. Limerick (after Ó Ríordáin, 1940, Fig. 2).

The entrance was a narrow lintelled doorway through the wall on the south side (Evans 1966, 134). Another important stone fort is Caher Ballykinvarga, Co. Clare (Harbison 1971, 203). This fort is 51·5 m in maximum diameter. The wall is over 4 m thick and 5 m in height. Like Staigue the wall has vertical joints on the outside face. Internally there are two terraces. The entrance was lintelled. The fort is almost completely surrounded by a *chevaux-de-frise* (see p. 228).

The origin of the ring-fort has not been satisfactorily established. Some authorities consider them as native and S. P. Ó Ríordáin (1953, 3) saw their forerunners in protected Neolithic or Early Bronze Age habitation sites at Knockadoon, Lough Gur. These sites consist of a circular enclosure defined by two concentric circles of upright stones. A stone enclosure excavated by O'Kelly at Carrigillihy, Co. Cork (O'Kelly 1951) has been dated by him to the Early Bronze Age. S. P. Ó Ríordáin proposed a Bronze Age date for the Cush sites. However, this dating is no longer tenable. Although by nature ring-forts are of simple plan, the enclosing of a circular area by a bank and ditch does not require much inventive power, and still there is no proof that the Knockadoon enclosures were forerunners of the ring-fort. It therefore seems more reasonable to consider that the ring-fort was introduced during the Iron Age,

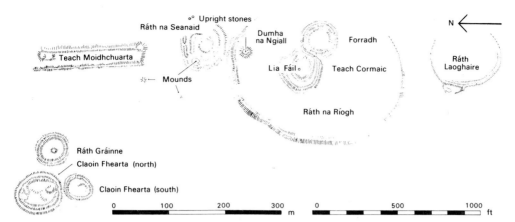

Figure 90   Tara, Co. Meath. Ground plan of the hill showing the principal sites.

but from whence it came is not yet clear. Stone ring-forts (*cashels*), such as the Staigue example, bear a close resemblance to Cornish stone forts like Chun Castle (Leeds 1926–7) and Leeds (esp. 235) has drawn attention, both on architectural grounds and on the finds, e.g. duck-stamped pottery, to similar features which occur in the Celtic areas of the north-west of the Iberian peninsula. However, in dealing with ring-fort origins another type of monument must be considered. These are the single or isolated farmsteads of Iron Age Britain. As Jope (*U.J.A.*, 17 (1954), 187) has pointed out, ring-forts closely resemble some of the British farmsteads (e.g. Micklemoor Hill, West Harling, Norfolk: Clark and Fell 1953, 6–10). Such farmsteads also occur in Scotland (e.g. West Plean, Stirlingshire: Steer 1955–6).

On the whole it does appear that the ring-fort is a new type of monument that was introduced during the Iron Age. Two alternative suggestions as to its origin have been put forward. It is difficult to know which one is correct but it may be the former and this point will again be returned to.

Another type of occupation site was the promontory fort. The promontory, in nearly all cases jutting into the sea, was naturally defended so it was only necessary to erect defences, a single or multiple bank and ditch, on the landward side. Some of the promontory forts have terraces on the inner faces of the banks (O'Kelly 1952b, 33). These features can be paralleled in Cornwall and Brittany. It therefore appears that the promontory fort was introduced from Atlantic Europe.

The most impressive occupation site of all is the hill-fort (Fig. 93, right). This is a fortified site, usually of several acres, that consists of a bank and ditch or more than one bank and ditch surrounding a hilltop. In some examples full advantage was taken of the natural setting and the bank and ditch follow the contour of the hill. Hill-forts may have served as tribal rather than as family centres. The hill-fort is a common monument throughout the Celtic world. Its origin goes well back into the Bronze Age (Piggott 1965, 202). At least fifty hill-forts are known in Ireland and these can be

227

divided into two main groups (Raftery 1972a), univallate sites (Group I) and multivallate sites (Group II). As the name implies, the univallate sites have a single line of defence (Fig. 95, top). Otherwise they vary in the extent of the area enclosed, in structure and in positioning. The area enclosed may vary from one acre as at Dunbeg, Co. Down (Inskeep and Proudfoot 1957) to almost forty acres as at Dún Ailinne, Co. Kildare (Wailes 1970). At some sites, Dún Ailinne, Ráth na Ríogh, Eamhain Macha (Plate 15a) and Clogher, the ditch occurs on the inside of the bank.

Most of the univallate forts occupy the summits of low, rounded hills that overlook good fertile agricultural land. They have a predominantly eastern distribution, from Antrim southwards to Kilkenny (Fig. 93, right). The presence of earlier monuments at a number of sites, for instance the Passage Grave within Ráth na Ríogh at Tara, suggests that the univallate hill-fort builders selected hilltops that already had an aura of sanctity attached to them (Byrne 1968). A number of places where univallate hill-forts occur were 'Royal' sites (see below). The dating evidence for univallate hill-forts is not very precise. It can only be said that they were lived in during the prehistoric Iron Age and that their use continued later.

The multivallate hill-forts mainly occur in the western part of the country from Cork to Donegal (Fig. 95, bottom). In view of their distribution they are usually built from stone, this being the material that was most readily available. The characteristic feature is a central citadel. The citadel is the most massively constructed of all the enclosing walls and structurally it is similar to some of the stone ring-forts, for example Staigue (p. 225). Lintelled doorways are known. On the inside of the walls terraces with steps give access to the top. The citadel is surrounded by a number, often three, of widely-spaced walls or banks. Although horseshoe-shaped in ground plan the great sites of Cahercommaun, Co. Clare and Dún Aengusa, Inishmore, Aran Islands must be related (Hencken 1938; Evans 1966, 118–21).

A feature of Dún Aengusa, at the promontory forts of Dubh Cathair, Aran and Doonamo, Co. Mayo, and at the stone ring-fort at Ballykinvarga, Co. Clare, is that there is a band of upright stones set close to each other presumably for the purpose of providing added defence. This feature is called a *chevaux-de-frise*. It is known from a small number of sites in Scotland, Wales and the Isle of Man. On the continent there is a limited number of sites in France and Germany but it is in Spain that the feature is most numerous (Harbison 1971).

On typological grounds multivallate hill-forts could have their origin in north-western Iberia. It may also be recalled that the type is found in Cornwall and west Devon (Fox 1961).

Royal Sites and Assembly Sites

At least six univallate hill-forts formed part of what is described in the literature as Royal Sites, places where kings lived. These are Ráth na Ríogh at Tara, Dún Ailinne, Eamhain Macha, Clogher, Cornaskee and Downpatrick. Except for Downpatrick the

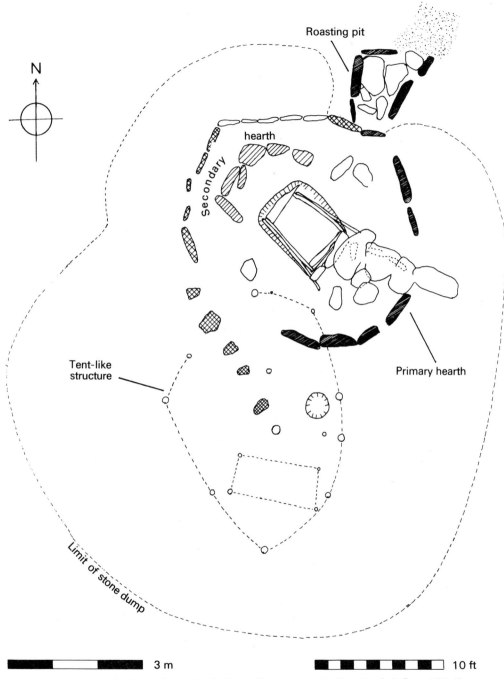

N

Roasting pit

hearth

Secondary

Tent-like
structure

Primary hearth

Limit of stone dump

3 m

10 ft

Figure 91 Ground plan of *fulacht fiadh*, Ballyvourney I, Co. Cork (after O'Kelly 1954, Fig. 2).

229

fosse is on the inside of the bank. Tara has the most complex series of earthworks (Macalister 1931; Ó Riordáin 1960) but at Eamhain Macha, Clogher and possibly Cornaskee there is a ring-fort within the enclosure (cf. Evans 1966, 60, 200, 115).

There are other royal residences at assembly sites that do not incorporate a hill-fort. Probably the most important of these is Rathcroghan (Cruachain), Co. Roscommon, the royal residence of the kings of Connacht (Killanin and Duignan 1967, 408–9). Here, the earthworks are scattered. Amongst the sites are ring-forts, barrows and other earthworks. The Hill of Uisneach in Co. Westmeath, anciently believed to have been the centre of Ireland, and its immediate neighbourhood is rich in monuments. The sites include four ring-forts, six mounds or cairns, three enclosures, one road, one rectangular platform of stones and a large ice-borne boulder (Aill na Míreann). Some of the sites were excavated in the 1920s (Macalister and Praeger, 1928–9; 1930–1). Both Cruachain and Uisneach were assembly places and it was at Uisneach that the Bealtaine festival was held annually on 1 May.

Other important assembly sites were Teltown (Tailteann) and Tlachtga, both in Co. Meath. The festival of Lughnasa – Aonach Tailteann – was held at Tailteann at the beginning of August. Today only two large monuments survive. One of these, Knockans (Crockans), consists of two banks and a ditch between. These are nearly 100 m long. One bank is close to 4 m in height; the other bank is much lower. It is just possible that this is the last remnant of a hill-fort. About half a mile away from Knockans there is a ring-fort, Rath Dubh. Tlachtga, or the Hill of Ward, close to Athboy, consists of a multivallate hilltop ring-fort. It was here that the assembly of Samhain (31 October) took place.

An earthwork that does not fit any of the foregoing categories occurs at Dorsey, Co. Armagh. This is an elongated enclosure of about 300 acres. On firm ground the enclosure is defended by one or two banks and ditches (Tempest 1930–2, 187–240; Davies 1940, 31–7; Evans 1966, 58–9).

Linear Earthworks

There is a series of earthworks across Ireland from south Down to south Donegal, the 'Black Pig's Dyke'. These earthworks usually consist of a bank between two ditches. They are not continuous but rather stretch between lakes and marshes. Kane (1908–9, 321; 1916–17, 539) put forward the view that the Black Pig's Dyke was the frontier of the kingdom of Ulster, but Davies (1955, 33) would simply consider them as short entrenchments that straddled roads or crossings so as to prevent cattle raiding. The Black Pig's Dyke may have been to some extent modelled on Roman frontier *limes*.

Souterrains

These are underground chambers which are associated with occupation sites, usually

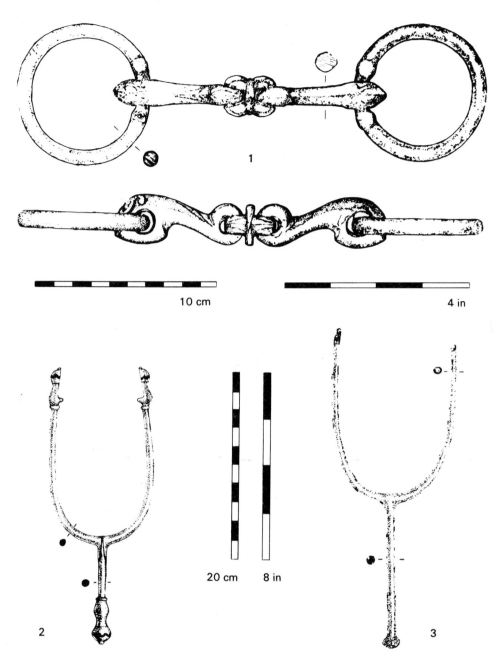

Figure 92 1 Bronze bridle-bit Clongill, Co. Meath (N.M.I. 1963: 101, found with 3); 2–3 Y-shaped bronze pieces, 2 Type I, Knockmany, Co. Tyrone (Co. Museum, Armagh 137–1956), 3 Type II, Clongill (N.M.I. 1963: 102). (Nos 1 and 3 after *J.R.S.A.I.*, 96 (1966), 13, Figs 2–3; No. 2 after Haworth 1971, Fig. 10.)

ring-forts. Evidence for the construction of souterrains during the Iron Age comes from Cush, Co. Limerick. Most of these are simple structures that consist of a more or less parallel-sided trench that was lined along the sides with dry-walling and roofed with lintels (Ó Ríordáin 1940, 92, 96, 97–100, 103, 113, 128–9, 131).

Cooking-places

These monuments which are often referred to as *fulachta fiadh* ('deer roasts') or *fulachta fiann* (cooking places of the Fianna) (Ó Ríordáin 1953, 43–5; O'Kelly 1954, esp. pp. 135–46) are more common in the southern part of the country, especially in Cork and Kerry, than in the northern part. Their location is a damp, low-lying area near a stream. The function of a *fulacht fiadh* was for boiling meat and basically the monument consisted of a wooden trough that was inserted into a rectangular-shaped pit (Fig. 91). The trough was filled with water and this was brought to the boil, and kept boiling, by dropping in hot stones. The stones were heated at a nearby hearth. Some of the sites such as Ballyvourney I and Drombeg both in Co. Cork had a complex of monuments such as a hut, a roasting oven and pits (O'Kelly 1954, 105–23; Fahy 1960). Drombeg was probably used for prolonged periods but the lack of evidence for permanent occupation indicated that *fulachta fiadh* were only used seasonally, possibly for short periods as hunting camps during the summer. The meagre evidence available suggests that the use of *fulachta fiadh* could have ranged from early in the Bronze Age down to mediaeval times (Ó Ríordáin 1953, 43–5). Their origin is unknown. Analogous sites occur in Wales and to a lesser extent in Scotland and England (O'Kelly 1954, 135–46).

Farming

A feature of Iron Age Ireland seems to have been protected farmsteads, crannógs and ring-forts (p. 224). At Cush, Co. Limerick a group of fields is associated with ring-forts (Fig. 89). The majority tended to be rectangular in plan; some were up to 213 m (700 ft) long and nearly 91 m (300 ft) wide. They were bounded by a bank and ditch. The ditch was 1 m (3 ft 3⅜ in) in depth and at the time of excavation the bank was 50 cm (20 in) in height (Ó Ríordáin 1940, 139–46).

Bones from excavated occupation sites at Feerwore, Cush, Freestone Hill and Dún Ailinne show that domestic animals were kept (Raftery 1944b, 49; Ó Ríordáin 1940, 173–4; Raftery 1969, 99, 104–7; Wailes 1970). Cattle were the most common animals but pigs, sheep and horse were also kept. The sheep were shorn with iron shears; there is an example from a human burial at Site B, Carbury, Co. Kildare (Willmot 1938, Fig. 5). Shears frequently occur in Iron Age contexts in France and in Britain (Déchelette 1927, 786–90).

Bronze bridle-bits and Y- or spur-shaped pieces indicate that the horse was harnessed, at least in parts of the country, around the first century B.C.–A.D. (Haworth

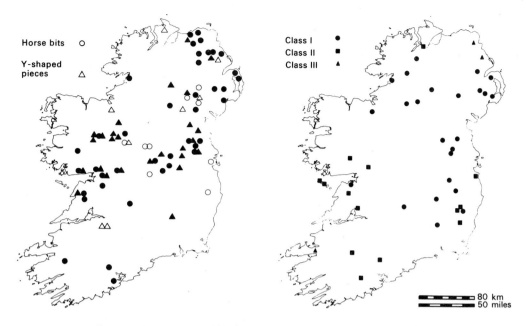

Figure 93 Left: Distribution of bridle-bits and Y-shaped pieces (based on Haworth 1971, Figs 12–13). Right: Distribution of hill-forts (based on B. Raftery 1972a, Fig. 14).

1971; see Fig. 93, left). The bits have a three-link mouth-piece and a ring on each side. The earlier forms, Haworth's Type A, is an adaptation of the English three-link bit. In Ireland the side links were pierced in the same place whereas in England they were pierced at right angles. In later and more native forms (Types B-E) the side links become bowed. Their outer end extends into the circumference of the ring and they are decorated (Fig. 92, 1). There are two forms of Y-shaped pieces (Fig. 92, 2–3). In Type I there are distinctive mouldings at the ends. In Type II the end of the shaft has a knot and the ends of the fork are flat and perforated. The precise function and place of origin of the Y-shaped pieces have not been established but they are a 'striking and exclusive feature of the Irish Iron Age' (Jope 1950, 59).

Positive evidence for vehicles is virtually non-existent (Greene 1972, for chariots). Two objects, allegedly from Lough Gur, may have been sheaths from the tips of draught poles of chariots (Fox 1950, 190–2). A wooden yoke from some place in Ireland might have been used for drawing a chariot (Piggott 1949, 192–3). A bronze terret, a Scottish second-century A.D. type, is claimed to have been found in Co. Antrim (Jope 1950, 59). Asymmetric wear on some bridle-bits provides evidence for paired draught (Jope 1955, 38).

Quern stones provide indirect evidence of corn-growing (Fig. 94). A new type, the rotary quern, was introduced. There are two types: one has flat, disc-shaped stones; in the other type the upper stone is bee-hive shaped. Bee-hive querns are mainly

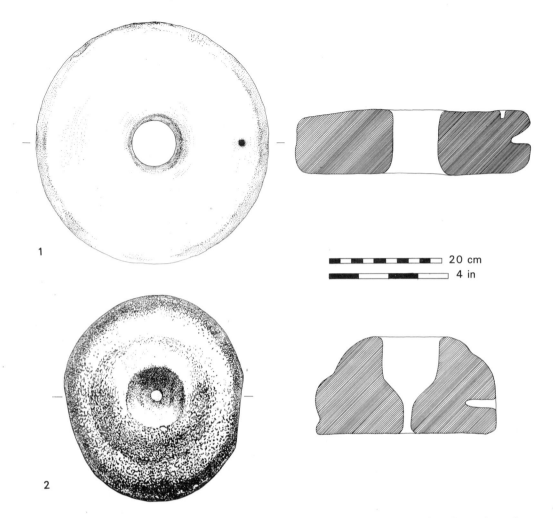

20 cm

4 in

Figure 94 Rotary querns: 1 disc-shaped quern, Cush, Co. Limerick; 2 bee-hive-shaped quern, Bunnafinglas, Co. Mayo (N.M.I. 1963: 72, after *J.R.S.A.I.*, 96 (1966), 19, Fig. 7).

found in the north-east and some are decorated with rectilinear or curvilinear motifs (Griffiths 1951).

Tools and Weapons

Iron slag and whetstones were found in the Cush and Feerwore ring-forts (Ó Ríordáin 1940, 154; Raftery 1944b, 32, 38). Whetstones are also known from other Iron Age sites (e.g. Freestone Hill, Raftery 1969, 51–8). Iron-smelting took place on the site of Ráth na Seanaid, Tara and on Freestone Hill. Enamel-working was also carried out on

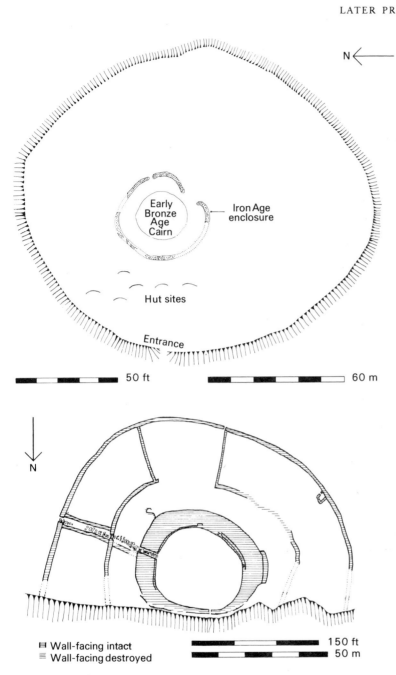

Figure 95 Top: ground plan of Group I hill-fort, Freestone Hill, Co. Kilkenny (after B. Raftery 1969, Fig. 3). Bottom: ground plan of Group II hill-fort, Cahercommaun, Co. Clare (after Hencken 1938, Pl. 2).

235

the Tara site and glass-making at Freestone Hill (Ó Ríordáin 1960, 22; Raftery 1969, 98). The chamber of a Passage Grave, Cairn H, at Loughcrew may have been used as a workshop. Significant finds from this site include bone plaques with compass-drawn designs, mainly loose curves in various combinations, on the surface. These plaques might have been pieces on which the bronze craftsmen tried out his designs before applying them to metal objects. Other finds include an iron punch, and the possible leg of a compass, green and blue glass beads, amber beads and iron rings (Conwell 1873, 51–8; Crawford 1925).

Regarding iron tools the presence of a punch and possibly a compass leg at Cairn H has already been noted. A small number of looped, socketed axeheads and 'shaft-hole' axeheads are known (Scott 1974, 12; Rynne 1958). Feerwore produced a non-socket chisel and tanged one-edged knives (Raftery 1944b, 34–5).

A number of iron spear-heads are known but it is difficult to isolate examples that can be assigned to the Iron Age. Possible examples are those from the neighbourhood of Castleconnell, Co. Limerick and Lisnacrogher, Co. Antrim (Armstrong 1923, 20, Pl. I: 1, Fig. 5). There are two main forms of spear-butt and both are made from bronze. One form is elongated and tapers from mouth to base (Fig. 96, 4); there is a moulding around the head and base. Line ornament often occurs and some had enamel settings. Due to their shape the second form have been termed 'door knob' spear-butts (Raftery 1951, 194). This type also occurs in Scotland (British Museum 1925, 158, Fig. 190).

The swords are shorter than their British and continental counterparts. Except for the fittings they are made from iron (Fig. 96, 1). There are two blade forms. In one (e.g. sword from Lough Gara; Rynne 1960) the blade tapers from the shoulder to the tip. It has a lozenge-shaped cross-section. In the other form (e.g. sword from Ballinderry; Armstrong 1923, Pl. I:2; Hencken 1950, Fig. 24:B) the blade is parallel-sided for most of its length and it has a mid-rib. In form the Irish swords are close to the continental La Tène II swords (Raftery 1939b). Their immediate place of origin is Britain (Rynne 1960).

Seven sword scabbard plates are known. These were found in or close to the valley of the lower Bann. They were made from beaten bronze and except for one piece the others are decorated (Jope 1954a). Engraving was the technique used. As Jope (1954a, 87) has shown, the chief characteristics of the Irish scabbard style are:

(a) The designs are laid out broadly on a sequence of S-figures or running waves.
(b) There is stylized plant ornament, sometimes this is twisted into fleshily swelling tails.
(c) Other principal motifs are, tightly-coiled hair-spring spirals, sickle-shaped or S-shaped finials, triangular 'teeth' on the round edges of the stems, hour-glass junctions with open or closed top and bottom.

The chapes that were attached to the base of the scabbards were pear-shaped at the

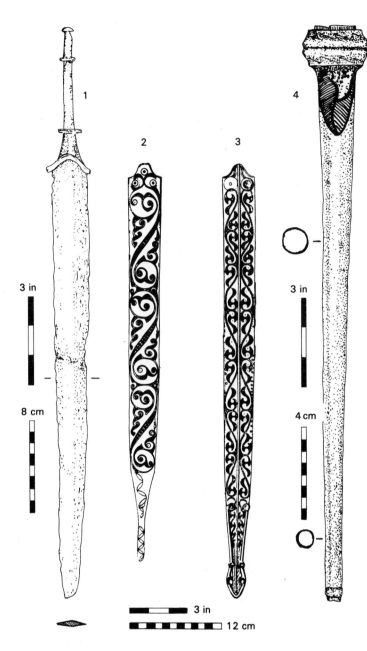

Figure 96 1 Iron La Tène sword, Cashel, Co. Sligo (N.M.I. 1958: 56, after Rynne 1960); 2 and 3 bronze La Tène scabbard plate, 2 Toome, Co. Antrim, 3 Lisnacrogher 2, Co. Antrim (after Jope 1954a, Fig. 1); 4 bronze spear-butt of elongated type, Ireland (after J. Raftery 1951, Fig. 226: 1).

bottom with extensions above. At the top there are sockets for taking settings, possibly of red enamel (Fig. 96, 2–3).

Scabbard mounts have been found on Lambay (Macalister 1928–9, 243, No. 24, Pl. 14:5). These type of mounts have a continental La Tène III background and they were probably derived from Belgic Britain (Piggott 1950, 21–2, 28).

Part of a bronze shield was found on Lambay (Macalister 1928–9, 243). The sub-rectangular wooden shield with leather covering from Clonoura, Co. Tipperary may also be Iron Age in date (*J.R.S.A.I.*, 92 (1962), 152).

Vessels

A cauldron from Drumlane, Co. Cavan was made from iron sheets riveted together. This piece may have been modelled on the Late Bronze Age cauldrons (Scott 1974, 16–17). There are two cauldrons of La Tène III type. Both are two-piece and they were made from bronze sheets riveted together (Armstrong 1923, 25; Hawkes 1951, 179–80, 182; Piggott 1952–3, 28, 30, called the Santon type in Britain).

At least four bronze cups are known. The best preserved example, from Keshcarrigan, Co. Leitrim, has an outwardly expanding rim, a concave neck and a swollen body (Jope 1954b, 92ff.; see Fig. 97, top). After casting these bowls were finished off with mechanical aids, such as spinning or rotational working. They belong, or are related to, a southern British group of bowls that were principally of Belgic workmanship (Fox and Hull 1948, 135–6).

Stone vessels with a hemispherical-shaped body from which a handle projects could have been lamps. They were probably derived from Scotland (Steer 1955–6, 243–6; see Fig. 97, bottom).

As far as can be judged the predominant type of pottery vessel in use during the Iron Age were bucket-shaped pots of coarse, gritty ware. The vessels are fairly homogeneous both in shape and in texture. The rims can be either rounded, flat-topped or internally bevelled. Sometimes perforations occur underneath. Some vessels have a slight shoulder. The pots tend to be undecorated but the flat-topped rims are often finger-impressed and when shoulders are present these sometimes have finger-impressions. This type of pottery is frequently found in hill-forts of Group I but what appears to be similar or related material has been found in ring-forts and burials (Kilbride-Jones 1950, 325, 326; Mogey, Thompson and Proudfoot 1956, 15–17, 24–8).

Personal Adornment

Tweezers (Jope and Wilson 1957, 81), bone combs (Crawford 1925, 22) and mirrors (Macalister 1928–9, 244; Jope 1954b, 94) were used. Seemingly all are based on British prototypes (combs – Bulleid and Grey 1911, 266–99; Callander 1931–2, 50 (weaving); and Stevenson 1966, 25, D-shaped, first-century A.D. from Scotland;

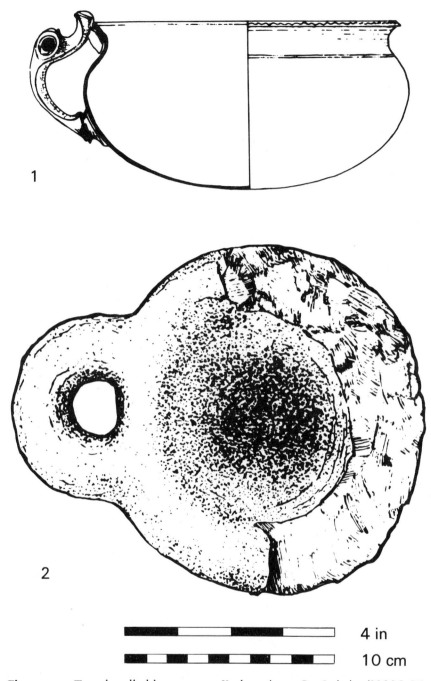

Figure 97 Top: handled bronze cup, Keshcarrigan, Co. Leitrim (N.M.I. W. 37, after Jope 1954b, Fig. 2). Bottom: handled stone cup, Rosduff, Co. Longford (N.M.I. 1958:85, after *J.R.S.A.I.*, 90 (1960), 23, Fig. 16).

239

mirrors – Fox 1948, 1958, 84–105, 1948 (with Hull), Fox and Pollard 1973). Necklaces of tiny blue glass beads were worn (i.e. Eogan 1968, 367) but more ornate beads are also known (Raftery 1972b). Spiral and penannular finger rings were also worn (Jope and Wilson 1957a, 79; Eogan 1968, 367). There is a small number of torcs, which are all in gold except for one example. Five varieties are represented. The buffer-terminal torc (Clonmacnois), the tubular torc (Broighter) and the beaded torc in bronze (Lambay) are represented by a single example each (Armstrong 1933, Nos 120, 117; Macalister 1928–9, 243). There are two loop terminal torcs both from Broighter (Armstrong 1933, Nos 118–19). A ribbon torc with a straight terminal forms part of the Somerset hoard (Raftery 1960b, 2, see p. 173) and another ribbon torc, but with bulbous terminals, may have been associated with the buffer-terminal torc from Clonmacnois. Ribbon torcs have La Tène associations on the continent (Keller 1965, Tf. 12:I; Bretz-Mahler 1971, 31–55). The immediate background to the beaded bronze torc is first–second century A.D. Scotland (Stevenson 1966, 26, 31; see Mahr 1941, 26, Middle La Tène in the Rhineland). The other three varieties have parallels in Britain.

Brooches (fibulae), a feature of the Iron Age world, are exceedingly rare in Ireland, some types are only represented by one or two examples. Those that occur have local characteristics. In some instances it would appear that the maker had only an acquaintance with the design of British or continental brooches (Jope 1954a, 89). There is only one definite La Tène II brooch, that from Navan (Eamhain Macha), Co. Armagh (Fig. 98, 1) and this probably dates to the first century A.D. (Jope 1961–2, 26; see also Dunning in Wheeler 1932, 67–70, Group B; Piggott 1957–8, 72–6, sub-type Bii). Three forms of La Tène III brooches are known, the Langton Down, Nauheim and 'flattened bow' types (Wheeler 1932, 71–2; Werner 1955; Jope 1961–2, 26ff.). The Langton Down and Nauheim types are of continental origin and in Britain they occur in fairly large numbers in the south. It was in that area that the flattened bow type developed (for type specimens see Fig. 98, 24–5).

Brooches of Roman type are represented by four forms, the dolphin, the thistle, the Navan and the 'poor man's brooch' (Fig. 98, 6, 7, 8, 3). Although inspired from the Roman world the Navan type is distinctively Irish (Jope 1961–2, 35–7). The other three forms are continental and at least the thistle and dolphin brooches have a La Tène III background. These three types became current in Britain about the middle of the first century A.D. and their period of use was not more than a century (Hawkes and Hull 1948, 311–12, 313, 314; Wheeler 1932, 72; Jope 1950, 54–6).

Pins are also rare and those that occur are late (Fig. 98, 9–13). Plain ring-headed pins, a southern British development out of the continental swan's neck pin (Dunning 1934; Hodson 1964, 103), and ring-headed pins with elaborately moulded head and neck are known (Seaby 1964; Jobey and Tait 1966, 29–32). This elaborate type may have developed in Yorkshire La Tène contexts (Stead 1965, 57). Ibex-headed pins were also introduced from Britain where the type developed (Dunning 1934, 280; Graham and Jope 1950, 55). Hand-pins, the earliest penannular brooches (Kilbride-

1a *Right* Chalk cliffs near the Giant's Causeway, Co. Antrim. (Photo: J. K. St Joseph, for the Cambridge University Collection)

1b *Below* Sunken drumlins, Clew Bay, Co. Mayo. (Photo: M. Herity)

2a   Sir James Ware.

2b   Gabriel Beranger.

2c   William Burton Conyngham.

2d   General Charles Vallancey.

3a   George Petrie.

3b   Sir William Wilde.

3c George Coffey
(After an unfinished portrait by
John Butler Yeats)

3d Professor R. A. S. Macalister.

4a Centre Court Cairn at Ballyglass, Co. Mayo, during excavation, looking north-west.
(Photo: S. Ó Nualláin)

4b Aerial view of Ballyglass Court Cairn and neolithic house, during excavation.
(Photo: L. Swan)

5a *Right* Aerial view of the tumulus of the New Grange Passage Grave, Co. Meath. (Photo: J. K. St Joseph, for the Cambridge University Collection)

5b *Below* Interior of the chamber of New Grange, looking east towards the passage. (Photo: J. Bambury, for the Commissioners of Public Works in Ireland)

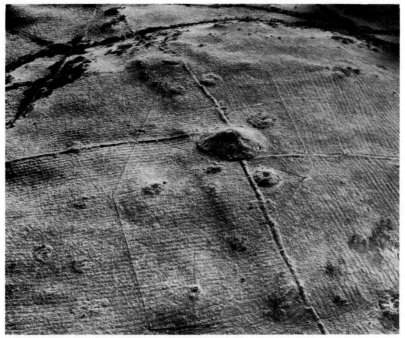

6a Aerial view of Passage Grave cemetery on Carnbane East, Loughcrew Cemetery, Co. Meath.
(Photo: J. K. St Joseph)
6b Denuded Passage Grave ('Dolmen') at Carrowmore with Maeve's Cairn, Knocknarea, in the background.
(Photo: J. Bambury, for the Commissioners of Public Works in Ireland)

7a   Ornamented kerbstone, Knowth Tumulus, Co. Meath.
(Photo: George Eogan)
7b   Ornamented stone basin, Knowth East Passage Grave, Co. Meath.
(Photo: J. Bambury, for the Commissioners of Public Works in Ireland)

8a Portal Dolmen, Pentre Ifan, Pembrokeshire.
(Photo: M. Herity)

8b Portal Dolmen, Ballykeel, Co. Armagh.
(Photo: A. E. P. Collins)

9a and b   Aerial views of the Knockadoon promontory, Lough Gur, Co. Limerick.
(Photos: D. Pochin-Mould)

10a　Mount Gabriel, Co. Cork, from the east.
(Photo: J. K. St Joseph, for the Cambridge University Collection)
10b　Stone circle, Drombeg, Co. Cork.
(Photo: J. Bambury, for the Commissioners of Public Works in Ireland)

11a Earthen enclosure, the Giant's Ring, Ballynahatty, Co. Down.
(Photo: J. K. St Joseph, for the Cambridge University Collection)

11b Earthen enclosure, Dowth, Co. Meath.
(Photo: J. K. St Joseph, for the Cambridge University Collection)

12a *Above* Terminal of one of three gold flange-twisted torcs from Tara, Co. Meath. (N.M.I.W. 192.)

12b *Left* Encrusted urn, Burgage More, Co. Wicklow (height 33 cm) (N.M.I. 1934 : 5647 A).

13a *Below left* V-notched shield, Clonbrin, Co. Longford, leather (diameter *c.* 50 cm). (N.M.I.)

13b *Below right* Wooden mould for making U-notched shields. Cloonlara, Co. Mayo (diameter *c.* 48 cm). (N.M.I.) (Photos: National Museum of Ireland)

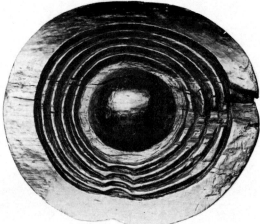

14a *Above left* Objects, probably part of a belt, made from horse-hair, Cromaghs, Co. Antrim.
(N.M.I. 1906: 13. After Coffey, 1906, Pl. 12.)
14b *Above right* Necklace of amber beads, Derrybrien, Co.Galway (width *c.* 30 cm).
(N.M.I.P. 1954: II.)
(Photo: National Museum of Ireland)
15a *Below* Hill-fort, Eamhain Macha, Co. Armagh.
(Photo: J. K. St Joseph, for the Cambridge University Collection)

15b *Above* Stone fort (cashel),
Staigue, Co. Kerry.
(Photo: J. Bambury, for the
Commissioners of Public Works
in Ireland)

16 *Left* Decorated stone, Turoe,
Co. Galway.
(Photo: J. Bambury, for the
Commissioners of Public Works
in Ireland)

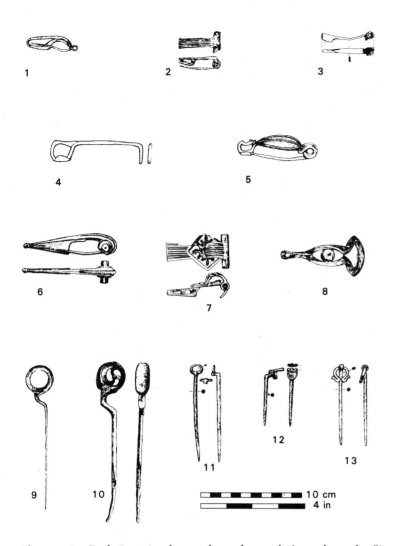

Figure 98 Early Iron Age bronze brooches and pins: 1 brooch of La Tène Type II, Eamhain Macha (Navan), Co. Armagh (N.M.I. 1906: 40); 2 brooch of Langton Down type, Lambay Island, Co. Dublin (after Macalister 1928–9, Pl. 24: 10, in N.M.I.); 3 'poor man's' brooch, 'Loughey', Co. Down (Ashmolean Museum, after Jope and Wilson 1957a. Fig. 1: 1); 4–5 brooches of flattened-bow type, 4 with rod-shaped bow, Lough Gur, Co. Limerick. 5 leaf-shaped bow, Eamhain Macha (Navan), Co. Armagh (both after Jope 1961–2, Fig. 2, Nos 6–7); 6 dolphin brooch, Lambay Island, Co. Dublin; 7 thistle brooch, Lambay Island (both after Macalister 1928–9, Pl. 24:8, 7, in N.M.I.); 8 brooch of Navan type, Eamhain Macha (Navan), Co. Armagh, (N.M.I. 1906: 39 after Jope 1961–2, Pl. 2a); 9 plain ring-headed pin, Ireland (after Dunning 1934, Pl. 1:1); 10 elaborate ring-headed pin, Ireland; 11 ibex-headed pin, Co. Wexford (N.M.I. 1959: 214); 12 hand-pin, Ballykinvarga, Co. Clare (N.M.I. 1964: 76); 13 'omega' pin, Maghera, Co. Donegal (N.M.I. 1959: 760).

241

Jones 1937), latchets (Raftery 1951, 203) and 'omega' pins (see Fig. 98, 11, 12, 13) also came into use before the end of the prehistoric period.

Other metal objects that were in use during the beginning of the first millennium A.D. include a massive bracelet from Newry, Co. Down (*Archaeological Survey, Co. Down*, 57–8). This is a Scottish type (M. Simpson 1968, Fig. 56). There are also pieces of uncertain use such as the Petrie Crown (Raftery 1951, 198, Fig. 233), the Cork horns (O'Kelly 1961), discs (cf. Fig. 99, 2) and the spoon-shaped objects (Fig. 99, 1). Objects of the latter form are known from Britain and France (Craw 1923–4; Davies 1929, 222; Way 1869; *Ant. J.*, 13 (1933), 464–5).

Hoards

A limited number of hoards have been found. That with the greatest variety of objects was found at Somerset, Co. Galway (Raftery 1960b). The majority of other hoards consist of a horse bridle-bit and a spur-shaped pendant (Haworth 1971, 39–40). The four Lough-na-Shade trumpets were probably part of a votive offering (below).

Religion, Ceremonies, Ritual

These events played a big part in the lives of the continental Celts and a priestly class, the Druids, were part of Celtic society (Piggott 1968). From the early literature it is also clear that ceremonies and religious practices were significant events in the lives of the Iron Age inhabitants of Ireland. The festivals of Bealtaine, Lughnasa and Samhain were important occasions and the surviving material remains at Uisneach, Tailteann and Tlachtga (see p. 230) confirm the literary accounts. The decorated horse harness trappings (see p. 232) would indicate that horses were used on ceremonial occasions; the trumpets, bronze discs (Jope and Wilson 1957b; Raftery 1951, Fig. 266; Macalister 1928–9, 243; Armstrong 1923, 27, Pl. 5) and some of the miscellaneous objects, like the 'Petrie Crown' (see above), may also have been the trappings of ritual practices. Furthermore, it is interesting to note that four trumpets were found together in the small lake, Lough-na-Shade, just below Eamhain Macha (Armstrong 1923, 22–3). Perhaps they were part of a ritual deposit. The only surviving piece has an elaborately repoussé decorated disc at the bell-end. Trumpets may have been a prominent Celtic object. One is portrayed on the statue of the Dying Gaul (Powell 1958, 255, Pl. 3). It is known that the ritual deposition of objects in water was a feature of Celtic ritualism. In Anglesey there is the deposit of Llyn Cerrig Bach (Fox 1946) and the practice has also been recorded on the continent (cf. Chadwick 1970, 148). In this context the nature of the Lisnacrogher site (p. 224) should again be raised. This might have been an occupation site but in the absence of precise details concerning discovery the possibility of a ritual deposit should be kept in mind.

Formal graves with grave-goods show that burial ceremony was common. The graves may be flat or they may have been covered by a mound. Within this dual

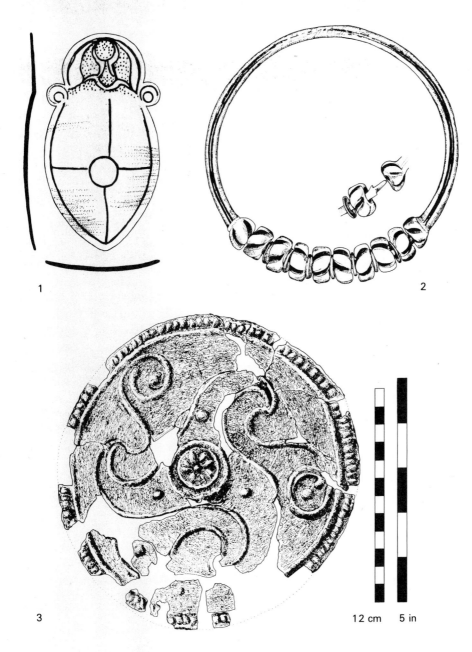

Figure 99 1 Spoon-shaped object, Ireland (after J. Raftery 1951, Fig. 231: 3); 2 beaded torc, Lambay Island, Co. Dublin; 3 bronze disc, Lambay Island, Co. Dublin (both after Macalister 1928–9, Pl. 24:1, 3, objects in N.M.I.).

division different burial rites occur, both groups containing inhumation and cremation graves. In the inhumation graves the body may have been placed in a flexed position or it may have been extended. According to second-hand information, a tanged one-edged iron knife 'lay' in a well constructed cist at Aghalahard, Co. Mayo (Raftery and Moore 1944, 171–2), but otherwise all well dated burials were in simple pits that were backfilled after the burial had taken place. A fair number of flat (i.e. unprotected) graves are known. At Knowth, Co. Meath at least eight such inhumation graves can be assigned to the Iron Age in view of the grave-goods, and a dozen other similar graves, but without grave-goods, may belong to the same period (Eogan 1968, 365–73; 1974a, 68–87). A contemporary burial but of uncertain type is known from New Grange (Flanagan 1960). The inhumation burials at Feerwore, Co. Galway and Kitale, Co. Meath may also be Iron Age in date (Raftery 1944b, 46–9; Rynne 1974, 270–1). Unprotected cremation burials were found at Kiltierney, Co. Fermanagh (unpublished, information from Mr L. N. W. Flanagan). The 'Loughey' objects may have been from a cremation burial (Jope and Wilson 1957a). There appears to have been a flat cemetery on Lambay but nothing is known about the type of grave, the burial rite or the deposition of the finds (Macalister 1928–9, 243–6).

Different forms of burial mound were erected. Tumuli 2 and 3 at Cush, Co. Limerick, the mound that was erected in the centre of the disused ring-fort at Lugg, Co. Dublin and to some extent the mound at Grannagh, Co. Galway can be described as bowl barrows (Ó Ríordáin 1940, 133–9; Kilbride-Jones 1950, 324–5; Macalister 1916–17, 508–10). Each had a surrounding ditch and the burial rite was cremation. At Cush the remains were cremated on the spot and the mound was then constructed over the ashes. At Lugg there were two unprotected burials. It appears that there were a number of unprotected burials at Grannagh. Subsequent excavations by Mr Etienne Rynne (personal communication) produced further cremation burials in the silted-up fosse. These were accompanied by grave-goods including bone beads and bronze fibulae.

Ring barrows were also constructed. There are dated examples from Oran Beg, Co. Galway (information from the excavator Mr Etienne Rynne), Mullaghmore, Co. Down, some of the Carrowjames, Co. Mayo mounds, especially Tumuli 7 and 8 (these sites had a low mound), and possibly Sites A and B at Carbury, Co. Kildare (Mogey 1949; Mogey, Thompson and Proudfoot 1956; Raftery 1938–9, 1940–1, 27–37, 53–9; Willmot 1938). Cremation was the burial rite. At Site B, Carbury there were also unprotected inhumation burials but these appear to have been secondary but still within the Iron Age. Ring barrows on the Curragh, especially Site 4 with its extended inhumation burials, may also be of Iron Age date (Ó Ríordáin 1950, 260). Four similar burials with iron fragments nearby were found under a low mound (No. 11) at Pollacorragune, Co. Galway (Riley 1936, 45–8, 55–6). At Tara a flat-topped mound at the Rath of the Synods covered inhumation and cremation burials. There were five inhumation burials within the fort (Ó Ríordáin 1960, 22).

A number of fashioned stones have been assigned to the Iron Age on stylistic grounds; none has been found in an archaeological context. There are two main forms – aniconic and iconic. These stones possibly also had a ritual significance.

There are three good examples of aniconic stones, Turoe, Co. Galway (Coffey 1902–4, 260–2; Raftery 1944b, 42–4), Castlestrange, Co. Roscommon (Coffey 1902–4, 262–3) and Killycluggin, Co. Cavan (Macalister 1922; O Ríordáin 1952, 68). These stones were free-standing and all were decorated with abstract designs – spirals, 'trumpets', meandering curves, trisceles, curvilinear lines and other motifs. Turoe is the most elaborately decorated (Plate 16). In Professor Duignan's view (personal communication) the designs were laid out in a manner appropriate to a four-sided pillar. Parallels for these stones have been cited in Brittany and in the Rhineland (Henry 1965a, 6).

Sculptures within the iconic group consist of heads. As Ross (1957–8, 11) has written, 'the head was the bodily member which was especially venerated by the Celts . . . the head was regarded by them as the seat of the soul, the centre of the vital essence, symbolic of the regenerative forces of life.' Dr Ross has further written that 'the cult of the head was the most widespread, typical and enduring of Celtic cults' (Ross 1967a, 127). The heads may be either single-, double- or triple-faced (Rynne 1972). There are two anthropomorphic figures in Caldragh graveyard, Boa Island, Co. Fermanagh. One is in its original position and is double-faced; the other is from Lustymore Island (Lowry-Corry 1933, 200–4). These sculptures may date from the Iron Age but it should be noted that there are primitive-looking sculptures, but of Early Christian date, from around lower Lough Erne (Lowry-Corry 1959, from White Island).

The Lia Fáil and the Cross of Adamnan at Tara may have been erected during the Iron Age. The latter has the remains of a very worn figure of indeterminate form (Macalister 1931, 30, 52).

Origins and Chronology

The origins and chronology of the later prehistoric events are not at present clear. However, evidence that is becoming available indicates that different influences reached different parts of Ireland. This view is based on the assumption that hill-forts provide evidence for a change in society and that this hill-fort building society had iron artifacts. As has been already pointed out (p. 228) univallate hill-forts have an eastern distribution and a British background. As yet, due to the lack of a find assemblage and the fact that coarse pottery cannot be dated closely, it is not known when the first univallate hill-forts were erected.

The dating of multivallate hill-forts is also uncertain. Only Cahercommaun has been excavated and while some of the finds can be assigned to the prehistoric period they do not provide close dating (Raftery 1972a, 51–3). On the evidence of ground plan an ultimate Iberian origin can be suggested for these forts. On the dating of the Spanish *castros* the builders of Group II hill-forts could have arrived in Ireland by the middle of the first millennium B.C. As further evidence for an Iberian connection at this time the *chevaux-de-frise* (p. 228) has been cited. Harbison (1971) has dismissed the Spanish connection in view of the fact that there it has an inland distribution (see also Mahr 1937, 409). But even if the *chevaux-de-frise* did not get to Ireland from Spain there is an assemblage of monuments that has an Atlantic European background. As Leeds pointed out, stone forts occur in north-west Iberia (Leeds 1926–7, 235). Promontory forts are at least known as far south as Brittany and they are also common in western Britain, especially in Cornwall and Pembrokeshire. Excluding Pembrokeshire, souterrains have also been found in those areas. So perhaps there was a movement of people up the Atlantic coast of Europe and on settling in Ireland they started to build a number of new types of settlement sites. While there are strong indications for suggesting that the Iron Age had a dual origin, when it commenced still remains an open question. But if future research proves that it was about the middle of the first millennium B.C. this date should not come as a surprise.

After the initial settlement it is not at present clear if there were subsequent settlements in the west and south-west. The story is different in the east and north-east, where there is evidence for successive intrusions. It has been previously mentioned that the earliest Iron Ages seem to have lacked a La Tène element. This appears to have come at a later stage and to be due to arrival in the north-east of the country of new people a century or so before the birth of Christ. The background to this new phase of the Iron Age may have been the La Tène 'culture' of Yorkshire (cf. Piggott 1950, 14–15) or even north Wales (Savory 1968, 19), although Jope (1954a, 87–8) has argued for direct continental contacts. The La Tène element, which probably represents a folk movement, includes swords and scabbard chapes (p. 236) and some other pieces (Rynne 1961a).

The next infusion of new types that Ireland received was during the first century A.D. These came from Britain and again the recipient area was the north-east and east. These novel types arrived not as a result of a settlement by foreigners but as a result of trading or raiding. Just before the end of the last century of the first millennium B.C. Class 1 bridle-bits and the earliest fibulae (representing the old La Tène tradition) appear. By that time southern Britain was dominated by the Belgae and objects that could be contemporary with the Belgic settlement, some may even have been derived from Belgic workshops, were arriving. These include mirrors, bronze bowls, and sword scabbard mounts. But these were only a few of the objects that arrived in Ireland during the first century A.D. Also arriving were other varieties of fibulae, pins, spiral finger rings, tweezers, cauldrons, stone cups, combs, torcs, glass beads. Southern Britain was the area from which most of the types arrived but some such as the cauldrons have a wider distribution, and the beaded torc and the stone cups came from Scotland. These first-century A.D. events should be considered against their historical background. In Britain that century was a disturbed period. There was the threat of the Roman invasion. It came in A.D. 43 when Claudius and up to 50,000 men landed in Kent.

The story of Ireland in the succeeding centuries is not very clear. There was no Roman invasion of Ireland, but very soon actual Roman types appear in the country, again no doubt due to trade or plundering. These objects include sherds of Samian ware, brooches of the thistle and dolphin types, ornaments like those in the New Grange hoard (Topp 1956), coins (e.g. New Grange, O'Kelly 1967, 84–5) and hoards of silver from Balline, Co. Limerick and Billinrees, Co. Derry (Ó Ríordáin 1947b; Bateson 1973). Apart from these Roman additions and some local development, as is demonstrated by such objects as the 'Petrie Crown' and the Cork horns, the Iron Age continued on uninterrupted down to the fifth century when, as will be shown below, the arrival of further new influences brought the prehistoric era to an end.

Discussion

Pending a wider knowledge of the regional groupings and a secure chronology one cannot, as yet, fully appreciate the communities who were responsible for the changes that took place during the later prehistoric period. The following comments are, therefore, of a generalized nature and they are not applicable as a whole to any regional group or phase.

The presence of hill-forts and 'Royal' sites is good proof for a tribal society and even kingship. The construction of a hill-fort would have been a formidable task and its building would have required the backing of a well organized social order. But in addition to the halls of the chiefs there were the ordinary farmsteads and from the animal bones that turn up on these occupation sites it appears that cattle were a very important economic factor, indeed some of the 'lords' of the hill-forts may have been cattle barons of their day. Quern stones are positive proof for grain growing and there is some evidence for field systems. Assembly sites indicate that gatherings, probably a mixture of festival, fair and religion, took place. Further evidence for ritual is provided by the stone sculpture, the Lough-na-Shade deposit and the burials with grave-goods.

The use of iron brought new technological problems which had to be mastered. Bronze, however, continued in use and, indeed, it is during what we call the Iron Age that some of the great achievements in bronze-working took place. This is clearly shown in the manufacture of the horse bridle-bits and the sword scabbard plates. In the decoration of the bronzes various techniques were used, repoussé (e.g. the box from the Somerset hoard, Raftery 1960b, 2, No. 157), incision, engraving and etching. The latter technique involves the scraping away of part of the surface so as to leave the designs in relief (O'Kelly 1961, 7–8). The craftsmen must have had a range of specialist tools (see p. 236; also cf. Lowery, Savage and Wilkins 1971). There were also considerable achievements in stone carving and sculpture as is shown by the iconic and aniconic carvings and also in the manufacture of quern stones. Wood must have been used abundantly as the evidence from excavated occupation sites of the period shows, e.g. houses and palisades. But wooden artifacts are rare, almost non-existent

(p. 238). If Iron Age in date, the shield from Clonoura shows that leather, in addition to wood, was skilfully used. At Freestone Hill some evidence for the curing of hides came to light (Raftery 1969, 98). The same site produced evidence for spinning and weaving. Glass was also made there and bone was worked. It is also during the Iron Age that we have the earliest indication for the use of enamel. A piece of red enamel occurs as a boss in the centre of one of the openwork mounts from the Somerset hoard (Raftery 1960b 3, No. 159). There is a band of red enamel around the edge of the Lisnacrogher scabbard mount.

Evidence for trade, travel or transport is not extensive. Native products are rarely found outside Ireland. The trumpet and possibly the bridle-bit from Llyn Cerrig Bach in Anglesey (Fox 1946, cf. p. 61) is about all that one can mention. Ireland, therefore, appears to have been the recipient, not the giver. Unless they were exclusively used for ceremonial purposes horses would have enabled people to move about fairly rapidly and if there is any historical basis in the story of the Táin Bó Cuailgne then large groups of people, together with their stock, could move right across Ireland. But perhaps the greatest achievement of the period under review is that it was at that time that the beginnings of historic Ireland took place.

From Prehistory to History

During the course of the fifth century A.D. the prehistoric period came to an end. But that century was one of those periods when changes took place not only in Ireland but in various other parts of Europe in addition. Again it was a period, as was the case at various times in the past, when the 'civilized' world contracted and the 'barbarian' world expanded. Now, that great Mediterranean civilization of Rome was on the retreat. The last of the legions left Britain about A.D. 410 and their grip on trans-Alpine Europe was loosened. To the north of the Roman world the 'barbaric' Germanic tribes were on the move and were about to issue forth in a series of migrations that were to change the course of events over large parts of Europe. Visigoths, Huns and Vandals pushed southwards across the Alps into Italy at the beginning of the century and the Emperor and Senate fled to Ravenna (Bullough 1965, 158). Closer to home, Germanic people, the Angles, the Saxons and the Jutes, arrived in south-east England around the middle of the fifth century and thereby laid the foundation of the Anglo-Saxon kingdom (cf. Wilson 1960, 25ff.).

Although not directly affected by the continental European changes, nevertheless a new age was dawning in Ireland and the major influences that contributed to its beginnings stemmed from Roman Britain. Christianity was now being adopted and it is hardly out of place to remark that the man to whom the major share in Christianizing Ireland is due, Patrick, is traditionally claimed to have arrived in Ireland as a slave from Britain in 432. About the same time the spread of literacy was taking place although the earliest evidence for writing, the Ogham script, is concentrated in the extreme south-west of the country (Macalister 1945, 1–305).

Indeed, the material remains of the earliest Christianity in the coastal areas of the south and west, which include distinctive architecture, stone carving and burials, may indicate direct continental contacts (for brief descriptions of some of the monuments and references to publications see Henry 1965a, 49–57, cf. page x for distribution of Eremitic monasteries).

New metal types also appear around the fourth century. These include hand-pins, latchets and hanging bowls (cf. de Paor 1958, 39–47). These objects could also have stemmed from the Roman world and they are of further interest in that they are decorated with 'Celtic' designs. Soon there were to be some borrowings from Anglo-Saxon Britain (Henry 1965b, 53ff.). But the eclipse of the Roman Empire led to the establishment of Irish colonies in Britain, notably in south-western Wales and in western Scotland where the Irish had their headquarters at Dunadd in Argyllshire (Christison, 1903–4, 224–33; 1904–5, 292–322; Laing 1975, 8–9, 41–2, 71–8, 92–9, 124–5).

In Ireland during the fifth century amalgamation was going on. Iron Age traditions, late Roman influences from Britain (spiritual, literary and technological), Anglo-Saxon borrowing, and possibly direct continental contact in the south and west were laying the foundations for the blossoming forth of the first stage of Early Christian Ireland. Monastic centres were becoming as important as political sites. This may have been the time when Old Kilcullen replaced Dún Ailinne, and close to Tara, Lagore was becoming a site of some importance. The monastic sites were also centres of great artistic achievement. By the second half of the sixth century the 'Cathach' had been compiled (Henry 1965a, 58ff.) and in this way the scene was being set for the subsequent production of some of the greatest works from Early Christian Europe such as the Book of Kells, the Tara Brooch, the Ardagh Chalice and the Moylough Belt-shrine (cf. Henry 1965a; de Paor 1958). During these centuries the Irish language was transformed and it was also at this time that the powerful dynasties of the Eoganacht in Munster and the Uí Néill further north were emerging (Mac Niocaill 1972, 1–12).

CHAPTER ELEVEN

Retrospect

By the time prehistoric man began to take a significant interest in Ireland, the island had developed much of its modern environmental personality, and the prehistory of Ireland can be viewed as the story of how her inhabitants recognized and exploited her environmental potential in soils, rocks and minerals, in flora and fauna, including a harvest of her rivers and the seas around her, and in her position in relation to the European continent. For the greater part of the era described in this book, the environment of Ireland differed significantly in two respects from that of today, however. For before a deterioration which set in about 1000 B.C. the climate was markedly better, with less cloudy and humid Atlantic weather and probably more blue skies, and with summer temperatures averaging two or more degrees Celsius higher. A consequence of this was that the blanket bogs of the west of Ireland (Fig. 2d), a product of a later change to the more humid climate of today, did not then exist, and considerable tracts of fertile soil as rich as any in Co. Meath grew their own attractive vegetation, both herb and woodland, which served to attract pioneer farmers particularly along the north Mayo coast. Both these differences are attested in the large numbers of prehistoric monuments found buried under blanket peat in the west of Ireland, and even more dramatically in the numbers of prehistoric farmsteads which have emerged from this peat in recent turf-cutting, and which were recorded as long ago as 1700 by the Archbishop of Dublin:

> 'Tis certain *Ireland* has been better inhabited than it is at present: mountains, that now are covered with boggs, have formerly been plowed; for when you dig five or six foot deep, you discover a proper soil for vegetables, and find it plowed into ridges and furrows . . . (King, in Molyneux 1726, 163)

That the potential of Ireland in rock and in soil was viewed with a shrewd and expert eye is clear from the rudely fashioned architecture and siting of 1200 megalithic tombs, mostly built of the ice-boulders with which Nature had strewed the face of the island. The clearance of Ireland's fertile morainic soils which is implied in the use of these boulders was followed by the production of cereal crops, mainly of wheat.

The heavy tree-cover which flourished before the arrival of the first farmers was cleared with axes made of polished stone and possibly with fire, these pioneers deliberately choosing to clear the stands of elm rather than of other trees, possibly because they judged that the soils in which elm flourished were most suitable for agriculture. In the earliest phases, it was the lighter upland soils that were cultivated, and it was probably also on these uplands that the imported cattle and sheep of these earliest farmers were grazed in a land which, even then, had the best cattle-land in Europe within her shores.

The organized exploitation of the mineral wealth of Ireland was begun surprisingly early with the mass-production of axeheads of igneous rock, which were used in clearance and possibly in the actual tilling of the soil; the axe-factory at Tievebulliagh in Antrim attests this. The jealousy with which the flint resources of Antrim and Down were regarded is documented in the siting of so many Passage Graves on or near the narrow band of chalk from which this flint can be harvested. This kind of overt record unfortunately appears to be no longer available in the case of the gold and copper deposits on which much of the industrial dynamism of the Bronze Age was founded, but it was undoubtedly on the dual foundation of metal resources exploited by expert craftsmen, and soil, plant and animal riches managed by solid farmers, that the pre-eminence of Ireland in the north-western province of Bronze Age Europe was established.

Though it might at first sight appear that Ireland was destined to be an Ultima Thule from her isolated position at the north-western edge of Atlantic Europe, she was in fact well placed to receive those immigrants who travelled north in the currents off that Atlantic façade, the more so if the warm moist south-westerlies of today blew with any frequency then. Indeed it appears that, with the ocean and wind currents behind them and with the lodestone of a rich and green land before them, prehistoric pioneers were virtually destined to come upon the Atlantic coasts of Ireland and to settle in great numbers there.

The north-eastern tip of Ireland, being only fifteen miles from Scotland, was destined also to attract visitors and colonists from Britain, even if the narrow sea-crossing was made hazardous by rushing tides. Trade in Tievebulliagh stone axeheads and in Antrim flint was a considerable attraction, and helped continue into Neolithic times older traditions of movement between the two islands which lasted throughout prehistory. But if for much of prehistory the people of east and north-east Ireland looked towards Britain, they also opened their windows to the part of Europe which lay beyond, to the North Sea and Jutland, and down the rivers Rhine and Elbe to the Danube, the Black Sea and the east Mediterranean. Ireland's relations with Britain in the Bronze Age, it could be said, derived in large measure from the situation further east. Prehistoric man was thus drawn along an Atlantic route to the west of Ireland by her position, by her fruitful soils and by her richness in minerals; he was drawn also by the same three forces into the east and north-east of the country, initially from Scotland and the rest of Britain and then along the roadways of the Rhine from the lands behind them, the gold of Leinster's El Dorado acting as the more powerful lodestone which began this movement about 2000 B.C.

The reconstruction presented here might incline one to conclude that the environment determined the course of Irish prehistory, but a closer examination of the record at present available shows that the cultural movements from Iberia to Ireland along the Atlantic façade tended to wane with the advent of the Bronze Age (probably because Iberia herself looked direct to Central Europe also), while Ireland's links with Central Europe and the area nearer home were even more strongly forged. A climax of this trend came in the Late Bronze Age with the dynamic rise of the Shannon estuary in the south-west, which, despite its position in the Atlantic façade, enjoyed strong contacts with the Nordic zone away to the east.

Islands are notoriously conservative, encouraging the retention of older traditions and resisting the introduction of newer ones; new movements into Ireland, therefore, tended to produce a more complex social environment. Almost invariably, each new wave of influence to reach Ireland is found mixed with the older, indigenous culture: Passage Grave and Late Neolithic material is found mixed with that of the Primary Neolithic; the looped spear-heads, rapiers and wing-flanged axeheads of the Urn complex persisted through some significant technological changes from 1400 till 700 B.C. If some new traditions, like the Irish/Scottish Food Vessel burials of the Early Bronze Age, appear in the record with little admixture, then the strength of their cultural impact appears the stronger.

The prehistory of Ireland also documents capricious variations in the archaeological record from one period to the next. Burial is unknown in the Mesolithic. It is a most important part of the Neolithic record, the megalithic tombs allowing many other assessments besides those of burial ritual to be made, about typological development, about distribution and characteristic siting, about small finds, about population size and social pattern: the contrast drawn in the early chapters of this book between the peasant society of the first farmers and the agglomerated, almost urban character of Passage Grave society demonstrates how far such evidence can be used in reconstructing these two contrasting faces of the Irish Primary Neolithic. This reconstruction itself raises new and difficult questions of how two communities so close in time and origin could differ so much in personality.

The Single Burials of the Late Neolithic and Earlier Bronze Age allow other kinds of assessment about the status and function of some individuals in a much-changed society; so far-reaching is this change and so radically different the affiliations of the new society in continental Europe that the Secondary Neolithic model might now be abandoned for Ireland and a new concept, Proto-Bronze Age, tried out (Piggott 1954, xviii). The archaeological record now forces the prehistorian to deal with metal technology, industries and their economics, luxury markets and trade, and to undertake new kinds of consideration of typology and chronology. It also presents him with a complex new ritual and even the possibility of developed astronomical science. Evidence of habitation is less easily recognized, however. Perhaps the flint and stone artifacts characteristic of Neolithic sites attract the lay eye more easily than the kind of distinctive material likely to be preserved in quantity on a Bronze Age habitation, coarse pottery and clay moulds, for instance? Perhaps the characteristic lowland siting of Bronze Age sites makes their destruction in recent farming more likely and their discovery more difficult? Perhaps Bronze Age studies have remained too long engaged merely with the industrial aspects of the period?

With the advent of the Celts and the Early Iron Age, the record changes again. Habitation and assembly sites are common, burials rare. Everyday objects are of the new metal, iron, and bronze and gold artificers find a new luxury market. The pattern of Early Iron Age communities is already foreshadowed in such aspects of Late Bronze Age society as the warrior chieftains, communal feasting, the lake dwelling and the beginnings of some Celtic princely sites, like Rathgall in Co. Wicklow. Many of the hilltop assembly sites of this new phase yield evidence of Neolithic habitation. Is it that two groups far removed in time make a similar environmental choice, or are there cultural factors at work, the Celts taking possession of places made sacred by an aboriginal presence and thus symbolically taking over the whole country itself?

Good archaeology is thus an art of the possible, understanding and adapting to each new body of evidence the better to recover to the full the story it can tell. Its best practitioners devise new strategies in the light of this understanding, in excavation and survey in the field, in understanding the ancient environment, in the study of objects in museums and laboratories. Much of their effort comes to nothing without good communication, in the form of clear and objective excavation reports, and well illustrated *corpus* studies by class of monument and object.

Today's prehistory is concerned with past lifeways, with greater insight into prehistoric environment, with a much fuller and subtler reconstruction of ancient communities. It asks more searching questions over a much broader spectrum of information, and attempts to understand how we have come to hold our present hypotheses. We need a new philosophical understanding of the actual and potential archaeological evidence and a new view of how our institutions are organized to collect it and make it available to the scientist and to the ordinary man.

Bibliographical Index

Abbreviations

Bibliographical Index

Figures in brackets at the end of each entry [ ] indicate the page in this book where the item cited is referred to.

Abercromby, John (1912), *The Bronze Age Pottery of Great Britain and Ireland*, 2 vols, Clarendon Press, Oxford. [135]

Addyman, P. V. (1965), 'Coney Island, Lough Neagh', *U.J.A.*, 28 (1965), 78–101. [142, 158]

Allen, I. M., Britton, D. and Coghlan, H. H. (1970), *Metallurgical Reports on British and Irish Bronze Age Implements and Weapons in the Pitt Rivers Museum*, Pitt Rivers Museum, Oxford. [119, 139]

Anati, Emmanuel G. (1963), 'New Petroglyphs at Derrynablaha, County Kerry', *J.C.H.A.S.*, 68 (1963), 1–15. [140]

Anderson, Joseph (1876), 'Notice of a Flint Arrow-head found at Fyvie, Aberdeenshire', *P.S.A.S.*, 11 (1874–6), 508–13. [43]

Anderson, R. S. G. (1941–2), 'A Cinerary Urn from Sandmill Farm, Stranraer, Wigtownshire', *P.S.A.S.*, 76 (1941–2), 79–83. [149]

Andrews, S. and Davies, Oliver (1940), 'Prehistoric Finds at Tyrone House, Malone Road, Belfast', *U.J.A.* 3rd ser., 3 (1940), 152–4. [45]

Annable, F. K. and Simpson, D. D. A. (1964), *Guide Catalogue of the Neolithic and Bronze Age Collections in Devizes Museum*, Wiltshire Archaeological and Natural History Society, Devizes. [149]

ApSimon, A. M. (1954), 'Dagger Graves in the "Wessex" Bronze Age', *Annual Report Inst. of Archaeology, London*, 10 (1954), 37–62. [148, 153]

ApSimon, A. M. (1958), 'Food Vessels', *Univ. of London Inst. of Archaeology Bulletin*, 1 (1958), 24–36. [135]

ApSimon, A. M. (1969a), 'An Early Neolithic House in Co. Tyrone', *J.R.S.A.I.*, 99 (1969), 165–8. [47, 135, 151]

ApSimon, A. M. (1969b), 'The Earlier Bronze Age in the North of Ireland', *U.J.A.*, 32 (1969), 28–72. [124, 129, 133, 152, 158]

An Archaeological Survey of County Down (1966), H.M.S.O., Belfast. [124, 125, 127, 242]

Armstrong, E. C. R. (1916–17), 'On Some Associated Finds of Bronze Celts discovered in Ireland', *P.R.I.A.*, 33 (1916–17), 511–26. [179]

Armstrong, E. C. R. (1917), 'The Great Clare Find of 1854', *J.R.S.A.I.*, 47 (1917), 21–36. [208]

Armstrong, E. C. R. (1920), *Catalogue of Irish Gold Ornaments in the Collection of the Royal Irish Academy*, Dublin, H.M.S.O. [13]

Armstrong, E. C. R. (1923), 'The La Tène Period in Ireland', *J.R.S.A.I.*, 53 (1923), 1–33. [236, 238, 242]

Armstrong, E. C. R. (1933), *Catalogue of Irish Gold Ornaments in the Collection of the Royal Irish Academy*, 2nd edition, Stationery Office, Dublin. [122, 131, 142, 158, 176, 178, 202, 209, 217, 240]

Arnal, Jean (1973), 'Sur les Dolmens et hypogées des pays latins: les V-boutons', in Glyn E. Daniel and Poul Kjaerum (eds), *Megalithic Graves and Ritual*, Moesgård, Jutland Archaeological Society, 221–6. [129]

Ashbee, Paul (1960), *The Bronze Age Round Barrow in Britain*, Phoenix House, London. [152]

Atkinson, R. J. C., Piggott, C. M. and Sandars, N. K. (1951), *Excavations at Dorchester, Oxon.*, Ashmolean Museum, Oxford. [131]

Bar-Adon, P. (1962), 'Expedition C – the Cave of the Treasure', *Israel Exploration Journal*, 12 (1962), 215–26. [121]

Bateson, J. D. (1973), 'Roman Material from Ireland: a Re-consideration', *P.R.I.A.*, 73C (1973), 21–97. [247]

Baudou, Evert (1960), *Die regionale und chronologische Einteilung der jungeren Bronzezeit im Nordischen Kreis*, Almquist & Wiksell, Stockholm. [201, 202, 214, 219]

Bell, John (1816), 'Letter from Mr John Bell', *Newry Magazine*, 2 (1816), 234–40. [31]

Bersu, G. (1947), 'A Cemetery of the Ronaldsway Culture at Ballateare, Jurby, Isle of Man', *P.P.S.*, 13 (1947), 161–9. [99]

Binchy, Eileen (1967), 'Irish Razors and Razor-knives', in Etienne Rynne (ed.), *North Munster Studies: Essays in Commemoration of Monsignor Michael Moloney*, Thomond Archaeological Society, Limerick, 43–60. [152, 158, 164, 166]

Blegen, C. W. (1963), *Troy and the Trojans*, Thames & Hudson, London. [167]

Borlase, William C. (1897), *Dolmens of Ireland*, 3 vols, Chapman & Hall, London. [12, 89]

Brennan, Mary Lou (1973), 'Robert Alexander Stewart Macalister 1871–1950, A Bibliography of his Published Works', *J.R.S.A.I.*, 103 (1973), 167–76. [13]

Bretz-Mahler, Denise (1971), *La Civilisation de La Tène I en Champagne*, (XXIII Supplement to *Gallia*), Paris. [241]

Briard, Jacques (1964), 'Note sur quelques faucilles à douille de l'Age du Bronze trouvées en France', *L'Anthropologie* 68 (1964), 133–8. [191]

Briard, Jacques (1965), *Les Depots Bretons et l'Age du Bronze Atlantique*, Travaux du Laboratoire d'Anthropologie Préhistorique de la Faculté des Sciences de Rennes, Rennes. [159, 163, 183, 219]

Briggs, Stephen, Brennan, James and Freeburn, George (1973), 'Irish Prehistoric Gold-working; some Geological and Metallurgical Considerations', *Bull. Historical Metallurgy Group*, 7 (1973), 18–26. [116]

Briscoe, Lady and Furness, Audrey (1955), 'A Hoard of Bronze Weapons from Eriswell, near Mildenhall', *Ant. J.*, 35 (1955), 218–19. [176]

British Museum (1925), *A Guide to the Antiquities of the Early Iron Age*, 2nd edn, London. [236]

British Museum (1953), *Later Prehistoric Antiquities of the British Isles*, London.

British Museum MSS., Stowe 1023, 1024. [5]

Britton, Dennis (1960), 'The Isleham Hoard, Cambridgeshire', *Ant.*, 36 (1960), 279–82. [195]

Britton, Dennis (1961), 'A Study of the Composition of Wessex Culture Bronzes', *Archaeometry*, 4 (1961), 39–52. [149]

Britton, Dennis (1963), 'Traditions of Metal-working in the Later Neolithic and Early Bronze Age of Britain: Part I', *P.P.S.*, 29 (1963), 258–325. [133, 139, 158, 195]

Broholm, H. C. (1953), *Danske Oldsager IV: Yngre Bronzealder*, Gyldendalske Boghandel, Copenhagen. [197]

Bruce, J. R., Megaw, E. M. and Megaw, B.R.S. (1947), 'A Neolithic Site at Ronaldsway, Isle of Man', *P.P.S.*, 13 (1947), 139–60. [99]

Bryce, Thomas H. (1902) 'On the Cairns of Arran – A Record of Explorations', *P.S.A.S.*, 36 (1901–2), 74–181. [51]

Buchvaldek, Miroslav (1967), *Die Schnurkeramik in Böhmen*, Universita Karlova, Prague. [111]

Buhigas, R. Sobrino (1935), *Corpus Petroglyphorum Gallaeciae,* Seminario de Estudos Galegos, Compostellae. [137]

Bulleid, Arthur and Gray, H. St George (1911 and 1917), *The Glastonbury Lake Village*, vol. 1 1911, vol. 2 1917, Taunton Castle, Taunton. [238]

Bullough, Donald (1965), 'The Ostrogothic and Lombard Kingdoms', in David Talbot Rice (ed.), *The Dark Ages*, Thames & Hudson, London. [248]

Burgess, C. B. (1968a), *Bronze Age Metalwork in Northern England*, Oriel Press, Newcastle upon Tyne. [183]

Burgess, C. B. (1968b), 'Bronze Age Dirks and Rapiers as illustrated by Examples from Durham and Northumberland', *Transactions of the Architectural and Archaeological Society of Durham and Northumberland*, 1 (1968), 3–26. [168, 169, 183]

Burgess, C. B. (1968c), 'The Later Bronze Age in the British Isles and North-western France', *Arch. J.*, 125 (1968), 1–45. [180, 182, 183, 186, 221]

Burgess, C. B. (1969a), 'Chronology and Terminology in the British Bronze Age', *Ant. J.*, 49 (1969), 22–9. [159, 164]

Burgess, C. B. (1969b), 'Some Decorated Socketed Axes in Canon Greenwell's Collection', *Y.A.J.*, 42 (1969), 267–72. [159]

Burgess, C. B. (1974), 'The Bronze Age', in Colin Renfrew (ed.), *British Prehistory: A New Outline*, Duckworth, London, 165–232. [158, 168, 183, 186]

Butler, J. J. (1960), 'A Bronze Age Concentration at Bargeroosterveld, with some Notes on the Axe Trade across Northern Europe', *Palaeohistoria* 8 (1960), 101–26. [193]

Butler, J. J. (1963), 'Bronze Age Connections across the North Sea', *Palaeohistoria*, 9 (1963), 1–286. [111, 122, 137, 144, 147, 168, 173, 176, 180]

Butler, J. J. and Smith, Isobel F. (1956), 'Razors, Urns and the British Middle Bronze Age', *University of London Institute of Archaeology Annual Report*, 12 (1956), 20–52. [152, 158]

Butler, J. J. and van der Waals, J. D. (1966), 'Bell Beakers and Early Metal-working in the Netherlands', *Palaeohistoria*, 12 (1966), 41–139. [132]

Byrne, F. J. (1968), 'Historical Note on Cnogba (Knowth)', *P.R.I.A.*, 66C (1968), 383–400. [228]

Calkin, J. Bernard (1962), 'The Bournemouth Area in the Middle and Late Bronze Age, with the 'Deverel-Rimbury' Problem Reconsidered', *Arch. J.*, 119 (1962), 1–65. [168]

Callander, J. Graham (1931–2), 'Earth Houses at Garry Iochdrach and Bac Mhic Connain, in North Uist', *P.S.A.S.*, 66 (1931–2), 32–66. [238]

Campbell, J. L. (1960), 'The Tour of Edward Lhuyd in Ireland in 1699 and 1700', *Celtica*, 5 (1960), 218–28. [5]

Case, H. J. (1961), 'Irish Neolithic Pottery: Distribution and Sequence', *P.P.S.*, 27 (1961), 174–233. [45, 93, 95, 100, 119, 129]

Case, H. J. (1966), 'Were Beaker-People the First Metallurgists in Ireland?', *Palaeohistoria*, 12 (1966), 141–77. [119, 121, 122, 131, 137, 139]

Case, H. J. (1969), 'Settlement-patterns in the North Irish Neolithic', *U.J.A.*, 3rd ser., 32 (1969), 3–27. [45]

Catling, H. W. (1964), *Cypriot Bronze-work in the Mycenaean World*, Clarendon Press, Oxford. [181]

Chadwick, Nora (1970), *The Celts*, Penguin, Harmondsworth. [224, 242]

Charlesworth, J. K. and Macalister, R. A. S. (1930), 'The Alleged Palaeolithic Implements of Sligo: a Summary', *P.R.I.A.*, 39C (1929–31), 18–32. [16]

Chart, D. A. (ed.) (1940), *A Preliminary Survey of the Ancient Monuments of Northern Ireland*, H.M.S.O., Belfast. [14, 72]

Childe, V. Gordon (1931), 'The Continental Affinities of British Neolithic Pottery', *Arch. J.*, 88 (1931), 37–66. [24, 27, 37, 56]

Childe, V. Gordon (1940), *Prehistoric Communities of the British Isles*, W. & R. Chambers, London. [35, 58, 124]

Childe, V. Gordon (1948), 'The Final Bronze Age in the Near East and in Temperate Europe', *P.P.S.*, 14 (1948), 177–95. [167]

Childe, V. Gordon (1957), *The Dawn of European Civilization*, 6th edn, Routledge & Kegan Paul, London. [116]

Childe, V. Gordon and Waterston, David (1941–2), 'Further Urns and Cremation Burials from Brackmont Hill, near Leuchars, Fife', *P.S.A.S.*, 76 (1941), 84–93. [149, 159]

Christison, David (1903–4), 'The Forts of Kilmartin, Kilmichael Glassary and North Knapdale, Argyle', *P.S.A.S.*, 38 (1903–4), 205–51. [249]

Christison, David (1904–5), 'Report on the Society's Excavations of Forts on the Poltalloch Estate, Argyll, in 1904–5', *P.S.A.S.*, 39 (1904–5), 259–322. [249]

Clark, J. G. D. (1932), 'Fresh Evidence for the Dating of Gold "Lunulae"', *Man*, 32 (1932), 40–1. [143]

Clark, J. G. D. (1935), 'The Prehistory of the Isle of Man', *P.P.S.*, 1 (1935), 70–92. [103]

Clark, J. G. D. (1936), *The Mesolithic Settlement of Northern Europe*, Cambridge University Press. [21, 24, 103]

Clark, J. G. D. (1937), 'Megalithic Research in the North of Ireland', *P.P.S.*, 3 (1937), 166–72. [35]

Clark, J. G. D. (1939), *Archaeology and Society*, 1st edn, Methuen, London. [13]

Clark, J. G. D. (1952), *Prehistoric Europe: The Economic Basis*, Methuen, London. [115, 187, 223]

Clark, J. G. D. (1954), *Excavations at Star Carr*, Cambridge University Press. [21]

Clark, J. G. D. (1960), *Archaeology and Society*, Methuen, London. [3]

Clark, J. G. D. (1963), 'Neolithic Bows from Somerset, England, and the Prehistory of Archery in North-west Europe', *P.P.S.*, 29 (1963), 50–98. [43]

Clark, J. G. D. (1975), *The Earlier Stone Age Settlement of Scandinavia*, Cambridge University Press. [24]

Clark, J. G. D. and Fell, C. I. (1953), 'The Early Iron Age Site at Micklemoor Hill, West Harling, Norfolk and its Pottery', *P.P.S.*, 19 (1953), 1–40.

Clark, D. L. (1970), *Beaker Pottery of Great Britain and Ireland*, 2 vols, Cambridge University Press. [122, 124, 126, 127, 129, 144, 149, 158]

Clarke, R. Rainbird (1954), 'The Early Iron Age Treasure from Snettisham, Norfolk', *P.P.S.*, 20 (1954), 27–86.

Coffey, George (1895), 'On a Double-Cist Grave and Remains at Oldbridge, Co. Meath', *P.R.I.A.*, 3 (1895), 747–52. [144]

Coffey, George (1897), 'Notes on the Prehistoric Cemetery of Loughcrew with a Fasciculus of Photographic Illustrations of the Sepulchral Cairns', *T.R.I.A.*, 31 (1896–1901), 23–38. [61]

Coffey, George (1902–4), 'Some Monuments of the La Tène Period recently discovered in Ireland', *P.R.I.A.*, 24C (1902–4), 257–66. [245]

Coffey, George (1904), 'Stone Celts and a Food Vessel found in the County Monaghan', *J.R.S.A.I.*, 34 (1904), 271–2. [70]

Coffey, George (1906), 'Two Finds of Late Bronze Age Objects', *P.R.I.A.*, 26C (1906), 119–24. [187, 199]

Coffey, George (1907a), 'Moulds for Primitive Spear-heads found in the County Tyrone', *J.R.S.A.I.*, 37 (1907), 181–6. [153]

Coffey, George (1907b), 'Find of Bronze Implements from Kilfeakle, County Tipperary', *J.R.S.A.I.*, 37 (1907), 86–9. [218]

Coffey, George (1908–9), 'Irish Copper Halberds', *P.R.I.A.*, 27C (1908–9), 94–114. [137]

Coffey, George (1909), *Guide to the Celtic Antiquities of the Early Christian Period*, Hodges Figgis, Dublin. [12]

259

Coffey, George (1912a), *New Grange and Other Incised Tumuli in Ireland*, Hodges Figgis, Dublin. [12, 58, 61, 66, 67]

Coffey, George (1912b), 'Some Recent Prehistoric Finds Acquired by the Academy', *P.R.I.A.*, 30C (1912), 83–93. [159, 193]

Coffey, George (1913), *The Bronze Age in Ireland*, Hodges Figgis, Dublin. [13, 169]

Coffey, George and Armstrong, E. C. R. (1914), 'Find of Bronze Objects at Annesborough, Co. Armagh', *P.R.I.A.*, 32C (1914), 171–5. [169]

Coghlan, H. H. and Case, Humphrey (1957), 'Early Metallurgy of Copper in Ireland and Britain', *P.P.S.*, 23 (1957), 91–123. [115, 119]

Coghlan, H. H. and Raftery, Joseph (1961), 'Irish Prehistoric Casting Moulds', *Sibrium*, 6 (1961), 223–44. [153, 160, 162, 163, 170, 193]

Coles, J. M. (1959–60), 'Scottish Late Bronze Age Metalwork: Typology, Distributions and Chronology', *P.S.A.S.*, 93 (1959–60), 16–134. [183]

Coles, J. M. (1962), 'European Bronze Age Shields', *P.P.S.*, 28 (1962), 156–90. [191, 195, 197, 217]

Coles, J. M. (1963), 'Irish Bronze Age Horns and their Relations with Northern Europe', *P.P.S.*, 29 (1963), 326–56. [210]

Coles, J. M. (1963–4), 'Scottish Middle Bronze Age Metalwork', *P.S.A.S.*, 97 (1963–4), 82–156. [164, 169]

Coles, J. M. (1965), 'The Archaeological Evidence for a "Bull Cult" in Late Bronze Age Europe', *Ant.*, 39 (1965), 217–19. [210]

Coles, J. M. (1968–9), 'Scottish Early Bronze Age Metalwork', *P.S.A.S.*, 101 (1968–9), 1–110. [133, 139]

Coles, J. M. and Taylor, Joan (1971), 'The Wessex Culture: a Minimal View', *Ant.*, 45 (1971), 6–14. [149]

Collins, A. E. P. (1952), 'Excavations in the Sandhills at Dundrum, Co. Down, 1950–1', *U.J.A.*, 3rd ser., 15 (1952), 2–30. [97]

Collins, A. E. P. (1954), 'The Excavation of a Double Horned Cairn at Audleystown, Co. Down', *U.J.A.*, 3rd ser., 17 (1954), 7–56. [32]

Collins, A. E. P. (1956), 'A Stone Circle on Castle Mahon Mountain, Co. Down', *U.J.A.*, 19 (1956), 1–10. [127]

Collins, A. E. P. (1957a), 'A Destroyed Burial Chamber at "Edenville", Ballygraffan, Co. Down', *U.J.A.*, 3rd ser., 20 (1957), 35–6. [47]

Collins, A. E. P. (1957b), 'Excavations at Two Standing Stones in Co. Down', *U.J.A.*, 20 (1957), 37–42. [128]

Collins, A. E. P. (1958), 'Ballygalley Hill, Co. Antrim', *P.P.S.*, 24 (1958), 218. [42]

Collins, A. E. P. (1959), 'Further Investigations in the Dundrum Sandhills', *U.J.A.*, 3rd ser., 22 (1959), 5–20. [97]

Collins, A. E. P. (1965a), 'Ballykeel Dolmen and Cairn, Co. Armagh', *U.J.A.*, 3rd ser., 28 (1965), 47–70. [88, 91]

Collins, A. E. P. (1965b), 'Cremation Burials from Cos Armagh and Derry', *U.J.A.*, 28 (1965), 71–7. [166]

Collins, A. E. P. (1966), 'Excavations at Dressogagh Rath, Co. Armagh', *U.J.A.*, 3rd ser., 29 (1966), 117–29. [46]

Collins, A. E. P. (1970), 'Bronze Age Moulds in Ulster', *U.J.A.*, 33 (1970), 23–36. [cf. Fig. 64]

Collins, A. E. P. and Evans, E. E. (1968), 'A Cist Burial at Carrickinab, Co. Down', *U.J.A.*, 31 (1968), 16–24. [134]

Collins, A. E. P. and Seaby, W. A. (1960), 'Structures and Small Finds Discovered at Lough Eskragh, Co. Tyrone', *U.J.A.*, 23 (1960), 25–37. [191, 212]

Collins, A. E. P. and Waterman, D. M. (1955), *Milliñ Bay, A Late Neolithic Cairn in Co. Down*, H.M.S.O., Belfast. [66, 127]

Collins, A. E. P. and Wilson, B. C. S. (1963), 'The Slieve Gullion Cairns', *U.J.A.*, 3rd ser., 26 (1963), 19–40. [66]

Conwell, Eugene Alfred (1873), *Discovery of the Tomb of Ollamh Fodhla*, McGlashan & Gill, Dublin. [11, 61, 236]

Cowen, J. D. (1951), 'The Earliest Bronze Swords in Britain and their Origins on the Continent of Europe', *P.P.S.*, 17 (1951), 195–213. [183]

Cowen, J. D. (1966), 'The Origins of the Flange-hilted Sword of Bronze in Continental Europe', *P.P.S.*, 32 (1966), 262–312.

Cowen, J. D. (1967), 'The Hallstatt Sword of Bronze: on the Continent and in Britain', *P.P.S.*, 33 (1967), 377–454. [219, 220]

Cowen, J. D. and Burgess, C. B. (1972), 'The Ebnal Hoard and Early Bronze Age Metalworking Traditions', in Frances Lynch and Colin Burgess (eds), *Prehistoric Man in Wales and the West: Essays in Honour of Lily F. Chitty*, Adams & Dart, Bath, 167–81. [150, 153]

Craw, James Hewat (1923–4), 'On Two Bronze Spoons from an Early Iron Age Grave near Burnmouth, Berwickshire', *P.S.A.S.*, 58 (1923–4), 143–60. [242]

Craw, James Hewat (1928–9), 'On a Jet Necklace from a Cist at Poltalloch, Argyll', *P.S.A.S.*, 63 (1928–9), 154–89. [143]

Crawford, H. S. (1925), 'The Engraved Bone Objects found at Lough Crew, Co. Meath', *J.R.S.A.I.*, 55 (1925), 15–29. [236, 238]

Croker, T. Crofton (1854), 'Notes on Various Discoveries of Gold Plates, chiefly in the South of Ireland', *Collectanea Antiqua*, 3 (1854), 131–52, 221–50. [122]

Curle, Alexander O. (1932–3), 'Account of Further Excavations in 1932 of the Prehistoric Township at Jarlshof, Shetland', *P.S.A.S.*, 67 (1932–3), 82–136. [170]

Danaher, Peter (1965), 'Bronze Age Burials at Rahinashurock, Co. Westmeath', *Ríocht na mídhe*, 3 (1965), 225–8. [151, 158]

Daniel, Glyn E. (1941), 'The Dual Nature of the Megalithic Colonisation of Prehistoric Europe', *P.P.S.*, 7 (1941), 1–49. [58]

Daniel, Gly E. (1950), *The Prehistoric Chamber Tombs of England and Wales*, Cambridge University Press. [54, 128]

Daniel, Glyn E. (1964), *The Idea of Prehistory*, Penguin, Harmondsworth. [10, 12]

Darbishire, R. D. (1873), 'Notes on Discoveries in Ehenside Tarn, Cumberland', *Archaeologia*, 44, pt 2 (1873), 273–92. [100]

Davies, D. Gareth (1967), 'The Guilsfield Hoard: a Reconsideration', *Ant. J.*, 47 (1967), 95–108.

Davies, Ellis (1929), *The Prehistoric and Roman Remains of Denbighshire*, privately published, Cardiff. [242]

Davies, Oliver (1936), 'Excavations at Dún Ruadh', *P.B.N.H.P.S.*, 2nd ser., I pt. 1 (1935–6), 50–75. [46]

Davies, Oliver (1937), 'Excavations at Ballyrenan, Co. Tyrone', *J.R.S.A.I.*, 67 (1937), 89–100. [89]

Davies, Oliver (1939a), 'Stone Circles in Northern Ireland', *U.J.A.*, 2 (1939), 2–14. [128]

Davies, Oliver (1939b), 'Excavations at the Giant's Grave, Loughash', *U.J.A.*, 2 (1939), 254–68. [119]

Davies, Oliver (1940), 'Excavations on the Dorsey and the Black Pig's Dyke', *U.J.A.*, 3 (1940), 31–7. [230]

Davies, Oliver (1941), 'Trial Excavation at Lough Enagh', *U.J.A.*, 3rd ser., 4 (1941), 88–101. [89, 100]

Davies, Oliver (1950), *Excavations at Island MacHugh*, supplement to *P.B.N.H.P.S.*, Belfast. [100, 110]

Davies, Oliver (1955), 'The Black Pig's Dyke', *U.J.A.*, 18 (1955), 29–36. [230]

Davies, Oliver and Evans, E. E. (1932), 'Excavations at Goward, near Hilltown, Co. Down', *P.B.N.H.P.S.*, (1932–3), 90–105. [13]

Davies, Oliver and Evans, E. E. (1934), 'Excavation of a Chambered Horned Cairn at Ballyalton, Co. Down', *P.B.N.H.P.S.*, (1933–4), 79–103. [35, 95]

Davies, Oliver and Mullin, J. B. (1940), 'Excavation of Cashelbane Cairn, Loughash, Co. Tyrone', *J.R.S.A.I.*, 70 (1940), 143–63. [119]

Deady, John and Doran, Elizabeth (1972), 'Prehistoric Copper Mines, Mount Gabriel, Co. Cork', *J.C.H.A.S.*, 77 (1972), 25–7. [115]

Déchelette, Joseph (1924, 1927), *Manuel d'archéologie préhistorique, celtique et gallo-romaine*, 2nd edn, Paris, Auguste Picard, 1924 (Bronze), 1927 (Iron). [180]

De Paor, Máire (1961), 'Notes on Irish Beakers', in G. Bersu (ed.), *Bericht über den V internationalen Kongress für Vor-und Frühgeschichte, Hamburg 1958*, Gebr. Mann, Berlin, 653–60. [119]

De Paor, Máire and Liam (1958), *Early Christian Ireland*, Thames & Hudson, London. [249]

Desborough, V. R. d'A. (1964), *The Last Mycenaeans and their Successors: An Archaeological Survey c. 1200–1100 B.C.*, Clarendon Press, Oxford. [167]

De Valera, R. (1960), 'The Court Cairns of Ireland', *P.R.I.A.*, 60C (1959–60), 9–140. [27, 31, 45, 56, 85, 90]

De Valera, R. (1961), 'The "Carlingford Culture", the Long Barrow and the Neolithic of Great Britain and Ireland', *P.P.S.*, 27 (1961), 234–52. [45]

De Valera, R. (1965), 'Transeptal Court Cairns', *J.R.S.A.I.*, 95 (1965), 5–37. [30, 54, 56, 58, 65]

De Valera, R. (1968), 'Pre-Celtic', entry in *Encyclopedia of Ireland*, Allan Figgis, Dublin, 80. [117]

De Valera, R. and Ó Nualláin, S. (1961, 1964, 1972), *Survey of the Megalithic Tombs of Ireland*, vols 1, 2, 3, Stationery Office, Dublin. [27, 31, 85, 90, 117, 119]

Dickinson, C. W. and Waterman, D. M. (1960), 'Excavations at Castle Skreen, Co. Down', *U.J.A.*, 3rd ser., 23 (1960), 63–77. [46]

Dunning, G. C. (1934), 'The Swan's-neck and Ring-headed Pins of the Early Iron Age in Britain', *Arch. J.*, 91 (1934), 269–95. [240, 241]

Elgee, H. W. and Elgee, F. (1949), 'An Early Bronze Age Burial in a Boat-shaped Wooden Coffin from North-east Yorkshire', *P.P.S.*, 15 (1949), 87–106. [149]

Eogan, George (1962), 'Some Observations on the Middle Bronze in Ireland', *J.R.S.A.I.*, 92 (1962), 45–60. [164]

Eogan, George (1963), 'A Neolithic Habitation-Site and Megalithic Tomb in Townleyhall Townland, Co. Louth', *J.R.S.A.I.*, 93 (1963), 37–81. [70]

Eogan, George (1964), 'The Later Bronze Age in Ireland in the Light of Recent Research', *P.P.S.*, 30 (1964), 268–351. [168, 169, 176, 178, 179, 183, 192, 193, 195, 197, 202, 205, 208, 210, 211, 213, 219, 222]

Eogan, George (1965), *Catalogue of Irish Bronze Swords*, Stationery Office, Dublin. [183, 193, 195, 217, 219, 220]

Eogan, George (1966), 'Some Notes on the Origin and Diffusion of the Bronze Socketed Gouge', *U.J.A.*, 29 (1966), 97–102. [195]

Eogan, George (1967a), 'The Associated Finds of Gold Bar Torcs', *J.R.S.A.I.*, 97 (1967), 129–75. [169, 176, 195]

Eogan, George (1967b), 'The Knowth (Co. Meath) Excavations', *Ant.*, 41 (1967), 302–64. [60]

Eogan, George (1968), 'Excavations at Knowth, Co. Meath, 1962–5', *P.R.I.A.*, 66C (1968), 299–382. [60, 240, 244]

Eogan, George (1969), 'Lock-rings of the Late Bronze Age', *P.R.I.A.*, 67C (1969), 93–148. [199, 209, 211, 214]

Eogan, George (1972), '"Sleeve-fasteners" of the Late Bronze Age', in Frances Lynch and Colin Burgess (eds). *Prehistoric Man in Wales and the West*, Adams & Dart, Bath, 189–209. [201]

Eogan, George (1974a), 'Report on the Excavations of some Passage Graves, Unprotected Inhumation Burials and a Settlement Site at Knowth, Co. Meath', *P.R.I.A.*, 74C (1974), 11–112. [60, 244]

Eogan, George (1974b), 'Regionale Gruppierungen in der Spätbronzezeit Irlands', *Archaologisches Korrespondenzblatt*, 4 (1974), 319–27. [208, 222]

Evans, E. Estyn (1930), 'The Sword-bearers', *Ant.*, 4 (1930), 157-72. [186]

Evans, E. Estyn (1933), 'The Bronze Spearhead in Great Britain and Ireland', *Arch.*, 83 (1933), 187–202. [183]

Evans, E. Estyn (1938a), 'Giants' Graves', *U.J.A.*, 3rd ser., 1 (1938), 7–19. [90]

Evans, E. Estyn (1938b), 'Doey's Cairn, Dunloy', *U.J.A.*, 3rd ser., 1 (1938), 59–78. [95]

Evans, E. Estyn (1945), 'Field Archaeology in the Ballycastle District', *U.J.A.*, 3rd ser., 8 (1945), 14–32. [67]

Evans, E. Estyn (1946), 'The Origins of Irish Agriculture', *U.J.A.*, 3rd ser., 9 (1946), 87–90. [110]

Evans, E. Estyn (1953), *Lyles Hill: A Late Neolithic Site in County Antrim*, Archaeological Research Publications No. 2, Stationery Office, Belfast. [46, 139, 147]

Evans, E. Estyn (1966), *Prehistoric and Early Christian Ireland. A Guide,* Batsford, London. [125, 226, 228, 230]

Evans, E. Estyn and Gaffikin, M. (1935), 'Belfast Naturalists' Field Club Survey of Antiquities: Megaliths and Raths', *I.N.J.*, 5 (1934–5), 242–52. [14]

Evans, E. Estyn and Jope, E. M. (1952), 'Prehistoric', in Emrys Jones (ed.), *Belfast in Its Regional Setting: A Scientific Survey*, British Association for the Advancement of Science, Belfast. [31, 43]

Evans, E. Estyn and Megaw, Basil R. S. (1937), 'The Multiple-Cist Cairn at Mount Stewart, Co. Down', *P.P.S.*, 3 (1937), 29–42. [135]

Evans, E. Estyn and Mitchell, G. F. (1954), 'Three Bronze Spearheads from Tattenamona, near Brookeborough, Co. Fermanagh', *U.J.A.*, 17 (1954), 57–61. [178]

Evans, E. Estyn and Paterson, T. G. F. (1939), 'A Bronze Age Burial Group from Kilskeery, Co. Tyrone', *U.J.A.*, 2 (1939), 65–71. [144, 166]

Evans, John (1881), *The Ancient Bronze Implements, Weapons and Ornaments of Great Britain and Ireland,* Longmans, Green, London. [153, 159]

Fahy, E. M. (1959), 'A Recumbent-stone Circle at Drombeg, Co. Cork', *J.C.H.A.S.*, 64 (1959), 1–27. [123]

Fahy, E. M. (1960), 'A Hut and Cooking-place at Drombeg, Co. Cork', *J.C.H.A.S.*, 65 (1960), 1–17. [232]

Fahy, E. M. (1962), 'A Recumbent-stone Circle at Reanascreena South, Co. Cork', *J.C.H.A.S.*, 67 (1962), 59–69. [123]

Fergusson, James (1872), *Rude Stone Monuments in All Countries*, John Murray, London. [11]

Filip, Jan (1960), *Celtic Civilization and its Heritage*, Czechoslovak Academy of Sciences & A.R.T.I.A., Prague. [224]

Flanagan, L. N. W. (1960), 'Bone Beads and Ring from Newgrange, Co. Meath', *U.J.A.*, 23 (1960), 61–2. [197, 244]

Flanagan, L. N. W. (1964), 'Necklace of Amber Beads, Kurin, Co. Derry', *U.J.A.*, 27 (1964), 92–3. [197]

Flanagan, L. N. W. (1966a), 'A Neolithic Site at Drumadonnell, Co. Down', *U.J.A.*, 3rd ser., 29 (1966), 76–82.

Flanagan, L. N. W. (1966b), 'An Unpublished Flint Hoard from the Braid Valley, Co. Antrim', *U.J.A.*, 3rd ser., 29 (1966), 82–90. [43]

Florescu, Adrian C. (1964), 'Contributii la cunoasasterea culturii Noua (Contribution à la conaissance de la civilisation de Noua)', *Archaeologia Moldavei*, 2–3 (1964), 143–216.

Fox, Aileen (1961), 'South-Western Hill-Forts', in S. S. Frere (ed.), *Problems of the Iron Age in Southern Britain*. University of London Occasional Paper No. 11, London, 35–60. [228]

Fox, Aileen and Pollard, Sheila (1973), 'A Decorated Bronze Mirror from an Iron Age Settlement at Holcombe, near Uplyme, Devon', *Ant. J.*, 53 (1973), 16–41. [240]

Fox, Cyril (1939a), 'The Socketed Bronze Sickles of the British Isles', *P.P.S.*, 5 (1939), 222–48. [183, 187, 191]

Fox, Cyril (1939b), 'A Second Cauldron and an Iron Sword from the Llyn Fawr Hoard, Rhigos, Glamorganshire', *Ant. J.*, 19 (1939), 369–404. [219, 223]

Fox, Cyril (1941), 'The Non-socketed Bronze Sickles of Britain', *Arch. Camb.*, 96 (1941), 136–62. [173]

Fox, Cyril (1946), *A Find of the Early Iron Age from Llyn Cerrig Bach, Anglesey*, National Museum of Wales, Cardiff. [242, 248]

Fox, Cyril (1948), 'Celtic Mirror Handles in Britain, with Special Reference to the Colchester Handle', *Arch. Camb.*, 100 (1948), 24–44. [240]

Fox, Cyril (1950), 'Two Celtic Bronzes from Lough Gur, Limerick, Ireland', *Ant. J.*, 30 (1950), 190–2. [233]

Fox, Cyril (1952), *The Personality of Britain*, 4th edn, National Museum of Wales, Cardiff. [123, 133, 150, 228]

Fox, Cyril (1958), *Pattern and Purpose: A Survey of Early Celtic Art in Britain*, National Museum of Wales, Cardiff. [240]

Fox, Cyril and Hull, R. M. (1948), 'The Incised Ornament on the Celtic Mirror from Colchester, Essex', *Ant. J.*, 28 (1948), 123–37. [238, 240]

Frazer, William (1889–91), 'On a Polished Stone Implement of Novel Form, and its Probable Use', *P.R.I.A.*, 17 (1889–91), 215–20. [153]

Frazer, William (1893), 'Incised Sculpturings on Stones in County Meath', *P.S.A.S.*, 27 (1892–3), 294–340. [61]

Giot, P. R. (1960), *Brittany*, Thames & Hudson, London. [123]

Glob, P. V. (1952), *Danish Antiquities 2: Late Stone Age*, ed. Therkel Mathiassen, Gyldendalske Boghandel, Nordisk Forlag, Copenhagen. [107, 109]

Graham, T. B. and Jope, E. M. (1950), 'A Bronze Brooch and Ibex-headed Pin from the Sandhills at Dunfanaghy, Co. Donegal', *U.J.A.*, 13 (1950), 54–6. [240]

Gräslünd, Bo (1967), 'The Herzsprung Shield Type and its Origin', *Acta Archaeologica* (Kopenhagen), 38 (1967), 59–71. [197]

Gray, William (1872), 'Stone Celts found near Belfast', *J.R.S.A.I.*, 12 (1872–3), 138. [45]

Greene, David (1972), 'The Chariot as Described in Irish Literature', in Charles Thomas (ed.), *The Iron Age in the Irish Sea Province*, Council for British Archaeology, Research Report 9, London, 59–73. [233]

Greenwell, William and Brewis, William Parker (1909), 'The Origin, Evolution and

Classification of the Bronze Spear-head in Great Britain and Ireland', *Arch.*, 61 (1909), 439–72. [149, 163]

Griffith, Richard (1844), 'On a Collection of Antiquities, Presented by the Shannon Commissioners to the Museum of the Academy', *P.R.I.A.*, 2 (1840–4), 312–16. [39]

Griffiths, W. E. (1951), 'Decorated Rotary Querns from Wales and Ireland', *U.J.A.*, 14 (1951), 49–61. [234]

Grimes, W. F. (1949), 'Pentre-Ifan Burial Chamber, Pembrokeshire', *Arch. Camb.*, 100 (1949), 2–23. [88]

Grimes, W. F. (1963), 'The Stone Circles and Related Monuments of Wales', in I. Ll. Foster and L. Alcock (eds), *Culture and Environment: Essays in Honour of Sir Cyril Fox*, Routledge & Kegan Paul, London, 93–152. [131]

Grinsell, L. V. (1941), 'The Bronze Age Round Barrows of Wessex', *P.P.S.*, 7 (1941), 73–113. [152]

Grose, Francis (1791, *recte* 1795), *The Antiquities of Ireland*, S. Hooper, London. [7]

Gurney, O. (1954), *The Hittites*, 2nd edn, Penguin, Harmondsworth. [167]

Hamilton, J. R. C. (1956), *Excavations at Jarlshof, Shetland*, Ministry of Works Archaeological Reports No. 1, Edinburgh. [212]

Harbison, Peter (1966), 'Mining and Metallurgy in Early Bronze Age Ireland', *N.M.A.J.*, 10 (1966), 3–11. [115]

Harbison, Peter (1967), 'Some Minor Metal Products of the Early Bronze Age in Ireland', *J.C.H.A.S.*, 72 (1967), 93–100. [129, 153]

Harbison, Peter (1968), 'Catalogue of Irish Early Bronze Age Associated Finds Containing Copper or Bronze', *P.R.I.A.*, 67C (1968), 35–91. [121, 122]

Harbison, Peter (1969a), *The Daggers and Halberds of the Early Bronze Age in Ireland*, Prähistorische Bronzefunde, Abteilung VI, I. Band, C. H. Beck'sche, Munich. [129, 137, 139, 146, 153, 157, 158, 159]

Harbison, Peter (1969b), *The Axes of the Early Bronze in Ireland*, Prähistorische Bronzefunde, Abteilung IX, I. Band, C. H. Beck'sche, Munich. [119, 153, 166]

Harbison, Peter (1969c), 'The Relative Chronology of Irish Early Bronze Age Pottery', *J.R.S.A.I.*, 99 (1969), 63–82.

Harbison, Peter (1971), 'Wooden and Stone *Chevaux-de-frise* in Central and Western Europe', *P.P.S.*, 37 (1971), 195–225. [226, 228, 246]

Harbison, Peter (1973), 'The Earlier Bronze Age in Ireland', *J.R.S.A.I.*, 103 (1973), 93–152. [124]

Harrison, Richard J. (1974), 'Origins of the Bell Beaker Cultures', *Ant.*, 48 (1974), 99–109. [117]

Hartmann, Axel (1970), *Prähistorische Goldfunde aus Europa*, Studien zum den Anfängen der Metallurgie 3, Gebr. Mann Verlag, Berlin. [116]

Hartnett, P. J. (1950), 'A Crouched Burial at Hempstown Commons, Co. Kildare', *J.R.S.A.I.*, 80 (1950), 193–8. [70, 134]

Hartnett, P. J. (1951), 'A Neolithic Burial from Martinstown, Kiltale, Co. Meath', *J.R.S.A.I.*, 81 (1951), 19–23. [84]

Hartnett, P. J. (1952), 'Bronze Age Burials in Co. Wicklow', *J.R.S.A.I.*, 82 (1952), 153–62. [144]

Hartnett, P. J. (1957), 'Excavation of a Passage Grave at Fourknocks, Co. Meath', *P.R.I.A.*, 58C (1957), 197–277. [125, 132, 139]

Harnett, P. J. (1971), 'The Excavation of Two Tumuli at Fourknocks (Sites II and III), Co. Meath', *P.R.I.A.*, 71C (1971), 35–89. [70]

Hartnett, P. J. and Eogan, George (1964), 'Feltrim Hill, Co. Dublin: A Neolithic and Early Christian Site', *J.R.S.A.I.*, 94 (1964), 1–37. [47]

Hartnett, P. J. and Prendergast, E. (1953), 'Bronze Age Burials, Co. Wexford', *J.R.S.A.I.*, 83 (1953), 46–57. [166]

Hawkes, C. F. C. (1942), 'The Deverel Urn and the Picardy Pin', *P.P.S.*, 8 (1942), 26–47. [168]

Hawkes, C. F. C. (1951), 'Bronze-Workers, Cauldrons, and Bucket-animals in Iron Age and Roman Britain', in W. F. Grimes (ed.), *Aspects of Archaeology in Britain and Beyond (Essays presented to O. G. S. Crawford)*, H. W. Edwards, London, 172–99. [238]

Hawkes, C. F. C. (1961), 'Gold Ear-rings of the Bronze Age, East and West', *Folklore*, 72 (1961), 438–74. [176]

Hawkes, C. F. C. (1962), 'Archaeological Significance of the Moulsford Torc Analysis', *Archaeometry*, 5 (1962), 33–7. [169]

Hawkes, C. F. C. (1965), 'The Celts: Report on the Study of their Culture and their Mediterranean Relations, 1942–62', in *L'Occident préromain*, (8ᵉ Congrès International d'Archéologie Classique, Paris 1963), Editions E. de Boccard, Paris, 61–79. [224]

Hawkes, C. F. C. (1969), 'Las Relaciones Atlanticas del Mundo Tartesico', in *Tartessos y sus Problemas, V Symposium International de Prehistoria Peninsular, 1968*, Universidad de Barcelona. [215]

Hawkes, C. F. C. and Clarke, R. R. (1963), 'Gahlstorf and Caister-on-Sea: Two Finds of Late Bronze Age Irish Gold', in I. Ll. Foster and Leslie Alcock (eds), *Culture and Environment: Essays in Honour of Sir Cyril Fox*, Routledge & Kegan Paul, London, 193–250. [199, 201, 202, 212, 214, 215]

Hawkes, C. F. C. and Hull, M. R. (1947), 'Camulodunum: First Report on the Excavations at Colchester, 1930–39', *Report XIV, Research Committee, Society of Antiquaries of London*. [240]

Hawkes, C. F. C. and Smith, M. A. (1957), 'On some Buckets and Cauldrons of the Bronze and Early Iron Ages', *Ant. J.*, 37 (1957), 131–98. [191, 202, 204, 215, 218]

Hawkes, Jacquetta (1941), 'Excavation of a Megalithic Tomb at Harristown, Co. Waterford', *J.R.S.A.I.*, 71 (1941), 130–47. [151, 158, 166]

Haworth, Richard (1971), 'The Horse Harness of the Irish Early Iron Age', *U.J.A.*, 34 (1971), 26–49. [231, 232, 242]

Hemp, W. J. (1935), 'The Chambered Cairn known as Bryn yr Hen Bobl near Plas Newydd, Anglesey', *Archaeologia*, 85 (1935), 253–92. [70]

Hencken, Hugh O'Neill (1932), *The Archaeology of Cornwall and Scilly*, Methuen, London. [116]

Hencken, Hugh O'Neill (1935), 'A Cairn at Poulawack, County Clare', *J.R.S.A.I.*, 65 (1935), 191–222.

Hencken, Hugh O'Neill (1938), *Cahercommaun: A Stone Fort in County Clare*, R.S.A.I., Dublin. [228, 235]

Hencken, Hugh O'Neill (1939), 'A Long Cairn at Creevykeel, Co. Sligo', *J.R.S.A.I.*, 69 (1939), 53–98. [29, 35]

Hencken, Hugh O'Neill (1942), 'Ballinderry Crannog No. 2', *P.R.I.A.*, 47C (1942), 1–76. [187, 188, 189, 202, 205, 207]

Hencken, Hugh O'Neill (1950), 'Lagore Crannog: An Irish Royal Residence of the 7th to 10th Centuries A.D.', *P.R.I.A.*, 53C (1950), 1–247. [224, 236]

Hencken, Hugh O'Neill (1968), *Tarquinia, Villanovans and Early Etruscans*, American School of Prehistoric Research, Bulletin 23, Peabody Museum, Harvard. [186]

Hencken, Hugh O'Neill and Movius, H. L. (1934), 'The Cemetery Cairn of Knockast', *P.R.I.A.*, 41C (1934), 232–84. [138, 153]

Henry, Françoise (1965a), *Irish Art in the Early Christian Period (to 800 A.D.)*, Methuen, London. [245, 249]

Henry, Françoise (1965b), 'On Some Early Christian Objects in the Ulster Museum', *J.R.S.A.I.*, 95 (1965), 51–63. [249]

Henshall, Audrey S. (1950), 'Textiles and Weaving Appliances in Prehistoric Britain', *P.P.S.*, 16 (1950), 130–62. [199]

Henshall, Audrey S. (1972), *The Chambered Tombs of Scotland*, vol. 2, Edinburgh University Press.

Herity, M. (1964), 'The Finds from the Irish Portal Dolmens', *J.R.S.A.I.*, 94 (1964), 123–44. [91]

Herity, M. (1969), 'Early Finds of Irish Antiquities'. *Ant. J.*, 49 (1969), 1–21. [6, 10]

Herity, M. (1970a), 'Rathmulcah, Ware and Mac Firbisigh', *U.J.A.*, 3rd ser., 33 (1970), 49–53. [4]

Herity, M. (1970b), 'The Early Prehistoric Period around the Irish Sea', in Donald Moore (ed.), *The Irish Sea Province in Archaeology and History*, Cambrian Archaeological Association, Cardiff. [16, 85]

Herity, M. (1970c), 'Cord-ornamented Beacharra Ware and the Single-burial Mode in Ireland', in Jan Filip (ed.), *Actes du VIIᵉ Congrès International des Sciences Préhistoriques et Protohistoriques*, l'Académie Tchécoslovaque des Sciences à Prague, 530–34. [49, 85]

Herity, M. (1971), 'Prehistoric Fields in Ireland', *Irish University Review*, 1 (1971), 258–65. [50]

Herity, M. (1973), 'The Prehistoric Period: Internal and External Communications', in Kevin B. Nowlan (ed.), *Travel and Transport in Ireland*, Gill & Macmillan, Dublin 11–17. [142]

Herity, M. (1974), *Irish Passage Graves*, Irish University Press, Dublin. [5, 58, 127, 137]

Herity, M., Evans, E. Estyn and Megaw, B. R. S. (1968), 'The "Larne" Material in Lord Antrim's Collection at the Ashmolean Museum, Oxford', *P.R.I.A.*, 67C (1968–9), 9–34. [42, 93]

Herring, Ivor (1941), 'The Tamnyrankin Cairn: West Structure', *J.R.S.A.I.*, 71 (1941), 31–52. [93, 95, 97]

Hestrim, Ruth and Tadmor, Miriam (1963), 'A Hoard of Tools and Weapons from Kfar Monash', *Israel Exploration Journal*, 13 (1963), 265–88. [121]

Hewson, L. M. (1938), 'Notes on Irish Sandhills', *J.R.S.A.I.*, 68 (1938), 69–90.

Hodges, H. W. M. (1954), 'Studies in the Late Bronze Age in Ireland: 1. Stone and Clay Moulds, and Wooden Models for Bronze Implements', *U.J.A.*, 17 (1954), 62–80. [193]

Hodges, H. W. M. (1956), 'Studies in the Late Bronze Age in Ireland: 2. The Typology and Distribution of Bronze Implements', *U.J.A.*, 19 (1956), 29–56. [170, 195]

Hodges, H. W. M. (1957), 'Studies in the Late Bronze Age in Ireland: 3. The Hoards of Bronze Implements', *U.J.A.*, 20 (1957), 51–63. [202]

Hodson, F. R. (1964), 'Cultural Grouping within the British Pre-Roman Iron Age', *P.P.S.*, 30 (1964), 99–110. [240]

Hundt, Hans-Jürgen (1955), 'Versuch zur Deutung der Depotfunde der Nordischen Jüngeren Bronzezeit unter besonderer Brücksichtigung Mecklenburgs', *Jahrbuch des Römisch-Germanischen Zentralmuseums Mainz*, 2 (1955), 95–132. [210]

Hunt, John (1967), 'Prehistoric Burials at Cahirguillamore, Co. Limerick', in Etienne Rynne (ed.), *North Munster Studies: Essays in Commemoration of Monsignor Michael Moloney*, Thomond Archaeological Society, Limerick, 20–42. [111, 128]

Inskeep, R. R. and Proudfoot, V. Bruce (1957), 'Dunbeg: A Small Hill-fort in Co. Down', *U.J.A.*, 20 (1957), 103–13. [228]

Iversen, Johs (1941), 'Land Occupation in Denmark's Stone Age', *Danmarks Geologiske Undersøgelse*, II, nr 66 (1941), 20–68. [24, 25]

Iversen, Johs (1949), 'The Influence of Prehistoric Man on Vegetation', *Danmarks Geologiske Undersøgelse*. IV, bd. 3, nr 6 (1949), 6–22. [25]

Jackson, John S. (1968), 'Bronze Age Copper Mines on Mount Gabriel, West County Cork, Ireland', *Archaeologia Austriaca*, 43, (1968), 92–114. [115]

Jacob-Friesen, Gernot (1967), *Bronzezeitliche Lanzenspitzen Norddeutschlands und Skandinaviens*, Augst Lax, Hildesheim. [195]

Jacob-Friesen, K. H. (1963), *Einführung in Niedersachsens Urgeschichte. II Teil, Bronzezeit*, 4th edn, ed. G. Jacob-Friesen, Augst Lax, Hildesheim. [180]

Jacobsthal, Paul (1944), *Early Celtic Art*, Clarendon Press, Oxford. [224]

Jankuhn, Herbert (ed.) (1970), *Vorgeschichtliche Heiliglümer und Opferplätze in Mittel-und Nordeuropa*, Vandenhoeck & Ruprecht, Göttingen. [210]

Jessen, Knud (1949), 'Studies in the Late Quaternary Deposits and Flora-history of Ireland', *P.R.I.A.*, 52B (1948–50), 85–290. [3, 19, 21]

Jessen, Knud and Helbaek, Hans (1944), 'Cereals in Great Britain and Ireland in Prehistoric and Early Historic Times', *Det Kongelige Danske Videnskabernes Selskab: Biologiske Skrifter*, vol. III, no. 2 (1944), 1–68. [27, 110, 158]

Jobey, George and Tait, John (1966), 'Excavations on Palisaded Settlements and Cairnfields at Alnham, Northumberland', *Archaeologia Aeliana*, 44 (1966), 5–48. [240]

Jope, E. M. (1950), 'Two Iron Age Horse Bridle-Bits from the North of Ireland', *U.J.A.*, 13 (1950), 57–60. [233, 240]

Jope, E. M. (1951), 'A Crescentic Jet Necklace from Rasharkin, Co. Antrim', *U.J.A.*, 14 (1951), 61. [144]

Jope, E. M. (1952), 'Porcellanite Axes from Factories in North-east Ireland: Tievebulliagh and Rathlin', *U.J.A.*, 3rd ser., 15 (1952), 31–55. [37, 39, 40, 50]

Jope, E. M. (1954a), 'An Iron Age Decorated Sword-Scabbard from the River Bann at Toome', *U.J.A.*, 17 (1954), 81–91. [236, 237, 240, 246]

Jope, E. M. (1954b), 'The Keshcarrigan Bowl and a Bronze Mirror-Handle from Ballymoney, Co. Antrim', *U.J.A.*, 17 (1954), 92–6. [238, 239]

Jope, E. M. (1955), 'Chariotry and Paired-Draught in Ireland during the Early Iron Age: the Evidence of some Horse-Bridle-Bits', *U.J.A.*, 18 (1955), 37–44. [233]

Jope, E. M. (1961), 'Daggers of the Early Iron Age in Britain', *P.P.S.*, 27 (1961), 307–43. [223]

Jope, E. M. (1961–2), 'Iron Age Brooches in Ireland: a Summary', *U.J.A.*, 24–5 (1961–2), 25–38. [240, 241]

Jope, E. M. and Wilson, B. C. S. (1957a), 'A Burial Group of the First Century A.D., from "Loughey", near Donaghadee, Co. Down', *U.J.A.*, 20 (1957), 73–95. [240, 241]

Jope, E. M. and Wilson, B. C. S. (1957b), 'The Decorated Cast Bronze Disc from the River Bann near Coleraine', *U.J.A.*, 20 (1957), 95–102. [238, 242, 244]

Kane, William Francis de Vismes (1908–9), 'The Black Pig's Dyke: the Ancient Boundary Fortification of Uladh', *P.R.I.A.*, 27C (1908–9), 301–28. [230]

Kane, William Francis de Vismes (1916–17), 'Additional Research on the Black Pig's Dyke', *P.R.I.A.*, 33 (1916–17), 539–63. [230]

Kavanagh, Rhoda M. (1973), 'The Encrusted Urn in Ireland', *P.R.I.A.*, 73C (1973), 507–617. [148]

Keller, Josef (1965), *Das Keltische Früstengrab von Reinheim*, Römisch-Germanisches Zentralmuseum, Mainz. [240]

Kenyon, Kathleen M. (1960), *Archaeology in the Holy Land*, Benn, London. [167]

Kenyon, Kathleen M. (1966), *Amorites and Canaanites*, British Academy, London. [116]

Kersten, Karl (1936), *Zur Älteren Nordischen Bronzezeit*, Karl Wachholtz, Neumünster. [173, 176]

Kilbride-Jones, H. E. (1937), 'The Evolution of Penannular Brooches with Zoomorphic Terminals in Great Britain and Ireland', *P.R.I.A.*, 43C (1937), 379–455. [240]

Kilbride-Jones, H. E. (1939), 'The Excavation of a Composite Tumulus at Drimnagh, Co. Dublin', *J.R.S.A.I.*, 69 (1939), 190–220. [81]

Kilbride-Jones, H. E. (1950), 'The Excavation of a Composite Early Iron Age Monument with "Henge" Features at Lugg, Co. Dublin', *P.R.I.A.*, 53C (1950), 311–32. [225, 238, 244]

Kilbride-Jones, H. E. (1954), 'The Excavation of an Unrecorded Megalithic Tomb on Kilmashogue Mountain, Co. Dublin', *P.R.I.A.*, 56C (1954), 461–79 [123]

Killanin, Lord and Duignan, Michael V. (1967), *The Shell Guide to Ireland*, 2nd edn, Ebury Press, London. [230]

Knowles, W. J. (1878), 'Flint Implements, and Associated Remains found near Ballintoy Co. Antrim', *Journal of the Anthropological Institute*, 7 (1878), 202–5. [99]

Knowles, W. J. (1889a), 'Report on some Recent "Finds" in County Antrim', *J.R.S.A.I.*, 19 (1889), 107–13. [99, 158]

Knowles, W. J. (1889b), 'Report on the Prehistoric Remains from the Sandhills of the Coast of Ireland', *P.R.I.A.*, 17 (1889–91), 173–87. [99]

Knowles, W. J. (1891), 'Report (Second) on the Prehistoric Remains from the Sandhills of the Coast of Ireland', *P.R.I.A.*, 17 (1889–91), 612–25. [97]

Knowles, W. J. (1895), 'Third Report on the Prehistoric Remains from the Sandhills of the Coast of Ireland', *P.R.I.A.*, 19 (1893–6), 650–63. [97]

Knowles, W. J. (1901), 'The Fourth Report on the Prehistoric Remains from the Sandhills of the Coast of Ireland', *P.R.I.A.*, 22 (1900–2), 331–89. [97, 99]

Knowles, W. J. (1906), 'Stone Axe Factories near Cushendall', *J.R.S.A.I.*, 36 (1906), 383–94. [37]

Knowles, W. J. (1909), 'On the Mounting of Leaf-shaped Arrowheads of Flint', *P.S.A.S.*, 43 (1908–9), 278–83. [42, 43]

Kossack, Georg (1959) *Südbayern Während der Hallstattzeit*, Römisch-Germanische Forschungen Band 24, Walter de Gruyter, Berlin. [186, 219, 221]

Kossinna, Gustav (1913), *Der Germanische Goldreichtum in der Bronzezeit, I: Der Goldfund von Messingwerk bei Eberswalde und die Goldenen Kultgefässe der Germanen*, Mannus Bibliothek nr 12, Kurt Kabissch, Würzburg. [209]

Kytlicova, Olga (1955), 'Hromadný Nález Bronzů od Starého Sedla (Okres Milevsko)', *Památky Archeologicke*, 100 (1955), 52–7. [176]

Lacaille, A. D. (1954), *The Stone Age in Scotland*, Oxford University Press, London. [18]

Laing, Lloyd (1975), *The Archaeology of Late Celtic Britain and Ireland c. 400–1200 A.D.*, Methuen, London. [249]

Lalor, M. W. (1879–82), 'Discovery of Kists and Human Remains at Luggacurren, Queen's Co.', *J.R.S.A.I.*, 15 (1879–82), 446–7. [144]

Lanting, J. N. and van der Waals, J. D. (1972), 'British Beakers as seen from the Continent', *Helinium*, 12 (1972), 20–46.

Lanting, J. N., Mook, W. G. and van der Waals, J. D. (1973), 'C14 Chronology and the Beaker Problem', *Helinium*, 13 (1973), 38–58. [117, 125]

Leask, H. G. and Price, Liam (1936), 'The Labbacallee Megalith, Co. Cork', *P.R.I.A.*, 43 250–2. [128]

Leask, H. G., and Price, Liam (1936), 'The Labbacallee Megalith, Co. Cork', *P.R.I.A.*, 43 (1936), 77–101. [14, 117]

Ledwich, Edward (1790), *Antiquities of Ireland*, John Jones, Dublin. [6]

Leeds, E. T. (1926–7), 'Excavations at Chun Castle, in Penwith, Cornwall', *Arch.*, 76 (1926–7), 205–40. [227, 246]

Leeds, E. Thurlow (1930), 'A Bronze Cauldron from the River Cherwell, Oxfordshire, with Notes on Cauldrons and Other Bronze Vessels of Allied Types', *Arch.*, 80 (1930), 1–36. [204]

Le Roux, C. T. (1971), 'A Stone-axe Factory in Brittany', *Antiquity*, 45 (1971), 283–8. [37, 56]

L'Helgouach, Jean (1965), *Les Sépultures mégalithiques en Armorique*, Travaux du Laboratoire d'Anthropologie Préhistorique de la Faculté des Sciences, Rennes. [121]

Liversage, G. D. (1968), 'Excavations at Dalkey Island, Co. Dublin, 1956–59' *P.R.I.A.*, 66C (1968), 53–233. [99, 124, 129, 130, 132, 142, 170, 191]

Longworth, I. H. (1961), 'The Origins and Development of the Primary Series in the Collared Urn Tradition in England and Wales', *P.P.S.*, 27 (1961), 263–306. [148]

Longworth, I. H. (1966a), 'Contracted Mouth Accessory Cups', *British Museum Quarterly*, 31 (1966), 111–22. [149, 152]

Longworth, I. H. (1966b), 'Two Gold Bracelets from Walderslade, Kent', *British Museum Quarterly*, 31 (1966), 131–3. [214]

Lowery, P. R., Savage, R. D. A. and Wilkins, R. L. (1971), 'Scriber, Graver, Scorper, Tracer: Notes on Experiments in Bronzeworking Technique', *P.P.S.*, 37 (1971), 167–82. [247]

Lowry-Corry, Dorothy (1933), 'The Stones Carved with Human Effigies on Boa Island and on Lustymore Island, in Lower Lough Erne', *P.R.I.A.*, 41C (1933), 200–4. [245]

Lowry-Corry, Dorothy (1959), 'A Newly Discovered Statue at the Church on White Island, County Fermanagh', *U.J.A.*, 22 (1959), 59–66. [245]

Lucas, A. T. (1950), 'Neolithic Burial at Norrismount, Co. Wexford', *J.R.S.A.I.*, 80 (1950), 155–7. [84]

Lucas, A. T. (1968), 'National Museum of Ireland: Archaeological Acquisitions in the Year 1965', *J.R.S.A.I.*, 98 (1968), 93–159 [40]

Lucas, A. T. (1972), 'Prehistoric Block-Wheels from Doogarymore, Co. Roscommon, and Timahoe East, Co. Kildare', *J.R.S.A.I.*, 102 (1972), 19–48. [187]

Lucas, A. T. (1973), *Treasures of Ireland*, Gill & Macmillan, Dublin.

Lynch, Frances (1967), 'Barclodiad Y Gawres – Comparative Notes on the Decorated Stones', *Arch. Camb.*, 116 (1967), 1–22. [58, 74]

Lynch, Frances (1969), 'The Megalithic Tombs of North Wales', in T. G. E. Powell (ed.), *Megalithic Enquiries in the West of Britain*, Liverpool University Press. [85, 89]

Lynch, Frances (1970), *Prehistoric Anglesey*, Anglesey Antiquarian Society, Llangefni. [149, 213]

Lynch, Frances (1971), 'Report on the Re-excavation of Two Bronze Age Cairns in Anglesey: Bedd Branwen and Treiorwerth', *Arch. Camb.*, 120 (1971), 11–83. [150]

Macalister, R. A. S. (1916–17), 'A Report on some Excavations Recently Conducted in Co. Galway', *P.R.I.A.*, 33C (1916–17), 505–10. [244]

Macalister, R. A. S. (1921a), *Ireland in Pre-Celtic Times*, Maunsel & Roberts, Dublin and London. [13]

Macalister, R. A. S. (1921b), *A Textbook of European Archaeology*, vol. I, Cambridge University Press. [13]

Macalister, R. A. S. (1922), 'On a Stone with La Tène Decoration Recently Discovered in Co. Cavan', *J.R.S.A.I.*, 52 (1922), 113–16. [245]

Macalister, R. A. S. (1928), *The Archaeology of Ireland*, Methuen, London. [13]

Macalister, R. A. S. (1928–9), 'On Some Antiquities Discovered upon Lambay', *P.R.I.A.*, 38C (1928–9), 240–6. [97, 238, 240, 241, 242, 243, 244]

Macalister, R. A. S. (1931), *Tara: a Pagan Sanctuary of Ancient Ireland*, Charles Scribner, London. [230, 245]

Macalister, R. A. S. (1932), 'A Burial Cairn on Seefin Mountain, Co. Wicklow', *J.R.S.A.I.*, 62 (1932), 153–7. [66]

Macalister, R. A. S. (1935), *Ancient Ireland*, Methuen, London. [13]

Macalister, R. A. S. (1937), 'Two Carved Stones in the Seefinn Carn', *J.R.S.A.I.*, 67 (1937), 312–13. [66]

Macalister, R. A. S. (1945), *Corpus Inscriptionum Insularum Celticarum*, vol. I, Stationery Office, Dublin. [248]

Macalister, R. A. S., Armstrong, E. C. R. and Praeger, R. Ll. (1912), 'Report on the Exploration of Bronze-Age Cairns on Carrowkeel Mountain, Co. Sligo', *P.R.I.A.*, 29C (1911–12), 311–47. [65, 70]

Macalister, R. A. S., Armstrong, E. C. R. and Praeger, R. Ll. (1913), 'A Bronze Age Internment near Naas', *P.R.I.A.*, 30C (1913), 351–60. [125, 128]

Macalister, R. A. S. and Praeger, R. Ll. (1928–9), 'Report on the Excavation of Uisneach', *P.R.I.A.*, 38C (1928–9), 69–127. [230]

Macalister, R. A. S. and Praeger, R. Ll. (1930–1), 'The Excavation of an Ancient Structure on the Townland of Togherstown, Co. Westmeath', *P.R.I.A.*, 39C (1930–1), 54–83. [230]

McAulay, I. R. and Watts, W. A. (1961), 'Dublin Radiocarbon Dates I', *Radiocarbon*, 3 (1961), 26–38. [25]

MacDermott, Máire (1949), 'Lough Gur excavations: Two Barrows at Ballingoola', *J.R.S.A.I.*, 79 (1949), 139–45. [121, 127]

MacHenry, Alexander (1888), 'Report on the Explorations at White Park Bay, Ballintoy', *P.R.I.A.*, 16 (1879–88), 463–4. [99]

McInnes, Isla (1968), 'Jet Sliders in Late Neolithic Britain', in J. M. Coles and D. D. A. Simpson (eds), *Studies in Ancient Europe: Essays Presented to Stuart Piggott*, Leicester University Press, 137–44. [128]

Mac Niocaill, Gearóid (1972), *Ireland Before the Vikings*, Gill & Macmillan, Dublin. [249]

MacWhite, Eoin (1944a), 'Amber in the Irish Bronze Age', *J.C.H.A.S.*, 49 (1944), 122–7. [197]

MacWhite, Eoin (1944b), 'The Bronze Socketed Gouge in Ireland', *J.R.S.A.I.*, 74 (1944), 160–5. [195]

MacWhite, Eoin (1945), 'Irish Bronze Age Trumpets', *J.R.S.A.I.*, 75 (1945), 85–106. [210]

MacWhite, Eoin (1946), 'A New View on Irish Bronze Age Rock-scribings', *J.R.S.A.I.*, 76 (1946), 59–80. [137]

MacWhite, Eoin (1951) *Estudios sobre las Relaciones Atlanticas de la Peninsula Hispanica en la Edad del Bronce*, Seminario de Historia Primitiva del Hombre, Madrid. [122]

Madden, Aedeen Cremin (1968), 'Beaker Pottery in Ireland', *J.K.A.H.S.*, I (1968), 9–24. [119]

Madden, Aedeen Cremin (1969), 'The Beaker Wedge Tomb at Moytirra, Co. Sligo', *J.R.S.A.I.*, 99 (1969), 151–9. [119]

Madsen, A. P., Müller, S., Neergaard, C., Petersen, J., Rostrup, E., Steenstrup, K. H. V. and Winge, H. (1900), *Affaldsdynger Fra Stenalderen i Danmark*, Reitzel, Copenhagen. [97]

Mahr, Adolf (1932), *Christian Art in Ancient Ireland*, vol. I, Stationery Office, Dublin. [14]

Mahr, Adolf (1934), 'A Wooden Cauldron from Altartate, Co. Monaghan', *P.R.I.A.*, 42C (1934), 11–29. [202]

Mahr, Adolf (1937), 'New Aspects and Problems in Irish Prehistory', *P.P.S.*, 3 (1937), 261–436. [14, 246]

Mahr, Adolf (1941), 'The Pagan Background', in Joseph Raftery (ed.), *Christian Art in Ancient Ireland*, vol. 2, Stationery Office, Dublin. [240]

Mahr, A. and Price, L. (1932), 'Excavation of Urn Burials at Clonshannon, Imaal, Co. Wicklow', *J.R.S.A.I.*, 62 (1932), 75–90. [152]

Manby, T. G. (1969), 'Bronze Age Pottery from Pule Hill, Marsden, W. R. Yorkshire and Footed Vessels of the Early Bronze Age from England', *Y.A.J.*, 42 (1969), 273–82. [127]

Marien, M. E. (1958), *Travailles du champ – d'urnes et des tombelles hallstattiennes de Court-Saint-Etienne*, Musées Royaux d'Art et d'Histoire, Brussels. [219]

Marshall, J. N. (1930), 'Archaeological Notes', *Trans. Buteshire Nat. Hist. Soc.*, (1930), 50–4. [99, 109]

Martin, Cecil P. (1935), *Prehistoric Man in Ireland*, Macmillan, London. [145]

Maryon, Herbert (1938), 'The Technical Methods of the Irish Smiths in the Bronze and Early Iron Ages', *P.R.I.A.*, 44C (1938), 181–228. [217]

May, A. McL. (1947), 'Burial Mound, Circles, and Cairn, Gortcorbies, Co. Derry', *J.R.S.A.I.*, 77, (1947), 5–22. [158]

May, A. McL. (1950), 'Two Neolithic Hearths at Gortcorbies, Co. Derry', *U.J.A.*, 13 (1950), 28–39. [121]

May, A. McL. (1953), 'Neolithic Habitation Site, Stone Circles and Alignments at Beaghmore, Co. Tyrone', *J.R.S.A.I.*, 83 (1953), 174–97. [128]

May, A. McL. and Collins, A. E. P. (1959), 'Cremation Burials at Gortfad, Co. Derry, with Some Remarks on Cordoned Urns', *U.J.A.*, 22 (1959), 33–41.

Megaw, B. R. S. and Hardy, E. M. (1938), 'British Decorated Axes and their Diffusion during the Earlier Part of the Bronze Age', *P.P.S.*, 4 (1938), 272–307.

Megaw, J. V. S. (1970), *Art of the European Iron Age. A Study of the Elusive Image*, Adams & Dart, Bath. [224]

Mitchell, G. F. (1951), 'Studies in Irish Quaternary Deposits: No. 7', *P.R.I.A.*, 53B (1950–1), 111–206. [3, 25, 72]

Mitchell, G. F. (1955), 'The Mesolithic Site at Toome Bay, Co. Londonderry', *U.J.A.*, 3rd ser., 18 (1955), 1–16. [23]

Mitchell, G. F. (1956), 'An Early Kitchen-midden at Sutton, Co. Dublin', *J.R.S.A.I.*, 86 (1956), 1–26. [19]

Mitchell, G. F. (1958), 'Radiocarbon-dates and Pollen-zones in Ireland', *J.R.S.A.I.*, 88 (1958), 49–56. [19]

Mitchell, G. F. (1965), 'Littleton Bog, Tipperary: An Irish Agricultural Record', *J.R.S.A.I.*, 95 (1965), 121–32. [50]

Mitchell, G. F. (1972), 'Further Excavations of the Early Kitchen-midden at Sutton, Co. Dublin', *J.R.S.A.I.*, 102 (1972), 151–9. [19]

Mitchell, G. F., O'Leary, M. and Raftery, J. (1941), 'On a Bronze Halberd from Co. Mayo and a Bronze Spearhead from Co. Westmeath', *P.R.I.A.*, 46C (1941), 287–98. [163]

Mitchell, G. F. and Ó Ríordáin, Seán P. (1942), 'Early Bronze Age Pottery from Rockbarton Bog, Co. Limerick', *P.R.I.A.*, 48 (1942), 255–72. [121]

Mitchell, G. F. and Sieveking, G. de G. (1972), 'Flint Flake, probably of Palaeolithic Age, from Mell Townland, near Drogheda, Co. Louth, Ireland', *J.R.S.A.I.*, 102 (1972), 174–77. [16]

Mogey, J. M. (1941), 'The "Druid Stone", Ballintoy, Co. Antrim', *U.J.A.*, 3rd ser., 4 (1941), 49–56. [72]

Mogey, J. M. (1949), 'Preliminary Report on Excavations in Mullaghmore Townland, Co. Down', *U.J.A.*, 12 (1949), 82–8. [244]

Mogey, J. M., Thompson, G. B. and Proudfoot, Bruce (1956), 'Excavation of Two Ring-Barrows in Mullaghmore Townland, Co. Down', *U.J.A.*, 19 (1956), 11–28. [238, 244]

Molyneux, Thomas, ed. (1726), *A Natural History of Ireland, in three parts, By Several Hands*, Geo. and Alex. Ewing, Dublin. [5, 250]

Moore, C. N. and Rowlands, M. (1972), *Bronze Age Metalwork in Salisbury Museum*, Salisbury Museum, Salisbury. [149]

Morris, Henry (1929), 'Ancient Graves in Sligo and Roscommon', *J.R.S.A.I.*, 69 (1929), 99–115. [134]

Morris, Henry (1940), 'Associated Finds from Co. Sligo and Co. Armagh', *J.R.S.A.I.*, 70 (1940), 94.

Morrison, M. E. (1959), 'Evidence and Interpretation of "Landnam" in the North-East of Ireland', *Botaniska Notiser*, 112 (1959), 185–204. [23]

Moscati, Sabatino (1968), *The World of the Phoenicians*, Weidenfeld & Nicholson, London. [215]

Movius, Hallam L. (1935), 'Kilgreany Cave, County Waterford', *J.R.S.A.I.*, 65 (1935), 254–96. [17, 193]

Movius, Hallam L. (1936), 'A Neolithic Site on the River Bann', *P.R.I.A.*, 43C (1935–7), 17–40. [103]

Movius, Hallam L. (1942), *The Irish Stone Age, its Chronology, Development and Relationships*, Cambridge University Press. [16, 17, 18, 21, 103]

Mozsolics, Amalia (1973), *Bronze und Goldfunde des Karpatenbeckens: Depotfundhorizonte von Forró und Ópályi*, Akadémiai Kiado, Budapest. [176]

Müller-Karpe, Hermann (1959), *Beiträge zur Chronologie der Urnenfelderzeit Nördlich und Südlich der Alpen*, Römisch-Germanische Forschungen, Band 22, Walter de Gruyter, Berlin. [167, 180, 186, 214]

O'Curry, E. (1861), *Lectures on the Manuscript Materials of Ancient Irish History*, James Duffy, Dublin. [9]

O'Curry, E. (1873), *On the Manners and Customs of the Ancient Irish*, 3 vols, ed. W. K. Sullivan, Williams & Norgate, London. [9, 11]

O'Flaherty, R. (1685), *Ogygia: Seu Rerum Hibernicarum chronologia . . . liber primus. . . .*, R. Everingham, London. [5]

Ó h-Iceadha, Gearóid (1946), 'The Moylisha Megalith, Co. Wicklow', *J.R.S.A.I.*, 76 (1946), 119–28. [123]

O'Kelly, Claire (1967), *Illustrated Guide to Newgrange*, John English, Wexford. [58, 125, 247]

O'Kelly, M. J. (1950), 'Two Burials at Labbamolaga, Co. Cork', *J.C.H.A.S.*, 55 (1950), 15–20. [136, 166]

O'Kelly, M. J. (1951). 'An Early Bronze Age Ring-fort at Carrigillihy, Co. Cork', *J.C.H.A.S.*, 56 (1951), 69–86. [226]

O'Kelly, M. J. (1952a), 'Excavation of a Cairn at Moneen, Co. Cork', *P.R.I.A.*, 54C (1952), 121–59. [127, 138, 166]

O'Kelly, M. J. (1952b), 'Three Promontory Forts in Co. Cork', *P.R.I.A.*, 55C (1952), 25–59. [139, 227]

O'Kelly, M. J. (1954), 'Excavations and Experiments in Ancient Irish Cooking-Places', *J.R.S.A.I.*, 84 (1954), 105–55. [229, 232]

O'Kelly, M. J. (1958), 'A Wedge-shaped Gallery-grave at Island, Co. Cork', *J.R.S.A.I.*, 88 (1958), 1–23. [Fig. 43, bottom]

O'Kelly, M. J. (1960), 'A Wedge-shaped Gallery-grave at Baurnadomeeny, Co. Tipperary', *J.C.H.A.S.*, 65 (1960), 85–115. [127]

O'Kelly, M. J. (1961), 'The Cork Horns, the Petrie Crown and the Bann Disc', *J.C.H.A.S.*, 66 (1961), 1–12. [242, 247]

O'Kelly, M. J. (1966), 'New Discoveries at the Newgrange Passage-grave in Ireland', *Sborník Národního Muzea v Praze*, 20 (1966), 95–8. [126, 131]

O'Kelly, M. J. (1969a), 'A Stone Mould for Axeheads from Doonour, Bantry, Co. Cork', *J.R.S.A.I.*, 99 (1969), 117–24. [139]

O'Kelly, M. J. (1969b), 'Radiocarbon Dates for the Newgrange Passage Grave, Co. Meath', *Antiquity*, 43 (1969), 140–1. [67]

O'Kelly, M. J. (1970a), 'Problems of Irish Ring-forts', in Donald Moore (ed.), *The Irish Sea Province in Archaeology and History*, Cambrian Archaeological Association, Cardiff, 50–4. [225]

O'Kelly, M. J. (1970b), 'An Axe Mould from Lyre, Co. Cork', *J.C.H.A.S.*, 75 (1970), 25–8. [132, 139, 143]

O'Kelly, M. J. (1972), 'Further Radiocarbon Dates from Newgrange, Co. Meath, Ireland', *Ant.*, 46 (1972), 226–7. [131]

O'Kelly, M. J. (1973), 'Current Excavations at Newgrange, Ireland', in Glyn Daniel and Paul Kjaerum (eds), *Megalithic Graves and Ritual*, Jutland Archaeological Society Publications, Jutland Archaeological Society, Moesgård. [67]

Ó Nualláin, Seán (1968a), 'A Ruined Megalithic Cemetery in Co. Donegal and its Context in the Irish Passage Grave Series', *J.R.S.A.I.*, 98 (1968), 1–29. [67]

Ó Nualláin, Seán (1968b), 'A Group of Portal-dolmens near Dunfanaghy, Co. Donegal', *Donegal Annual* 7 (1968), 289–99. [89]

Ó Nualláin, Seán (1971), 'The Stone Circles of County Kerry', *J.K.A.H.S.*, 4 (1971), 5–27. [123]

Ó Nualláin, Seán (1972), 'A Neolithic House at Ballyglass near Ballycastle, Co. Mayo', *J.R.S.A.I.*, 102 (1972), 49–57. [30, 47]

Ó Ríordáin, A. B. (1958), 'Early Bronze Age Hoard from Co. Leitrim', *J.R.S.A.I.*, 88 (1958), 143–5. [166]

Ó Ríordáin, A. B. (1967), 'Cordoned Urn Burial at Laheen, Co. Donegal', *J.R.S.A.I.*, 97 (1967), 39–44. [151, 152, 166]

Ó Ríordáin, Seán P. (1936), 'Excavations at Lissard, Co. Limerick, and Other Sites in the Locality', *J.R.S.A.I.*, 66 (1936), 173–85. [152]

Ó Ríordáin, Seán P. (1937), 'The Halberd in Bronze Age Europe', *Arch.*, 86 (1937), 195–321. [137]

Ó Ríordáin, Seán P. (1938), 'A Bronze Age Find from Oldtown, Kilcashel, Co. Roscommon', *J.G.A.H.S.*, 18 (1938), 40–2. [202]

Ó Ríordáin, Seán P. (1940), 'Excavations at Cush, Co. Limerick', *P.R.I.A.*, 45C (1940), 83–181. [225, 226, 232, 234, 244]

Ó Ríordáin, Seán P. (1946), 'Prehistory in Ireland, 1937–46', *P.P.S.*, 12 (1946), 142–71.

Ó Ríordáin, Seán P. (1947a), 'Excavation of a Barrow at Rathjordan, Co. Limerick', *J.C.H.A.S.*, 52 (1947), 1–4. [107, 127]

Ó Ríordáin, Seán P. (1947b), 'Roman Material in Ireland', *P.R.I.A.*, 51C (1947), 35–82. [247]

Ó Ríordáin, Seán P. (1948), 'Further Barrows at Rathjordan, Co. Limerick', *J.C.H.A.S.*, 53 (1948), 19–31. [127]

Ó Ríordáin, Seán P. (1950), 'Excavation of Some Earthworks on the Curragh, Co. Kildare', *P.R.I.A.*, 53C (1950), 249–77. [244]

Ó Ríordáin, Seán P. (1951), 'Lough Gur Excavations: The Great Stone Circle (B) in Grange Townland', *P.R.I.A.*, 54C (1951), 37–74. [125, 127, 130]

Ó Ríordáin, Seán P. (1952), 'Fragment of the Killycluggin Stone', *J.R.S.A.I.*, 82 (1952), 68. [245]

Ó Ríordáin, Seán P. (1953), *Antiquities of the Irish Countryside*, 3rd edn, Methuen, London. [137, 152, 226, 232]

Ó Ríordáin, Seán P. (1954), 'Lough Gur Excavations: Neolithic and Bronze Age Houses on Knockadoon', *P.R.I.A.*, 56C (1954), 297–459. [49, 104, 107, 121, 129, 170, 171, 172]

Ó Ríordáin, Seán P. (1955), 'A Burial with Faience Beads at Tara', *P.P.S.*, 21 (1955), 163–73. [158]

Ó Ríordáin, Seán P. (1960), *Tara: The Monuments on the Hill*, 3rd edn, Dundalgan Press, Dundalk. [225, 230, 236, 244]

Ó Ríordáin, Seán P. and Daniel, Glyn E. (1964), *Newgrange and the Bend of the Boyne*, Thames & Hudson, London. [58]

Ó Ríordáin, Seán P. and de Valera, Ruaidhrí (1952), 'Excavation of a Megalithic Tomb at Ballyedmonduff, Co. Dublin', *P.R.I.A.*, 55C (1952), 61–81. [119]

Ó Ríordáin, Seán P. and Ó h-Iceadha, Géaróid (1955), 'Lough Gur Excavations: The Megalithic Tomb', *J.R.S.A.I.*, 85 (1955), 34–50. [119]

Pegge, S. (1789), 'Observations on Some Brass Celts, and Other Weapons Discovered in Ireland, 1789', *Arch.*, 9 (1789), 84–95. [163, 178]

Péquart, M., Péquart, St J. and Le Rouzic, Z. (1927), *Corpus des signes gravés*, Auguste Picard, Paris. [40, 77]

Petrie, G. (1837), 'On the History and Antiquities of Tara Hill', *T.R.I.A.*, 18 (1839), 25–232. [8]

Petrie, G. (1845), *The Ecclesiastical Architecture of Ireland, Anterior to the Anglo-Norman Invasion*, Hodges & Smith, Dublin. [9]

Piggott, C. M. (1946), 'The Late Bronze Age Razors of the British Isles', *P.P.S.*, 12 (1946), 121–41. [151, 152, 197]

Piggott, C. M. (1949), 'A Late Bronze Age Hoard from Blackrock in Sussex and its Significance', *P.P.S.*, 15 (1949), 107–21. [180]

Piggott, Stuart (1931), 'The Neolithic Pottery of the British Isles', *Arch. J.*, 88 (1931), 67–158. [24, 45]

Piggott, Stuart (1938), 'The Early Bronze Age in Wessex', *P.P.S.*, 4 (1938), 52–106. [144, 148, 149, 153, 159]

Piggott, Stuart (1949), 'An Iron Age Yoke from Northern Ireland', *P.P.S.*, 15 (1949), 192–3. [233]

Piggott, Stuart (1950), 'Swords and Scabbards of the British Early Iron Age', *P.P.S.*, 16 (1950), 1–28. [238, 246]

Piggott, Stuart (1952–3), 'Three Metal-Work Hoards of the Roman Period from Southern Scotland', *P.S.A.S.*, 87 (1952–3), 1–50. [238]

Piggott, Stuart (1954), *The Neolithic Cultures of the British Isles*, Cambridge University Press. [54, 103, 252]

Piggott, Stuart (1957–8), 'Excavations at Braidwood Fort, Midlothian and Craig's Quarry, Dirleton, East Lothian', *P.S.A.S.*, 91 (1957–8), 61–77. [240]

Piggott, Stuart (1963), 'Abercromby and After: The Beaker Cultures of Britain Re-examined', in I. Ll. Foster and Leslie Alcock (eds), *Culture and Environment: Essays in Honour of Sir Cyril Fox*, Routledge & Kegan Paul, London, 53–91. [117, 124, 129, 139]

Piggott, Stuart (1965), *Ancient Europe from the Beginnings of Agriculture to Classical Antiquity*, Edinburgh University Press. [114, 116, 224, 227]

Piggott, Stuart (1968), *The Druids*, Thames & Hudson, London. [242]

Piggott, Stuart and Powell, T. G. E. (1947), 'Notes on Megalithic Tombs in Sligo and Achill', *J.R.S.A.I.*, 77 (1947), 136–46 [65]

Pilcher, J. R. (1969), 'Archaeology, Palaeoecology, and ¹⁴C Dating of the Beaghmore Stone Circle Site', *U.J.A.*, 32 (1969), 73–90. [128]

Pilcher, J. R., Smith, A. G., Pearson, G. W. and Crowder, Adèle (1971), 'Land Clearance in the

Irish Neolithic: New Evidence and Interpretation', *Science*, 172 (1971), 560–2. [25, 49]

Plunkett, Thomas and Coffey, George (1896–8), 'Report on the Excavations of Topped Mountain Cairn', *P.R.I.A.*, 20 (1896–8), 651–8. [144]

Pococke, R. (1773), 'An Account of Some Antiquities Found in Ireland', *Arch.* 2 (1773), 32–41. [6]

Pollock, A. J. and Waterman, D. M. (1964), 'A Bronze Age Habitation Site at Downpatrick', *U.J.A.*, 27 (1964), 31–58. [158]

Powell, T. G. E. (1938a), 'Excavation of a Megalithic Tomb at Ballynamona, Co. Waterford', *J.R.S.A.I.* (1938), 260–71. [90]

Powell, T. G. E. (1938b), 'The Passage Graves of Ireland', *P.P.S.*, 4 (1938), 239–48. [58]

Powell, T. G. E. (1950), 'A Late Bronze Age Hoard from Welby, Leicestershire', *Arch. J.*, 105 (1950), 27–40. [213]

Powell, T. G. E. (1958), *The Celts*, Thames & Hudson, London. [224, 242]

Powell, T. G. E. (1963), 'The Chambered Cairn at Dyffryn Ardudwy', *Ant.*, 37 (1963), 19–24. [88, 89, 90, 176]

Powell, T. G. E. (1966), *Prehistoric Art*, Thames & Hudson, London. [176]

Powell, T. G. E. (1973), 'Excavations of a Megalithic Chambered Cairn at Dyffryn Ardudwy, Merioneth, Wales', *Arch.*, 104 (1973), 1–50. [90, 224]

Powell, T. G. E. and Daniel, Glyn E. (1956), *Barclodiad Y Gawres*, Liverpool University Press. [58]

Prendergast, Ellen (1958), 'Stone Mould for Flat Axeheads', *J.R.S.A.I.*, 88 (1958), 139–43.

Prendergast, Ellen (1959), 'Prehistoric Burial at Rath, Co. Wicklow', *J.R.S.A.I.*, 89 (1959), 17–29. [84]

Prendergast, Ellen (1960a), 'Burial Mound of the Bronze Age at Kilmore, Co. Westmeath', *J.R.S.A.I.*, 90 (1960), 5–9.

Prendergast, Ellen (1960b), 'Amber Necklace from Co. Galway', *J.R.S.A.I.*, 90 (1960), 61–6. [197]

Prendergast, Ellen (1962), 'Urn Burial at Maganey Lower, Co. Kildare', *J.R.S.A.I.*, 92 (1962), 169–73. [Fig. 56. 1]

Price, Liam (1934), 'The Ages of Stone and Bronze in County Wicklow', *P.R.I.A.*, 42C (1934), 31–64. [125]

Price, Liam (ed.) (1942), *An Eighteenth Century Antiquary: the Sketches, Notes, and Diaries of Austin Cooper*, Falkiner, Dublin. [7]

Radford, C. A. Ralegh (1958), 'The Chambered Tomb at Broadsands, Paignton', *P.D.A.E.S.*, 5 (1957–8), 147–66. [58]

Raftery, Barry (1969), 'Freestone Hill, Co. Kilkenny: An Iron Age Hillfort and Bronze Age Cairn', *P.R.I.A.*, 68C (1969), 1–108. [137, 235]

Raftery, Barry (1970), 'The Rathgall Hillfort, County Wicklow', *Ant.*, 44 (1970), 51–4. [37, 192]

Raftery, Barry (1971), 'Rathgall, Co. Wicklow: 1970 Excavations', *Ant.*, 45 (1971), 276–98. [201, 210, 215]

Raftery, Barry (1972a), 'Irish Hill-forts', in Charles Thomas (ed.), *The Iron Age in the Irish Sea Province*, Council for British Archaeology Research Report 9, London, 37–58. [228, 233, 245]

Raftery, Barry (1972b), 'Some Late La Tène Glass Beads from Ireland', *J.R.S.A.I.*, 102 (1972), 14–18. [240]

Raftery, Barry (1973), 'Rathgall: a Late Bronze Age Burial in Ireland', *Ant.*, 47 (1973), 293–5. [84]

Raftery, Barry (1974), 'A Prehistoric Burial Mound at Baunogenasraid, Co. Carlow', *P.R.I.A.*, 74C (1974), 277–312. [84]

Raftery, Joseph (1938–9), 'The Tumulus Cemetery of Carrowjames, Co. Mayo, Part I', *J.G.A.H.S.*, 18 (1938–9), 157–67. [152, 244]

Raftery, Joseph (1939), 'An Early Iron Age Sword from Lough Gur, Co. Limerick', *J.R.S.A.I.*, 69 (1939), 170–2. [236]

Raftery, Joseph (1940), 'Hoard of Gold Objects from Co. Kerry', *J.C.H.A.S.*, 45 (1940), 56–7. [14, 202]

Raftery, Joseph (1940–1), 'The Tumulus Cemetery of Carrowjames, Co. Mayo, Part II, Carrowjames II', *J.G.A.H.S.*, 19 (1940), 16–88. [244]

Raftery, Joseph (ed.) (1941), *Christian Art in Ancient Ireland*, vol. 2, Stationery Office, Dublin. [240] 14

Raftery, Joseph (1942a), 'Knocknalappa Crannog, Co. Clare', *N.M.A.J.*, 3 (1942), 53–72. [187, 191]

Raftery, Joseph (1942b), 'Finds from Three Ulster Counties', *U.J.A.*, 5 (1942), 120–31. [218]

Raftery, Joseph (1944a), 'A Neolithic Burial in Co. Carlow', *J.R.S.A.I.*, 74 (1944), 61–2. [84]

Raftery, Joseph (1944b), 'The Turoe Stone and the Rath of Feerwore', *J.R.S.A.I.*, 74 (1944), 23–52. [225, 232, 234, 236, 244, 245]

Raftery, Joseph (1951), *Prehistoric Ireland*, Batsford, London. [236, 237, 242, 243]

Raftery, Joseph (1960a), 'A Bronze Age Tumulus at Corrower, Co. Mayo', *P.R.I.A.*, 61C (1960), 79–93. [139]

Raftery, Joseph (1960b), 'A Hoard of the Early Iron Age', *J.R.S.A.I.*, 90 (1960), 2–5. [240, 242, 247, 248]

Raftery, Joseph (1963), 'A Matter of Time', *J.R.S.A.I.*, 93 (1963), 101–14. [17]

[Raftery, Joseph] (1966), 'National Museum of Ireland: Archaeological Acquisitions in the Year 1963', *J.R.S.A.I.*, 96 (1966), 7–27.

[Raftery, Joseph] (1967), 'National Museum of Ireland: Archaeological Acquisitions in the Year 1964', *J.R.S.A.I.*, 97 (1967), 1–28. [40]

[Raftery, Joseph] (1969). 'National Museum of Ireland: Archaeological Acquisitions in the Year 1966', *J.R.S.A.I.*, 99 (1969), 93–115. [40, 232, 234, 236, 248]

Raftery, Joseph (1970a), 'Prehistoric Coiled Basketry Bags', *J.R.S.A.I.*, 100 (1970), 167–8. [37]

Raftery, Joseph (1970b), 'Two Gold Hoards from Co. Tyrone', *J.R.S.A.I.*, 100 (1970), 169–74. [202]

Raftery, Joseph (1971), 'A Bronze Age Hoard from Ballyteagan, County Laois', *J.R.S.A.I.*, 101 (1971), 85–100. [192, 199]

Raftery, Joseph (1973), 'A Neolithic Burial Mound at Ballintruer More, Co. Wicklow', *J.R.S.A.I.*, 103 (1973), 214–19. [84]

Raftery, Joseph and Moore, Allerton (1944), 'Two Prehistoric Burials in Co. Mayo', *J.R.S.A.I.*, 74 (1944), 171–6. [244]

Randsborg, Klaus (1968), 'Von Periode II zu III', *Acta Archaeologica* (Copenhagen), 39 (1968), 1–142. [180]

Reeves, T. J. (1971), 'Gold in Ireland', *Geological Survey of Ireland Bulletin*, 1 (1971), 73–85. [116]

Reinecke, Paul (1965), *Mainzer Aufsätze zur Chronologie der Bronze -und Eisenzeit*, (Nachdrucke aus: Altertümer unserer heidnischen Vorzeit, 5 (1911), und Festschrift des Römisch-Germanischen Zentralmuseums, 1902), Rudolf Habelt, Bonn. [219]

Riley, F. T. (1936), 'Excavations in the Townland of Pollacorragune, Tuam, Co. Galway', *J.G.A.H.S.*, 17 (1936), 44–64. [244]

Ritchie, P. R. (1968), 'The Stone Implement Trade in Third-Millennium Scotland', in J. M.

Coles and D. D. A. Simpson (eds), *Studies in Ancient Europe*, Leicester University Press, 117–36. [50]

Roe, F. E. S. (1966), 'The Battle-Axe Series in Britain', *P.P.S.*, 32 (1966), 199–245. [153]

Ross, A. (1957–8), 'The Human Head in Insular Pagan Celtic Religion', *P.S.A.S.*, 91 (1957–8), 10–43. [245]

Ross, A. (1967a), *Pagan Celtic Britain*, Routledge & Kegan Paul, London. [245]

Ross, A. (1967b), 'A Three-faced Head from Wiltshire', *Ant.*, 41 (1967), 53–6.

Roth, Helmut (1974), 'Ein Ledermesser der atlantischen Bronzezeit aus Mittelfranken', *Archäologisches Korrespondenzblatt*, 4 (1974), 37–47. [193, 218]

Rotherham, E. Crofton. (1895), 'On the Excavation of a Cairn on Slieve-na-Caillighe, Loughcrew', *J.R.S.A.I.*, 25 (1895), 311–16. [61]

Rowlands, M. J. (1971), 'A Group of Incised Decorated Armrings and their Significance for the Middle Bronze Age of Southern Britain', *British Museum Quarterly*, 35 (1971), 183–99. [168]

Royal Irish Academy MS., Antiquarian Portfolio I. [84]

Rusu, Mircea (1963), 'Die Verbreitung der Bronzehorte in Transsilvanien vom Ende der Bronzezeit bis in die mittlere Hallstattzeit', *Dacia*, 7 (1963), 177–210. [167]

Ryan, M. FitzG. (1973), 'The Excavation of a Neolithic Burial Mound at Jerpoint West, Co. Kilkenny', *P.R.I.A.*, 73C (1973), 107–27. [84]

Rynne, Etienne (1958), 'Iron Axe-head of La Tène Date', *J.R.S.A.I.*, 88 (1958), 149–50. [236]

Rynne, Etienne (1960), 'La Tène Sword from near Lough Gara', *J.R.S.A.I.*, 90 (1960), 12–13. [236, 237]

Rynne, Etienne (1961a), 'Cist-Burial at Caltragh, Co. Galway', *J.R.S.A.I.*, 91 (1961), 45–51. [158, 246]

Rynne, Etienne (1961b), 'The Introduction of La Tène into Ireland', in G. Bersu (ed.), *Bericht Über den V. Internationalen Kongress für Vor- und Frühgeschichte, Hamburg 1958*, Berlin, 705–9. [246]

Rynne, Etienne (1961–3), 'Notes on Some Antiquities found in Co. Kildare', *J.K.A.S.*, 13 (1961–3), 458–62. [156, 158]

Rynne, Etienne (1963a), 'The Decorated Stones at Seefin', *J.R.S.A.I.*, 93 (1963), 85–6. [66, 74]

Rynne, Etienne (1963b), 'Two Stone Axeheads found near Beltany Stone Circle, Co. Donegal', *J.R.S.A.I.*, 93 (1963), 193–6. [158]

Rynne, Etienne (1963c), 'Bronze Age Burials at Drung, Co. Donegal', *J.R.S.A.I.*, 93 (1963), 169–79. [149, 152]

Rynne, Etienne (1964a), 'Middle Bronze Age Burial at Knockboy, Co. Antrim', *U.J.A.*, 27 (1964), 62–6. [151]

Rynne, Etienne (1964b), 'Two Stone Axeheads from Killamoat Upper, Co. Wicklow', *J.K.A.S.*, 14 (1964), 50–3. [42]

Rynne, Etienne (1966), 'Bronze Age Cemetery at Scarawalsh, Co. Wexford', *J.R.S.A.I.*, 96 (1966), 39–46. [152]

Rynne, Etienne (1972), 'Celtic Stone Idols in Ireland', in Charles Thomas (ed.), *The Iron Age in the Irish Sea Province*, Council for British Archaeology Research Report 9, London, 79–93. [245]

Rynne, Etienne (1974), 'Excavations at "Madden's Hill", Kiltale, Co. Meath', *P.R.I.A.*, 74C (1974), 267–75. [244]

Sandars, N. K. (1957), *Bronze Age Cultures in France*, Cambridge University Press. [173, 180, 195]

Sandars, N. K. (1968), *Prehistoric Art in Europe*, Penguin, Harmondsworth. [224]

Sandars, N. K. (1971), 'From Bronze Age to Iron Age: a Sequel to a Sequel', in John

Boardman, M. A. Brown and T. G. E. Powell (eds), *The European Community in Later Prehistory: Studies in Honour of C. F. C. Hawkes,* Routledge & Kegan Paul, London, 1–29. [180]

Sangmeister, Edward (1964), 'Die schmalen "Armschutzplatten"', in Rafael von Ulsar and Karl J. Narr (eds), *Studien aus Alteuropa, Teil I*, Böhlau Verlag, Köln Graz, 93–122. [129]

Savory, H. N. (1948), 'The "Sword-bearers". A Reinterpretation', *P.P.S.*, 14 (1948), 155–76. [186]

Savory, H. N. (1968), *Early Iron Age Art in Wales*, National Museum, Cardiff. [246]

Savory, H. N. (1972), 'Copper Age Cists and Cist-Cairns in Wales', in Frances Lynch and Colin Burgess (eds), *Prehistoric Man in Wales and the West*, Adams & Dart, Bath, 117–39. [135]

Scott, Brian G. (1974), 'Some Notes on the Transition from Bronze to Iron in Ireland', *Irish Archaeological Research Forum*, I (1974), 9–24. [223, 236, 238]

Scott, J. G. (1964), 'The Chambered Cairn at Beacharra, Kintyre, Argyll, Scotland', *P.P.S.*, 30 (1964), 134–58. [35, 99, 109]

Scott, J. G. (1969a), 'The Clyde Cairns of Scotland', in T. G. E. Powell (ed.), *Megalithic Enquiries in the West of Britain*, Liverpool University Press. [37, 51]

Scott, J. G. (1969b), 'The Neolithic Period in Kintyre Argyll', in T. G. E. Powell (ed.), *Megalithic Enquiries in the West of Britain*, Liverpool University Press. [50]

Scott, J. G. and Powell, T. G. E. (1969), 'A Bronze Horse Figurine found near Birkwood, Lesmahgow, Lanarkshire', *Ant. J.*, 49 (1969), 118–26. [219]

Seaby, W. A. (1964), 'A Ring-headed Bronze Pin from Ulster', *U.J.A.*, 27 (1964), 67–72. [240]

Shee, Elizabeth (1972), 'Three Decorated Stones from Loughcrew, Co. Meath', *J.R.S.A.I.*, 102 (1972), 224–33. [134, 137]

Shee, Elizabeth (1973), 'Techniques of Irish Passage Grave Art', in Glyn E. Daniel and Poul Kjaerum (eds), *Megalithic Graves and Ritual*, Moesgård, Jutland Archaeological Society, 163–72, (1973). [76]

Shee, Elizabeth and Evans, D. M. (1965), 'A Standing Stone in the Townland of Newgrange, Co. Meath', *J.C.H.A.S.*, 70 (1965), 124–30. [128]

Shee, Elizabeth and O'Kelly, M. J. (1971), 'The Derrynablaha "Shield" Again', *J.C.H.A.S.*, 76 (1971), 72–6. [76]

Simon, J. (1749), *An Essay towards an historical account of Irish Coins, and of the Currency of foreign monies in Ireland*, S. Powell, Dublin. [6]

Simpson, D. D. A. (1965), 'Food Vessels in South-West Scotland', *Trans. Dumfries and Galloway Nat. Hist. and Archaeological Society*, 42 (1965), 25–50. [135]

Simpson, D. D. A. (1968), 'Food Vessels: Associations and Chronology', in J. M. Coles and D. D. A. Simpson (eds), *Studies in Ancient Europe: Essays Presented to Stuart Piggott*, Leicester University Press, 197–211. [133, 135, 137]

Simpson, D. D. A. (1971), 'Beaker Houses and Settlements in Britain', in D. D. A. Simpson (ed.), *Economy and Settlement in Neolithic and Early Bronze Age Britain and Europe*, Leicester University Press, 131–52. [129, 158]

Simpson, D. D. A. and Thawley, J. E. (1972), 'Single Grave Art in Britain', *Scottish Archaeological Forum*, 4 (1972), 81–104. [137, 145]

Simpson, Morna (1968), 'Massive Armlets in the North British Iron Age', in J. M. Coles and D. D. A. Simpson (eds), *Studies in Ancient Europe: Essays Presented to Stuart Piggott*, Leicester University Press, 233–54. [242]

Smith, A. G. (1970), 'Late- and Post-glacial Vegetational and Climatic History of Ireland: A Review', in Nicholas Stephens and Robin E. Glasscock (eds), *Irish Geographical Studies in Honour of E. Estyn Evans*, Queen's University, Belfast, 1970. [110]

Smith, A. G. and Collins, A. E. P. (1971), 'The Stratigraphy, Palynology and Archaeology of

Diatomite Deposits at Newferry, Co. Antrim, Northern Ireland', *U.J.A.*, 3rd ser., 34 (1971), 3–25. [23, 25, 103]

Smith, A. G., Pearson, G. W. and Pilcher, J. R. (1970), 'Belfast Radiocarbon Dates I, II', *Radiocarbon*, 12 (1970), 285–97. [128, 131]

Smith, A. G. and Willis, E. H. (1962), 'Radiocarbon Dating of the Fallahogy Landnam Phase', *U.J.A.*, 3rd ser., 24–5 (1961–2), 16–24. [25, 110]

Smith, C. (1746), *The Antient and Present State of the County and City of Waterford*, Edward and John Exshaw, Dublin. [6]

Smith, C. (1750), *The Antient and Present State of the County and City of Cork*, 2 vols, J. Exshaw, Dublin. [6]

Smith, C. (1756), *The Antient and Present State of the County of Kerry*, Ewing, Faulkner, Wilson and Exshaw, Dublin. [6]

Smith, M. A. (1959), 'Some Somerset Hoards and their Place in the Bronze Age of Southern Britain', *P.P.S.*, 25 (1959), 144–87. [164, 168, 169, 173, 176, 180, 181]

Smith, M. A. and Blyn Stoyle, A. E. (1959), 'A Sample Analysis of British Middle and Late Bronze Age Materials using Optical Spectrometry', *P.P.S.*, 25 (1959), 188–208. [217]

Sprockhoff, Ernst (1953), 'Armringe mit kreisförmiger Erweiterung', in Gorbert Moro (ed.), *Beiträge zur älteren europäischen Kulturgeschichte II. Festschrift für Rudolf Egger*, Verlag der Geschichte für Karnten, Klagenfurt, 11–28. [199]

Sprockhoff, Ernst (1956), *Jungbronzezeitliche Hortfunde der Südzone des Nordischen Kreises (Period V)*, Katalog des Römisch-Germanischen Zentralmuseums zu Mainz, Nr. 16, Mainz. [187, 199, 201, 214, 218]

Stead, I. M. (1965), *The La Tène Cultures of Eastern Yorkshire*, Yorkshire Philosophical Society, York. [240]

Steer, K. A. (1955–6), 'An Early Iron Age Homestead at West Plean, Stirlingshire', *P.S.A.S.*, 89 (1955–6), 227–51. [227, 238]

Stephens, N. and Collins, A. E. P. (1960), 'The Quaternary Deposits at Ringneill Quay and Ardmillan, Co. Down', *P.R.I.A.*, 61C (1960–1), 41–77. [23]

Stevenson, Robert B. K. (1955), 'Pins and the Chronology of Brochs', *P.P.S.*, 21 (1955), 282–94.

Stevenson, Robert B. K. (1966), 'Metal-work and Some Other Objects in Scotland', in A. L. F. Rivet (ed.), *The Iron Age in Northern Britain*, Edinburgh University Press, 17–44. [238, 240]

Stjernquist, Berta (1962–3), 'Präliminarien zu einer Untersuchung von Opferfunden', *M.L.U.H.M.* (1962–3), 5–64. [210]

Stone, J. F. S. and Thomas, L. C. (1956), 'The Use and Distribution of Faience in the Ancient East and Prehistoric Europe', *P.P.S.*, 22 (1956), 37–84. [149]

Sweetman, P. David (1971), 'An Earthen Enclosure at Monknewtown, Slane: Preliminary Report', *J.R.S.A.I.*, 101 (1971), 135–40. [125, 132]

Taylor, Joan J. (1968), 'Early Bronze Age Gold Neck-Rings in Western Europe', *P.P.S.*, 34 (1968), 259–65. [122, 143]

Taylor, Joan J. (1970). 'Lunulae Reconsidered', *P.P.S.*, 36 (1970), 38–81. [131, 143, 147]

Taylour, William (1964), *The Mycenaeans*, Thames & Hudson, London. [167]

Tempest, H. G. (1930–2), 'The Dorsey, some Notes on the Large Entrenchment in the Townland of Dorsey in the South of the County of Armagh', *Co. Louth Archaeological Jour.*, 7 (1930–2), 187–240, 407–10. [230]

Thomas, Nicholas (1968), 'Note on the Carrickinab Awl', *U.J.A.*, 31 (1968), 23–4. [129]

Thrane, Henrik (1958), 'The Rattle-pendants from the Parc-y-Meirch Hoard, Wales', *P.P.S.*, 24 (1958), 221–7. [187, 214]

Thrane, Henrik (1962), 'The Earliest Bronze Vessels in Denmark's Bronze Age', *Acta Archaeologica* (Copenhagen), 33 (1962), 109–63. [204]

Tohall, P., de Vries, H. and van Zeist, W. (1955), 'A Trackway in Corlona Bog, Co. Leitrim', *J.R.S.A.I.*, 85 (1955), 77–83. [142]

Topp, Celia (1956), 'The Gold Ornaments Reputedly Found near the Entrance to New Grange in 1842', *Twelfth Annual Report of the University of London Institute of Archaeology* (1956), 53–62. [247]

Topp, Celia (1962), 'The Portal Dolmen of Drumanone – Co. Roscommon', *Bulletin of the University of London Institute of Archaeology*, 3 (1962), 38–46. [88]

Torbrügge, Walter (1959), *Die Bronzezeit in der Oberpfalz*, Materialhefte zur Bayerischen Vorgeschichte Heft 13, Kallmunz. [173]

Torbrügge, Walter (1960), 'Die bayerischen Inn-Funde', *Bayerische Vorgeschichts Blätter*, 25 (1960), 16–69. [210]

Torbrügge, Walter (1970–1), 'Vor- und frühgeschichtliche Flussfunde', *Bericht der Rönisch-Germanischen Kommission*, 51–2 (1970–1), 1–146. [210]

Tratman, E. K. (1928), 'Report on Excavations in Ireland in 1928', *P.B.S.S.*, 3, no. 3 (1928), 109–25. [17]

Trump, Bridget (1962), 'The Origin and Development of British Middle Bronze Age Rapiers', *P.P.S.*, 28 (1962), 80–102. [169, 183]

Vallancey, Charles (1770–1804), *Collectanea de Rebus Hibernicis*, 6 vols, Thomas Ewing, Dublin. [6, 10]

Van Wijngaarden-Bakker, Louise H. (1974), 'The Animal Remains from the Beaker Settlement at Newgrange, Co. Meath: First Report', *P.R.I.A.*, 74C (1974), 313–83. [129]

Von Merhart, Gero (1952), 'Studien über einige Gattungen von Bronzegefässen', *Festschrift des Rönisch-Germanischen Zentralmuseums in Mainz zur Feier seines hundertjahrigen Bestehens 1952*, Band II, Mainz, 1–71. [202]

Waddell, John (1970), 'Irish Bronze Age Cists: A Survey', *J.R.S.A.I.*, 100 (1970), 91–139. [135, 139, 142, 144]

Waddell, John (1974), 'On Some Aspects of the Late Neolithic and Early Bronze Age in Ireland', *Irish Archaeological Research Forum*, 1 (1974), 32–8. [135]

Wailes, Bernard (1970), 'Excavations at Dún Ailinne, Co. Kildare', *J.R.S.A.I.*, 100 (1970), 79–90. [46, 228, 232]

Wakeman, W. F. (1848), *A Handbook of Irish Antiquities*, James McGlashan, Dublin. [11]

Wakeman, W. F. (1879–82), 'On Some Recent Antiquarian Discoveries at Toam and Killicarney, near Blacklion, in the County of Cavan', *J.R.S.A.I.*, 15 (1879–82), 183–200. [158]

Wakeman, W. F. (1883), 'Lisnacroghera, near Broughshane, Co. Antrim', *J.R.S.A.I.*, 16 (1883), 375–406. [224]

Wallace, J. N. A. (1938), 'The Golden Bog of Cullen', *N.M.A.J.*, 1 (1938), 89–101. [202, 208]

Walshe, P. T. (1941), 'The Excavation of a Burial Cairn on Baltinglass Hill, Co. Wicklow', *P.R.I.A.*, 46C (1940–1), 221–36. [66, 70]

Ware, Sir James (1764), *Works Concerning Ireland*, ed Walter Harris, 3 vols, Robert Bell and John Fleming, Dublin. [5]

Waterman, D. M. (1963), 'A Neolithic and Dark Age Site at Langford Lodge, Co. Antrim', *U.J.A.*, 3rd ser., 26 (1963), 43–54. [46]

Waterman, D. M. (1964), 'The Stone Circle, Cairn and Alignment at Drumskinny, Co. Fermanagh', *U.J.A.*, 27 (1964), 23–30. [128]

Way, Albert (1869), 'Notices of Certain Bronze Relics of a Peculiar Type, Assigned to the Late Celtic Period', *Arch. J.*, 26 (1869), 52–83. [242]

Werner, J. (1955), 'Die Nauheimer Fibel', *J.R.-G.Z.-M.M.*, 2 (1955), 170–95. [240]

Westropp, T. J. (1901), 'The Ancient Forts of Ireland: Being a Contribution towards our Knowledge of their Types, Affinities, and Structural Features', *T.R.I.A.*, 31 (1901), 579–730. [225]

Wheeler, R. E. M. and Wheeler, T. V. (1932), *Report on the Excavation of the Prehistoric, Roman, and Post-Roman Site at Lydney Park, Gloucestershire*, Research Report 9, Society of Antiquaries of London. [240]

Whelan, C. Blake (1928), 'A Prehistoric Hearth at Greenoge, Dunmurray, County Antrim', *I.N.J.*, 2 (1928–9), 94–8. [46]

Whelan, C. Blake (1934a), 'Further Excavations at Ballynagard, Rathlin Island, Co. Antrim', *P.B.N.H.P.S.*, (1933–4), 107–11. [72]

Whelan, C. Blake (1934b), 'Studies in the Significance of the Irish Stone Age: The Campignian Question', *P.R.I.A.*, 42C (1934–5), 121–43.

Wilde, W. R. (1857, 1861, 1862), *A Descriptive Catalogue of the Antiquities of Stone, Earthen, and Vegetable Materials (1857), Animal Materials and Bronze (1861), and Gold (1862) in the Museum of the Royal Irish Academy*, Hodges, Smith, Dublin. [10, 42, 84, 130, 131, 158, 209]

Wilde, W. R. (1870), 'Memoir of Gabriel Beranger and his Labours in the Cause of Irish Art, Literature, and Antiquities from 1760 to 1780', *J.R.S.A.I.*, 11 (1870–1), 33–64; 121–52, 236–60; 12 (1872), 445–85; 14 (1876), 111–56 [7]

Wilkins, J. (1961), 'Worsaae and British Antiquities', *Ant.*, 35 (1961), 214–20. [10]

Willmot, G. F. (1938), 'Three Burial Sites at Carbury, Co. Kildare', *J.R.S.A.I.*, 68 (1938), 130–42. [232, 244]

Wilson, David (1960), *The Anglo-Saxons*, Thames & Hudson, London. [248]

Woodman, P. C. (1967), 'A Flint Hoard from Killybeg', *U.J.A.*, 3rd ser., 30 (1967), 8–14. [43]

Woodman, P. C. (1973), 'Mount Sandel', *Excavations 1973. Summary Accounts of Archaeological Work in Ireland*, ed by T. G. Delaney, The Association of Young Irish Archaeologists, Belfast, 9. [24]

Woodman, P. C. (1974), 'The Chronological Position of the Latest Phases of the Larnian', *P.R.I.A.*, 74C (1974), 237–58. [24]

Wood-Martin, W. G. (1886), *The Lake-Dwellings of Ireland*, Hodges Figgis, Dublin. [11]

Wood-Martin, W. G. (1888), *The Rude Stone Monuments of Ireland (Co. Sligo and the Island of Achill)*, Hodges Figgis, Dublin. [11, 65]

Wood-Martin, W. G. (1895), *Pagan Ireland*, Longmans, Green, London. [12, 13]

Index